The
London
Traveletter
Guidebook

The London Traveletter Guidebook

Clark Siewert

B T Batsford Ltd   London

ISBN 0 7134 6024 5

Photoset by Deltatype Ltd, Ellesmere Port, Cheshire
Printed in Great Britain by
Dotesios (Printers) Ltd, Trowbridge

for the publishers B. T. Batsford Ltd
4 Fitzhardinge Street, London W1H 0AH

Contents

Introduction

Thank you for choosing this London guidebook, which I confidently believe will live up to your expectations. Why? Because this book is the outgrowth of the same four years of hard work that went into our newsletter **London Traveletter**, and the aim is the same: to present a friendly, personal, critical look at 'everybody's favourite big city', a place that attracts millions of visitors each year. Of course, many other guidebooks have been published. The launch of this, yet another book, is sure to prompt the same question we had with the start of the **Traveletter**: 'Why another newsletter/guidebook in a market already saturated with travel literature?'

Exactly. Much of what is on offer is too much. Too many ads, too many listings and too much wonderful prose about too many hotels, restaurants and attractions. Advertising and public relations people have their jobs to do, but London can't always be wonderful. At **London Traveletter**, we have taken on the job of sifting through this morass of information and bringing it up to date. For the last four years we've told our readers what we, as London residents, have found to be good value for the money or the experience. Since our newsletter neither takes advertising nor undertakes public relations work for anybody, these considerations do not influence us. This same principle guides our book.

We do not seek to patronize our readers, whom we see to be much like ourselves. Unlike some other books, we recognize that most readers are neither budget nor luxury travellers. Most of us spend money on things we enjoy and scrimp on the things we don't. Some visitors economize by going on package tours, then splurge on good restaurants or shopping at Harrods. Others don't care much for food, but will spend a lot on a hotel room or a day trip. People are individuals, not marketing profiles. When giving a real choice, they often surprise those who think tourists only want the touristy.

So we offer intelligent, critical advice on all kinds of places you may enjoy. It does no great service to provide a huge listing, with bland descriptions, nor to say what's chic or merely cheap. Instead, we present London as a selection of *experiences* that we have found to be particularly memorable, enjoyable, pleasant, valuable or somehow 'unmissable'. Perhaps you do have to trust my judgment a little, but this guidebook is also the product of the critical opinions of our contributing newsletter writers and subscribers who let us know about their own London experiences. It derives from a stimulating and dynamic process. With the publication of **The London Traveletter Guidebook**, I am sure that it will continue.

Clark Siewert
Editor, **London Traveletter**

How to use this guidebook

This guidebook is a carefully-selected compilation of some of **London Traveletter's** most valuable tips, recommendations and favourite London experiences. More than anything else, our aim is to point you in the right direction — for you. After all, isn't that what a guide is supposed to do? The organization is designed to parallel your visit — getting here, arrival, places to stay, entertainment, sights and discoveries beyond. But you'll benefit most if you at least skim the whole book beforehand, with particular attention to the tips at the beginning of most chapters. You may want to make plans or book ahead. And you'll know where to look for further information once you're here. Rather than spend a lot of time on the usual gee-whizz statistics and corny historical anecdotes, we concentrate on good commonsense advice, based on our experience, and on introducing you to some of the best London has to offer. Then, you're on your own.

1   *Potted London history*

Historical matters need not be dwelt upon at length. Every aspect of London has its own book-size or larger saga; it is better to seek out the amount and subject matter that most appeals to you. Perhaps no place else in the world has so much history: it stares out at you from every street corner, and what you can't look at for free will certainly be for sale.

We don't all like the same things. What is fascinating to some is boring to others. Nevertheless, we do think you will enjoy your visit more and make better use of your time if you read our bare essentials account of London's last two millenia below. Better still, make an early stop at the **Museum of London** to help visualize the city's story and/or the **National Portrait Gallery** to be better able to put faces with places and dates (see *Sights*).

Seeing London's heritage

While it is true that London has ancient origins, it's important for first-time visitors to dispel the notion of the city as a quaint medieval town. Most of that vanished in the Great Fire of 1666, which levelled all but the fringes and outlying parts of the old walled, wooden and half-timber town. Like most of London, 'Gothic' or 'Tudor' buildings are likely to be less than 300 years old: the product of one of the numerous architectural revivals that took place in the last century.

The fact is that the vast majority of buildings in the central area are Georgian,

Victorian or modern. This is not just the result of the Great Fire but also due to the simple reason that London's greatest surge in population and urban expansion occurred between 1800 and the First World War, when the number of inhabitants grew from about 1 million to 4.5 million. Today, there are only 2.5 million in this same old 'County of London' area, while Greater London has 6.5 million inhabitants — a figure also in decline since 1939 when 8.6 million people made London the world's most populous metropolitan area.

Although the famed seventeenth-century architect Sir Christopher Wren re-designed St Paul's and many beautiful baroque churches after the fire, most of these were within the limits of the old City and its outlying districts, which then barely stretched beyond today's Covent Garden area. In Wren's time, Westminster Palace, the site of today's Parliament, was the king's home — an intentional arm's length from the London of fires, riots and disorders. Until the mid-nineteenth century, places like Kensington and Hampstead were just small towns surrounded by farms and country estates.

The huge industrial and commercial expansion of the Georgian and Victorian period created a different concept of 'London' from that of previous times. The City of London, the historic square mile area which had received the medieval city charter, became just one part of a vast urban conglomeration of still-distinct areas, often described as 'villages', that grew together to produce the London of today. You'll notice that the buildings along major streets and central shopping areas of these 'villages' are often older than their outlying parts.

Today's London sprawl is more diverse and cosmopolitan than any before, but still deeply rooted in the heritage of the past. To know London, you should know something of its history, and this is best glimpsed in those buildings and other relics that have survived the ravages of time, fire, floods, bombs and urban redevelopment.

Prehistoric (?–AD43) and Roman (AD43–410)

Prehistoric sites in the vicinity of today's urban sprawl indicate that a number of Celtic tribes may have lived in the area prior to the Roman conquest in AD43; but there is no record of a significant pre-Roman settlement on the spot they picked for Londinium. (One theory has it that the name is a latinization of 'Lyndin', a musical Celtic word meaning 'waterside fortress'.) It is known that wealth and power in ancient Britain was already concentrated in south-east England (much as it is today), and it is not surprising that the Romans picked this easily-fortifiable site on navigable water at the centre of this region for their military and administrative base.

Londinium, stretching along the Thames from near the present Tower of London to St Paul's and inland to the site of today's Barbican, was never a very large city in our modern terms, but it was big by ancient standards. At the height of its power the Roman city had a population of about 30,000 and was the fifth largest north of the Alps. Londinium had a forum, a basilica, temples and fine houses, but less remains of it than of many other Roman settlements in Britain.

Parts of the city walls are still visible in a small park next to **Tower Hill** underground station and in other spots. Most notable is at the edge of the Barbican on **London Wall**. Nearby is the **Museum of London**, which contains a number of relics. At the **Walbrook Mithraeum** on Queen Victoria Street are the foundations of a temple to the god Mithras. A short day trip to **St Albans**, a commuter town just north of London, provides a rewarding opportunity to see a well-preserved mosaic floor of a Roman house and the substantial remains of a Roman theatre.

The Anglo-Saxon Period (c.AD410–1066)

From around AD200 the Romans in Britain came under attack from northern Celtic tribes and then from Germanic raiding parties. For another century and a half the Empire maintained its fortified borders and sea coasts. Roman citizenship was extended to the conquered Britons: the Romans themselves became assimilated. As other frontiers were increasingly beleaguered and Rome itself was threatened, the Roman legions were withdrawn. An appeal from British magistrates for military aid was rejected by the Emperor Honorius in 410, and later that year the city of Rome was sacked by Alaric the Goth. British Romans looked to their own defences, but these soon crumbled before Saxon and Danish invaders. Reigning warlords brought in Saxon mercenaries, but these people, now known as the 'Anglo-Saxons', began to flood in and push out the ancient Britons.

Until near the end of the period there is little mention of London in the old chronicles, and it did not reappear as the capital of an Anglo-Saxon kingdom. The city seems to have retained some importance, because soon after 597, the year St Augustine was sent to England from Rome, the first St Paul's Cathedral was founded by Aethelburt, the King of Kent.

The early Anglo-Saxons were not city dwellers. Much of what they did construct was destroyed by the invading Danes and, later, by the Normans. Anglo-Saxon features can be seen in many country churches and ruins, but in London about all that remains is the round Saxon arch of the church of **All Hallows by the Tower**, portions of several church crypts, and the relics in London's museums.

The Normans and the Houses of Plantagenet, York and Lancaster (1066–1485)
William the Conqueror re-established London as the pre-eminent centre of national economic and political power shortly after the invasion and his coronation as King of England at **Westminster Abbey** on Christmas Day, 1066. Though the Abbey itself had been built only shortly before by Edward the Confessor (1042–1065), 'the last English King', the early structure was a copy of Romanesque churches in Normandy and thus belonged to this later period. Most of what we see today actually dates from the later Plantagenet King, Henry III. Another building on Parliament Square, **Westminster Hall**, next to the Houses of Parliament, dates from this period, when it served the Norman law courts.

The other great Norman monument in London is, of course, the **White Tower**, the central stronghold of the fortress we know today as the **Tower of London**. Virtually every king of the period added to the fortress; an extensive amount of building took place during the reign of Edward I (1272–1307).

The Normans and their successors were great castle and cathedral builders. Some of their best castles are in Wales, but **Windsor Castle** is, of course, an excellent example much nearer (a day or half-day trip) to London.

Little is left of medieval London because it was a walled, mostly wooden town of open sewers, subject to frequent fires and plagues. There were few public buildings as we know them. A major fire destroyed an early St Paul's in 1136, and in 1349 the Black Death decimated London's population. But Richard I's grant of a corporation form of government to the City of London, and the growth of a powerful network of craft, trade and professional guilds, gave London a resilience that allowed it to survive each calamity and laid the foundations for the 'square mile' of the City's future pre-eminence in international finance and trade. Perhaps the best symbol of this spirit is the much-restored medieval commercial building, the **London Guildhall**, which dates from the fourteenth century, though visitors should bear in mind that it was badly damaged in the fire of 1666 and the German blitz, and much of what you see is restoration work. Nevertheless, the Hall gives a certain impression of the bustling commercial centre that teemed to the almost unheard of size of 50,000 by the end of the medieval period. In size, importance and power, London already dwarfed any English rival.

The Tudors (1485–1603)
London continued to spread out towards Westminster, which was growing up around Henry VIII's court at Whitehall Palace. By the end of the Tudor period, in 1605,

metropolitan London had a population of over 250,000, more of whom lived outside the walls than inside, and a growing number of whom lived at the far end of London Bridge in Southwark on the south bank of the River Thames.

Little remains of much of the distinctive brick and half-frame architecture of the city of Elizabeth I, Shakespeare, Raleigh and Drake. Some of the finest surviving London examples include the *Old Hall* at *Lincoln's Inn* (1490), the *Middle Temple Hall*, parts of *Fulham Palace*, and the *Gatehouse* at Lambeth Palace. Go and see *Staple Inn* on Holborn to get an idea of Tudor London's look. But the most beautiful Tudor architectural legacy is the country house, and the most famous of these is *Hampton Court Palace* — another day or half-day trip.

The Stuarts (1603–1714)

The City of London backed England's rise to world power with men and money, but deference to the King's power was not to last much longer. The confidence of the early Stuart regime is well expressed at the remarkable *Banqueting House* — all that remains of the Royal Palace of Whitehall, which burned down in 1698. Commissioned by James I, the building was the work of the distinguished Palladian architect Inigo Jones in 1619–1622. It celebrates the 'divine right' of James I, especially in an immense Rubens ceiling installed during the subsequent reign of Charles I. James is depicted as a saint, with allegorical scenes of the union of England and Scotland. The claim to 'divine right' did not endear Charles I to the leading figures in the City of London, who believed that his monarchy was damaging trade interests. London became a stronghold for Cromwell and Parliament during the Civil War (1642–1651). Ironically, when Charles was executed in 1649, he stepped onto the scaffold through a window of the Banqueting House.

Shortly after the restoration of the monarchy in 1660, London was hit by another plague (1664–66), which wiped out 75,000 inhabitants. This was quickly followed by the Great Fire of 1666, which swept away much of the medieval and Tudor city. Most of the buildings that remained were outside the city walls in the area of Holborn and the Strand, or on the south bank. This point is well illustrated by the fact that the early Jacobean *Prince Henry's Room* is on Fleet Street, across from Chancery Lane, and is claimed to be the oldest house (1610) in London. Today the atmospheric interiors contain mementos of the diarist Samuel Pepys, who lived nearby. Although buildings in this area survived the fire, few seem to have survived later construction and redevelopment.

Shortly after the fire, the great architect Sir Christopher Wren was hired to redesign the whole of the city. If his plans had been carried out, London would look more like an Italian city, with broad geometric thoroughfares and piazzas. However, the merchants rejected his proposals and rebuilt in brick (half-timbering was banned because of the fire risk) along slightly wider and straightened versions of the ancient curving streets and lanes.

It is for the new *St Paul's Cathedral*, the *Greenwich Observatory* and the *Chelsea Hospital* and two dozen still-standing churches that Wren is now remembered. His classical style, which combined some of the best of the baroque, was influential in the restoration of London. But he did not succeed in remaking the city: development continued in the same disorganized, higgledy-piggledy way as before. Merchants built what was economic, and property speculators produced housing designed to appeal to the taste of potential residents. Restored eighteenth-century London was to become a combination of brick boxes and elegant terraces.

Wren was also adept at designing country houses. *Kensington Palace*, now the residence of the Prince and Princess of Wales, bridges the gap between the Jacobean baroque manor and a more classical design. The Palace was redesigned by Wren for William and Mary, and became the favourite residence of Queen Anne (1702–1714) — a deeply religious monarch who gave her name to the famous baroque school of design.

The Georgian and Regency Period (1714–1837)
In 1714, the throne of Britain passed to the nearest Stuart relatives, the Hanoverian Kings, and the first four, all named George, gave their name to an era of classical taste and design in which Britain reasserted its mastery of the seas, started the Industrial Revolution, defeated Napoleon and founded new colonies across the globe. As the capital of a successful great power, London's fortunes grew with the empire.

At the beginning of the Georgian era, James Gibbs established his masterpiece of *St Martin in the Fields* (1726) as a model for Anglican churches all over the world. But not all was classic lines and colonnades: many Georgian terraces and commercial buildings that still stand are simple and only slightly adorned brick and plaster. Most of London's West End tourist and hotel areas were built during the Georgian period and the early part of the Victorian era that followed.

The elegant terraces, squares and crescents of Belgravia, Marylebone, Bayswater and Regents Park are Georgian or Regency. ('Regency' refers to a Georgian style that was influential for most of the first half of the nineteenth century, though the actual Regency period lasted only from 1810 to 1820, when George IV presided as regent for his father George III, who had gone mad.) Many of the buildings in these areas are the work of the famous architect John Nash, as are many of the West End's public streets, buildings and parks (*Regent Street, Carlton Terrace* on *The Mall, Buckingham Palace, Marble Arch*). William Wilkins designed the *National Gallery* and Sir Robert Smirke designed the *British Museum* in neo-Grecian style.

London boomed and bloomed in other ways during this golden age. The Georgian era was the time of painters like Gainsborough, Reynolds, Turner, Hogarth, Romney and Raeburn; furniture makers like Chippendale, Kent, Sheraton and Hepplewhite; and writers like Samuel Johnson, Wordsworth, Byron, Shelley, Coleridge and Keats. Furniture, silver, pottery and crafts from the period are today's highly-prized antiques.

The Victorian and Edwardian Eras (1837–1914)
The foundations of the new *Houses of Parliament* were laid in 1837, the last year in the short reign of King William IV (1830–37), and the first year in the long reign of his niece Queen Victoria (1837–1901). More than any other building, it symbolizes the beginning of the Victorian era, because it is so strongly medieval in decorative appearance and a clear rejection of Georgian classicism. The decorative details were designed by Augustus Pugin, an influential architect who called for a return to medieval principles, which he identified as religious, and an abandonment of classical architecture, which he saw as pagan.

John Ruskin and his disciple George Street also called for a Gothic revival. Street's *Royal Courts of Justice* (1881) and George Gilbert Scott's *Albert Memorial* (1872) and *St Pancras Station* (1868) are other prominent examples of buildings that are so neo-gothic they have fooled many tourists into thinking they were genuine medieval relics. Countless churches, town halls and vast residential and commercial areas of London are also based on Victorian neo-gothic decorative ideas, but few are as extravagant as these. Towards the end of the century, a whole series of 'revivals' gave the look greater diversity.

Charles Dickens scarcely exaggerated the crime, poverty and squalor of this period in London's history, but we should not forget that it was also a time of rapid mechanization and technological progress (values which much of the architecture rejected), as well as runaway population growth and social problems. Railways connected London to all corners of the kingdom, and architects clearly saw the railway station as the modern cathedral. London's underground railway system was the first in the world, and has remained the world's largest.

New Thames bridges were built and the old ones rebuilt. Cheap transport encouraged the population to spread out to farflung suburbs. A massive new sewer system was the engineering wonder of the age. Wealth was certainly not evenly distributed, but for the first time masses of people were able to afford cheap, standardized goods.

As the capital of the biggest empire with the largest navy and the highest credit surplus, London reached its apogee in population, power and world-wide influence during the reign of Victoria's playboy son, King Edward VII (1901–1910). London's 'villages' had grown together to make London the most populous city in the world; geographic 'London' was roughly the same in extent as the place we know today.

After the First World War a long period of decline, in both population and influence, set in and did not begin to reverse itself until the 1960s.

The modern era (1914–the present)
Few would deny that the end of the Great War marked a watershed for exhausted Britain and London, but for a while no one seemed to notice that centre stage was gradually being yielded to the United States and New York. New York, with its vitality and its dynamic polyglot population, became the focus of attention as American movies, jazz, records and popular culture came to dominate the entertainment scene world-wide and even in London. The first multinational companies, like Ford, arrived in Britain, and American art, science and technology were increasingly admired. The United States ended the war as a creditor nation, and its overwhelming wealth brought about a gradual shift in world financial leadership from London to New York. Disarmament and appeasement gradually eroded much of Britain's international political influence and, with it, London's status in the eyes of the world. Only America's isolationist sentiments helped postpone the passing of political leadership until the Second World War.

Everyone has heard of the tremendous bravery shown by Londoners in the face of nightly German bombardment in the Blitz that lasted from 1940–45 (the worst year was 1940–41, before the US entered the war, and Britain stood alone) when 30,000 people were killed. Whole sections of the East End and the City were virtually obliterated. Incendiary cluster bombs spread fire beyond bomb sites, which also pock-marked the West End. Only a few outlying areas were lucky enough to escape war damage. Most public buildings suffered and millions of houses were damaged in some way.

The war changed the face of London. Reconstruction began immediately afterwards, and great efforts were made to restore famous and historic structures, but rebuilding was severely hampered by shortages of money and materials. New town planning acts and the new post-war (1945–51) Labour government's emphasis on housing and state enterprise brought about the transformation of whole areas into vast public housing estates. Modern 'international-style' office blocks appeared everywhere, even outside the City's new skyline. Perhaps the most controversial of these were the glass and concrete high-rise buildings such as *New Zealand House* in the Regency Haymarket area, and *Centre Point*, which towered above its Victorian and Georgian surroundings at the corner of Oxford Street and Tottenham Court Road. It was far easier to rebuild bomb sites in the mostly bland, modern forms that appeared. Planning restrictions also helped to limit innovation, and few modern London buildings have achieved international critical acclaim.

Eventually, a wave of reaction to some of the more extreme designs of modern architects and planners appeared. Schemes for the wholesale vandalization of historic areas such as Soho and Covent Garden for office blocks and parking lots were stopped, but the battle still continues today.

By the 1960s London had largely recovered from the war, and most of the scars had disappeared. Having ceased to be the capital of an empire, London found a new identity as a major city in the European Community and emerged again as a world financial and cultural centre, in competition with New York. Pop music and Carnaby Street fashions drew world-wide attention, as did London's leadership in art and antique sales and auctions, and in the performing arts. London became a prominent international meeting centre as well as the headquarters (or European headquarters) for many multinational corporations.

A stream of immigration from the Commonwealth and all parts of the globe made London a more cosmopolitan city than ever before. In the new London you could buy anything or eat any kind of food from anywhere in the world. For the first time these exotic items became available to the masses, and a tourist boom began which shows no sign of abating.

Tourism changed the face of the city, too: once-polite Edwardian terraces have become rows of budget hotels; every major shopping street seems to have an American fast food joint on it, and some dubious 'tourist attractions' have sprouted. But tourism is now a major industry on which the life of London depends — tourists buy a third of theatre tickets and pay for a fifth of the public transport revenues. Without the tourists, choices now available in restaurants, shops and theatres would be considerably reduced, and public transport would be more expensive.

In 1986 the Greater London Council, London's elected governing body, was abolished for political reasons by the Conservative Government. Although a few London-wide functions passed to a residuary body, 'London' is now a geographical name for a vast urban region of 32 independent boroughs, rather than a single unified city.

During the eighties, Britain's renewed economic growth and vigour have been particularly strong in London, along with an increased interest in preserving the heritage of the past. It is this vital combination which continues to make London a world capital in a much broader sense than ever before, as well as one of the world's favourite visitor destinations.

2 Getting there

From other parts of Britain
Air, rail and **coach** connections are, of course, available from all parts of the kingdom. Please see our comments in Chapter 12, *London's Britain*. These transportation hints apply equally to travel *to* London. Visitors should also investigate the numerous 'minibreak' deals available that include transport and accommodation for a bargain price.

From North America

Air
Twelve years ago, there were only a few US 'gateway cities' with direct flights to London. These were New York, Boston, Chicago, Miami, Washington, Seattle, Los Angeles and San Francisco. The huge growth in demand for air travel has added Atlanta, Dallas, Houston, St Louis, Tampa, Minneapolis, Denver, Pittsburgh, Cincinatti and even Charlotte, North Carolina (home of Piedmont Airlines), with the prospect of additional cities.

Unfortunately, deregulation has also led to a decrease in the choice of carriers and continued uncertainty over fares. Laker Airways, which pioneered cheap trans-atlantic travel, did not survive its 'fare wars' with major IATA (International Air Transport Association — in the view of many, a price-fixing cartel) carriers, and disappeared in 1982. Soon it was succeeded in this role by *People Express*. Until

1986, when People Express was swallowed by the growing giant Continental, it offered a very cheap alternative to the major carriers for people from all parts of the States through its domestic feeder routes to their gateway at Newark, New Jersey. **Continental** has continued with very good deals, but not at the same bargain levels offered by People Express.

This has left **Virgin Atlantic** as the only serious, non-IATA, bargain airline in the Laker mould. Most travellers from the New York (Newark Airport) or Miami metropolitan areas or adjacent parts of the East Coast will find that this small British airline offers the best fares to London. The major disadvantage is that, as a non-American carrier, it has no internal feeder network, and has not been very useful to people in the Midwest, Southwest and West. Despite low fares, standards of service have remained fairly high and our readers have been mostly satisfied. New routes to Boston and Los Angeles are planned for 1989. A small Scottish competitor, Highland Express, appeared and disappeared in 1987. New bargain air lines are constantly rumoured.

One cheap alternative for US travellers from regions distant to Virgin's Newark base has been the '**bucket**' or 'consolidated tickets' available through some agents who advertise heavily in the travel sections of US newspapers. These tickets are basically unsold space made available by the airlines through certain agents at reduced prices and often with heavy restrictions. A certain number of these tickets would seem to be on **Continental** or airlines like **Air India**, who fly a leg of their New York–Bombay route through London. Commonly, travellers with these tickets do not know the carrier or departure time until the day before.

Another way to London is the **charter flight**, but these are less common than they were in the days before 1978, when Laker Airways upset the airlines' protected high fare structure. Charters to London these days are most often available through university and student organizations, and, again, through ads in newspapers. Beware: charters fill up early and are subject to cancellation (you can lose your money if you don't have insurance), and long delays and flight time changes are common.

From time to time the major airlines offer **standby** seats at much reduced prices. You can buy these tickets in advance, but you are not guaranteed a seat and you have to be willing to risk long waits (and hotel bills) in peak season. Standby prices and policies have varied erratically from season to season and airline to airline. They are mostly for the young and flexible, but during periods other than mid-June to mid-September and the Christmas holidays they can be a fairly safe bet; some airlines even make daily predictions.

For most people, especially those who must begin their journeys away from gateway cities, the easiest and most useful alternative is the **Advance Purchase Excursion Fare (APEX)**. Usually, the minimum requirements are that you purchase the ticket 21 days in advance and that you must stay for a minimum of 7 days and for a maximum of 90 days. Sometimes you can buy the ticket 'open jaw' (arriving at and departing from different cities). Nowadays most Apex ticket return dates can be changed for a fee of about £50.

This new Apex flexibility means that only those who must fly at short notice, or truly long-stay visitors, should pay the high premium for regular ordinary air fares. Apex and regular economy rates differ only very slightly between the major IATA carriers. The main change is seasonal: the highest fares are during the two high seasons (Christmas and May–September); the low season usually lasts from December 1–12 and December 28 to March; shoulder seasons are October–November and March–April. There may be more variation in **first** and **business class** fares and policies. If you can afford these upper bracket fares, you might want to check whether extra goodies are on offer and on the type of seating available. For many business travellers these become major considerations in choosing an airline.

The choice for economy passengers on major IATA airlines usually comes down to whether a particular airline offers a package deal like car hire (fly-drive), whether they feel swayed by a slight difference in ticket price, or perhaps just a gut feeling about the airline's service, reliability, or image. The last is hard to quantify, and comes down to personal quirks, but over the last two years our readers' most consistent praise has been for the high standards of efficiency and service on the new **British Airways**. This is perhaps surprising, both as the reaction of a largely American subscribership and for an airline that only ten years ago was renowned for strikes, unhelpful stewardesses and indifferent service. A new attitude has been aggressively pushed by the management of this slimmed-down, newly-privatized giant airline, with startling results. Perhaps at a time when their American competitors have been dogged by the agonies of internal deregulation and union disputes, British Airways has consistently won or been placed highly in recent travellers' surveys. For the moment, and with fares being roughly equal, we would rate it a very worthy choice.

Another reason for choosing an airline may be the destination airport. Foreign visitors who are touring elsewhere in Britain may want to fly into one of the provincial or major city airports. Numerous British cities now have service from the major continental cities. North America is now linked by regular scheduled service to Prestwick (near Glasgow) and Manchester, and there are proposals for flights to Birmingham and Cardiff. But even if you're flying to London, when you choose an airline you also choose an airport, and you might want to see our section on London's airports in Chapter 3.

It may pay to shop around when buying a transatlantic air ticket. Read the ads in newspaper travel sections; consider whether Virgin Atlantic or charters are of any use to you; visit more than one travel agent. Air fares and the airline industry have been in constant flux in recent years. It's impossible for us to predict what sort of deal you might turn up by the time you read this book. Just make sure you make your enquiries early enough if you plan to go during high season, or, if your schedule is not flexible.

Canadian travellers have had a greater choice of fares and airlines since 1987 when the UK and Canada concluded a greatly liberalized air treaty. **Nationair** and **Wardair** have introduced new, value schedule services to London and Prestwick, to add to those already run by **Air Canada** and **Canadian Airlines**. Those living on both sides of the border near Vancouver, Winnipeg, Toronto and Montreal should compare fares and exchange rates.

Ship

North Americans should give serious consideration to an outward or return journey on the **Cunard** Line's *Queen Elizabeth II*. Why? The five day crossing is simply the experience of a lifetime. The ship is the last of its kind, and ocean liner crossings (though not cruises!) may not be with us much longer. Passage is not too unreasonable, if, for example, you sail one direction and fly the other under the package deals available from Cunard and British Airways. Standby fares are often available at reduced rates.

Perhaps we should mention that we know of several past instances in which Americans 'resident' in Britain (this has included teachers on sabbatical) have been able to purchase single fares at the pound rate, often lower than the dollar fares charged in the US. We do not know whether this situation will still prevail at the time of reading, or whether the pound/dollar exchange rate would make the difference worthwhile. Cunard's US office is at 555 Fifth Avenue, New York NY 10017 (Tel 800 880 7500). the UK office is at 30a Pall Mall, London SW1 (Tel. 01-491 3930).

From the Continent

Air or ship
European air fares have remained so high that, until recently, travellers from nearby parts of the Continent — northern France, the Low Countries, north Germany and Scandinavia — have found the many ferry and rail/ferry links to be much more economical, if not the most convenient. The beginnings of a liberalization of inter-European air fares has changed this situation.

The French travel company **Nouvelles Frontières** won a long court case which has enabled it to offer bargain Paris–London fares. Agreements between the UK and the Netherlands and Belgium have allowed much cheaper, though generally restricted, fares on airlines like **Transavia** and **Air Europe**. **Virgin Atlantic** has been allowed to run an inexpensive service from Maastricht with few restrictions. This city has speedy connections with nearby Aachen, Dusseldorf, Paris, Brussels and Amsterdam. A recent European treaty will push more airlines in this direction.

Ferry services are almost too numerous to mention. Until the Channel Tunnel opens in 1993, these and the fewer (but quicker) hovercraft services will be the only other practical access to the island capital from the Continent. The main channel routes are: (from France) Calais — Dover or Folkestone; Dunquerque — Dover or Ramsgate; Cherbourg — Weymouth or Portsmouth; Dieppe — Newhaven; (from Belgium) Zeebrugge — Felixstowe or Dover; Oostende — Dover or Folkestone; (from Holland) Vlissingen or Hook of Holland — Harwich. Other ferry services operate from Spain, Germany, Norway, Sweden and further down the French coast. For most travellers a choice of ferry route will be based on nearness to home or the relevant point in travel.

3   *Getting oriented*

On arrival

London's airports

Heathrow and Gatwick are the world's two busiest international airports. (These statistics, of course, exclude domestic traffic and, thus, American hubs, but nonetheless give some idea of their immense importance.) Some scheduled international traffic now goes to nearby Stansted or Luton airports. Stansted has been designated as the third London airport. The new London City Airport can take only small airliners and, as yet, tickets to it are expensive and only for those with **City** business. For the immediate future, most visitors will continue to arrive at Heathrow or Gatwick. Your choice of airline might be influenced by the London airport where it lands. Both airports have full facilities, but for various reasons you may find one more convenient than the other.

Heathrow

Reasons for choosing Heathrow

- Transfer to central London is by the easy access airport **underground** (subway) stations (Heathrow Central and Terminal 4) on the Piccadilly Line, which runs through many central hotel areas or by the limited stop **Airbus**. Gatwick is further from town and passengers use the British Rail Gatwick Express to Victoria

Station. Although travel time is actually slightly quicker, the fare is higher and most visitors are then faced with a queue for a taxi at Victoria Station.

• Taxi passengers will find Heathrow to be a quicker and cheaper ride — about £20 to central London, as compared with £35 from Gatwick.
• Weather conditions are marginally better (less risk of fog).
• Passengers for the western parts of London or western Britain (a bus connects to Reading Station) will find Heathrow more convenient.
• Some authorities think Heathrow is safer — Gatwick has only one runway.

Details
Heathrow is the largest of London's airports and the home base of British Airways, sprawling over a vast acreage on the city's western outskirts. Since it was first established as London's main airport in 1946 it has grown like Topsy. Confused planning has run behind demand, adding one terminal after another, with a still only barely adequate connecting bus service. A fourth terminal opened in 1986 and a fifth is planned. The whole place has an atmosphere of organized chaos during heavy summer and Christmas use.

The terminals
Each one is meant to be self-contained, but they aren't. For example, only Terminal 2 has a post office. Buffet facilities have improved, and all the terminals have a sitdown restaurant, though the food is unexciting and highly-priced. Terminals 1, 2 and 3 are connected by bus and long underground walkways: Terminal 4 by bus.

Terminal 1 Serves domestic, Irish and Channel Island routes, and some (mainly European) international destinations.
Airlines: Aer Lingus, Air UK, British Airways (UK and most European flights except Paris and Amsterdam), British Midland, Brymon, Cyprus, DanAir, El Al, Euroair, Icelandair, Manx, Sabena, South African Airways.

Terminal 2 The terminal for European and North African carriers tries to have a continental flavour in the food and shops on offer. After passport control there is even a specialty food shop in the departure lounge. The check-in area is low-ceilinged and claustrophobic. Upstairs, the arrivals hall is very spacious after customs. Terminal 2 has Heathrow's only post office.
Airlines: Aeroflot, Air Algerie, Air France, Alitalia, Austrian Balkan, CSA, Finnair, Iberia, JAT, LOT, Lufthansa, Luxair, Malev, Olympic, Royal Air Maroc, SAS, Swissair, TAP, TAROM, Tunis and Turkish.

Terminal 3 Most North Americans and Intercontinental passengers who are not on British Airways will arrive at this terminal. Arrivals and departures are actually in two separate, recently-renovated buildings.
Airlines: Air Canada, Air India, Air Mauritius, Alia Royal Jordanian, Bangladesh Biman, BWIA, Egyptair, Ethiopian, Ghana, Gulf Air, Iran Air, Iraqi Airways, Japan, Kenya, Kuwait, Malaysian, Middle East, Nigeria, Pakistan, Pan American, Qantas, Saudia, Singapore, Sudan, Syrian, Thai, TWA, VARIG, VIASA, Zambia Airways.

Terminal 4 The design of the new Terminal 4 has eliminated many of the space and bad design problems of the other terminals. Intelligently and efficiently planned, most of its slots were pounced on by British Airways for its intercontinental, Concorde, Paris and Amsterdam flights. Terminal 4 is another good reason for flying British Airways from the US, Canada and other intercontinental destinations. The

main negative aspect for transfer passengers is its distance from Terminals 1, 2 and 3, which are clustered together.
Airlines: Air Malta, British Airways (intercontinental, Concorde, Paris and Amsterdam services), KLM and NLM.

Passport control and customs (all terminals)
Passport control can be slow at early morning rush hours, when queues build up at the desks marked 'Other' — where non-British and non-EEC passengers must wait. Customs is generally speedy. It operates on the Green (nothing to declare) and Red (dutiable alcohol, tobacco and gifts) system. In general, you can walk straight through the Green channel if you have no more than your duty free allowance of spirits, cigarettes and gifts for people in the UK, are not carrying any drugs and have only your personal effects with you. Customs people have a sixth sense which alerts them to dodgers, and few obvious North American tourists are stopped as they push their baggage trolleys past the inspectors (Miami flights are a notable exception). In all terminals, you emerge through sliding doors to an arrival hall with facilities for exchange, hotel bookings, car rental and transportation to London.

Transfers

UK destinations If you are flying on to another UK destination, you must proceed through immigration, collect your baggage, pass through customs, then look for the 'Transfer Bus' signs to a 'landside' transfer bus to Terminal 1.

Transfer to Gatwick Airport Transfer passengers must clear immigration and customs. Unfortunately, the quick and efficient helicopter 'Airlink' is no more. You must use the **Speedlink** Express Coach service, which operates from 0600 to 2300 daily. Look for the 'Speedlink' check-in area signs in the arrival area. Coaches run every 20 minutes from 0600 in the morning, half hourly in the afternoon, and hourly from 1840 to 2240. Journey time is supposed to be 50 minutes, but this can be considerably lengthened during rush hours on the M25 motorway (0730–0930; 1630–1830). Fares are £9.00 adult or £5.00 child.

Arrival facilities

Currency exchange Facilities in Terminal 1 and Terminal 2 are open from 0700 to 2300 daily. The Bank in the Terminal 3 arrivals hall is open 24 hours, and the branch in the departures hall is open from 0630 to 2130 daily. The Travellers Exchange Corporation in Terminal 4 is open 24 hours. We recommend that you change only as much as you require to get into London and for immediate needs until you familiarize yourself with the money and exchange rates.

Telephones Available in most arrival halls. Some take credit cards.

Shops and restaurants Generally to be found in the departure, rather than arrival, halls, except in Terminal 2.

Information All arrival halls have desks for airport information, bus and underground services, British Rail services, hotel bookings and car hire. These are generally open from around 0700 to 2300.

Getting into London and settling in
If you have not pre-arranged all your transportation and accommodation requirements, you will now have to make a decision about how to get into London and where to stay.

Hotels The 'Hotels Plus' desk or the London Tourist Board accommodation service in Heathrow Central underground station will make hotel bookings in several price brackets for a small fee. Unless you know exactly where you want to stay, and especially if you've come off a lengthy flight, we recommend that you book a place for one night or so only, to give you time to recover and get your bearings.

If the accommodation doesn't suit you, you can then call other hotels or consult the **British Travel Centre** at 12 Regent Street, or the **London Tourist Board** at Victoria Station, and by that stage you'll have a better idea of how much you can afford within your budget.

Transportation
A **Heathrow Transfer Ticket** can be bought from travel agents abroad that is valid for either bus or underground services. But you may want a look at the alternatives below.

Underground This is clearly the fastest and cheapest (about £1.90) transportation to central London. If your hotel is near a station on the Piccadilly Line, and you feel comfortable carrying your own luggage, this is obviously the most attractive option. If you have a lot of luggage and/or must manage one or more underground station changes, the 'tube' may be more trouble than it's worth.

The Underground connects with all British Rail's London terminals, and if you want to take the Underground part of the way to save money, these are the obvious places to find a taxi, along with major street intersections and hotels. Journey time to central London is 40 to 50 minutes.

Airbus The Airbus is more expensive than the Underground, but worth consideration if one of the two routes stops near your destination and/or you are carrying heavy luggage. You might also want to ride these buses to a central London point and then hail a taxi. For example, you might take the Airbus to the Kensington Hilton stop (£4.00 single, £6.00 return), then take a taxi to your hotel, if this is say, a short distance away (£2.00), but out of walking distance of a tube station. You will have spent £6.00 rather than the £20.00 a full taxi journey would have cost.

Journey time on the Airbus depends on traffic; it normally takes about an hour, but can be longer in the morning and afternoon rush hours. Airbuses have wheelchair lifts and connect at **Victoria** and **Euston** with **Carelink**, London's wheelchair-accessible bus service between railway stations.

Taxi This works out best for those travelling in a group, or if there are up to four people travelling together. A shared taxi stand is located at Terminal 2. A taxi into the centre costs £20.00 (so £5.00 each for four). It would cost four adults £16.00 on the Airbus and £7.60 on the underground. As noted above, you might want to use a taxi for only part of your journey. Taxis can take well over an hour if the traffic is heavy.

Other bus services These mostly operate from the Central Bus Station, linked by subway walks to Terminals 1, 2 and 3 and are most useful for London suburban and commuter towns in south east England. If you're going to one of these places rather than central London, a bus from this station might save you time, money and aggravation. Check with the Airport Information Desk.

Bus to British Rail There is a bus link to the Reading British Rail station — most useful to those who are going first to somewhere in the west like Bath, Bristol, Plymouth or Cardiff.

Gatwick

Reasons for choosing Gatwick
- British Rail train service is available from a station in the South Terminal to London Victoria Station on the non-stop Gatwick Express, or by a route to London Bridge, Farringdon, and King's Cross Stations and through-London trains to the North called Thameslink. Although these services are more expensive than the Underground links between Heathrow and central London, and passengers will usually need to switch to taxis, bus or Underground to complete their journey, the train service may be handier for passengers with heavy luggage (porters, trolleys and lifts are available most of the way).

- The airport is more centralized than Heathrow, and services are more accessible. The two terminals and the satellite are connected by a rapid transit railcar — not the awkward buses as at Heathrow.

- Generally fast and highly-regarded baggage delivery and reclaim.

- Transfers to other airlines are easier and less fraught than at Heathrow. Again, you don't have to rely on buses.

- Gatwick is more convenient to passengers whose destinations are in south or east London, or who are staying around Victoria Station.

- Passengers leaving London on British Airways via Gatwick can check in their baggage at Victoria Station.

Gatwick is the second-largest London airport and was, until recently, the homebase of British Caledonian Airways, now merged with British Airways. Originally only a charter airport with few scheduled services, Gatwick is now the world's second-busiest international airport. Fortunately, growth has been better planned and controlled. Gatwick can get very crowded in the summer months with holiday flight delays, and the check-in lines can get alarmingly long, but somehow it still manages to seem more self-contained and user-friendly.

Arrival
Facilities at both terminals are relatively speedy, but new North Terminal's walkways to Passport Control are shorter than those at South Terminal. British and EC nationals are often through passport control in seconds. Other passport holders may have a short wait in the 'Other' queue that is especially long when early morning flights arrive. Baggage is mostly efficient: sometimes your bags await you. Customs is the same Red and Green system as found in other British airports (see *Heathrow: Passport control and customs*).

In either terminal, you will emerge through sliding doors to arrival facilities for 24-hour exchange, hotel bookings, car rental and transportation to London. North Terminal arrivals should take the quick (free) shuttle to South Terminal's rail station to catch the **Gatwick Express** or other trains to London. Shopping and food facilities at the new North Terminal are quieter than those at the old South Terminal.

Transfers
Passengers transiting Gatwick airport for another international destination should not go through Passport Control, but report to the transfer desk for directions. Those travelling on to another UK destination should clear immigration and customs and take their baggage to the domestic check-in area. If you are going to Heathrow, look for the **Speedlink** bus service sign (*see p. 14*).

Getting into London from Gatwick
If you have not pre-arranged all your transportation and accommodation requirements, you will now have to make a decision about how to get into London and where to stay.

Hotels You can either make a hotel reservation at the 'Hotels Plus' desk (open from 0700 to 2300), or you can wait until you get to Victoria Station, where the **London Tourist Board** or one of the private services is available for booking accommodation. The fairly expensive **Gatwick Hilton** is connected to the main terminal; the similarly priced **Gatwick Penta** is also sited at the airport.

Unless you know exactly where you want to stay, and especially if you've come off a lengthy flight, we recommend that you book a place for one night or so only, to give you time to recover and get your bearings. If it doesn't suit you, you can then call other hotels or consult the **Tourist Board** (above) or the **British Travel Centre** at 12 Regent Street, and by that stage you'll have a better idea of how much you can afford within your budget.

Transportation

Rail By far the quickest and easiest way to get into central London from Gatwick (30–40 minutes). The British Rail station is in the South Terminal building.

Be sure to collect a free baggage trolley before you leave the arrivals hall, because the walk to the station gate can seem awfully long. It can also be a good idea to buy your ticket at the British Rail desk just behind passport control, because long lines often form at the station ticket windows. Britrailpass holders can, of course, use their passes, but as the validity period begins on first use, you might prefer to wait until you are ready to start touring outside London. If you will be returning to Gatwick within three months, it may be convenient to buy a return (£10), rather than a single (£5) ticket.

One of the most annoying things about BR's station at Gatwick is that you are not allowed to take trolleys through the station gate and down to the platform. Hire a porter if you have a lot of bags, or save your back by carrying them on to the lift (elevator). (This is straight in front of the gate, but not well-signposted).

Most visitors to central London will probably want to take the **Gatwick Express** to Victoria Station, where taxis and information are plentiful and major underground and bus stations are situated. The Gatwick Express runs in both directions every fifteen minutes between 0620 and 2235, and then hourly throughout the night.

Alternatively, the **Thameslink** connects Gatwick to London Bridge, Farringdon and King's Cross stations from 0700 to 2209, and may be useful to visitors staying at the Tower Hotel or near the City financial district. The same express provides through-London direct service to Bedford and other points north of London. Services are also available to Brighton and the south coast towns.

Bus or coach Green Line and other buses into London are cheaper but much slower than the train, especially in periods of heavy traffic, and are recommended only if you hate trains. But if your destination is a suburban or commuter town, especially in the southern outskirts of London, it might be quickest to go by bus. The coach/bus station is signposted below concourse level.

Taxis We do not recommend taxis from Gatwick into London because of the price (£35), distance, time and delays due to traffic congestion *en route*. London taxis are readily available from a separate Gatwick Express rank at Victoria Station, and queues are moving much faster than previously.

Railway stations

London has eight major termini: **Paddington** (north-west and west); **Euston** (north, west and western Scottish); **St Pancras** (north); **Kings Cross** (east, north-east and eastern Scottish); **Liverpool Street** (east); **Charing Cross** (south and east); **Victoria** (south and south-east) and **Waterloo** (south and west).

All British Rail stations are also connecting points for two or more underground stations. Victoria Station is only a short walk from the **Victoria Coach Terminal**, where buses depart for suburban towns and cities throughout the country.

Foreign visitors travelling by rail from north-west Germany, Holland and Belgium may arrive at **Liverpool Street**, where renovations are in progress. Currency and hotel booking facilities are available, but much better to arrive at **Victoria**, which has a vast array of facilities.

Finding your way around

Unless you try to get some concept of the layout of London's enormous sprawl into your head, efforts to see or do much at all can be self-defeating. Here are a few of our tips.

Orientation tips

- Obtain the excellent BTA (British Tourist Authority) map of London's central area on arrival (available from their Travel Centre at 12 Regent Street SW1 and their other information centres at airports and stations).

- Buy a map and street index book, commonly known here as an '**A–Z**' (Americans note: this is pronounced 'eh to zed'). If you just want to see the major sights in the central area, you can probably get by without an A–Z, but it becomes essential when you're trying to find a small shop or restaurant on a tiny, obscure street somewhere. A–Z's are available at a variety of reasonable prices from £1.95 upwards. Buy one that is convenient to carry around but covers more than just central London — you've already got that on your BTA map.

- Make a list of places you want to go to while you're here. Consult your map and index book to see where they are and which are close to one another, and where they are in relation to tubes and bus lines.

- Take one of the half-day or day bus tours that go past the major sights to get an idea of distances.

- Think of the location of places of interest in relation to the location of your hotel (which you should mark on your map), or to **Piccadilly Circus**, which is smack in the middle of 'tourist London'. Several underground and bus lines meet there, and it is central, though not necessarily within walking distance of many theatres and attractions of all kinds. You might even want to walk in several directions from Piccadilly Circus to help get your bearings. North along **Regent Street** will take you toward the **Regent** and **Oxford Street** shops; south — towards **Trafalgar Square** and **Whitehall**; east — towards **Leicester Square** and the theatres; west along **Piccadilly** towards **Mayfair**, **Green Park**, and **Hyde Park**.

- Learn to use the postal district codes that follow addresses (e.g. W1, WC2) as clues to where places are located (see below).

- Develop a reasonable plan for seeing London based on the time you have available and the nearness of your destinations to one another and to means of transport. Make sure you leave time for wandering or just relaxing.

Directions

Learn to think of London in terms of its obvious divisions: directions, postal districts and neighbourhoods.

North-south

If you look at a map of the whole metropolitan area, the big urban mass of London appears to be divided in two by the River Thames. But this geographical division is by no means equal in other terms. Most of the London of interest to visitors and businessmen is north of the Thames, and some North Londoners will speak disparagingly of those areas and people 'south of the river'. Although most of the attractions, hotels, restaurants, major shops, corporation headquarters and smart neighbourhoods are indeed north of the Thames, the south is not just residential and industrial areas. A major arts complex (the **National Theatre**, the **National Film Theatre**, the **Hayward Gallery** and the **Royal Festival Hall**) is on the South Bank, the **Old Vic** is just behind Waterloo station, and several important attractions, like the **Imperial War Museum** are also there, but many tourists never venture south of the river.

East-west

North of the Thames, the main division runs along east-west lines.

East

This generally refers to the **East End** — which is the home of the Cockney, the traditional London working-class — though geographically it spreads east and north-east from the point where the Strand becomes Fleet Street, and includes the City financial district, as well as neighbourhoods like Islington, Stepney, Hackney, Poplar, Whitechapel and Bethnal Green. Much of the East was badly bombed in the war; today a lot of it is an area of aging terraces and vast council (public housing) estates.

West

Most tourist attractions, hotels, restaurants, famous shops, major stores, large public parks and elegant neighbourhoods are concentrated in the west and south-west parts of central London. The **West End** refers to what was the west end of London in the eighteenth and early nineteenth centuries: loosely, it includes Covent Garden, Soho, St James, Piccadilly and Mayfair. Sometimes it is used to refer to the whole of 'tourist London' in the west. Probably 90 per cent of tourists spend 90 per cent of their time in London in the west.

Postal districts

Having learned to think of London in directions, the letter and number following a London address will provide you with a good clue to its location. The letter, of course, stands for the direction, and (sometimes but not always) the lower the number of the postal district, the nearer it may be to the centre of London, which is reckoned by the Post Office to be Trafalgar Square/Charing Cross. For example, W1 stands for West One (Mayfair) which is nearer to Trafalgar Square than W11, West Eleven (Notting Hill). The system can still be confusing. It must be pointed out, for instance, that SW addresses can be on either side of the Thames (though all SE addresses are south of the river).

Some postal districts

EC   East Central   The Tower of London (4); Bank of England (2); St Paul's (4); Barbican (1)

WC	West Central	Lincoln's Inn Fields (2); Covent Garden (2); Leicester Square (2)
W	West	Soho (1); Piccadilly Circus (1); Paddington Station (2)
SW	South West	St James's (1); Harrods (1); Chelsea (3); Buckingham Palace (1)
SE	South East	Waterloo Station (1); Imperial War Museum (11); Greenwich (10)
N	North	Kings Cross Station (1)
NW	North West	Madame Tussaud's (1); Regent's Park (1)

Historic neighbourhoods from east to west

Now, thinking from east to west, mostly on the north side of the Thames, learn the names of some of the historic central London neighbourhoods.

East

Docklands
An area in the East End, formerly derelict from Blitz destruction and London's rundown as a port after containerization, now a rapidly-developing area of new industry and new upmarket dwellings. Most easily seen from the **Docklands Light Railway**, a new, high-tech elevated system that runs from the **Tower of London** to **Island Gardens**, connected by an under-the-Thames passenger tunnel to **Greenwich**.

East End
The largely working-class eastern parts of London to the City, including the Docklands. It used to be rare for the tourist to visit the scattered attractions here — the **Bethnal Green Museum of Childhood**, the **Brick Lane Market**, and the haunts of **Jack the Ripper** — but the new Docklands Light Railway may soon change all that.

The City of London or The City
This refers to the historic 'square mile' stretching along the Thames from near the Tower to just east of St Paul's and the Barbican — once the original site of walled Roman Londinium and the medieval city. Today it is London's financial district, the equivalent of New York's Wall Street 'downtown', and a separate borough with its own Lord Mayor of London (who is mayor only of The City and not of greater London, which has no mayor).

Like most financial districts, it has an ever-growing skyline of modern high-rises and is almost deserted after dark. The cost of precious floor space to the corporation lawyers, insurance companies, stockbrokers, accountants and banks, banks and more banks that occupy most of its buildings is continually escalating. The City was badly bombed during the war and many of its present buildings are new, unexciting and functional, so, except for **St Paul's**, the **Wren churches**, and the **Tower of London**, many tourists skip it entirely. But if you have the time, perhaps on one of the many inexpensive walking tours, it is worth a walk to see sights like the **Bank of England**, the **Guildhall**, the **Stock Exchange**, **Lloyds** and the **National Westminster Tower**, Britain's tallest skyscraper. You can also take in ancient street names like **Cheapside**, gaze at some of the opulent interiors of some of the older bank lobbies, or eat in an old-fashioned City pub with pinstriped bankers and brokers.

West central

Holborn
Extends between the City and **Covent Garden**. Originally grew up outside the walls of the medieval city along the highway now called Holborn Street. **Lincoln's Inn** and **Gray's Inn** are here, and the tiny streets and alleys are still heavily populated by lawyers, law courts, bookshops and related industries.

Fleet Street
Runs from near **St Paul's** to **St Clement Danes** church. Formerly the centre of the newspaper industry, though most of the major national newspapers have now moved their printing away, leaving behind some staff in interesting Art Deco buildings like the **Daily Express** and **Sunday Telegraph** buildings.

The Strand
Just beyond the Aldwych traffic island, **Fleet Street** becomes **The Strand**, running down to **Trafalgar Square**. Some theatres, London's most famous stamp shops and several notable pubs are located along it.

The West End
Includes the districts that were the 'west end' of London around 1800. Also refers to the heavy population of London's mainstream theatres in this area. For most tourists today it is London's city centre or 'downtown'.

Covent Garden
An area of little streets, trendy restaurants and specialty shops that surround London's most successful development project — the revitalization of Covent Garden's derelict market. The former fruit, vegetable and flower pavilion set in an Italian-inspired piazza is now a busy shopping centre with craftsmen, souvenir sellers, small branch stores and cafés.

Soho
Lying between **Oxford Street** and **Coventry Street**, Soho was until recently a semi-derelict area of X-rated cinemas, striptease joints, sex shops, nightclubs and cheap ethnic restaurants. Now there are fewer strippers and the restaurants are getting increasingly expensive, though it is still a good place to find a wide selection of restaurants in a small area. The southern part is London's **Chinatown**, centred on Gerrard Street. Generally, Soho is pretty tame nowadays.

Leicester Square
On the edge of Soho is a pretty green square surrounded by massive cinemas and tourist-oriented shops. Most new blockbuster films have their British premières here.

Piccadilly
The general name for the area surrounding **Piccadilly Circus** and **Piccadilly** (the street). Until about ten years ago, Piccadilly Circus was becoming steadily more and more derelict, but it is now being revitalized at some cost to the traditional look of an area that is filling up with burger, pizza and rib chains. The former 'circus' is no longer a traffic circle or roundabout, and the central statue of Eros now sits off to the side. But the famous lightboard still flashes big garish messages and the streets teem with tourists and Shaftesbury Avenue theatregoers. Piccadilly (the street) has remained a rather elegant, long, wide street graced with the **Burlington Arcade** and famous traditional shops like **Fortnum & Mason** and **Hatchards** bookshop.

St James's
Lying between Piccadilly and St James's Park, this is an elegant Georgian area of embassies, arcades, expensive hotels and traditional upper-class shops. **Jermyn Street** and **St James's Street** are particularly worth a stroll to savour this atmosphere.

Regent Street
An elegant curving street flanked by grand Regency high-rises. Considered a posh address by airlines and tourist offices, the street is also the home of famous stores

like **Hamley's**, considered to be the world's largest toy store, and **Liberty's**, London's most beautiful department store.

Oxford Street
At **Oxford Circus**, Regent Street intersects Oxford Street, London's biggest generally middle- to down-market shopping street. Most of the traders are major department stores or branches of most of Britain's shoe, clothing and jewellery chains.

Mayfair
Probably London's most up-market area. **Savile Row** tailors, **Cartier's**, **Asprey's** and **Tiffany's**, and streets like **New Bond Street** and **Old Bond Street**, just ooze high prices and exclusive looks to those who can't afford them. Embassies, including America's at Grosvenor Square, and some of the world's best hotels, like **The Connaught** and **Claridges**, help fill out the area.

South, west and further west

Westminster
A whole London borough that takes in most of the West End. However, the name of Westminster also refers to the area that grew up around the King's court, the current site of the **Houses of Parliament**, and later around the Parliament and the main British government buildings along **Whitehall** and adjacent streets, such as **Downing Street**, where the residence and office of the British Prime Minister may be found at Number 10. Across the lovely **St James' Park** to the west is the monarch's residence since the mid-nineteenth century — **Buckingham Palace**.

The South Bank
Across the river from **The Embankment** and **Westminster**, a narrow strip bordering the Thames contains the **National Theatre**, the **National Film Theatre**, the **Royal Festival Hall** and the **Hayward Gallery**. Just behind Waterloo Station, separated from most of its peers, is the famous **Old Vic Theatre** and its fringe offspring.

Belgravia
Between Victoria Station, Buckingham Palace and Knightsbridge lie the Regency terraces of Belgravia, one of the city's most expensive residential areas.

Knightsbridge
This is the exclusive area around **Harrods** and **Brompton Road**, stretching north to **Hyde Park**.

Chelsea
Brompton Road curves into Fulham Road south of Harrods, and what was Knightsbridge imperceptibly shades into Chelsea, which stretches down to the Thames. At the centre is **King's Road**, high-spot of sixties fashion boutiques and showground for the colourful plumage of the punks in the seventies. Chelsea used to be an avant-garde artists' colony; nowadays few artists, or indeed most members of the middle classes, could afford to live there. Tiny two-up, two-down mews houses fetch high prices. Gentrification is spreading steadily southwards along King's Road to Fulham, displacing the traditional butchers and bakers with more chic upmarket delis, restaurants and yuppie shops.

Kensington
The westernmost section of London, attracting large numbers of tourists, with two parts.

South Kensington
Mostly like upmarket Chelsea, but many more of the elegant terraces have been turned into inexpensive tourist hotels. This is particularly true of the scruffy neighbourhood around **Earl's Court**, with its bed-sitters, huge transient community of tourists and vast selection of fast food joints. **Holland Park** and **Kensington High Street** form a central area of elegant high-priced houses. Nearer to Knightsbridge are the **Natural History, Science** and **Geology museums.**

Notting Hill Gate
The more southerly part is an expensive Regency neighbourhood; further north it is full of rapidly-gentrifying Victorian terraces and big council blocks.

Bayswater and Paddington
The area north of Hyde Park. Some parts are elegant Regency; others are decaying bed-sits and bed-and-breakfast hotels, many of which are now being used to house the homeless.

Well-known outer parts of London

Greenwich
Considered by many to be part of the East End, Greenwich is nevertheless south of the river, and more distinguished than many of its neighbours as the home of the **Greenwich Observatory** where GMT was calculated, and as the mooring of several famous ships. Easily reachable by train, light railway (plus foot tunnel) or riverboat.

Richmond and Kew
Also on the Thames, but on the opposite, west, side of London are the polite middle-class areas of Richmond, with its charming riverfront and views, and Kew, home of the world-famous **Kew Gardens**. Richmond and Kew are the last two stops on a District Line spur of the underground.

Hampstead
This is a wealthy, rolling North London neighbourhood bordering the huge green expanse of **Hampstead Heath.**

4 Getting around London

Once you know where you are and where you want to go, consult your map. Is there an Underground station nearby? If not, check a bus map (available free from tourist offices) for a route. Or there might be a British Rail station in the area from which you might walk or take a taxi. In fact, you often have a choice of several methods of transportation for getting around the 650 square mile London sprawl, particularly in the well-served central tourist area and some parts of the north and west. Those visitors going very far south of the river or to some parts of the East End might have to rely on British Rail or minicabs. To help you make a choice we give below some tips and list some passes and discounts to help you save time and money.

- Useful phone numbers: **London Travel Information**: 222 1234; **Travelcheck** (recorded advice on delays and cancellations): 222 1200.

- Unless you must make several connections, the Underground (subway or metro system) will usually get you to your destination in the shortest time with a minimal amount of fuss.

- The Underground and the buses are relatively safe at night, and much safer than their New York counterparts, especially in the well-lit, heavily-travelled central zone.

- A drawback of Underground travel is that it closes down between about 0030–0100 and 0630–0700. During the early morning hours you must rely on taxis or on the excellent but few and far between Night Bus system.

- A double-decker bus journey provides a more interesting slice of local life. For visitors, the main problem is knowing where to get off, especially now that conductors are being phased out in favour of driver-only buses.

- Other than for the excellent sightseeing from their top decks, buses are at their best for short trips, but, unlike taxis, they must stop at appointed places and are more easily snagged in traffic snarls.

- Bus journeys are only slightly less expensive or the same price as the comparable Underground journeys.

- Black cabs, either the familiar, traditional FX4, or its slightly sleeker new rival, the Metrocab, now come in a variety of colours, but they remain the most expensive way of getting around.

- Even black cabs are not that expensive if you split the fare. Example: cab fare is £4.40; an Underground ticket to the same destination is 90p. If there are four of you and you split the fare, a cab will cost you £1.10 each, or only 20p more per person.

- Minicabs are cheaper than black cabs for trips to the airports or outer London.

- **Travelcards** and **Capitalcards** (see below) are two travel passes which provide unlimited travel for a set price and can help beat the two main difficulties of London's transportation system: expense, and the fact that tickets rarely allow you to transfer between different modes of transport or even between red buses.

Passes

London Regional Transport and tourist boards heavily push the **Travelcard** and **Capitalcard**, though London Transport has been considering the introduction of separate bus and tube passes by 1990. Some tourists buy one-day cards every day for convenience. Should you automatically buy one? If you know you will be making more than one round trip journey in central London or beyond during the day, or you know you will need to use bus and Underground, then it's probably worthwhile to buy a one-day Travelcard. If you're making a journey by bus or Underground *and* British Rail outside the five-zone Greater London area, then you're probably better off with a Capitalcard. Still confused? Read on . . .

Zones
For purposes of these passes, London Regional Transport divides the Greater London area into five concentric zones. Zone 1 encompasses the whole of the main tourist area of central London and most of the major tourist sights. Zone 2 encompasses a few other tourist sights like Greenwich and the Docklands. The other three zones encompass scattered places of interest, vast tracts of suburbia and Heathrow Airport. In other words, Zone 1 is where you'll probably spend most of your time unless your hotel is in an outer zone.

Visitor Travelcards
These have replaced the former Explorer Pass and can only be bought overseas from travel agents or tour operators. Like the ordinary Travelcard sold here, they allow unlimited rail, bus and tube travel and come in one-day and weekly versions. Unlike the Travelcard, the longer period Visitor Travelcard does not require a photo and is also available in three and four day versions. It comes with discount vouchers for products and services you may or may not want to use. At press time, buying an all-zone Visitor Travelcard had no price advantage over Travelcards bought here.

Travelcards
These are available in one-day and seven-day versions from Underground stations. The one-day version is the best bargain. For only £2.30 it now allows unlimited red bus, tube and rail travel in all five Greater London zones after 0930 Monday to Friday and all day on weekends. Most visitors buying a seven-day card will prefer to purchase only a one-zone (£6.40) or two-zone (£8.20) (if, for example, your hotel is in Zone 2) card; why pay considerably more for all five zones (£17.70) unless you're going to make a number of forays into outer zones 3–5? These areas contain only a few visitor attractions. You might want to buy daily all zones Travelcards as you need them (if you buy seven – this is still a total of only £16.10). Or, buy a cheap day return on the day you need to go out to Heathrow in zone 5. A small drawback of the seven-day card is that you must supply a little British passport-sized photo, but you can easily obtain these from the automatic photo machines in many stations (four poses for £1.00). A photo is not required for a one-day card. One-day cards can now be bought from the new computerized station ticket machines — but even they will refuse your money before 0930 Monday–Friday.

Capitalcards
If you want to go to or from somewhere outside Greater London that's most easily reached by British Rail, and you will also travel by bus and tube within the five zones, then you might want to investigate the new **Capitalcard** to see whether there is any price advantage over combined rail/tube tickets to the destination. Like the Travelcards, they include buses, tubes and rail in Greater London and are valid from 9.30 Monday–Friday and all day Saturday and Sunday.

Children
Children aged 5–16 pay only 80p for an all-zone one-day Travelcard and half the adult price for Capitalcards.

Means of transport

The Underground
The first thing most visitors notice about getting around London is that the easiest method is undoubtedly the Underground (or 'tube'), the city's enormous 251-mile metro or subway network, the world's first and still the world's largest. (Americans should note that 'Subway' signs in London will lead them to pedestrian underpasses not the tube.) The system is also undoubtedly one of the easiest to find your way around. Stations are not difficult to identify — just look for the famous circle-with-a-line-through-it symbol. Otherwise the ease of use has nothing to do with the actual lay-out — the plan is anything but logical, having grown from a hodge-podge of old local railway lines and later projects — but has everything to do with **the map**, found at every station entrance, on every station platform, and now on many T-shirts.

The map is an award-winning classic, a triumph of everyday graphic design. Bright colour-coding clearly demarcates each of the variously-named route lines. Interchanges are marked with an obvious symbol. Find the departure station and the destination station on the map and follow the colour route to the desired station, or the nearest interchange for transfer to another coloured route. The map is reproduced everywhere, and if you study it before you start out, you shouldn't get lost. There are, however, a few other things you need to know.

Stations
Some of London's stations are simple affairs, with only a ticket hall and two platforms, while others, especially interchange stations like **King's Cross** and **Baker Street**, are unnecessarily labyrinthine, with long, exhausting, maze-like tunnels.

2F

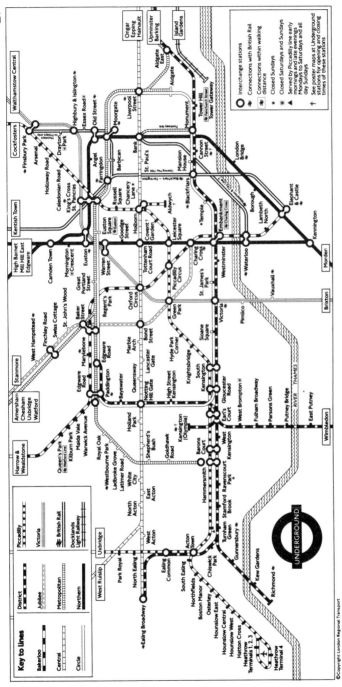

Nevertheless, as long as you keep your desired route line, direction (north, south, east, west) and colour code in mind, and follow the signs, even in the mad panic of rush hours (0800–0900 and 1630–1800) you'll find your way to the correct platform. Most station platforms have a display board which indicates how far your train will be going. If not, you'll have to look out for the sign on the front of your train to note whether that final destination is beyond yours, or on a fork or branch line. In some of the larger stations different route lines may even share the same platforms. Again display boards will advise you whether to wait for the next train. A loudspeaker announcement repeating 'Mind the gap' as you get ready to board means that there is a dangerous space you must step over as you board the train. Smoking is now prohibited throughout the Underground system.

Foreign tourists may find the 'Way Out' exit signs to be slightly crazy, but to the British that is what the phrase literally means.

Changing trains in a very few stations, like **Hammersmith**, requires travellers to hold on to their tickets and cross the street to another route station. In any case, you should clutch your ticket until the final collector's barrier, or you'll have to pay twice. Look around when you've passed the barrier for the 'Local Map' on the station wall for local directions. But don't forget to enjoy the stations themselves — some are of a charming Edwardian or Art Deco design and many are now being restored or redecorated with a local theme. **Baker Street**, for example, has tiled silhouettes of Sherlock Holmes.

Tickets

Tickets work on the same zonal system as Travelcards, the bargain all-inclusive travel pass described above. If you don't want, or you don't need, a Travelcard, the set adult fare in Zone 1 (Central Zone) is currently 60p. Children pay only 50p. If you travel to a destination in the next zone, the fare goes up to 90p (40p for children). For return trips to the three further-out zones (including Wimbledon, Richmond and Heathrow) and back on the same day, you'll save money by buying a **Cheap Day Return** or a one-day **Travelcard**.

Buses

Countless tourist guide books have advised that the best way to see London is from the top of a red double-decker bus. This statement is probably still true — if you take London Regional Transport's excellent City Tour or if you have plenty of time. The chief drawback of the buses is their speed — or rather lack of it: they must pick up and drop off passengers at appointed bus stops. In doing so, they inevitably get caught up in traffic snarls and slow downs.

If you want to see London from the top of a double-decker you can't do better than to follow Route 15 or 52 from end to end. Route 15 begins in the **East End** and takes you past the **Tower of London**, **St Paul's**, the **Strand**, **Trafalgar Square**, **Piccadilly Circus**, **Regent Street**, **Oxford Street**, **Marble Arch**, **Paddington Station**, and the **Portobello Market**. Route 52 begins at **Victoria Station** and passes round the back of **Buckingham Palace Gardens**, **Hyde Park Corner**, near **Harrods**, then past **Hyde Park**, **High Street Kensington**, **Kensington Church Street**, **Notting Hill Gate**, and the **Portobello Market**. Other routes recommended for sight-seeing: 11, 16, 24, 31, 74, 88, 134, and 159. Otherwise, the red double-deckers are best on short distances or to supplement an Underground or train trip.

Be aware that the entire bus system is undergoing privatization and deregulation. As outer and long-distance routes are privatized or contracted out, the process will eventually reach the central city. The red double-decker is not threatened at present, but be aware that you will encounter two types. The older models have more charm for the adventurous because (in theory if not strictly legally) you can jump on or off at the back at any time, and (mostly) friendly conductors sell tickets, make change and dispense advice and information about the sights and where to get off. The passing of the conductor is a matter of great regret to those who love to travel on the buses and don't know the city.

Eighty per cent of London's buses are now the more modern one-man, pay the driver at the front type. Drivers still offer change for small denominations (except on the single-decker Red Arrow routes, where there is a flat fare of 40p), but this rare luxury is due to be phased out because it slows down traffic and the bus itself. Once you're on, you can't get off unless the driver opens the door — so be sure to ring the button by the door. These buses are cleaner and roomier than the old models. On both types you should try to sit in front upstairs to enjoy the view (smokers are restricted to the rear upstairs seats).

Bus maps are available free from London Transport. Check the appropriate numbered route and then find a stop. Stops have metal 'flags' at the top of a pole, indicating which route numbers stop there and whether it is a 'request stop'. If it says 'Request', then you must stick your arm out if you want the driver to stop for you. At other stops, the driver will stop automatically. Many poles also have an eye-level plaque that gives the schedule of routes stopping there and indicates whether the bus is going in the direction you want to go. The buses themselves are numbered to correspond to route numbers, though you should also look at the destination sign on the front of the bus to see whether it will be going all the way.

We hope you will join the famous queue to board: it's a civilized British custom that is sadly beginning to die out.

Hoppas and Red Arrows

Hoppas are 'midibuses' — red medium-sized buses that are part of the same system as the red double-deckers, but are meant to be more frequent and convenient for tourists and shoppers (Mondays–Saturdays every 6–7 minutes). The current Central Hoppa runs from **Waterloo Station** to **Kensington High Street** and stops at **Westminster Abbey**, **Victoria Station**, **King's Road**, **Knightsbridge** (Harrods) and **South Kensington** (Museums), to name but a few. Fare is a flat 60p for adults and 50p for children, and all Travelcards and Capital Cards valid for the Central Zone are accepted. Red Arrows are direct buses from the major railway stations to important London points. The fare is a flat 50p and, again, London Transport passes are valid.

Night Buses

After midnight most bus routes close for the night, and only a few 'Night Bus' routes are available. If you can't afford a taxi home, get a bus map or phone for the schedule of these hourly buses.

Green Line buses

These go the airports, the suburbs, some attractions and nearby towns. Phone 01-668 7261 for information and schedules.

Tickets

Red bus fares seem to be constantly on the increase. In Zone 1 fares are currently 40p or 60p. When you cross into Zone 2, the fare goes up to 90p and rises in increments as you go further out. Hoppas are a flat 60p. Because there is no facility for transferring tickets between buses, or between buses and the Underground or British Rail, Travelcards and Capitalcards are very valuable to those who plan on doing a lot of travel by bus, but you must buy these at Underground stations and designated shops as they are not sold on buses.

Taxis

When a Londoner wins the pools or a lottery (or maybe when they write a best-selling guidebook) and are asked what this means to them, an unsurprising number have said, 'I can take a taxi whenever I want without worrying about the cost'. This is unsurprising because London cabs are roomy, comfortable and efficient. Black cab drivers must pass a rigorous 'knowledge' test which requires them to know all streets and routes within central London and to identify obscure streets and sights. Many aspirants don't make it. Most drivers keep the sliding glass window that separates you from them open to only a small crack — enough to hear you if you want to talk to them (and enough to strain to eavesdrop if the backseat chat sounds desperately interesting). All this adds to the basic convenience of a taxi — you get in, and get out at your destination: no worrying about a long walk from the station, finding your directions, or getting lost; no growing frustration as your bus creeps from stop to stop in excruciatingly slow traffic. You can sit back and relax in luxurious splendour.

When you consider all this, London black cab fares don't seem that exorbitant. By world standards, they aren't, especially if you're splitting the fare. Fare-splitting usually means between you and your party; fare-splitting between strangers is now allowed from a stand at Heathrow Terminal 2 and throughout central London, but the idea is not popular with cabbies and has not been promoted. Still, one person's journey from Notting Hill to Soho costs, for example, just £5. There are small surcharges for travel after 8 pm and at weekends and holiday, and for luggage. A few tips:

● Yellow 'For Hire' signs in cab windows and a lighted yellow lamp on the top of the cab indicate that the driver is on duty and looking for a fare. If you hail him he should stop. If the sign is turned off and the lamp not lit (and no passenger is in the back), hail him anyway — he may stop to find out if you are on his route home.

● A black cab driver 'For Hire' may not refuse to take you if the journey is less than 6 miles and within the Greater London area.

● Don't hesitate to ask if you think your driver is going the long way round. There are a few unscrupulous drivers who should know better.

● To report a driver who fails to observe the above rules, or is rude or discourteous, phone 278 1744. Standards are strictly upheld and all complaints are investigated.

● You can call a black cab to pick you up (Tel. 286 0286 or 272 0272), but the meter will already be running. Most minicab companies (see below) don't impose a pre-pick-up charge, and you can book a minicab in advance.

Minicabs

Most minicabs are not 'mini' at all. A surprising number are estate cars (station wagons) or older Mercedes-Benz. Often, they are private cars belonging to individual drivers who pay a fee to work for a minicab firm that maintains a booking service and dispatches them to pick up fares. For this reason, the quality of drivers and vehicles varies. Some are rude and may know London less well than you do, but other minicabbies are very professional and take great pride in their vehicles and their work.

Minicabs are considerably cheaper than black cabs for long-distance trips, especially to the airports. Generally speaking, they do not use meters, so it's a good idea to get a fare quote over the phone and then confirm it with the driver. Within the central area, the fare difference when compared with black cabs isn't that great, usually not much more than a pound. The other major difference is that you can't hail them, you must phone. Ask at your hotel for recommendations, or look in the Yellow Pages or on local noticeboards, because companies are predominantly local.

Delta (01-453 1111) is a recommended company with high standards, but we find they are very popular. Another notable company is **City Cars** (01-488 4223).

British Rail suburban trains
British Rail goes to a number of places in outer London where the tube doesn't, particularly south of the river. Sometimes, you even have a choice; you'll need to check a map of the local area and fares to see which is more convenient. Underground stations can sell designated combined tube/BR tickets to some stations within Greater London, but you might find it cheaper to buy an all zone **Travelcard** (see above), which allows unlimited tube, bus and train travel within Greater London for one day.

5 Other practical matters

More information

London's two major information centres are the **London Tourist Board Information Centre** at Victoria Station (Tel. 01-730 3488), open daily from Easter–October, Mon–Sat 0900–1900 and Sun 0900–1700; November–Easter, Mon–Sun 0900–1700; and the **British Travel Centre** at 12 Lower Regent Street (Tel. 01-730 3400), open 0900–1830 Mon–Fri, Sat–Sun 1000–1600.

In our experience, the Victoria Station office has better London information because it is run by the London Tourist Board and Convention Bureau, though it is more crowded. The British Travel Centre, run by the BTA, provides nationwide information, rail and hotel bookings. Both can make local bookings. Sometimes it's interesting to compare their different approaches to the same subject. For example, they each publish pamphlets on 'Renting a London Apartment'.

There are separate information counters at **The Tower, Harrods, Selfridges, Heathrow** and **Gatwick**. The **Scottish Tourist Board** is at 19 Cockspur Street SW11 (Tel. 01-930 8661), and the **Wales Tourist Board** is at 34 Piccadilly W1 (Tel. 01-409 0969). *The Daily Telegraph Information Bureau* (almost any topic) (Tel. 01-538 6293).

North America

British Tourist Authority (BTA) offices:

40 West 57th Street, New York NY 10019; Tel. (212) 581 4700

John Hancock Center, 875 North Michigan Avenue, Chicago, II 60611; Tel. (312) 787 0490

World Trade Centre, 350 Figueroa Street, Suite 450, Los Angeles, California 90071; Tel. (213) 628 3525

Cedar Maple Plaza, 2305 Cedar Springs Road, Dallas, Texas 75201; (214) 720 4040

94 Cumberland Street, Toronto, Ontario M5R3 N3; Tel. (416) 925 6326

City tours

Many companies offer basic London sightseeing tours at competitive rates from the top end of Trafalgar Square, Parliament Square, Coventry Street (between Piccadilly Circus and Leicester Square) and other locations, but London Transport's own *Original Sightseeing Tour* (£6) is hard to beat. (*The Sunday Times* found this tour had the best guides.) It departs several times a day from Victoria Station and other spots and lasts an hour and a half. For information, ring 01-222 1234. *Harrods* runs upmarket half and full day trips in posh buses at premium prices. Other companies run a variety of themed London and day tours (information readily available from tourist offices and most hotels), but to get a real feel for the city, try one of the numerous walking tours. Phone one of the companies for a schedule. You then simply show up at the meeting point, pay the fee (usually £1.50 to £4) and enjoy the stroll and the story. All kinds of areas and subjects (Jack the Ripper, Ancient Pubs, Legal London etc.) are covered by a number of companies but we specially recommend Alex and Peggy Cobban of *Discovering London*. (Tel. (0277) 213704). Other useful companies: try *Streets of London* (Tel. 01 882 3414) or *Citisights* (Tel. 01 739 2372). If you want a pampered, private tour service, you can't do better than Simon Anderson of *Friends in London* (P.O. Box 163 London WC2; Tel. 01-240 9670). He also runs a Rolls Royce/Jaguar airport greeting service.

Money and currency exchange

In general, the wisest advice is still to carry **travellers' cheques/checks**, which can be replaced if lost or stolen. Almost all cheques issued by major financial institutions are readily redeemable in the UK. It is less common for retailers to accept travellers' cheques than it is in the United States and some other countries, but, in London, many of the major stores and a number of restaurants accept pound cheques. A few, like Harrods, will take dollar travellers' cheques (or even US currency) at a rate which is usually less favourable than a bank's. American Express, Thomas Cook and VISA are the most widely accepted. Major credit cards can be valuable because you don't pay commission when your account is debited (but see below).

Some cash is always practical for foreign visitors to have on hand in the form of small denominations of British money. Money makes the world go round and currency is most obviously money. For this reason we never travel abroad without $10–20 worth of US$1 bills for unforeseen tips and emergencies.

British money

Foreign visitors will find British money far less confusing than they may have thought. Forget about crowns, florins, shillings and ha'pennies. Since decimalization in 1971 these terms are out, though 'one shilling' (5p) and 'two shilling' (10p) coins are still in circulation and a few older people still call a 5p piece a 'bob'.

Now there is simply 100p ('pee') or pennies to the £1 (pound), in denominations of 1p, 2p, 5p, 10p, 20p, 50p and £1. Notes come in £5, £10, £20 and £50. If you go up to Scotland you will still find £1 notes. The slang for £1 is a 'quid'.

Exchange

The pound is constantly fluctuating in value in relation to most major currencies. The best rates may change with legislation or practice, but, in four years of publication, we have found the following tips have held generally true:

• *Currency notes*   Your best deal is usually at one of the major British banks. Over the years we've found the **National Westminster Bank** best of all because their policy has been to charge a flat commission plus a fair exchange rate. Commission has varied between £1–£1.50. Bank policy is always changing, but other banks have charged commission on a percentage basis (usually ½ to 1½%). This can be penal if you are changing large amounts, and there's no stated maximum. Check both the commission and the exchange rates charged.

• *Rates from bureaux de change and street traders*   Perhaps no group has generated so much heat from tourist authorities as the operators of the many foreign exchange/*bureaux de change* chain shops. Widespread complaints have arisen about deceptive practices such as posting only *selling rates* for the dollar (the lower rate that British tourists pay to buy US dollars) rather than the *buying rate* (the higher rate that US tourists must pay to purchase pounds) and unfair rates of exchange behind 'no commission' signs. Sometimes it's late and the banks are closed: if you must go somewhere else, look for posted buying and selling rates, and the small sign that shows it adheres to the London Tourist Board's Code of Practice. Small shop traders sometimes give favourable rates of exchange though these may be offered in the expectation that you will buy something.

• *Major stores*   Their rates are not far off those of the banks, though you need to watch commission charges. Harrods operates its own bank, **The Harrods Trust**, and many Americans have opened 'checking accounts'. We've found Harrods rates to be competitive.

• *Travellers' cheques/checks*   The best to have are Barclays/VISA, Thomas Cook/Midland Bank or American Express, because, at least at presstime, you won't pay commission twice if you go to the issuer to redeem them. Thus, American Express holders should go to American Express, Thomas Cook holders to Thomas Cook or Midland Bank and Barclays/VISA holders to Barclays Bank. Some favoured customers of these institutions may have paid no original sales commission, either. Holders of other cheques should redeem them at the issuer's branch if possible, or at one of the other major banks.

American Express	6 Haymarket, SW1. Tel. 01-930 4411. Hours, 9–6 Mon–Fri, 9–5 Sat, 10–6 Sunday. Piccadilly Circus underground.
Thomas Cook	(Best for its own travellers' cheques.) Opposite Tourist Information in Victoria Station, and many other locations. Cheques also favourably redeemed at Midland Bank branches.
VISA	Redeemable at all Barclays Bank branches.

• *Hotel rates*   Larger hotels will exchange cheques/currency for guests, but amounts accepted for cash are small and the rate is not favourable.

• *Credit cards*   It's very sensible to carry one of the major credit cards (VISA, Access/Master Card or American Express). These cards are widely accepted all over the UK, but even if you don't want to use them, they can be very helpful in an emergency, especially if you know your secret PIN (personal identification number), with which you can actually get cash from the cash dispensers of UK banks (check with your card issuer before leaving home). And if you don't know your PIN, you can still get cash up to a stated limit during office hours from participating local banks (look for the appropriate window sticker).

It may just be luck, but we've found we've often come out best in exchange terms by using 'plastic money' because there's no commission and the exchange rate is often a favourable international one. Of course, you can lose out badly if, for example, you are a US tourist and the rate for the dollar goes against you in between the time you pay for the goods and the moment the merchant relays the charge to the credit card company. But with increased computerization and improved communications, lengthy time lags are becoming less common.

Banking hours
Banks are open from 0930–1530 Monday to Friday, with the exception of national or regional holidays (see below). Some branches of Barclays and National Westminster are open on Saturday morning. 24-hour exchange is available at airports. Victoria Station's exchange booths and many *bureaux de change* have long hours.

Communication

Post offices
Hours vary, but most branches are open at least 0930–1700 Monday to Friday, and 0930–1200 on Saturdays. Lines can be long because post offices are also the place where customers get their car and TV licences and pick up welfare payments, and the Post Office also has its own bank (Girobank — though at press time this is a new candidate for privatization) — but few branches have foreign exchange facilities. For speedier service go to a large main post office with separate windows for different services. From July 1989, some shops will sell stamps.

The Post Office says that the fastest overseas deliveries go from the main post office at King Edward Street, EC1 (where *poste restante* or general delivery mail is automatically sent if you don't specify otherwise), but the most convenient post office for visitors is probably the **Trafalgar Square Branch Office** at 24–28 King William IV Street, WC2, Tel. 01-930 9580, Underground: Charing Cross. It has long opening hours (0800–2000 Monday to Saturday, 1000–1700 Sundays), and staff are well-versed in the requirements of international mail. There is a Post Office Shop next door for paper, string, cards, stationery and officially-acceptable and suitably-sized mailing boxes.

Postage rates (as of early 1989)
North America
Cards   27p
Letters   32p, then 15p for each additional 10 grams.

EEC (and other European Countries*)
Cards   19p, 23p*
Letters   19p up to 20 grams, 23p up to 20 grams*, then 39p up to 60 grams for both.

Australia, New Zealand
Cards   27p
Letters   35p up to 10 grams, then 16p for each additional 10 grams.

An inexpensive way to send airmail letters anywhere in the world is the Aerogramme (27p each; pack of 6 for £1.50). Available from post offices only. Swiftair is an extra £1.65, but gets letters there a little faster.

Hong Kong, Malaysia, Singapore
Cards   27p
Letters   32p then 15p for each additional 10 grams

Japan, Korea
Cards   27p
Letters   35p up to 10 grams, then 16p for every extra 10 grams

Telephones

Hotel service rates are mostly outrageous, and some of the larger hotels even admit that international calls are a good source of profit! You can get round this problem in four ways.

Coin-operated phones

These are OK for local calls, if you can find one that's working. Many London phone boxes are constantly jammed — due to vandals and slow repair work by British Telecom.

The new coin pay-phones flash 'INSERT MONEY' on a digital display as soon as the receiver is lifted. Insert the relevant coins: the display unit will tell you how much you have left as you talk, and flashes when you need to add more money. Dial the number. You'll then hear a purring ringing sound of two tones, or a rapid repeated tone. The latter means the line is 'engaged' (busy). When you replace the receiver, unused money is refunded.

Older-style phones have no digital display and you insert your coins only when the phone is answered — you'll hear a series of high-pitched pips which stop when you put in enough money. More pips sound when you need to add more money. Coin phones are a cumbersome way of making international calls. If you have to use them for this purpose, get plenty of 50p pieces beforehand. It is generally better to buy a high-denomination *phonecard*.

Phonecards

Phonecards are available from many newsagents and general stores. It might suit you to buy a high-denomination card (you can buy £10 and £20 cards) to last you for your trip. Card-operated phones are more efficient, the boxes (booths) are less likely to be vandalized, and you don't have to worry about sticking in more coins when the pips start.

Credit card phones

Get an international phone credit card before you leave home. With it, Americans can make calls home on **USA Direct** (0800-89-0011). Some public phones (mostly at airports and railway stations) will accept VISA cards or Access/Master Cards.

Private rates

This is the cheapest way. If you can get your host to agree, call from a private home or bed and breakfast — and watch the time.
Direct dial time charge bands to the US and Canada
(Correct at presstime, but call 100 for latest rates.)
Cheap rate   2000–0800 and all day Saturday and Sunday: 61p per minute
Peak rate   1500–1700: 81p per minute
Standard rate The rest of the time: 71p per minute
Direct dial time charge bands to Western Europe
Cheap rate   2000–0800: 36p per minute
Peak rate   0800–2000: 46p per minute
Direct dial time charge bands to Hong Kong, Australia and New Zealand
Cheap rate   1430–1930, 2400–0700: 81p per minute
Peak rate   0700–1430, 1930–2400: 102p per minute

Useful numbers

Operator	100
Emergency	999
London directory enquiries	142
Rest of Britain enquiries	192
International Operator (North America)	155
US Embassy	01-499 9000
Canadian High Commission	629 9492

Telegrams, telex
International cables or telexes can be sent by dialling 190, but it's usually cheaper just to phone home. Telexes can also be sent from the ***Westminster Communications Centre***, 1A Broadway SW1 (Mon–Sat 0900–1900), Tel. 01-222 4444. Calls can also be made from here but there's a minimum extra charge of £1.50.

Medical matters

Doctors
British visitors can, of course, attend the local doctor's surgery as a temporary resident. Citizens of the EEC and other countries should check to see if their country has reciprocal arrangements. There is no reciprocal agreement with the USA — American visitors will have to pay. However, individual doctors may not ask for payment for minor problems because they don't want to undertake the necessary paperwork.
 If you fall ill you have several options:

● Your hotel will have a doctor on call or a list of doctors. The local police usually have a list.

● You can phone or pop into a local doctor's office (called a 'surgery') and see if they'll treat you or recommend someone.

● ***Medical Express***, Chapel Place, W1 (Tel. 01-499 1991) is just off Oxford Street (Bond Street or Oxford Circus undergrounds). Basic charge for a visit is £45, but they also run tests, take X-rays, etc. Opening hours: Monday to Friday 0800–2000, Saturday 0900–1800.

● Finally, you can hail a taxi and ask the driver to take you to the nearest hospital Casualty (or Accident and Emergency) Department. There's no charge for a genuine emergency, but you may start to incur charges after the first day. So, if you're not eligible for the National Health, or your country has no reciprocal agreement, it's very important to review your foreign travel health insurance coverage before you leave.

Dentists
Again, call or visit a local surgery, or ring 01-400 0400 for directions to a nearby dentist.

Glasses
It's a good idea to bring a copy of your prescription with you. The fastest place to get it filled is ***Selfridges Optical*** in the department store, 400 Oxford Street, W1, Tel. 01-629 1234, ext. 3889. Most take 2–3 hours. More complicated prescriptions may take longer. You pay over the odds, but most other places will take several days.

Drugs
What the Americans call a 'drugstore' the British usually call a 'chemist'. Chemist shops are everywhere, but most close by 1800–2000. ***Bliss*** at 50–56 Willesden Lane,

NW6, Tel. 01-624 8000 is open 0900–0200. There are chemists in most areas that are open at night; the police have a list of these.

Habits

Cigarettes
Most US brands and many other foreign brands are available at very high prices (heavily taxed). If you've got a big habit, make sure you bring your duty free allowances (400 from outside the Common Market) with you. Smoking is banned on the Underground and on the lower deck of double-decker buses. Otherwise, London is less anti-smoking than New York and other major cities, though of course courtesy is always appreciated.

Alcohol
The drinking age is 18. Children under 16 must be accompanied by parents in special rooms, and many pubs exclude children altogether. Pubs may now open from 1100 or 1130 to 2300 Monday to Saturday under new legislation, but a number still keep to the old afternoon closing period of 1430–1700 or 1730. Sundays hours are now 1200–1500 and 1900–2200. Retail Sales hours are the same as most normal business and grocery shop hours, except on Sundays, when alcohol can only be sold during Sunday pub hours. Customs generally allow you to bring in one bottle duty free.

Laundry

Dry cleaners and laundries are everywhere. Check whether they have a 'same day' or 'next day' service. Launderettes or coin-operated laundries are fairly expensive, but cheaper than laundries. In most, an extra small fee will allow you to leave your clothes for a 'service wash' that you pick up later. Since launderettes seldom have ironing facilities, you might want to bring a small travel iron with you.

Electricity and appliances

British electric current is 240 volts AC (50Hz). If you're bringing along a hairdryer, shaver or other electrical appliance, you need not only a transformer but an adaptor that will convert to British electric plugs.

Time

All of Britain is in one time zone. London is five hours ahead of New York; six hours ahead of Chicago; seven hours ahead of Denver and eight hours ahead of Los Angeles and San Francisco. Paris is one hour ahead of London. Between late March and late October, Britain is on British Summer Time, which means that clocks are set one hour forward for daylight saving.

Public Holidays

New Years Day (January 1 (or the Monday after a weekend New Year))
New Years Monday (Scotland)
St Patrick's Day (March 17 — N. Ireland)
Good Friday
Easter Monday (not Scotland)
May Day Bank Holiday (first Monday in May)
May Bank Holiday (last Monday in May)
Battle of the Boyne (mid-July — N. Ireland)

August Bank Holiday (first Monday in August — Scotland; last Monday in August — England and N. Ireland)
Christmas Day
Boxing Day (December 26th or the Monday after a weekend Christmas)

Opening Hours

Offices
Usually 0900–1700, but 0930–1730 is also common. Lunch is most popular between 1300 and 1400, but most offices stay open. Banks open 0930–1530 Monday–Friday.

Shops
0900 or 1000 to 1730 or 1800 Monday to Saturday. Some have a late closing night when they stay open for an extra hour or two, and many supermarkets are now open 0800–2000. Wherever you are you will probably find a corner shop or delicatessen open until 2000. It is illegal for most shops to open on Sundays, but some do it anyway.

Museums and galleries
Times vary, but very few are open on Sunday mornings.

Hairdressers

Men's
If you are just looking for a trim, you can usually find a barber or men's hairdresser at department stores, hotels and major railway stations. Mayfair still has two old fashioned 'gentlemen's barbers' where a shave and a haircut is a special treat of superb service in elegant surroundings. **Truefit & Hill** (23 Old Bond Street W1, Tel. 01-493 2961) has a photo of patron Prince Philip on the wall. **Trumper's** (9 Curzon Street W1, Tel. 01-499 1850) has individual velvet-curtained cubicles. Both sell interesting men's toiletries. Neither is unreasonably expensive, but you need to book.

Women's
Ask at your hotel. Two places we recommend are **Ellis Helen** (75 Walton Street SW3, Tel. 01-589 8519) (men also) and **Cazaly & Co.** (61 Monmouth Street WC2, Tel. 01-240 4973). Both are reasonable, but if you want quality at very low prices try the **Vidal Sassoon School** at 56 Davis Mews W1 (men too) (Tel. 01-629 4635). Fashionable, critically-acclaimed places include **Trevor Sorbie** (10 Russell Street WC2, Tel. 01-240 3816); **Neville Daniel** (by appointment to the Queen) (175 Sloane Street SW1, Tel. 01-245 6151); **The Head Gardener of Hyde Park** (37 Knightsbridge SW1, Tel. 01-235 4994), and **Harrods** own is highly rated (Tel. 01-730 1234).

Senior Citizens Discounts

Take along proof of age, and ask. Some places only give discounts to holders of British pension books. O.A.P. means 'Old Age Pensioner' (a woman over 60 or a man over 65). Many of our senior American subscribers have taken advantage of OAP discounts.

Weather and clothing

London weather is unpredictable at any time of year. Some summer days require a light sweater; winter gloom is occasionally broken by golden, brilliant days. If you're travelling elsewhere in the country, conditions can vary markedly within a few miles.

Travel west, and especially north-west, and rainfall increases to 60 inches a year or more (Cloudy London gets only a deceptive 23 inches, spread fairly evenly over the year). Our recommendations below are based mainly on London, so remember that it may be colder if you are headed north or up into the hills. Recorded *weather information* is on 0898 500 480.

January/February
January and February are the coldest months. The damp cold seldom allows the mercury to climb up above 10°C (50°F). Snow might remain on the ground for a few days, but Britain has relatively mild winters compared to Northern continental Europe and the northern half of the United States.

What to wear
Dress warmly. Bring heavy woollens and rubber boots or shoe covers for outdoors, and lighter woollens for indoors (rooms may have low heating levels). You might want to wait until you get here to buy some knits in the January sales.

March/April
Spring arrives tentatively in early March with buds, crocuses and flowers in the parks. There is still the threat of more freezes and snowfalls on the hills and in the north. By April, the weather changes to alternate between sunny cool days and damp, chilly, dreary periods. Temperature variation: −1°C (30°F)–12°C (50s°F). There are not a lot of new leaves or blossoms until mid-April to the beginning of May, even in London. For most of March it's best to stay south and enjoy spring at its early best.

What to wear
Come prepared to dress in layers (i.e. shirt or blouse, sweater, jacket and/or medium-weight coat that you can peel off if you're uncomfortable). Heavy woollens can be dispensed with, but you still need to be warmly dressed if you're going to hillier elevations, northern parts or windy areas of the coast. Expect some indoor temperatures to drop as heating levels are reduced.

May/June
By early May the trees are leafing and flowering. There'll be dull grey, damp days dipping down to 4–10°C (40°sF), but more days will be warmer, some with 15–20°C (60°sF) temperatures.

What to wear
During the summer, always have a cotton pullover handy. The weather is so changeable that a hot, sunny day can suddenly become cold and damp. Bring a few with you (and a woollen sweater if you've got a cold nature or are visiting coastal or highland areas — where a light to medium jacket will also come in handy). Alternatively, Marks and Spencer sell beautiful cotton sweaters at reasonable prices. Long-sleeved shirts and blouses are more useful than short-sleeved. Many hotel dining rooms still require jacket and tie.

July/August
This period is supposed to be the hottest time of the year, but in Britain, never count on long periods of sunny days. Mornings are generally above 10°C (50°s); it can then warm up to 21°C (70°F) or even 26°C (80°F), but 15–23°C (low 60s–low 70sF) is the average range. Higher ground and beach areas can be plagued by chilly winds. Rain is always possible.

What to wear
Play it safe. Bring your bathing suit, cotton shirts, blouses (long-sleeved are

preferable), light skirts and dresses, but either bring or buy cotton or light wool sweaters and a windbreaker or light jacket. Only in holiday areas are shorts very often seen on adults, but many Britons who are stuffy at other times of the year are casual in summer and most people care even less what visitors wear. Each summer I notice fewer diners in ties, but it will be many years before British women take to 'trouser suits' with the same enthusiasm as their American counterparts. Generally, it's OK to go bare-legged here in the summer.

September/October
Summer starts to fizzle out slowly in September. There may be some dark cool days, but usually there is no genuine autumn cold until late in the month. Most places in southern England don't have a very good 'leaf show' until at least mid-October, but this depends on what the weather has been like. Temperatures range from 8–21°C (high 40°s–low 70°sF) from September to mid-October, and there is always the hope of a pleasant Indian Summer. From mid-October, you begin to notice a more consistent chill.

What to wear
From mid-September onwards the easiest thing to do is come prepared to dress in layers. Bring at least a medium coat and a medium sweater that you can pull on and off to match the temperature changes. Except in the far north, at higher elevations and on unusually chilly evenings, you won't really feel comfortable in medium wool suits and dresses until some time in October.

November/December
November usually brings the first few scattered days of honest-to-goodness winter weather, but is mainly a time of damp autumn temperatures, 8–12°C (40°s and 50°sF), that are penetratingly chilly but not freezing. It may freeze a few times, and snow may fall in the higher Pennines, Wales and the Scottish Highlands. December is a transition month between autumn and the cold months of January/February. Expect freezes but don't be surprised by mild days.

What to wear
Have your really warm things ready. A lined topcoat or raincoat is useful. But don't forget lighter sweaters, skirts and tweed sports coats. These come in handy in many lightly-heated British hotels and homes. Heating is usually too little, or, in the case of places with a large American clientele, too much. Winter is a more formal time than summer, but a comfortable suit or good dress suffices almost everywhere these days.

Babysitters

You can get your hotel to recommend someone for £5 an hour or more. Or, we use **Babysitters Unlimited** (271 King Street, Hammersmith W6, Tel. 01- 741 5566). Rates are £1.75 per hour by day or £2.00 in the evening, plus transportation fares (these are usually not high because they try to find sitters who live nearby). If you are a visitor to London, there is also a session fee of £3, or if you're staying longer you can pay the annual membership of £20.00. Babysitters can be hard to find in the summer, or on some weekends, so book in advance. Two other good agencies are: **Childminders** (Tel. 01-935 2049) and **Universal Aunts** (Tel. 01-351 5767).

Finding Toilets/Restrooms

Sometimes it's the most pressing of human needs, and when the call strikes, it's usually the time that no 'public conveniences' are in sight. Perhaps earlier in the day you passed two or three. Actually, there are fewer and fewer public toilets as time goes by, despite the appearance of futuristic automated outhouses, the 'Superloo', on a few street corners (give them a try — after all, they are another London experience). And more toilets have a 10p entrance charge — local councils try to deter tramps from camping in them. Don't despair: if you remember the hints below, you should be able to avoid disaster. We also let you know about a few places that are, well . . . uh . . . more pleasurable than others. Some could even be tourist attractions in themselves.

Hints

- Look around or check your map for any signs with a man and/or woman figure or that say 'Gents', 'Ladies', 'WC', 'Toilets', or 'Public Conveniences'. Occasionally, you'll see one simply marked 'loo' — it's the British slang word for toilet.

- Major department stores and bigger shops are actually your best bet for quality accessible loos. Signs may say 'For Customers Only', but if you're looking then you're a customer, aren't you?

- If you're near a railway station or free museum you should find a place of comfort there. Only the biggest underground stations tend to have them. Railway stations often impose a 5p or 10p charge for facilities that are variable in cleanliness and quality.

- Changes in licensing hours now permit pubs to remain open from 1100 to 2300. Most publicans don't mind the occasional non-customer slipping in to use their clearly-marked toilets. Conditions vary — and inevitably decline as it gets later in the evening.

- Major hotels often have beautifully decorated and maintained WCs with extras like free packets of cologne, scented warm towels, etc. The only problem is that toilets are often cleverly hidden to ensure that you walk past reception. Still, it's unlikely that you'll be stopped: if you are, just say you're looking for the bar or picking up a brochure!

- McDonalds and a number of modern fast food chains often maintain clean toilets.

- After 2300 or even 2200 most public facilities close. If you're going to be out you may want to plan ahead.

Areas

Oxford Street
The department stores all have at least adequate loos. The Gents tends to be on the top floor to deter tramps. *Selfridges* has several frequently-recommended loos, and the Ladies at *Selfridges Hotel* is peaceful and carpeted.

Marylebone
Public toilets opposite the *Planetarium* are OK. The *Wallace Collection* has beautiful Victorian loos. *Durrants* and the public conveniences on *St Christopher's Place* have good facilities. Some of *Regent's Park's* (off the Inner Circle near Queen Mary's Rose Garden) are clean, with some entrances covered in refreshing foliage.

Soho, Leicester Square and theatre-land
The public toilets in *Great Marlborough Street* (near Carnaby Street) have interesting tile work. Along with the automatic loos on the south side of Leicester Square, the north side has two vast, cavernous underground public Ladies and Gents with pretty mosaic tile work and a 10p entry fee. The *Trocadero's* are also 10p. Many theatres have old-fashioned tiling and facilities, but are reserved for customers only. If you

have an excuse to be in the *Café Royal*, free Ashbourne Water is on offer.

Covent Garden
Public toilets on the west side of the piazza appear to be in the crypt of *St Paul's Church* and have long hours (0630–2330), but the Ladies often has a long queue. Treat yourself to the beautiful marbled loos of the *Savoy Hotel* (down the staircase and left). Reportedly, you can ask the attendants for many free 'extras' (shoe polish, buttons, Malvern Water) but don't forget to tip. It is worth a visit to the famous American Bar upstairs.

Trafalgar Square
Forget public facilities and go to the free toilets downstairs at the *National Portrait Gallery* for some of the best loos in London. Ladies and Gents are on either side of a carpeted lounge with three sofas, a phone and maps.

Mayfair and St James's
St James's Park has well-kept toilets in little brick buildings just off the Mall, and others just off Horseguards Parade, but more interesting toilets abound in these two areas. The best are at *Brown's Hotel* (down the stairs outside St George's Bar). The Gents is marbled, mirrored, mahoganied and carpeted, with a writing desk and magazines. I'm told the Ladies is equally charming. Again, worth a visit to the bar! *Duke's* is famous for free emergency sewing kits. The *Inn on the Park* recently won the 'Kimberley Clarke Certificate of Excellence' for 'Britain's Best Ladies Hotel Washroom' — carpeted, brass fittings and oyster pink dressing tables. The *Connaught Hotel* (straight through the lobby near the staircase) has a marble and mahogany Gents with free Alka Seltzer and mouthwash; the Ladies has flowers, plants and shell-shaped sinks. *Claridges'* Ladies has stuffed armchairs, potted plants and free soap, face powder and mineral water.

Victoria
The station has clean, if unexciting, toilets at a charge of 10p. Those of the *Grosvenor Hotel* next door may be more appealing.

Chelsea
Sloane Square has borough-run public toilets. Those of nearby department store *Peter Jones* are cleaner and quieter.

Knightsbridge
Harvey Nichols has a good, easy-to-find Ladies. *Harrods* has a number of Gents and Ladies facilities. The most interesting is the big underground Gents near the *Green Man* pub: the best Ladies is reputedly on the fourth floor, next to the Trafalgar Bar, and is supposed to be very luxurious.

The City
Jonathan Routh, author of the *Initial Good Loo Guide* (Banyan Books, £2.95) awards three stars to the public loos of the *Guildhall* as a 'palace' that is the 'survivor of a more gracious age of toileteering' with brass, mosaics, cut-glass, marble and antique porcelain.

Tipping

Many hotels add a service charge, but, even so, staff may expect small change for services rendered. Porters or bellhops should get about 50p per bag for one or two bags. Head porters or concierges should be tipped only if they've performed any special services for you. Some people tip hairdressers 10–15% for a good service in a fancy shop. Bar personnel are not tipped except for table service. Courteous taxi drivers are happy with 10% or reasonable change on a note. See Restaurant tips for further advice.

6 Hotels and accommodation

Few aspects of visiting Britain attract as much disappointment and criticism as London hotels. At the bottom of most complaints are the accommodation price levels — some of the highest in the world. If services, cleanliness and furnishings were, at least in most cases, value for money, there would be few complaints. Sadly, the average hotel double is now over £70 a night. For much under £50 you are usually talking about a bed and breakfast or a tiny flowered-wallpaper hotel room with squeaky floorboards and a bathroom down a corridor. Americans pay that same price for a top-quality motel room.

It is something of a paradox that at the top price levels London has some of the best hotels in the world. Few can match **Claridges**, the **Connaught**, the **Berkeley** and the **Savoy** for services, atmosphere, taste and overall quality. But, of course, you have to pay for it.

In the mid-range, London hotels vary greatly in quality and value. Unless you know a great deal about a hotel, you're usually better off to pick a modern hotel in preference to an older one for the same price. Aside from a few listed below, most less-expensive older London hotels don't really offer much Olde England charm. Several areas of London now seem to consist mostly of Georgian and Victorian terraces indifferently turned into hotels for inexpensive tour groups. Other rooms are let to individual travellers for outrageous prices in summer.

At the bottom of the scale, we are really talking about the *bed and breakfasts*, and the *bed and breakfast hotels*. Although some establishments are in a grey area between the two, there is an important difference. Central London has few real bed and breakfasts — which in Britain normally means no more than two or three extra rooms let out for extra income by a family who reside in the house. Around **Victoria, Paddington, King's Cross** and **Earl's Court** stations are many bed and breakfast hotels. Usually they don't offer much else, but many have 10 or more rooms, with or without bath. Increasingly, these hotels are part of cheap chains owned by foreign-registered companies more interested in property speculation than good-value hotel-keeping.

In the past, Britons stayed in real B and Bs, or boarding houses, when away from home. There was little tradition of small family-owned and -run city hotels such as you find in many continental cities. During the last 30 years many excellent continental-type hotels have opened in the country, but London still has few. One reason is London's phenomenal property market, in which many people have seen rises of 100 per cent in the last four years. Many hotel owners invest minimum amounts of capital in room decor and upkeep; if they are going to fill the rooms at £50 each with package tours, why bother? Sell the building, make a profit and let the next owner worry about it.

Not many new hotels have been built in the past decade, few are on the drawing board and restrictive planning laws make approval a slow process, so the problem is not going to go away. Still, the city seldom fills up entirely. *Something* is usually available in summer peak periods, but with a little research and advance investigation you can arrange accommodation in your price range that will be at least adequate. Our hope is that the selections below will provide an idea of what some establishments are like.

The alternative for those staying at least a week is to rent a self-catering flat. This too is becoming expensive, as it gets more popular, but in many cases it compares favourably with the overall expense of staying in a hotel — considering service charge, VAT, tips and restaurant meals.

Hotel hints

- Combined air/hotel or (within Britain) rail/hotel deals are frequently real bargains when you consider London hotel rates and charges. It's best if you ask your travel agent to check the description and ordinary rates of the hotel(s) on offer.

- At most periods other than mid-June to late September, arriving in London without a reservation presents few problems except at top bracket and popular hotels. Of course, if you want to stay in a particular hotel of any type, it's wise to book in advance.

- Transatlantic travellers would do well to book at least the first night in advance to give time to get over jet lag, collect their wits and decide where they really want to stay. Alternatively, you can book a night when you arrive through the reservation desks at the **airports, Victoria Station** or the **Tourist Information Centre** there, or the **BTA Travel Centre** at 12 Regent Street. Then ponder your options. Booking a whole week while still bleary-eyed is a recipe for disaster.

- Many of London's top bracket hotels are really extraordinary places, but they are *very* expensive. For a once-in-a-lifetime treat, you might splurge on two nights at the end of your stay at **Claridges**, the **Connaught** or one of the other famous hotels.

- Hotel chains offer bargain breaks and value deals during the winter and other off-season periods. Even luxury class hotels occasionally offer two-for-one packages. Always ask.

- Budget and tourist hotels will often negotiate or offer cheap weekly rates during the winter low season. Again, it doesn't hurt to ask.

- Always be sure to ask whether quoted rates include full breakfast, VAT (15 per cent) and any service charge (often 10–15 per cent).

- The areas around these stations — **King's Cross, Paddington, Victoria** and **Earl's Court** — contain many budget and bed and breakfast hotels, many of which advertise cheap rates on front doors and windows. None of these neighbourhoods is particularly salubrious. King's Cross and Earl's Court have drug, prostitution and crime problems. Hotels around Paddington should be avoided unless you know they have no council bed and breakfast clients. (Several London boroughs have been paying B and B hotels in this W2 postal district to house their homeless; unless you want to experience some of the worst of London's housing crisis, with needy families of four or more in one room, give this area a miss.) At least ask. The area around Victoria is probably the most convenient and wholesome of the four, if not the cheapest.

- The BTA's Crown Classification can be of some use in evaluating the basic standards of a hotel or a B and B, but do bear in mind that the crowns are indicative of quantitative rather than qualitative factors. The 1–5 crown system just tells you how many facilities are offered. For example, a 3-crown hotel is one with, among other things, one third or more bedrooms having a bath, shower or WC *en suite*. Some 5-crown hotels are impersonal overpriced glass and concrete blocks, while there are 1-crown hotels with outstanding rooms with private bath and friendly personal service as one of many free, unquantifiable, extras. The present Crown Classification has not been an unqualified success. Hotels have to agree to pay for an inspection, and several large chains have boycotted it. Reform of the crown system as it operates in England will probably soon be undertaken to bring it into line with the Scottish system, where qualitative factors are considered.

- Discounts (up to 40 per cent off) on chain and moderately-expensive hotels are often available from these brokers:

  Room Centre UK　　　　　　01-328 1790
  Hogg Robinson's Hotel Service 01-405 1245

  Superbreak operates good hotel discounts and value minibreaks all over the UK (**Tel.** 01-278 0383)

- In many less-expensive hotels only some or even none of the rooms have private baths. (*En suite* means the room has a private bath.)

- Most hotel rates include breakfast — either *continental*: usually bread, toast or rolls with butter, jam and marmalade; or *English*: which includes at least eggs, bacon or ham, and toast.

- Rooms on higher floors of older hotels tend to be smaller but quieter.

- If you're visiting London on a budget and staying in a bed and breakfast hotel, you'll enjoy your visit most if expectations are kept to a minimum — quality for money just doesn't compare with the US or elsewhere in Europe.

Hotel selections

The listings below should be considered as no more than qualified recommendations. All London hotels have something wrong with them — some a great deal. Even the top notch hotels have a defect: their outrageous prices. Most of our inexpensive hotels have been selected for adequacy rather than excellence. Please remember that hotels change with ownership and management, and prices are always on a steadily upward march. For that reason, we have not listed by price but by price category, to give you an idea rather than a specific quote which may change before publication. Since travel is usually in twos, rates are for doubles. Single rates may be as much as two thirds or more the double rate.

A	Luxury	Most doubles over £130
B	Expensive	Most doubles £90–130
C	Moderate	Most doubles £50–90
D	Inexpensive	Most doubles less than £50

Charming or atmospheric hotels

So many letters ask the same question: 'Can you give me the name of a London hotel like the one Miss Marple [or other film, literary or television characters] stayed in . . . with the charm and service of bygone London . . . [then comes the kicker] for under £50 a night [or other low prices]?' I think I know what they're after: understated, quiet, wood-panelled surroundings; attentive, smooth service by sharp septuagenarians who've been there forever; a chance to have tea in the lounge with colonels, maiden aunts and debutantes down for the season; silver service of roast beef in the restaurant; four poster beds in the rooms (but let's not forget the colour TV and modern *en suite* plumbing), . . . and all presided over by the likes of the Duchess of Duke Street.

Alas, the old-fashioned gentleman's London of song and story mostly vanished with the onslaught of mass tourism in the 1960s. Modern London is a tourist city in which the average room rate is over £70 a night. At least 60 per cent of the clientele of hotels like the Savoy, Dorchester, Claridges and the Connaught are well-heeled Americans; very few of the remainder are British, much less British lords, ladies, vicars or sleuths. Nowadays, Miss Marple either couldn't afford to stay in her type of hotel, or would find it too internationalized for her comfort. She'd probably look up distant cousins instead.

But bits and pieces of an older, more graceful London survive in the hotels we've selected below. Mostly you've got to be able to pay for it. Is it worth £130 plus a night? This is not for me to say. All depends on your outlook and personal preferences. (I once paid a painful amount to stay at Tiger Tops Jungle Lodge in Nepal, but I've never regretted a single penny, because the experience remains a treasure in my memory.) One answer might be to have a few days at the beginning of your trip in a value-for-money (by London standards anyway) modern hotel, then a couple of days at the end at a more expensive, charming hotel, where you can luxuriate in civilized comfort . . . for once in your life.

The Athenaeum

Some years ago the Athenaeum was renovated and given a new look, but the tradition of excellent service was kept up, and 70 per cent of their business is repeat. And there's the famous bar with over a 100 varieties of Scottish malt whisky.

A   116 Piccadilly W1, Tel. 01-499 3464 (112 rooms)

Bailey's Hotel

The first London hotel to install an elevator in 1880. Recently renovated, but there's still a certain Victorian ambience, though we've heard a few complaints about the service. The highly-regarded **Bombay Brasserie** is on the premises.

C   Gloucester Road SW7, Tel. 01-373 6000 (150 rooms)

Basil Street Hotel

A big point is made of maintaining an Edwardian atmosphere with oriental carpets, potted palms, fresh flowers and oak panelling, and some assistance is offered by the presence of a Ladies Club that still has some country gentry members (female hotel guests are automatic members). This and the proximity to Harrods means that a large number of the guests are women shoppers. Only two subscribers have complained about poor food and service. Some of the rooms are tiny; request a larger room when booking far in advance. Only a few rooms do not have a private bath.

C 8 Basil Street SW3, Tel. 01-581 3311 (100 rooms)

Berkeley Hotel
The Berkeley has moved into new quarters since the days when it was a Noel Coward hang-out, but still has a very English feel. Perhaps it's the old-fashioned service. People keep telling us that they have the service just right — friendly, but polite and correct. Rooftop pool. Some rooms have balconies.

A Wilton Place SW1, Tel. 01-235 6000 (160 rooms)

Blakes Hotel
Created from a row of nineteenth-century houses, it's a peculiar combination of modern black-and-white revival Art Deco and Art Nouveau features. A place to run into Steven Spielberg rather than Miss Marple. Avoid if you hate trendies.

A 33 Roland Gardens SW7, Tel. 01-370 6701 (65 rooms)

Brown's Hotel
Trusthouse Forte has not managed to destroy Brown's. Many of the clientele are foreign businessmen who are repeat customers. They like the old-fashioned elegant service, individualized rooms and the comfortable Victorian feel of the reception and restaurant. No two of the modernized traditional bedrooms are alike; request one of the larger rooms. Possibly the best traditional breakfast and one of the best-served afternoon teas of any London hotel, but it also helps to be a guest.

A 19–20 Dover Street W1, Tel. 01-493 6020 (125 rooms)

Capital Hotel
Probably the least-known and most underrated because its room decor was previously very dull. Be sure to ask for a room in the charmingly-redecorated Edwardian wing that was once the fashionable Squires Hotel in the 1920s. The restaurant is one of the best in town. Very close to Harrods.

A 22 Basil Street SW3, Tel. 01-589 5171 (56 rooms)

Chesterfield Hotel
Pleasant Georgian-façade hotel with panelled bar, quiet luxury and decent-sized bedrooms with *en suite* bathrooms and many extras.

A 35 Charles Street W1, Tel. 01-491 2622 (113 rooms)

Claridges and **The Connaught**
If money's no object, these two hotels dating from the Victorian era are, in our opinion, the best in London. They are very near to one another in genteel Mayfair, and share other similarities — antiques, oil paintings, oak panelling (though Claridges has more of a preserved Art Deco look). Service in both is old-fashioned and absolutely impeccable. Both are famous for splendid private bathrooms. Club-like, but guests are automatically club members. Trouble is, it's almost impossible to get in, so reserve far in advance. What's the difference? The Connaught is smaller and has the best food — possibly in town. Claridges has a restaurant/grill, **La Causerie**, that is most famous for its smörgåsbord luncheon and after-theatre suppers.

Claridges **A** Brook Street W1, Tel. 01-629 8860 (205 rooms)
Connaught **A** Carlos Place W1, Tel. 01-499 7070 (90 rooms)

Dorchester *and* Grosvenor House Hotels

I would have the same criticism of these two Park Lane hotels — too much of a big, institutionalized hotel feel. The former is in a slightly higher class. Now owned by the Sultan of Brunei, the Dorchester has restored much of its 1930s splendour; the service is very good, and, if you like nouvellish cuisine, you can't do much better. During most of 1989 the Dorchester will be closed for room refurbishment.

Dorchester   A   Park Lane W1, Tel. 01-629 8888 (275 rooms)

Grosvenor House   A   90 Park Lane W1, Tel. 01-449 6363 (468 rooms)

Dorset Square Hotel

A recommended, little-known small hotel not far from Baker Street, with Regency charm, real fires, antiques and marble bathrooms. Each room is different. Overlooking the square where cricket was born. Charming service in both hotel and the **Country Manners** restaurant.

B   39 Dorset Square NW1, Tel. 01-723 7874 (30 rooms)

Duke's Hotel

One of the best-located up-market hotels in London for the non-business visitor, and the tariffs reflect its St James's address. Only 52 rooms, but recent renovation has made them brighter and larger (ask for upper floors or book a suite). The hotel has not lost its old feel, with familiar oil paintings. Reception areas with patterned plaster ceilings and the panelled bar complete the ambience of this small, intimate place, which strives more successfully than most to maintain the air of an exclusive private residence.

A   35 St James' Place SW1, Tel. 01-491 4840 (52 rooms)

Durrants Hotel

Set in a traditional eighteenth-century terrace, this is one of London's best-value atmospheric hotels, but rates have been rising rapidly. Still makes the *Good Hotel Guide*, and there's now a feeling that it's now on the up and up. Ask for one of the larger rooms on the lower floors. A very pleasant place to stay. Most rooms have baths.

C   26–32 George Street W1, Tel. 01-935 8131 (96 rooms)

Ebury Court Hotel

Made up of five contiguous houses near Victoria Station with funny little passages where the houses join; the rooms are small, the decor quiet and the furniture mostly plain. Food is plain too. Again, the idea is supposed to be the country hotel in town, and the Ebury won an award from the *Good Hotel Guide* for 'maintaining old-fashioned hotel virtues in the metropolis'. Only 14 rooms have private bath. Perhaps this is the reason a few of the guests we've met have come away disappointed; surprising, because the atmosphere is home-like. Family-managed.

C   26 Ebury Street SW1, Tel. 01-730 8147 (39 rooms)

Goring Hotel

Around the corner from the Mews at Buckingham Palace. Despite the address, this hotel is a recommendable, less-expensive, alternative for those looking for traditional English atmosphere and service. Rooms vary in size and shape. Things were a bit run down, but some redecoration has improved matters without losing the Edwardian look. Built in 1910, it was the first London hotel in which all rooms had a private bath. Service is good; many staff have been with this family-owned and run hotel for many years. One drawback is the food, which tends towards the pricey and uninteresting. Ask for a room overlooking the garden. Men may enjoy the drawings hung in the Gents.

B Grosvenor Gardens SW1, Tel. 01-834 8211 (90 rooms)

Hyde Park Hotel
If you can't stay at Claridges or the Connaught, see if you can get one of the better rooms at this hotel — in the back, overlooking Hyde Park. Some have backdoors to wide terraces. Big rooms are high-ceilinged with huge closets and some original brass fittings in good working order. Public areas have a well-preserved Edwardian magnificence with white marble stairs, crystal chandeliers and potted palms. Dine in the **Park Room** overlooking the park, or the dark oak-panelled **Cavalry Grill**.

A 66 Knightsbridge SW3, Tel. 01-235 2000 (186 rooms)

Montcalm Hotel
This hotel has one of the many handsome Georgian/Regency façades in the area. Inside is a modernized, restful, chocolate-brown decor. Interesting split-level suites are available.

A Great Cumberland Place W1, Tel. 01-402 4288 (115 rooms)

Portobello Hotel
The hotel combines two Victorian terrace houses looking on to a lush green private park. Victorian military theme — brass, mahogany, scarlet curtains, military prints. Good base for the Portobello Market, but some rooms are notoriously tiny places to store shopping loot. Relaxed atmosphere — the kind of place you either love or hate. Nice basement bar and, unusually for a small hotel, 24-hour room service.

C 22 Stanley Gardens W11, Tel. 01-727 2777 (25 rooms)

Ritz Hotel
Its devotees claim it has not been ruined by repainting and renovation, and many of them think the restaurant the most beautiful in Europe. Definitely a romantic place to eat — with its famous well-spaced tables where Edward dined with Mrs Simpson — but the food is better at other hotels. The hotel exudes a heavy elegance befitting its name: gold leaf, marble and potted palms. Rooms are fully modernized, but on the whole it seems a bit much, taken together with the gold-laden clientele. Some people say the service is snobbish. Personally, I'd prefer to be a voyeur and go there for tea rather than spend the night in perhaps too-splendid surroundings.

A Piccadilly W1, Tel. 01-493 8181 (128 rooms)

Savoy Hotel
Built by the famous Richard D'Oyly Carte in 1889, the Savoy was considered by some to be London's finest hotel between the wars. Some still think so. The grand marbled and frescoed entrance hall has too much bustle for me; as does the fabled **American Bar**. The rebuilt **Savoy Grill** is not what it was; but the **River Restaurant** has fine views and the food is regaining its old reputation under a new chef. Many of the rooms have been refurbished in the ultra-modern style. Still, no two are alike, and if it's nostalgia you're looking for, then book one of the magnificent **Edwardian Riverside Suites** with their original marble bathrooms. A good location, handy to the theatres, but there is a definite big hotel feel to the place.

A Strand WC2 Tel. 01-836 4343 (200 rooms)

St James's Court Hotel
The old St James's has been gutted and modernized by the Taj group. Rooms are redecorated in modernized traditional styles. Wonderful outdoor façades and Art

Deco in the public areas. A high standard of old-fashioned service merits its inclusion in this section.

A   St James's Court, Buckingham Gate SW1, Tel. 01-834 6655 (391 rooms)

Stafford Hotel

A small, elegant, turn-of-the-century hotel in the St James's area, the Stafford takes pride in serving its own special food and wine selections. This ambience carries over to the rest of the hotel, which looks like, but is more relaxed than, genuine English clubland. Perhaps it's also due to the high number of genuine aristocratic regulars. The bar opens on to a cobbled summer patio.

A   16 St James Place SW1, Tel. 01-493 0111 (65 rooms)

Swiss Cottage Hotel

Eccentric, hard-to-get-into Victorian gem. Subscribers report varied rooms, occasionally noisy plumbing and sometimes *Fawlty Towers* service, but they are somehow enchanted to book again. Most rooms with bath.

C   4 Adamson Road NW3, Tel. 01–722 2281 (72 rooms)

Waldorf Hotel

Refurbishment has made this formerly-downcast Trusthouse Forte hotel, convenient to Covent Garden, recommendable again. Nostalgia is one of its big selling points. Tea dances are still held on Fridays, Saturdays and Sundays in the Palm Court lounge.

B   Aldwych WC2, Tel. 01-836 2400 (310 rooms)

Wilbraham Hotel

A reasonably-priced Victorian charmer with individualized-rooms furnished with antiques and a high standard of service. Like many London hotels, the main problem is too many small rooms. Request one of the larger rooms far in advance. Some cheaper rooms are without bath. Restaurant. Well located near Sloane Square.

C   Wilbraham Place SW1, Tel. 01-730 8296 (52 rooms)

International chain and modern luxury hotels

For my part, I cannot understand why anyone would come to London and stay at a Hilton, Intercontinental, Hyatt or Sheraton when, in the same price bracket, they could enjoy the charm and special British ambience of Claridges, the Savoy, the Dorchester or the Connaught. Actually, I think there are two good reasons. First, these famous hotels are frequently booked up by repeat customers. Second, staying in the international chains is slightly less of a hassle for business people and the traveller in a hurry, with features like express checkout and coffee shops.

Staying in the hotels listed below is much like staying in the counterparts elsewhere in the world. Standards of accommodation and service are high, there are no surprises and few hassles. So we've tried to mention any specially distinguishing features.

Churchill Hotel

Our favourite of the big modern exterior/panelled Regency interior type. Superb service, elegant interiors, well-appointed and equipped bedrooms and baths. Excellent open-late coffee shop. Good location for Oxford Street shoppers.

A   30 Portman Square W1, Tel. 01-486 5800 (489 rooms)

Hilton

In 1987, all Hiltons outside the USA were bought by **Ladbroke's**, a British betting shop and hotel chain. London has two of the hotels that belonged to the old Hilton chain, and there's another conveniently connected to Gatwick's South Terminal. The big one is called the **London Hilton** on **Park Lane**. The 27-storey skyscraper has always been a particularly bland place to stay — except for the great views and, now, the interesting **British Harvest Restaurant**. We prefer the **Hilton International Kensington** in pleasant leafy Holland Park, where a good pub practically next door and charming nearby walks and restaurants give a real sense of being in England. Holland Park and Shepherds Bush tubes are a short walk away. All other London hotels now described as 'Hilton' or 'Hilton National' are former Ladbroke's. Generally, the old Ladbroke's are not up to 'Hilton' standards, but they are being improved in this direction. 'Hilton National' seems to aim for a Holiday Inn standard.

London Hilton A 22 Park Lane W1, Tel. 01-493 8000 (500 rooms)
Hilton Kensington A 79 Holland Park Avenue W11, Tel. 01-603 3395 (600 rooms)
Hilton Hotels A 37 Claringdon Road, Watford, Tel. (0923) 244 400

Howard Hotel
Not much personality, but a very efficient, well-run modern hotel. The main attraction is Thames-view rooms which you must be sure to request.
A Temple Place, Strand WC2, Tel. 01-836 3555 (136 rooms)

Hyatt Carlton Tower
Hyatt has just the one London hotel, but they seem to have splurged on it. Everything is sumptuously appointed. The Chinoiserie lounge is regarded as a great place to have tea, and the **Chelsea Room** is one of London's better-rated restaurants. Location is good — overlooking Cadogan Gardens and near to Knightsbridge and the King's Road, Chelsea.
A 2 Cadogan Place SW1, Tel. 01-235 5411 (221 rooms)

Inn on the Park
An award-winner for both 'London's best' *and* 'London't most expensive' hotel. Why? Seems to be for the generously-sized, beautifully-decorated rooms, with plenty of extras, the superb standard of service and well-appointed lounges and public areas — all in an unlikely-looking modern tower block. The **Four Seasons Restaurant** has beautiful views over Hyde Park. All said, rooms are pretty expensive.
A 11 Hamilton Place W1, Tel. 01-499 0888 (228 rooms)

Intercontinental
Since **Intercontinental** was British-owned, it's not surprising that London has four. The central **Intercontinental** is set in an ugly concrete block that does nothing for the beauty of traffic-mad Hyde Park Corner but provides a very central location for its business clientele. Good and useful coffee shop. The **Britannia Intercontinental** is set behind a more relaxed, colonnaded Georgian façade near the American embassy in elegant Mayfair. Anglo-American food in the interestingly-named **Best of Both Worlds** restaurant. The **Portman Intercontinental** is, again, ugly on the outside, traditional revival on the inside. Bedrooms are attractively decorated. Good location for Oxford Street shoppers. The **Mayfair Intercontinental** has a famous marble staircase and particularly spacious rooms with many extras.

Intercontinental A 1 Hamilton Place W1, Tel. 01-409 3131 (491 rooms)
Britannia Intercontinental A Grosvenor Square W1, Tel. 01-629 9400 (356 rooms)
Portman Intercontinental A 22 Portman Square W1, Tel. 01-486 5844 (278 rooms)
Mayfair Intercontinental A Stratton Street W1, Tel. 01-629 7777 (322 rooms)

London Marriot
Once the Hotel Europa, known for tiny rooms. **Marriot** eliminated many of them in the renovations. As a result Executive Rooms are large, with sitting areas. The small

lobby gives a somewhat impersonal and claustrophobic feeling, despite the traditional decor; but, like the rest of the chain, this is a very good, well-run hotel.
A   Grosvenor Square W1, Tel. 01-493 1232 (229 rooms)

Le Meridien Picadilly
Behind an Edwardian façade, the old Piccadilly Hotel has been totally transformed into a slightly French-flavoured luxury hotel by the respected Paris-based chain. Rooms are equipped with many extras. Guests can use the pool or health club. Possibly London's best-located hotel — a few steps from Piccadilly Circus.
A   19 Piccadilly SW1, Tel. 01-734 8000 (284 rooms)

Mountbatten Hotel
A new, well-located hotel, for some reason themed on the life of the late Earl of Burma. Rooms are double-glazed against noise, and bathrooms are a luxurious Italian marble. Two subscribers have commented favourably on the service. Perhaps this is what the rates reflect, or maybe it's the convenience to Covent Garden and the theatres.
A   Seven Dials, Covent Garden WC2, Tel. 01-836 4300 (127 rooms)

Sheraton Park Tower
An 18-storey skyscraper, seemingly built to match the rival Hilton a mile away, whose main attraction is, again, the views from upper rooms. I find the foyer to be noisy and exposed to continual foot traffic. Spacious bedrooms and highly-regarded suites. Very convenient to Harrods and Harvey Nichols in Knightsbridge. The more intimate **Belgravia Sheraton**, not far away, is preferable. It, too, is a modern tower block, but somehow on a more human scale. Both rooms and service are more individualized. Good value buffet lunch.
Sheraton Park Tower   A   101 Knightsbridge SW1, Tel. 01-235 8050 (295 rooms)
Belgravia Sheraton   A   20 Chesham Place SW1, Tel. 01-235 6040 (90 rooms)

Other upmarket chains
Both standards and prices are generally high in these mostly British-based chains. They also offer frequent deals, discounts and minibreaks, so you might ask when making an advance booking. Hotel room brokers (see *Hotel hints* at the beginning of this section) are also able to offer discounts on some of these chain hotels.

Holiday Inn
There are four of these — the ultimate in standardized chain hotels. The **Holiday Inn (Mayfair) (B/A** — 3 Berkeley Street W1; 186 rooms) is the most central. The **Holiday Inn (Marble Arch) (B/A** — 134 George Street W1; 235 rooms) has an indoor pool and plenty of parking. The **Holiday Inn (Chelsea) (B/A** — 17 Sloane Street SW1; 206 rooms), conveniently located for Harrods and Chelsea, also has an indoor pool and ample parking. None is cheap by US standards, but the **Holiday Inn (Swiss Cottage) (B/A** — 128 King Henry's Road SW3; 304 rooms), near Regent's Park, has an indoor pool and slightly lower rates.
Holiday Inns   10 New College Parade NW3, Tel. 01-722 7755

Rank
Besides the very upmarket **Athenaeum**, this British firm owns four other major London hotels. A distinctive feature of each is a Reserve Floor to cater especially for businessmen. The modern **Royal Garden (A** — 395 rooms) next to green Kensington Gardens can be a very pleasant place to stay, in one of the parkview rooms. The **Royal Lancaster (A** — 418 rooms) overlooks Hyde Park; again, request a parkview room. I

know at least one frequent visitor who always stays here. The **Gloucester (A** — 531 rooms) is slightly cheaper, in South Kensington; the lobby gives the impression of being heavily patronized by Middle Eastern visitors. The **White House (B** — Albany Street NW1; 580 rooms) is pleasantly located near Regent's Park. Like the others, it is modern, with high standards, but the tariff is somewhat less.

Rank Hotels   1 Thameside Centre, Brentford, Middlesex, Tel. 01-569 7120

Thistle Hotels

Thistle Hotels seem to be trying to corner the market, but at least they do seem to keep some rates from going right through the roof. The **Kensington Palace Thistle (C/B** — 298 rooms) is less expensive than some of the more centrally-located members, near Kensington Gardens. The **Lowndes Thistle (A** — 79 rooms) is a quiet, attractive hotel convenient to both Knightsbridge and Chelsea. The **Royal Horse-guards Thistle (B/A** — 284 rooms) overlooks the Thames near Parliament. The **Royal Westminster (B/A** — 135 rooms) is convenient to the Palace, and the **Royal Trafalgar (B** — 108 rooms) is on a quiet road, but still in the heart of theatre-land. **Selfridge's Hotel (A** — 298 rooms), attached to the store, now belongs to Thistle. All the hotels feature modern bedrooms, often with traditional themes.

Thistle Hotels   5 Victoria Road W8, Tel. 01-937 8033

Trusthouse Forte

A huge UK and worldwide hotel empire that includes several excellent hotels we've mentioned elsewhere, including **Brown's, Hyde Park** and **Grosvenor House** (all **A**) and the **Kensington Close (C** — 524 rooms). Other well-known THF hotels include the massive, uninspiring **Cumberland (B** — 905 rooms), the somewhat gloomy Victorian **Russell Hotel (B** — 320 rooms) and the modern, well-run **Cavendish (A** — 253 rooms). The giant chain seems to be alternately loved and hated by businessmen, but they do offer frequent value weekend and short break deals. The **Strand Palace (C** — 770 rooms) and **Regent Palace (C** — 1000 rooms) have excellent all-you-can-eat roast carveries.

Trusthouse Forte   24–30 New Street, Aylesbury, Bucks HP20 2NW. Reservations 01-567 3444

Useful value-for-money moderate hotels

These mostly modern hotels are either good value for money because they're only slightly out of the way or because they frequently feature value deals — though prices are on the rise as more people discover them.

Clifton-Ford Hotel

More centrally located and slightly pricier than some hotels listed below, this modern hotel nevertheless offers good value for the location and is frequently overlooked. Comfortable piano bar.

C/B   47 Welbeck Street W1, Tel. 01-486 6000 (220 rooms)

Hotel Ibis

Another hotel owned by a French chain offering quality low-cost accommodation in a modern hotel. The neighbourhood is not too salubrious — but you won't find many other up-to-date hotels with rates at £22 per person single or £47 double. Breakfast is extra.

D   3 Cardington Street NW1, Tel. 01-388 7777 (300 rooms)

They also operate a similarly inexpensive modern hotel in Greenwich — within easy commuting distance of London (Tel. 01-305 1177)

Kensington Close
Across the road from the Tara, is this hotel which is as good if you book one of the 'superior' bedrooms. Added bonus is an indoor pool and gym. Close to Kensington High Street shopping.
C   Wrights Lane W8, Tel. 01-937 8170 (524 rooms)

Hotel Lily
Value inexpensive modern hotel, just up the road from the Ramada Inn London West. Compact rooms with bath and colour TV. Friendly staff. Slightly out of the way location helps keep prices down.
C   23 Lillie Road SW6, Tel. 01-381 1881 (100 rooms)

New Barbican
One of the few modern hotels within walking distance of the Barbican Centre and the City, the New Barbican is mainly promoted to business and overlooked by many visitors, who may find it otherwise convenient enough.
C   Central Street, Clerkenwell EC1, Tel. 01-251 1565 (400 rooms)

Novotel
Another French chain offers good rates in this big glass box a bit out of the way in Hammersmith. Not much personality either in the hotel or in the rooms, but it's modern, clean and everything works. Nearby King Street, Hammersmith, has plenty of shopping, and a pleasant Thameside walk with good pubs is just a stroll away. Hammersmith tube provides easy access to central London.
C   1 Shortlands, Hammersmith W6, Tel. 01-741 1555 (633 rooms)

President
Massive, less-expensive modern hotel dating from the 1960s, with TV, private baths, late coffee shop and most big hotel facilities.
D/C   Russell Square WC1, Tel. 01-837 8844 (450 rooms)

Ramada Inn London West
A functional modern block, slightly out of the way, but near enough to West Brompton or Earl's Court tubes.
C   47 Lillie Road SW6, Tel. 01-385 1255 (498 rooms)

Stakis St Ermins
This modernized late-Victorian hotel is well-managed, handy to the sights, and retains some touches of period charm. Many room extras add to overlooked location value, but prices are on the way up.
B   Caxton Street SW1, Tel. 01-222 7888 (300 rooms)

London Tara
When I lived in Aberdeen and visited London on business or pleasure, the Tara was my favourite place to stay on account of its relatively low rates for small but functional, light, airy bedrooms with modern facilities. All the advantages of a major chain without the cost.
C   Scarsdale Place, Wrights Lane W8, Tel. 01-937 7211 (831 rooms)

Special-mention, upmarket bed and breakfast and unusual accommodation

The Beaufort
Originally, this 'bed and breakfast' was intended to be an upmarket home away from

home for businesswomen and lady shoppers. Decor is still feminine, but men are welcome too. The idea is your own front door key. Personal service. Very convenient to Harrods.

B 33 Beaufort Gardens SW3, Tel. 01-584 5252 (29 rooms)

Claverly Hotel
Down the street from the Beaufort is this less expensive neighbour, which has won several BTA awards. Spotless, cheerful, well decorated and the service is warm. All rooms have TV, but only a few have private bath. The big bonus is, again, location.

D/C 14 Beaufort Gardens SW3, Tel. 01-589 8541 (35 rooms)

Eleven Cadogan Gardens
The idea is that you are staying in an English aristocrat's townhouse while he's away. The lounge and stairways are elegant with panelling and paintings. Some rooms are simpler and homey, but many are furnished with antiques and mahogany furniture. Breakfast is served in your room. Private garden and porter service, but no restaurant or hotel-type range of services.

B 11 Cadogan Gardens SW3, Tel. 01-730 3426

Fortyseven Park Street
Very elegant, very expensive luxury bed and breakfast adjoining **Le Gavroche** (access by private door). Only for the wealthy. Twin bedded suites with kitchen.

A 47 Park Street W1, Tel. 01-491 77282 (54 rooms)

Hazlitt's
A small, well-regarded, new hotel in Soho. Quiet, pleasant bedrooms where continental breakfast is served each morning as part of the package.

C 6 Frith Street W1, Tel. 01-434 1771 (22 rooms)

Knightsbridge Hotel
Somehow this small affordable hotel near Harrods has managed to resist the temptation to become high-priced luxury flats. Your own front door and room key. Cheerful service. One of a kind.

C 10 Beaufort Gardens SW3, Tel. 01-589 9271 (20 rooms)

Knightsbridge Green Hotel
This pleasant, now renovated, little hotel, also near Harrods, has long been an open secret. Some 'rooms' are really small suites and prices are really very reasonable considering size and location. All rooms with bath, TV, phone and tea- making. Reserve far in advance.

C 159 Knightsbridge SW1, Tel. 01-584 6274 (22 rooms)

L'Hotel
Very pretty, with designer wallpaper, brass bedsteads and fittings, and pine desks in the rooms. Breakfast is served in the hotel's excellent, award-winning **Le Metro** wine bar, or in your room. Staff are friendly and professional. Book far in advance and ask for one of the larger rooms, or a suite with gas coal-fire.

B 28 Basil Street SW3, Tel. 01-589 6286 (Only 12 rooms)

Number Sixteen
Once privately owned, this popular upmarket bed and breakfast is now part of a chain. The former owner still lives there, but doesn't manage, so it's not clear whether high standards of personal service will be kept up. Four Victorian houses

joined together. Each of the beautifully-decorated rooms (most with private facilities) is different. Many are complemented by prints and well-chosen antiques. Pretty garden.

B   16 Sumner Place SW7, Tel. 01-589 5232 (32 rooms)

Worth a mention moderate to less expensive hotels

Alexander Hotel
A designer version of the same idea as Number 16 across the road. Several joined nineteenth-century houses with smartly-decorated rooms and a garden.

C/B   9 Sumner Place SW7, Tel. 01-581 1591 (37 rooms)

Chelsea Knights
Slightly out-of-the-way hotel offers good value doubles. English and Middle Eastern restaurant.

D/C   422 Fulham Road SW6, Tel. 01-385 8561 (40 rooms)

Coburg
Nothing fancy, though well-maintained, attractive bedrooms, next to Hyde Park. Not all rooms have bath.

C   129 Bayswater Road W2, Tel. 01-229 3654 (125 rooms)

Columbia
Well-maintained, good-value family hotel is a favourite of a tour director friend from California on her frequent business trips. Formerly the American Officers' Club.

C   95 Lancaster Gate W2, Tel. 01-402 0021 (93 rooms with bath)

Crest Hotels
This is a value-for-money chain that offers modernized rooms with a few extras and all the usual features for lower prices than many similar standard hotels. The **Bloomsbury Crest (C** — 239 rooms) is on Coram Street, just off Russell Square. The **Regent Crest (C/B** — 322 rooms) is more stylish, and handy for Oxford Street and Regent's Park. Standards of service are high in the refurbished elegant Edwardian **Marlborough Crest (B** — 169 rooms), also in Bloomsbury.

Crest Reservations: Bridge Street, Bunbury, Oxon, Tel. 01-236 3242

Colonnade Hotel
Some visitors overlook this hotel near out-of-the-way but charming Little Venice. Some suites and better doubles are more expensive in this Georgian house. Most rooms with bath.

D/C   2 Warrington Crescent W9, Tel. 01-289 2167 (53 rooms)

Embassy House
Restored and redecorated, near Hyde Park and Harrods.

C   31–33 Queen's Gate SW7, Tel. 01-584 7222

Gore Hotel
All the recently-revamped bedrooms have baths or showers. Family-owned and run.

C   189 Queen's Gate SW7, Tel. 01-584 6601 (54 rooms)

The Hallam Hotel
Good value, well-located family-run bed and breakfast in a Victorian town house.

Breakfast room and resident's bar. Location near Oxford Circus very handy for shoppers.

C 12 Hallam Street, Portland Place W1, Tel. 01-580 1166 (23 rooms)

Mornington Hotel
Friendly, attractive, Swedish-owned, modernized hotel. All bedrooms have bath or shower.

C 12 Lancaster Gate W2, Tel. 01-262 7361 (70 rooms)

Pastoria
Small, friendly, well-located hotel. Reasonable rates considering proximity to Leicester Square. All rooms with bath.

C St Martin's Street WC2, Tel. 01-930 8641 (58 rooms)

Regent Palace
A great-value place to stay — a few steps from Piccadilly Circus — if you don't mind a bathroom down the hall.

C 12 Sherwood Street W1, Tel. 01-734 7000 (1000 rooms)

Rubens
Not-bad hotel, with good rates for the location. Small, modern-style bedrooms with many extras.

C Buckingham Palace Road SW1, Tel. 01-834 6600 (193 rooms)

Sandringham Hotel
Quiet, out-of-the-way bed and breakfast hotel, 25 minutes from central London, near Hampstead Heath. Strictly family style and family-run. Downstairs is an honesty-system refrigerator and drink facility. A frequent *Good Hotel Guide* entry, much beloved by one of our subscribers. Only 5 rooms have bath.

D 3 Holford Road NW3, Tel. 01-435 1569 (15 rooms)

Strand Palace
Massive hotel without much character, but most bedrooms are now refurbished with baths. Frequent value deals. Carvery.

C 372 Strand WC2, Tel. 01-836 8080 (800 rooms)

Willett Hotel
One of London's better, simple hotels, set in an interesting Victorian house. All rooms have radio and TV, and most have private bath.

D 32 Sloane Gardens SW1, Tel. 01-824 8415 (17 rooms)

Adequate inexpensive bed and breakfast hotels
These hotels have been given a favourable mention by *London Traveletter* subscribers for cleanliness, adequate facilities and friendly service at 'budget' prices (mostly somewhere under £50 for a double). Nothing spectacular — expect tiny bedrooms with homely furniture and decor, though many now have TV. Private bathrooms, when available, tend to be very compact. Few have restaurants, just breakfast rooms, but most are located in tourist areas with fast food and other cheap eating places. Again, exclusion does not imply criticism — we may not know anyone who's stayed there.

Victoria/Belgravia

Alison House
Only one room out of eleven has private facilities, but very popular. Book one of the larger rooms.
82 Ebury Street SW1, Tel. 01-730 9529

Arden House
35 rooms — only 14 have bath.
10–12 St George's SW1, Tel. 01-834 2988

Chesham House
All rooms have TV but no private baths. Clean, with friendly service and extras.
64 Ebury Street SW1, Tel. 01-730 8513

Collin House
Clean, friendly. 13 rooms — 8 with private bath/shower.
104 Ebury Street SW1, Tel. 01-730 8031

Granada Hotel
16 bedrooms — all with private bath or shower.
73 Belgrave Road SW1, Tel. 01-821 7611

Bloomsbury

Academy Hotel
Recently refurbished. All 23 rooms have TV but only half have bath or shower.
19 Gower Street WC1, Tel. 01-631 4115

Lonsdale Hotel
Clean, well-kept, cheaper hotel near British Museum, but only 2 of 34 rooms have private bath.
9 Bedford Place WC1, Tel. 01-636 1812

Marylebone

Hart House
Very popular. Most rooms with TV and private bath.
51 Gloucester Place W1, Tel. 01-935 2288

Merryfield House
Little hotel in which all 7 decent-sized rooms have bath/shower.
42 York Street W1, Tel. 01-935 8326

Paddington/Bayswater

Beverley House
Most of the 20 rooms have TV and bath or shower.
142 Sussex Gardens W2, Tel. 01-723 4615

Craven Gardens
Brighter than usual budget hotel with small bedrooms, all with TV and bath/shower.
16 Leinster Terrace W2, Tel. 01-262 3167

Lancaster Gate
Some rooms have view of Hyde Park. All have TV and bath/shower. 60 rooms. 106 Lancaster Gate W2, Tel. 01-402 5111

Chelsea/Knightsbridge

Blair House
Quiet little hotel convenient to Sloane Square and Harrods. 18 rooms — all with colour TV and half with bath/shower.
34 Draycott Place SW3, Tel. 01-581 2323

South Kensington/Earl's Court

Abcone Hotel
Most of the 30 rooms have private bath and colour TV.
10 Ashburn Gardens SW7, Tel. 01-370 3383

Aster House
All 12 rooms in this bright, friendly hotel have TV, minibars, and shower rooms.
3 Sumner Place SW7, Tel. 01-581 5888

Eden Plaza
Recently-improved tourist hotel — all rooms with TV and bath/shower. Also public sauna.
68 Queen's Gate SW7, Tel. 01-370 6111

Number Eight
Pleasant 8-room hotel, all with bath or shower, TV and many extras.
8 Emperor's Gate SW7, Tel. 01-370 7516

Prince Hotel
Cheerful 20-room hotel in two Victorian houses. All large rooms, with TV and bath or shower.
6 Sumner Place SW7, Tel. 01-589 6488

Other Areas

Frognal Lodge
Value hotel in **Hampstead** — 7 of 17 rooms have TV and private bath/shower. 14 Frognal Gardens NW3, Tel. 01-435 8238

Charlotte Restaurant & Guest House
Good value place in **West Hampstead**. Simple rooms in a house with an excellent inexpensive central European restaurant. Hard to beat accommodation/meal packages.
221 West End Lane NW6, Tel. 01-794 6476

Yardley Court
The 9 rooms — all with TV — in this award-winning hotel are full of extras. 5 rooms have private facilities.
18 Court Yard, Eltham Street SE9, Tel. 01-850 1850

Real bed and breakfasts
If you didn't see anything that appeals in the above suggestions, or it still all sounds too expensive, you might want to opt for the famous British bed and breakfast. Generally, London is not the best place to try it out. Most of the better places are not very central, and home atmospheres are not quite as friendly and relaxed. In an international city like London many hosts do it mostly for the money, and prices are high. In places like York, Bath and less-visited towns, more people offer real bed and breakfast — a clean, simple room or two, in their homes — for the additional pleasure

of it all. Americans should not expect too much: bed and breakfast in the USA seems to have become a much more lavish and expensive affair than in its birthplace.

The **London Tourist Board and Convention Bureau's** information office at Victoria Station, or the **British Travel Centre** at 12 Regent Street can help book you into a bed and breakfast once you arrive. Through the BABA (Book A Bed Ahead system), they can help you arrange a B&B anywhere in the country. Or you can contact one of the organizations below to arrange a B&B in advance from a range of choices. Either way, it's all a matter of luck. You might stay with a host who becomes a friend for life; you might come and go without seeing much of them, or you might wind up in an unfriendly landlord's run-down room.

World Wide Bed and Breakfast Association
Every year, this company produces a book entitled *The Best Bed and Breakfast in the World*, listing hundreds of carefully-screened British B&Bs. At the last count, they offered more than 35 in London, costing from £17 per person upwards.

WWBA, PO Box 134, London SW10, Tel. 01-370 7099 (24 hours)

Other useful agencies

London Homes
Screened B&Bs in West London, Richmond Hampstead and nice areas — for transportation, decoration and friendliness.

Flat 6, 6 Hyde Park Mansions NW1, Tel. 01-262 0900

Bed & Breakfast (GB)
A big private booking organization. They publish a miniguide, available from British Tourist Authority (BTA) offices overseas. Prices start at £16.

Box 66, Henley-on-Thames, Oxon., Tel. (0491) 578803

London Home to Home
Covers West London. Minimum single rate £16 per person.

19 Mount Park Crescent, Ealing W5, Tel. 01-567 2998

London Homestead Services
Covers Greater London. Minimum single rate £12.

154 Warwick Road W14, Tel. 01-371 1411

Accommodation for students and rock-bottom budget travellers

Youth hostels
Important to reserve in advance, particularly for the summer months. The maximum stay is four nights, and curfews may be inconvenient. All require YHA or IYHF membership. Book through your local organization or direct — months ahead if possible. If you arrive without a reservation, enquire at YHA Headquarters:

YHA London Headquarters, 14 Southampton Street WC2, Tel. 01-836 8541

Holland House, in a restored Jacobean mansion in Holland Park W8 (Tel. 01-937 0748) and **Hampstead Heath** in a lovely, if inconvenient, location at 4 Wellgarth Road NW11 (Tel. 01-458 9054) are preferred. Other locations include: 36 Carter Lane EC4 (near **St Paul's**), Tel. 01-236 4965; 38 Bolton Gardens SW5 (**Earl's Court**), Tel. 01-373 7083; and 84 Highgate West Hill N6 (**Highgate**), Tel. 01-340 1831, also pleasant, but mainly groups. More hostels may open during the summer season.

Private hostels
A place in a hostel (several strangers of the same sex to a room) is cheap, but of course there's little privacy, though a few have some individual rooms. Some clean preferred places are: **Fieldcourt House**, 32 Courtfield Gardens SW5, Tel. 01-373 0152;

Baden-Powell (you don't have to be a scout), Queen's Gate SW7, Tel. 01-584 7030.
The **Driscoll House Hotel**, 172 New Kent Road SE1, Tel. 01-703 4175, charges £100 a
week for its 200 single rooms. A simple but friendly place.

Earl's Court and **King's Cross** areas have many very cheap, very seedy hotels, but
bear in mind that crime, prostitution and the drug trade are also very visible in these
districts. **Victoria** and **Bloomsbury** are more wholesome budget hotel areas, but may
be slightly pricier.

Renting a flat or house

For stays of a week or more, you should consider renting a flat or house.
Unfortunately, many visitors now have the same idea, and so renting is less of a
bargain and some very poorly-maintained properties are on offer. Nevertheless,
when you consider all the hotel charges, including VAT, service, tips, restaurant
meals and other extra expenses, it can still be value for money. A week in a tourist
hotel can now easily cost more than £500, exclusive of restaurant meals, so the idea
of renting still merits your consideration.

How do you go about finding an apartment? We provide some leads that our
subscribers have found satisfactory. I am sorry we are not able to provide more, but
so many London flats received decidedly mixed reviews. And the last few years have
seen many changes of ownership, with, in some cases, big changes in quality.
Clearly, the most satisfied renters are those who've rented from friends, relatives or
friends of friends with flats in London. These arrangements are usually closed to the
general public, and must be found through the grapevine.

More addresses of apartments and accommodation are available from the BTA
overseas. Americans and Canadians have a number of home-based agents who list
London flats and apartments. They would be wise to compare prices, because extra
commissions and exchange rates sometimes make a big difference when you pay in
dollars. On the other hand, these agents tend to list the kind of quality flat that North
Americans prefer.

Alternatively you can wait until you get here to begin your search. The longer your
stay, the more worthwhile is this approach, because you have the opportunity to
compare the wide variety of units on offer, and perhaps even negotiate the price.
From mid-June to mid-September, London can get very crowded. Flats are still
available, but choice is much more limited.

More addresses of holiday self-catering flats or apartments are available from
London tourist information offices, or check with estate agents in the area in which
you want to stay. Few local agents are interested in lets of less than a month, though
they sometimes have the odd gem and can be a great reference to other
opportunities. The best bargains are found by ads in the local papers or the *Evening
Standard*, on neighbourhood notice boards or from small letting agencies who
advertise in these media — though it's usually a good idea to inspect the premises
before making a commitment. Try some of the nice outer areas like Hampstead or
Richmond.

What should you expect? The situation is similar to hotels: you get what you pay
for. But London rental flats may not have everything a North American visitor
expects. Dishwashers, washing machines and separate showers (or even overhead
showers) are still rare. Few flats have automatic gadgets like food processors or
blenders. A rental flat should have a refrigerator, cooking facilities, an adequate
supply of glasses, cutlery, crockery and linen, and basic furnishings such as dining
table, beds, dressers, couches and chairs. Probably a TV will be provided, but you
should check. Carpets and furniture are often worn — as you would expect in a place
with frequent changes of occupancy. Some places offer a daily maid service; others
just a weekly change of linen. Cleanliness and general upkeep vary tremendously,
but maid service may be worth paying extra for.

Check to see whether electricity and gas are included. In Britain, local calls are charged, even to private customers, so a flat may not include a telephone, or a charge and hefty extra deposit may be required for the use of one. In some places, opting not to pay the deposit means that people can phone you, but you can't phone out.

Of course, if you're willing to pay more, you should get more, and, again, it's very important to compare prices. Some places feature access to a pool or health club, or give an excellent view of parks. Price is also a function of location. Most holiday flats are in central London, but the futher away you go from the preferred areas and the centre, the more you may get for your money. If a flat is a short walking distance from a tube station on a direct line into London, being out of the centre may not make much difference.

The preferred areas are the ones you would expect: W1 (**Mayfair** and **Marylebone**), SW1 (**Belgravia**, **Knightsbridge** and **Westminster**), SW3 (**Chelsea**) and W8 (**Kensington**). Prices in these districts are often at a premium. Many flats in SW10 and SW6 (**Fulham**), SW5 (**South Kensington**), W11 (**Notting Hill**) and W2 (**Paddington** and **Bayswater**) are almost as central. Avoid streets close to major railway stations like **Waterloo** (SE1) and **King's Cross** (N1).

As a rule of thumb (though there are plenty of exceptions) you should expect to pay a minimum of £250 a week for an acceptable one bedroom flat in a fairly central area. £500–800 is now the more usual. Studio flats (one big room) are seldom good value: the bed is often a fold-out couch. For £1000 or more, you should be getting something really special. Some places demand all or most of the rent in advance as a deposit. Expect also to part (temporarily, you hope) with a big deposit to cover breakages.

Full houses on short let are more difficult to find, and are often only available in the holiday season, but they may work out cheaper for large parties who want to split the rent. Two drawbacks: many are in far-flung suburbs, and they may not include linen, so you have to bring or buy your own.

Selected apartments and agencies
We realize that these rates may seem fairly expensive, but the lower down the scale the apartments, the more subscriber-complaints we receive.

St James's Court Hotel and Apartments
If money were no object, I have no doubt that this would be my first choice. First, everything — furnishings, decor, service — is not only of the highest quality, but also brand new. Second, it offers the best of both worlds: apartment renters get all the same services as the hotel guests next door — laundry, messages, concierge, maids, health club, two restaurants and 24-hour room service. It's an attractive and atmospheric place to stay. St James's Court comprises eight turn-of-the-century mansion blocks, several storeys high and built around a quadrangle with a huge mock-baroque fountain.

No two of the apartments are alike and each has its own character — expressed in traditional themes with modern taste and all the modern amenities. In fact, I'd say that the room decor and colour schemes are the most sumptuous and at the same time the most pleasing of any London rental apartments I've seen. Restrained, but not too minimal like some other rental units. Wall coverings and prints are well-chosen and placed. All the little touches have been thought of — for example, it isn't necessary to ask whether every bathroom has a shower as well as a bath. A choice of videos as well as colour TV is provided.

The location is great too. **Victoria** and **St James's Park** stations are nearby, as are **Buckingham Palace**, **St James's Park**, **Green Park**, **Whitehall** and the **Houses of Parliament**. **Knightsbridge**, **Regent Street** and **Piccadilly** are not far away for shopping. If you really want to use your fully-equipped kitchen, there's a large Sainsbury's just around the corner on Victoria Street.

Booking information
A 1-bedroom is £230 daily, £1380 weekly. A 1-bedroom with study as well as living room is £270 daily, £1620 weekly. A 2-bedroom is £300 daily, £1800 weekly. A 3-bedroom is £400 daily, £2400 weekly. Rates exclude VAT.
Reservations to: **St James Court**, Buckingham Gate, London SW1 6AF Tel. 01-834 6655. Telex. 938075/919557 TAJJMAG. Taj Hotels, Utel or in USA 1-800-458 8825

The Athenaeum
My second choice would be another famous hotel-with-apartments. Second only because there's no room service. Otherwise, renters enjoy the same services as the guests in the 90-room 4-star hotel that strives hard to retain its venerable traditions of personal service. Seventy per cent of the business is repeat, and hotel personnel go to great lengths to keep you happy. They will even stock your refrigerator with requested favourite items from **Fortnum and Mason** (just down the road) or **Harrods**. Marvellous location on Piccadilly near Hyde Park Corner, close to Mayfair shopping and restaurant facilities.
The other matter in which the **Athenaeum** takes great pride is the privacy afforded to its guests. The Apartment entrance is on a side street. This attention to privacy means that many guests have been prominent film personalities.
The apartments have been redecorated in traditional style. Old features, such as mock-Adam mantelpieces, are retained to give a very homely, cosy feeling to smartly-designed and maintained decor. Each has a fully-equipped kitchenette (but they did seem a bit small), bathroom with shower and bath, either one or two double bedrooms and a sitting room with colour TV, in-room films, radio, direct dial and switchboard telephone service.

Booking information
The Athenaeum is a little cheaper than the St James Court: £850 weekly for a 1-bedroom; £1100 for a 2-bedroom. The management is willing to negotiate odd extra days and for periods of less than a week when they are not busy. Reduced rates can apply from January to March, and, surprisingly, in July and August, when many regularly customers are 'on family holidays rather than in London'.
Reservations to: **Athenaeum Hotel**, 116 Piccadilly, London W1V 0BJ Tel. 01-499 3464. Telex. 261589. Or Rank Hotels in USA (800) 223 5560

Arlington House
In another hard-to-beat location, just behind the Ritz and overlooking Green Park. Many subscribers tell us that this big modern block with many full-time residents as well as renters is the best value thing they've come across at the top end of the market. Reasons? Apartments are relatively roomy. Decor is restrained English traditional, and many of the views look out over Green Park or the St James's area. Good, friendly security. The brochure says 'Porters can arrange to have groceries and papers delivered daily'.
The overall impression is that the apartments are spacious and well-maintained. That may not sound exciting, but by the standards of many tiny dirty and expensive London rental units, it can seem almost heaven. Features like separate WCs and walk-in closets (one I saw even had a window) are common.
Some people like being near the complex's fashionable restaurant, **Le Caprice**. The relaxed Sunday brunch attracts many renters as well as celebrities. The **Blue Posts**, a pub with a restaurant, over the street, has been very co-operative in supplying guests with carryout food. The **Ritz** is practically next door, and those who really want to live it up can buy their groceries at **Fortnum and Mason**.

Booking information
Rate structure is complicated, depending on time of year and unit desired. Studios

rent at £336 per week. Large 1-bedrooms go for £504–609 per week. 2-bedrooms, 1-bath £665. 2-bedrooms, 2-baths £708–994. 3-bedrooms, 2-baths £1071–1155. 4-bedrooms, 2-baths £1267. All rates include VAT. Minimum letting periods — April–September, 3 weeks; October–March 1 week. Minimum deposit of £300 required to secure reservations.

Reservations to: **Lupus Properties**, 94a Brompton Road, London SW3 1ER. Tel. 01-581 8481.

Dolphin Square

Not quite so opulent, but both good-quality and value for money. A kind of between-the-wars survivor with pervading Art Deco atmosphere. A huge complex built in 1935, it was originally all residential. Now one of the sections, **Rodney House**, is let to short-term visitors.

The apartments are comfortably furnished in sensible, attractive styles, and are of medium size. The ones I inspected have a light, airy atmosphere, created by large windows and light backgrounds. Thirties-style electric fireplaces give a relaxed, old-fashioned feeling. Kitchens are basic and their looks could do with some updating, but this is probably under way now as a floor-per-year renovation programme is operative. Not the place to stay if you want to hold receptions or impress status-conscious friends, but a good place for a relaxed holiday visit.

Renters can use the residents' big swimming pool. You might see some of Dolphin Square's famous residents, including David Steel (former leader of the former Liberal Party), a number of MPs and other theatrical and entertainment personalities. The pool is free, but other health facilities, sauna and squash courts require a small fee. With the exception of the **Tate Gallery** (a few blocks away), **Dolphin Square** is not well located for easy walking access to restaurants and attractions. But there are plenty of local shops; Pimlico Station and several bus lines are two minutes away; and, better yet, Dolphin Square is self-contained, with its own butcher, baker, grocer, greengrocer, hairdresser and newsagent to serve both residents and renters. I'm a fan of the **Dolphin Square Brasserie and Restaurant** overlooking the pool — Thirties' atmosphere, grand piano and jazz evenings with famed artists like George Melly. Arrangements will soon permit the restaurant to provide room service to renters.

Booking information
A 2-room apartment (lounge and bedroom) costs £420–456 a week. 3 rooms (lounge and two bedrooms) cost £540–600. There is an exceptionally nice 3-bedroom apartment that rents for £840 a week. Apartments are also rented on a daily basis (£74 a night for a 2-room). All have separate kitchen and bathroom and Monday–Friday maid service.

Reservations to: **Dolphin Square Trust Ltd**, Dolphin Square, London SW1V 3LX. Tel. 01-834 9134. Essential to book well in advance — a percentage of rooms are always booked up by an American holiday firm. A week's rent is required as deposit at the time of booking.

Other companies and agents

These firms are either generally well-reputed or have drawn mostly favourable reviews from our writers and subscribers. Exclusion does not necessarily imply criticism.

Holiday Flats

Offer many adequate properties at lower prices in safe, but less desirable areas like Kilburn or Swiss Cottage.

1 Princess Mews, London NW3, Tel. 01-794 1186

Taylings
A range of London houses and flats at reasonable prices; sometimes no linen is provided. Still, you might save, especially in a group. **Taylings** does advise: 'Many overseas visitors may not find older, simpler, less expensive properties suitable for their needs'.

14 High Street, Godalming, Surrey GU7 1ED, Tel. (04868) 28522

Josephine Butcher
An interior designer who lets a few luxurious homes to those with references in the Chelsea/Knightsbridge area for £600–1500 a week.

25 Hasker Street SW3, Tel. 01-584 1898

Aston's
Extremely popular agency with one-bedroom budget lets in South Kensington.

39 Rosary Gardens London SW7, Tel. 01-370 0737

Tourist Accommodation Booking Service
Fully-equipped flats at a bargain rate of £8 per person per night in four Victorian houses in the **Parliament Hill** area. Despite listings in many guidebooks, this friendly couple (the Sheppards) keep their rates low because they are 'satisfied'.

8 Woodsome Road, London NW5, Tel. 01-267 1782

Crawford's Holiday Flats
Basic, inexpensive accommodation in the **Marylebone** area.

10 Wyndham Place W1, Tel. 01-402 6165

Eyrie Mansion
A hidden service-flat bargain just off **Piccadilly**.

22 Jermyn Street, London SW1, Tel. 01-734 2353

Clearlake Apartments
Bargain flats, some with views of **Hyde Park**. One subscriber stays here every year.

18 Prince of Wales Terrace, London W8, Tel. 01-937 3274

Draycott House
Quality, comfortable 1–3 bedroom flats near **Sloane Square**. £600–1500 in high season.

10 Draycott Avenue, London SW3, Tel. 01-584 4659

Greengarden House
Recently redone 1-2 bedroom flats with maid service, just off **Oxford Street**. £500–700 per week (minimum stay — two weeks).

Sally Woolard, Greengarden House, St Christopher's Place, London W1, Tel. 01-935 9191

7   *Eating out in London*

London is becoming an important world gastronomic centre. Only two decades ago, this statement would have drawn smirks and derisive laughter; it still does — from the ignorant who haven't heard the good news, and from certain superior Frenchmen. London now has several world-class chefs and many highly-regarded restaurants. The criticism is often made that many of these cooks and restaurants are not British. This is true. Perhaps only New York rivals London for the sheer variety of restaurants and cuisines on offer (While Paris is world leader in French and haute cuisine, some might say it is only now learning to appreciate other styles.) London offers French, German, Italian, Russian, Polish, Swedish, Indian, Burmese, Malay, Ethiopian, and Caribbean cuisine, to name just a few. But what about the old stereotype, the much-maligned awfulness of English food?

Britain is slowly developing a simple but sophisticated style of its own, which some are calling Modern British Cuisine. The style has yet to be defined; in fact, it evades easy definition because it willingly partakes of many influences, but generally it has these characteristics: an emphasis on fresh, quality ingredients (often the menu changes with the markets); vegetables are prominent; light gravies prevail over sauces and are used with chutneys and relishes; fruit and herb flavourings are common, and meats tend to be plain and offset by other flavourings on the plate. Along with this development has come a rediscovery of the glories of very English cheeses like Blue Stilton, Wensleydale and matured cheddars. Two places where you can sample these influences at work in the hands of innovative young British chefs are **Alastair Little** and **Clarke's** (see below), but more and more 'English' restaurants are adopting similar ideas.

Superior exceptions apart, what will the visitor think of the average English restaurant? I think it is important first to go back and examine some of the prejudices about British food. What most of the critics have always missed about the cuisine of these islands is that they are homestyles — and in these homestyles good British cooks have always made use of some of the qualities supposedly rediscovered by modern British cuisine.

Undeniably, Britain has always had more than its share of uncared-for meats and over-cooked vegetables; but most critics and travellers experienced British cooking only in hotels and the homes of the aristocracy, because Britain once had no restaurant culture outside London. For most people, 'eating out' meant eating in a hotel restaurant — either during their travels or for a special occasion. Hotels, then as now, tried to please everyone and ended up pleasing no one, serving the infamous brown Windsor soup, heavy, starchy potato and gravy dishes, soggy vegetables and bread puddings. Roasts were generally well-prepared. Prominent people remembered the cooking styles they found in country houses.

Much of the English aristocracy had an ascetic attitude to fine food and drink, regarding it as somewhat vulgar. Only recently I had dinner with just such a family. Though quite well off, the hostess served everyone a tiny boiled potato, a gnarled piece of roast beef and a few overcooked shreds of carrot on fine china plates (and they were not trying to imitate nouvelle cuisine!). Eleven years of rationing during and after the last world war did nothing to help matters. But even before the war, as now, there were a few restaurants serving unadulterated traditional roast game or fish with plain but carefully-cooked vegetables not smothered in heavy gravies.

You can still sample good traditional British restaurant food in places like **Rules**, **Simpsons-in-the-Strand** and the **Savoy Grill**. These restaurants are expensive, of course, and at lower price levels it is true that you are unlikely to find much that is terribly exciting about British restaurant food, though you will find good things in bits and pieces, mostly as fast food: **Geale's** fish and chips, **Justin de Blank's** excellent Cornish pasties, the 'ploughman's lunch' offered in many pubs, scones and cream with afternoon tea at good hotels and patisseries.

The old-style greasy 'caff' or café is pretty awful indeed, but many serve good breakfasts. Somerset Maugham once said that 'to eat well in England you should eat breakfast three times a day'. A good, well-cooked traditional English breakfast of eggs, bacon, ham, sausage, and toast is a glory. Sometimes there are exotic specialities on offer like kippers, mackerel, scones, fried mushrooms, grilled tomatoes or black pudding. The French are said to be insisting that 'full English breakfast' be served on the new Channel Tunnel trains in 1993. Try the huge breakfasts on Pyrex plates at the **Fox and Anchor** pub.

What most visitors are likely to encounter in their hotels, tourist-oriented restaurants and many central pubs is not bad food but the same bland international style food served up everywhere in the western world: burgers, steaks, ribs, chicken, salads, spaghetti bolognese, pizza and pancakes. We have often heard American visitors to central London repeating the cliché about how bad English food is, only to find they had been eating the same foods they would order at a Denny's fast food restaurant at home. Unfortunately, London imitators do not always match Denny's prices; even more sadly, they don't match Denny's quality.

If you like to eat in this unfussy, relatively inexpensive way, then that is fine. But if you really want to enjoy London as a gastronomic centre, get out and sample all the cosmopolitan delights today's London has to offer.

If money's no problem, eat at fine French restaurants like **Tante Claire** or the Roux brothers' **Le Gavroche**. Though the latter is expensive, these same excellent French brothers offer some of the same food at a much-reduced price in their staff training grounds, **Gavvers** and **Les Trois Plats**. Bistros and brasseries like **Mon Plaisir** and **Le**

Routier and many wine bars offer French food at reasonable prices. London has atmospheric and stylish Italian restaurants, like the newly-renovated Covent Garden **Bertorelli's**, and the celebrity favourite **San Lorenzo**; but if you just want a cheap dish of spaghetti, all-you-can-eat pasta bars now abound. The world's best Indian restaurants are in London, not Delhi. Some of the world's best Chinese and Greek food is in Soho, as is the world-renowned Hungarian restaurant, **The Gay Hussar**. London has a Burmese and several Thai and Malaysian restaurants; sushi and terriyaki bars; at least two satay take-aways; Spanish tapas bars; Jewish kosher cafés; East European restaurants patronized by vanquished counts and Ruritanian field marshals, and many more. A moving feast is there for those prepared to seek it out.

Of course, restaurant likes and dislikes are a matter of personal taste. Some like Thai food — others find it inedible. Dieters are thrilled by nouvelle cuisine, while hearty eaters consider the minuscule portions an unconscionable rip-off. By all means, explore London's restaurants on your own and find your own favourites. To help you out, we offer some selections below that have pleased us or our subscribers or are worth noting. These selections are based as much on the special quality of venues — their particular blend of atmosphere, service, uniqueness — as the quality of the food. But first, a few tips . . .

Tips for eating out

- **Booking** Essential to book in advance if you want to go to a specific popular or famous restaurant. Multiple bookings by no-shows are frowned upon here and considered rude. Booking policies vary: the **Connaught Hotel** and **Le Gavroche** take bookings weeks in advance (and you'll probably need to book them that far ahead, particularly for a Friday); but some, like **The Gay Hussar**, will not take bookings more than a week in advance. You can usually get a table at less-popular places by phoning the afternoon before. If you know where you want to go, book to avoid disappointment.

- **Dress** A number of places still specify jacket and tie for gentlemen, but in the vast majority of restaurants people wear what they like, especially in the summer. Of course the more expensive or renowned the restaurant, the more elegant your fellow diners will be. To avoid feeling uncomfortable requires no more than commonsense.

- **Hours** The British generally do not meet for a restaurant lunch before 1pm; an evening meal is seldom before 8pm. But restaurant hours don't run late — last orders are seldom after 11pm except in some theatre-oriented places.

- **Value** Eating out in London is expensive — relatively more expensive than in the United States and most European capitals. Good medium-priced restaurants are few. You can get round this problem by ordering a value set meal. Most commonly these are available at lunch, though some restaurants also offer evening set meals. Some of the most expensive restaurants offer this bargain. Another option is to go to a **wine bar** — many serve inexpensive bistro-type food.

- **Payment** Credit cards are accepted by most restaurants. Visa and Access (Mastercard) are the most common, but some restaurants (rather eccentrically these days) accept only one or none. Ask in advance. Beware the 'credit card trick' (see below)

- **Tipping** This is becoming a very controversial matter. Most restaurants impose a 10 per cent service charge and most people we know don't add anything else except for extraordinary or beyond-the-call-of-duty service. At fancy or expensive restaurants some people feel that they are somehow obliged to leave more. It's up to you, but I wouldn't advise you to go along with the 'credit card trick' practised by many otherwise reputable restaurants. A service charge is added to the bill, then the total is left blank on the credit card slip to encourage the unsuspecting to pay service twice. Only if *no* service charge is added to the bill and service has been adequate do we leave a tip of 10–12 per cent.

To confuse you even further, it's only fair to add that some London food critics disagree with us and say you should leave at least 12–15 per cent for good service (in other words, add a little extra if only 10 per cent is put on the bill). Others, like the **Good Food Guide**, are anti-tipping. And we know that some of our subscribers enjoy tipping in a big way; we wish they wouldn't, because it inflates expectations and makes an evening more and more expensive.

Restaurant areas

As you browse these streets, note that many restaurants have menus posted outside. If nothing is on view, don't hesitate to ask to look at a menu before you sit down.

Soho
Soho now has few bargain bistros, but if you don't know where you want to go, stroll along **Greek, Frith, Romilly** and adjoining streets for the many small and atmospheric Italian, Greek, French, oriental and other restaurants. Soho has a wider selection of restaurants in a small area than anywhere else in London. Contrary to myth, the area is no more unsafe to walk in after dark than elsewhere in central London.

Gerrard Street
Just off Shaftesbury Avenue in Soho. This and adjoining streets are choc-a-bloc with Chinese restaurants of all kinds.

Covent Garden
Now an area for trendy yuppie-oriented nouvellish restaurants. But some of the older places survive.

Charlotte Street
The section lying between Tottenham Court Road and Percy Street and adjoining streets have some interesting Italian, Greek, French and other restaurants.

Fulham Road
Between Sydney Place and Elm Place, and further down between Elm Park and St Stephen's Hospital, are areas of fashionable restaurants. Good Italian food here and elsewhere in Chelsea.

Earl's Court
Many inexpensive ethnic restaurants and fast food take-aways.

Queensway and Westbourne Grove
An area of ethnic — Chinese, India, Arabic — and other restaurants.

Note
London has thousands of restaurants. We've chosen a few of the more interesting ones in the next few sections. The amount per person is only a rough guide for three courses with a house or less-expensive bottle of wine. We've done our best, but prices are always on the rise. *Please phone and book beforehand*. Most of our selections are established restaurants, but even so, they come and go.

London Traveletter's favourite restaurants

These restaurants are favourites with ourselves and our subscribers. They all have an indefinable 'something' that makes for a unique London experience.

Anna's Place

Gorgeous Swedish cooking. Try the *gravad lax* as a starter — it's properly marinated. My adventurous friend ordered the *smoked reindeer with caraway bread*. You'll like it, according to the said friend, if you want to be that barbaric (who chauffeured Santa Claus around, after all?). A good alternative would be the *blue cheese, apple and celery soup* — rich but light; the *Swedish caviar* is also good, but not that distinctive.

There is a lovely little garden open in the summer, and an extensive wine list. **Anna's** is a cafe which also has a bar, so you can, as the Islington residents do, drop in for a snack or for a full meal. Anna herself is friendly and circulates solicitously from time to time among the guests. The atmosphere is light yet intimate; there are only 15–20 tables, and there is a rather eclectic mix of artwork around the room, with a bit of unstained wood and greenery. It is fair to say that the restaurant is international, but I would stick to the Swedish specialties. Booking well ahead is essential. About £30 for two, with wine. I'll probably be sitting at the next table. (J.E.)

90 Mildmay Park, N1, Tel. 01-249 9379. Bus 30, 38 or taxi. Hours: Tues–Sat 1900–2230; lunch 1200–1430

La Barca

A place best enjoyed for what it is — an Italian theatre restaurant behind Waterloo Station on the South Bank. To do this, you should see the current production at the historic **Old Vic** nearby, or a little further away at the **National Theatre** or the **National Film Theatre**. The **Old Vic** is the former home of the National Theatre, and has been bought and beautifully restored by Canadian businessmen 'Honest Ed' Mirvish. Original Victorian features were retained, except for the seating, which is now some of the most comfortable in town. **La Barca** is very convenient to the **Old Vic**, just down the street. In fact, it is the best choice south of the river, an unfashionable district with few good restaurants.

Truly a theatre restaurant, **La Barca's** walls are lined with photos, autographs and certificates from showbiz notables. The menu is lenghty and, in our limited experience, the food is good, but the main attractions are the aforementioned walls, the bustle of waiters and a look at the late-night mix of up-market London — genuine celebrities, yuppies, sloanes, trendies and other less-exhibitionistic creatures. Book both the **Old Vic** and **La Barca** for an entertaining double-bill. If the play bores you, **La Barca** may still delight. About £20 per person with wine.

80–81 Lower March SE1, Tel. 01-261 9221 U: Waterloo. Hours 1200–1430; 1900–2330.

Bombay Brasserie

The opening of this luxurious Indian restaurant in **Bailey's Hotel** was delayed until astrologers advised on the most propitious day. It seems to have been worth the wait. Although London has dozens of fine Indian restaurants, the **Bombay Brasserie** attracts the 'in crowd'. The decor sets it apart from other Indian restaurants, for one thing — wicker chairs, sepia photographs, palms and lazily-rotating fans take you back to the days of the Raj. At lunchtime there is a set buffet only, but in the evening you can indulge yourself on more ambitious *à la carte* dishes like the Parsee wedding speciality of tender *mutton with dried apricots*, preceded perhaps by *crab malabar* — baked flaked crab, richly spiced with grated coconut and fresh curry leaves.

This is not our usual idea of an Indian restaurant — a place where several friends can split the bill and share several dishes economically — but the food and the splendid atmosphere of this restaurant merit a visit. If you haven't tried Indian food before, the **Bombay Brasserie**, is a good, though relatively expensive, place to begin. £20–£25 per person. (M.C.)

Bailey's Hotel, Courtfield Close SW7, Tel. 01-370 4040. U: Gloucester Road. Hours: Mon–Sun 1230–1430; 1930–2400.

Capital Hotel Restaurant

A few steps away from Harrods, this lovely little place has some of the best French food in London. Recently redecorated in sumptuous peaches, creams and teals, with pretty wall-coverings in rich, elegant fabrics. Flattering low lighting, without requiring candles or cane. Service efficient — a bit over-efficient, so we asked for time to relax!

We tried the *salad of rabbit*, with light mayonnaise and tomato sauce, which passed the test: neither too gamey nor tender to the point of flavourless mushiness. The *scallops mousseline* were light and well-flavoured, and far from insipid; best with their horseradish cream. The *fillets of duck breast* were delicious, but lacked a properly crisped skin. Red cabbage and potatoes provided an uninspired side dish, but with an excellent honey and lemon glaze. The *nage of turbot*, with cucumber in tarragon sauce, was simple and very good. The dessert proved to be a real *pièce de résistance*, to serve up a cliché: try the *marquise au chocolat blanc, sauce au café*. Excellent selection of French cheese.

The food was beautifully presented and the wine list well chosen and quite extensive. What endears the Capital to me, among other things, is that they alone are prepared to serve you — without puzzled looks — *Canari*, an after-dinner digestif: hot water with carved lemon peel. Even the Dorchester falls down on that last elegant touch. Highly recommended for that special dinner. About £60 for two with good wine. Elegant, elegant. (J.E.)

22 Basil Street SW3, Tel. 01-589 5171. U: Knightsbridge. Hours: Mon–Sat 1230–1430; 1830–2230 (Sun 1900–2200).

Le Caprice

A restaurant that performs the almost impossible task of pleasing everybody with its long eclectic menu for all cuisines and styles. There are skimpy trendy dishes for the diet-conscious, and heartier fare for the hungry. The shiny black and white interior, with full windows on one side and David Bailey black and white photographs on the inside walls, gives the impression that you are in the ultimate slick up-market diner for the fashionable. And you do regularly see famous faces here. But the staff are professional and courteous even if you are famous only for a 50-minute visit. Carefully-selected house wines. The Sunday brunch is a special treat, with traditional favourites, or *eggs Benedict* and the like. About £23–£25 per person.

Arlington House, Arlington Street SW1, Tel. 01-629 2239. U: Green Park. Hours: daily 1200–2400.

Caravanserai

An Afghan restaurant almost as exotic as its name. Afghan food is very similar to northern Indian, except some dishes seem to be more strongly or subtly spiced (and this is indicated on the menu). You get the impression that some dishes that show a stronger Persian or Arabic influence are genuinely Afghan. With others, you wonder whether 'Afghan' isn't just an excuse for clever innovations on run-of-the-mill Indian dishes. For example, if Afghanistan is a country with no sea-coast, how come there are prawn and marinated fish dishes? Try the Afghan 'complete dishes' with rice and lentils. The pretty rugs, wall hangings and charming staff make this place an essential stop for those who collect cuisine experiences. About £30–£40 for two.

50 Paddington Street W1, Tel. 01-935 1208. U: Baker Street. Hours: Mon–Sat 1200–1500; Mon–Thurs 1800–2300; Fri–Sat 1800–2330.

Chuen Cheng Ku or New World
Both of these are huge restaurants that are at their best for the wonderful London Chinatown institution of Sunday lunch *dim sum*. What is *dim sum*? Trolleys of inexpensive Chinese dishes are wheeled past your table by waitresses chanting their names in Chinese. When you see something appealing, stop the waitress and order. Most speak reasonably-fluent English and can explain dishes with names like *duck webs*. Most choices have more prosaic names — delicious dumplings, cold roast pork, noodle soup at prices that average £1 or less each. Kids love it. *Dim sum* is also served at weekday lunches, but the atmosphere is best at Sunday lunch times when huge Chinese families get together to order vast arrays of dishes. For regular evening meals both these restaurants are fine examples of the high-quality cuisine in London's Chinatown. *Dim sum* will probably cost less than £10 per person.

Chuen Cheng Ku: 17 Wardour Street W1, Tel. 01-437 1398; New World: Gerrard Place W1, Tel. 01-734 0677. U: Piccadilly Circus. Hours: Mon–Sun 1100–2345.

Clarke's
Tucked away among Kensington Church Street's seemingly-endless antique shops is a little gem of a restaurant that is producing some of the city's most unusual combinations of tastes and flavours. **Clarke's** is only a few years old; the creation of Sally Clarke, a charming young British restaurateur whose training included some time in California. Combine that background with a good, modern English style of cooking; some smells, aromas and ingredients from the south of France; the best local cheeses and a highly unusual wine list, and what you have is a very creative mix that has won steady praise.

There is no choice on the set four course meal with coffee (a whole jug is brought to your table at the end!). But what a good thing — you might never have tried some extremely innovative dishes that can scarcely fail to delight.

Sally Clarke, a lovely, tall, stylishly-dressed brunette, is herself constantly on the scene — looking after her patrons, doing a bit of the serving and giving advice on the wine. Many of the customers are regulars, well-known to her. The old ideal of restaurant atmosphere . . .

Almost perfect, but we've hardly mentioned the food. Absolutely no complaints. And so innovative you almost want to stand up and cheer. Have you ever heard of a small crisp pizza, topped by fresh diced salmon, as a starter? The salmon is from the restaurant's private daily supply, and the flavour combination really works. This was followed by char-grilled chicken breast stuffed with pine nuts. Not dry, but served with the delicious saved drippping, deep-fired celeriac root chips and other nouvellish vegetables in sensible quantities on the main plate.

English cheese provided the perfect follow-up, and we felt sufficiently inspired to splurge on half a bottle of dessert wine (why don't restaurants realize they would sell more sweet wines if they'd provide more half bottles?). We asked Ms Clarke's advice on this and, later, on brandy. In both cases she suggested little-known Californian brands that must be rare on London bar lists. A pity, because they travelled well. I won't name them — I don't want to share everything about our wonderful evening with you. So I'll stop here, but I will say that dessert — a kind of apple pie and ice cream purée — was yet another highlight, followed by a long linger over coffee and brandy. If you don't mind a no-choice set meal (menu changes daily), make a point of booking Clarke's on your next visit. Set dinner £25.00. Lunch £14–16.

124 Kensington Church Street W8, Tel. 01-221 9225 U: Notting Hill Gate. Hours: Mon–Fri 1230–1400; 1930–2300. Closed for two weeks in summer.

Connaught Hotel Restaurant
Hotel food needn't be bad or bland. There is another tradition of hotel food that borrows heavily from the French without losing an essentially English character.

Meats, grills, sole and salmon are the main features on the menu, but these are served with complexity and style. Vegetables are delicately cooked with just the right timing. It is recognized that even potatoes can be delicious when prepared with due respect.

This same tradition also accepts another French maxim that Anglos still find hard to swallow — that eating is a total experience that is at its best in the right atmosphere of sights, smells, sounds *and* tastes. The ambience must be appropriate. In the English hotel context, this means starched linen, silver service, polished oak panelling and waiters with a smoothness that never misses a beat. Perhaps this idea is best expressed by the story about the **Connaught Hotel Restaurant**. A harried Canadian businessman was rude enough to order a hamburger (which, of course, has never been on the menu). Without a flinch, the waiter calmly retorted, 'I am sorry, sir, that is off today'.

But before I go on, let me warn you. You'd better go on a special occasion to justify the price to yourself. Or invent one. Maybe we'll celebrate Ground Hog Day there. The menu is mostly in French, except for the upper corner listing of dishes of the day and statements about VAT, service charge (both included) and credit cards (for some reason only Access or MasterCard is accepted). There is a set price after the main course — a total that includes a huge choice of appetizers and the sweet trolley at the end. The cheapest is *ox tongue* at £18.80; most expensive is *homard* at £38.70, and a wide range in between.

Expect to spend a total of at least £45 per person. In the Grill Room, the menu is shorter but similar. You pay for each course rather than for three courses in the restaurant. Book well ahead, because most tables are reserved for hotel guests.

Carlos Place W1, Tel. 01-499 7070. U: Green Park. Hours: lunch 1230–1430; dinner 1830–2215.

El Bodegon
One of our favourite places, just off Fulham Road. I haven't ever seen it in many 'best of London restaurants' type guidebooks — but it's been around for years and has a small enthusiastic following.

Well-presented is the word that describes **El Bodegon**. The welcome is very warm and informal, but polite in the Spanish way. Walls are decorated with pictures and certificates from astronauts and other notables. There is a big picture of King Juan Carlos, but I don't know if he came here in his younger days.

In the centre of the room is a long table with huge trays of beautiful appetizers. When you order your meal, the waiter will juggle each one of these up to your table to give you a good look. But there are even more on the menu. Last time, I ordered the *crab pancakes*, and will do so again next time. Of course, they have *gazpacho* if that's what you want.

For first-timers to Spanish food, I would recommend the seafood *paella* — it is generously endowed with fresh prawns in just-right, ungreasy saffron and herb rice. Steaks and more familiar dishes are available to those who don't want to risk anything too new. But I'll warn you that the desserts are undistinguished.

What we like most is the spirit of the place: Spanish pride, dignity and simple elegance. Waiters enjoy showing off the restaurant's appetizers, but their attitude is: you choose, you know what's best. This extends to the wine list — full of good reasonably-priced Riojas. The restaurant's spirit is best exemplified by a friendly waiter's response to my question about the price of Spanish brandies: 'Sir, the most expensive is £3.50, the cheapest, you can have for free'. About £18–£20 per person with wine.

9 Park Walk SW10, Tel. 01-352 1330 U: South Kensington, but a long walk, so take a 14 bus or taxi from there). Hours: daily 1200–1500, 1900–2400

The Gay Hussar
No, this isn't a 'gay' restaurant, but a London institution with possibly the best Hungarian food outside Hungary, and a distinctive old-fashioned ambience that few other restaurants can match. The cosy decor is paprika red and, funnily enough, the former owner had a long-standing relationship with the moderate wing of the Labour party. Political luminaries and a sizeable number of publishers and journalists are weekly patrons, so it can be hard to book. Service is attentive, and friendly advice is readily given when requested.

Because Hungarian restaurants are few and far between, you might be excused for not being familiar with the cuisine. Try the goose, veal, or carp — off-set with spicy red cabbage and potatoes. The more adventurous can try *cold cherry* — or *'hangover' soup*. Our favourite is the indescribably delicious *roast duck with apple sauce* — we have a hard time ordering anything else.

Make an evening of it, because the restaurant is excellent value for a small place that seats only 35 and can fill up any night it wants to open. Order the Hungarian *Merlot, Mori Ezerjo* or *Egri Bikaver* wine, than have a sweet and tasty dessert glass of *Tokay* with your applecake. As the Good Food Guide says, 'Everyone is a regular after five minutes'. An evening out for two will run to £40–£50; special set lunch is £10.50. Book early, though the last time we checked they would not accept bookings more than a week in advance.

2 Greek Street W1V 6NB, Tel. 01-437 0973. U: Tottenham Court Road. Hours: Mon–Sat 1230–1430, 1730–2230.

Gordon's Wine Bar
Push open the plain brown door, descend a steep flight of steps, and you will find yourself in **Gordon's Wine Bar**, near Charing Cross Station. Here you can eat and drink in what is probably the oldest wine bar in London. Time seems to have stood still. Sitting at tables lit by candles flickering in the top of old wine bottles, customers can drink their wine under the low brick arches in what used to be the Duke of Buckingham's powder magazine, where gunpowder for the army was stored.

The house itself has many interesting associations with literary and theatrical personalities. In a room overhead Rudyard Kipling wrote *The Light That Failed*, and both he and G. K. Chesterton drafted several of their books in the little parlour of the wine bar. Frequently, famous actors and actresses such as Sir Laurence Olivier and Vivien Leigh would enjoy a glass of wine here when acting in the **Player's Theatre** opposite. The present owner, Luis Gordon, who has run the wine bar for the past 16 years, is an expert on wines of all varieties. Indeed, his family has spent over 200 years in the wine trade. He is very proud of a magnificent collection of English wine bottles, dating back to 1630, once owned by his father.

This is not a bad place to eat, either. There is a good selection of food prepared by the chef Mike Smith, who even cooks his own pork pies — something of a rarity in London. The menu changes every day and among the dishes are poached salmon, casseroles, chicken, giant sausages and a wide selection of cheeses, all in prime condition. Around the walls are pages from old newspapers and prints from the early 1900s. Apart from the excellent wines and food, the ambience generated by all those people who, over the centuries, came here to enjoy convivial glasses and good conversation, is quite unique. The average price is about £3 a head plus wine, and this includes a variety of help-yourself salads. (A.N.)

47 Villiers Street WC2, Tel. 01-930 1408. U: Charing Cross/Embankment. Hours: Mon–Fri 1100–1500; 1730–2200. Closed Saturday and Sunday.

Khan's
If you can imagine lofty square rooms with no decor but palm posts, arches, small Casablanca-like fans, cool blue walls — one blotchy (either by design, or perhaps

they forgot the wallpaper) — high ceilings, and lots of card tables jammed together and covered with linen cloths . . . you're on your way. Add lots of people, half scruffy, half yuppie, lots of bustle and noise: a Bombay version of McDonalds at lunch hour. If you don't mind speed eating, then try **Khan's** for good Indian food. My dish was still wet with suds, and the cutlery was dashed down in a clattery bunch in front of us, but the food is still undeniably good.

Don't let them tell you nothing is pre-prepared. It is — and served so hastily you'll think it's all lined up assembly-style. Still here? Then try the *butter chicken*, the best in London. The *chana masala* (chick peas with garlic, ginger, chilli paste) is wonderful. The *chicken jalfrezi* is a hot curry that's strictly for the hardiest of taste buds — but subtle as well with its mixture of spices. The *yogurt and cucumber raita* is nothing special, but makes a complementary cool side dish, as does the *palak* (spiced spinach). There are half a dozen red and white wines at £4–£6 a bottle, as well as cocktails. We ate very well for £16. Try the *iced sorbet in orange* for dessert. **Khan's** is speedy but somehow endearing. (J.E.)

15 Westbourne Grove W2, Tel. 01-727 5420. U: Bayswater. Hours: Mon–Sun 1200– 1500; 1800–2400.

Kleftiko

Slightly off the beaten track for most people — just off the Shepherds Bush roundabout, about midway between Holland Park and Shepherd's Bush (Central Line) tube stations, on Holland Park Avenue — **Kleftiko** is very handy to the Kensington Hilton, across the street. Otherwise, we think it is worth the short hike for the very warm welcome from the two Greek Cypriot brothers who treat all their guests like regulars in this cosy bistro restaurant. The special is lamb **kleftiko**, as you might have guessed, but don't miss delicious Greek starters like hummus, sausages and olives, or you might choose succulent pork or fish as a main course alternative. Wash your kleftiko down with a bottle of *Othello*. About £12–£15 per person.

186 Holland Park Avenue W11, Tel. 01-603 0807. U: Holland Park or Shepherds Bush. Hours: Mon–Sat 1200–1500; 1800–2330

Phoenicia

Wonderful Lebanese food is served at this charming restaurant in a pleasant neighbourhood just off Kensington High Street, but the outstanding attraction is their £7 all-you-can-eat Lebanese set lunch, served daily except Sundays from huge tables of salads, hummus, kibbeh, tabbouleh, lamb, pitta bread with fillings and chicken in all forms. If you haven't tried Lebanese food before, it's a delicious collection of flavours from all over the Eastern Mediterranean region. This is one of the few London Lebanese restaurants that welcomes non-Arab and Arab with equal warmth. Go and sample London's best restaurant bargain — I'm sure you'll find something you'll like — then linger over the included cup of murky coffee for as long as you like. An *à la carte* evening meal will probably run to £40 or more with wine for two.

11–12 Abingdon Road W8, Tel. 01-937 0120. U: Kensington High Street. Hours: Mon–Sun 1200–2400.

Rules

Rules predates Simpsons-in-the-Strand by a good many years — it claims to be the oldest restaurant in London. It was opened by Thomas Rule in 1798 as an oyster bar, and contemporary food writers were soon extolling its 'porter (beer), pies and oysters' as well as the quality of the clientele — 'rakes, dandies and superior intelligences'. The list of famous authors and actors who have dined and wined here would fill pages, but the memorabilia on the walls — playbills, photographs, cartoons and paintings — gives some idea. The most famous names associated with

Rules are those of the Prince of Wales (Edward VII) and actress Lily Langry, who were such frequent patrons that a special door was installed to enable the Prince to come and go without walking through the restaurant.

The food at Rules is as British as you can find anywhere, with *roast ribs and scotch beef, steak, kidney and mushroom pie,* and — for the daring — *tripe and onions* on Wednesdays or the esoteric *East End eel, mash and peas* on Fridays. Game in season is a feature here; *Loch Fyne oysters* are by the half dozen, and try the *Cornish crab salad.* About £25 per person. (M.C.)

35 Maiden Lane, Covent Garden WC2, Tel. 01-836 5314. U: Charing Cross/ Embankment. Hours: Mon–Sat 1200–2400.

San Frediano
'San Fred's', as some of the waiters' shirts proclaim, is a Fulham Road institution with many regulars who are enthusiastically welcomed. But first-time patrons are just as warmly greeted. The problem, for some, is the noise and bustle. We just accept it as part of the authentic Italian atmosphere. You have to catch the waiters as they run past, but they still manage to take orders and serve with the expected amount of style. They really make you believe you are in a fashionable café in Rome.

Prices, for both food and wine, are less than in other fashionable Italian places in London, but the menu is a good deal more innovative, though some old favourites have simply been cleverly renamed. For the most interesting choices, look at the right-hand side of the menu, where new daily choices are handwritten. How many London Italian restaurants serve *guinea fowl,* for example? Mine was delicious, as was the *tagliatelli* beforehand. The wine list is more than adequate, though in summer we usually stick with light dry *Frascati* — otherwise it might be difficult to walk out of the door. About £18–£20 per person.

62 Fulham Road SW3, Tel. 01-584 8375. U: South Kensington. Hours: Mon–Sat 1230–1430; 1915–2315.

Critic's choice

These restaurants have won high accolades from many food critics (though don't expect them all to agree). The main reason they are not included in the list above is that they are not special or sentimental favourites with us. High prices may have something to do with it. Most of these restaurants are a great evening out, but you should expect to pay for it.

Alastair Little
Very simple place with a cleverly thought-up English menu that changes every day. Eccentric, but the quality of the cooking is so high that many critics rave about this small Soho restaurant. Only the best produce is used, and the flexible menu means that what's used is always what's freshest — including lamb and especially fish. The well-chosen wine list is getting more expensive (most are over £10), though Little seems to be trying to hold prices down. Service from Little's two women partners is informal and well-informed. Fashionable with media people. If you don't mind having your preconceptions challenged about what a restaurant should be like, you should give this place a try. Cost is about £50 for two with wine.

49 Frith Street W1, Tel. 01-734 5183. U: Piccadilly Circus. Hours: Mon–Fri 1230–1500; 1900–2330.

L'Arlequin
Small, simply-decorated French restaurant just over the Battersea Bridge. Well presented — perhaps too much so. On the last look, the food was very nouvelle, so

avoid it if you don't like very small portions. Expensive for both food and wine at £30 per person, but the set lunch is only £14.50.

123 Queenstown Road SW8, Tel. 01-622 0555. U: Clapham Common. Hours: Mon–Fri 1230–1400; 1930–2300.

Dorchester Terrace and Grill

This restaurant achieved celebrity under famous chef Anton Mosimann, who invented something called *cuisine naturelle,* which is a no-additive, no-sugar version of nouvelle cuisine. Fitness enthusiasts may find his sophisticated, unadulterated, good-looking small portions to be nothing short of heaven. Those put off by these ideas will find the **Grill** to be more to their liking: another place to enjoy more traditional English food. £80–£100 for two. The Dorchester is closed for renovation during most of 1989.

Park Lane W1, Tel. 01-629 8888. U: Hyde Park Corner. Hours: Mon–Sat 1800–2330; Grill 1230–1500; 1830–2300 (Sun 1900–2230).

Le Gavroche

If you want to blow £120–£160 on a meal for two at a Michelin three-star restaurant, probably the best temple of French food in these islands, look no further. This is unquestionably the place. Many critics rate it as perfect or near-perfect in nearly all respects — superb food service and atmosphere (though a few don't like the decor). Run by French chef Albert Roux, who, with his brother Michel (creator of the **Waterside Inn**, Britain's other three-star), is now almost legendary in British culinary or 'foodie' circles; much of the style is neither traditional nor nouvelle, but something much better called New Classic Cuisine. Too much fuss is made of this place for us to find it very appealing, but we can't deny that **Gavroche** is one of the best. It can be affordable if you go for the *Menu Exceptionnel* (£35 per person), or book the set lunch at £19.50. Otherwise, we've already indicated what you may spend *à la carte.*

43 Upper Brook Street W1, Tel. 01-408 0881. U: Marble Arch. Hours: Mon–Fri 1200– 1400; 1900–2300.

Inigo Jones

A genteel temple of nouvelle cuisine with superb service, artistic presentation and high prices. 'Cuisine bourgeoise' choices are sometimes offered for those less than enthusiastic about Paul Gaylor's nouvelle creations, and there are useful pre-theatre and vegetarian menus. A la carte diners will pay upwards of £90 for a meal for two with wine, but most will opt for the excellent set lunch at £17, or dinner at £27.

14 Garrick Street WC2, Tel. 01-836 6456. U: Covent Garden. Hours: Mon–Sat 1200– 1430; 1730–2300.

Langan's Brasserie

Considering the transitory nature of anything 'fashionable', it amazes me that **Langan's Brasserie** is still, almost 15 years after it opened, packing in some of the most talked-about people in London. The fact that one of the owners is film star Michael Caine does help, of course, but many like **Langan's** more because it's cosmopolitan and fun than because of the celebrities. Paintings, prints and photographs clothe the walls, and there is an air of old-fashioned bustle. For around £25 a head you can have a three course meal from a long and wide-ranging menu which majors in British dishes and some classic French cooking — tiny spinach soufflés with anchovy sauce, or *bisque de crevettes* to start, and tripe and onions or poached turbot with Hollandaise sauce to follow, and a recommendable *crème* brulée to finish. Lots of media people around, so dress is relatively informal, but in the smartest way. (M.C.)

Stratton Street W1, Tel. 01-493 6437. U: Green Park. Hours: Mon–Fri 1230–1445; 1900–2345; Sat 1900–0045.

Ma Cuisine
This small, quality French restaurant can sometimes be hard to book. A mixture of modern and bourgeois French food in unusual combinations like veal sweetbreads and kidneys roasted and served in a light sauce of juniper berries. A meal for two with wine would be about £60.

113 Walton Street SW3, Tel. 01-584 7585. U: South Kensington. Hours: Mon–Fri 1230–1400; 1930–2300.

Le Mazarin
Quality French restaurant set in a pink pastel Chelsea basement. Again, the place is run by another ex-Le Gavroche chef, René Bajard, who obviously learned his skills with sauces and fish. If you can't afford Le Gavroche or can't get into Gavvers, this place has related styles of food with a set value dinner price of £22.50 and a house wine for only £8.

30 Winchester Street W1, Tel. 01-828 3366. U: Victoria. Hours: Mon–Sat 1900–2330.

Memories of China
Ken Lo's light and airy — almost Scandinavian-style — restaurant with its elegant façade is not far from Victoria Station. Ken Lo is a gentle tennis-playing veteran whose name — thanks to his innumerable cook books and articles — is synonymous with Chinese cooking. His menu might be described as the best of the best, since it concentrates on the specialities of those regions most famous for their food. He once introduced me to a simple fish dish, a whole steamed bass cooked with ginger, which exemplified all he was most proud of in Chinese cuisine — it was fresh, wholesome and flavoursome. Still, a *Shantung chicken* in garlic sauce might be more in your line, or one of the regional dinners, which allows you the choice of the hot and spicy dishes of Szechuan as well as the gentler food of Peking. About £60 for two with wine. Set lunch £16 or set dinner £22.67. (M.C.)

67 Ebury Street SW1, Tel. 01-730 7734. U: Victoria. Hours: Mon–Sat 1200–1430; 1900–2300.

Rue St Jacques
A shooting star in the restaurant firmament, **Rue St Jacques** was awarded two stars in Egon Ronay's guidebook only a year after opening. Such gastronomic precocity has attracted the rich and fashionable to this small restaurant dominated by classy mirrors. The menu is similarly rich — rich in cream, foie gras, lobster and truffles — but these are used with discretion and to great effect in quite sensational sauces. There is a magnificent cheese board with no less than 35 different cheeses seductively displayed, and desserts to rave about — *strawberry tart, soufflé au chocolat au rhum, vacherin of summer fruits,* for instance, all beautifully presented. Wines are expensive — a *Fleurie* at £10 a bottle is about the cheapest on the list. A vintage champagne is £40 a bottle, and a *Chateau Giscours '79* recommended at £15.50. Dinner for two is about £90. (M.C.)

5 Charlotte Street W1, Tel. 01-637 0222. U: Goodge Street. Hours: 1230–1430; 1930–2315.

Simply Nico
Every time chef Nico Ladenis opens a new restaurant (this is his third), he is immediately lauded by the critics. If he leads a charmed professional life, it is not undeserved. Ladenis is a master of clever ingredients and flavourings that don't always work out, but when they do, his cooking is wonderful. Basically, the food is French, inspired by Provence and influenced by the chef's Greek background. Despite the chef's early dissatisfaction with and departure from mainline nouvelle cuisine orthodoxy, Michelin inspectors were in a big hurry to award his newest restaurant two stars. Wines are very expensive (no house wine). Book far in advance for the £16.50 set lunch, otherwise you'll pay upwards of £80 for dinner for two.

48a Rochester Row SW1, Tel. 01-630 8061. U: Victoria. Hours: Mon–Fri 1230–1400; 1930–2300.

La Tante Claire
If you were here before 1985, you'll find this Michelin two-star to be much improved in background atmosphere; with more space and beautifully-set tables, it's larger, lighter and more restful. The owner-chef, Pierre Koffmann, was once a trainee at **Le Gavroche**, and his style is basically nouvellish modern French, but with great innovation, attention to detail and willingness to experiment. Expensive menu and wine list (about £100 dinner for two). Save with the great value set lunch (£18) and French country wines.

68 Royal Hospital Road SW3, Tel. 01-352 6045. U: Sloane Square. Hours: Mon–Fri 1230–1400; 1900–2300 Closed for three weeks in August/September.

A pleasant meal out

Most of us have a pleasant image in the back of our minds of a charming little restaurant — perhaps candlelit, with checked tablecloths, or smart linens and stylish waiters — or one of many other fantasies of a venue for that special, perhaps romantic, evening out, or long lazy lunch that we'll always remember. The ingredients are usually caring service, delicious food and a unique atmosphere. It also helps if the bill doesn't spoil it all. The trouble is — it also depends on the mood of the diners. Everything needs to come together at once to make it work. We've listed some restaurants here that you might try, not because they are or aren't highly graded by gastronomes or favoured by the fashionable, but because they have a different or pleasant ambience which you may find enjoyable.

British (including Anglo-French) traditional and modern
Most good traditional British cooking has a strong French influence, but many of these places also serve a good roast beef and Yorkshire pudding and roast potatoes — the real thing. These restaurants serve mostly traditional food, but modern influences are strong and growing.

- **Connaught Hotel** (see *Favourites*)
- **Rules** (see *Favourites*)
- **Gordon's Wine Bar** (see *Favourites*)

Baron of Beef
If you're out in the City at lunchtime and want somewhere 'atmospheric', try this well-named restaurant for its prime roasts, grills and Whitstable oysters. Situated in an old part of London, it caters for a mainly stockbroker clientele (you should wear jacket and tie) with *roast sirloin of prime Scotch beef with Yorkshire pudding* from the trolley, *beefsteak and kidney pie*, even *jugged hare* and *roast sucking pig*. Unlike **Simpson's**, however, there are no homely English puddings to follow — fruit and

cheese are all that's on offer. The decor is modern baronial — wood-panelling, plush upholstery and sporting prints. About £45 for two.

Gutter Lane EC2, Tel. 01-606 6961. U: St Paul's. Hours: Mon–Fri 1200–1500; 1730–2100.

The English House and The English Garden

In case you think the restaurants offering traditional English food are too macho or huge-portion oriented, visit one of these Chelsea restaurants, under the same management. You won't get the huge sides of beef on grand silver trolleys, but there is a range of interesting English dishes cooked to traditional recipes: *chilled Stilton soup, Huntingdon fidget pie* and *oyster-stuffed chicken*, for instance, and always the most delicious puddings. **The English House** is in the front 'parlour' of a tiny terraced Chelsea house, and is stylishly furnished with flowered wallpaper and country antiques. **The English Garden** is a lovely place to eat: it could be a set for *The Importance of Being Earnest*, and works out slightly cheaper (about £50 for two) than the **House**.

The English House: 3 Milner Street SW3, Tel. 01-584 3002. U: Sloane Square. Hours: Mon–Sun 1230–1430; 1930–2330.

The English Garden: 10 Lincoln Street SW3, Tel. 01-584 7272. U: Sloane Square. Hours: Mon–Sat 1230–1430; 1930–2330; Sun 1230–1400; 1930–2330.

The Greenhouse

Not as expensive as the grand hotel dining rooms, but an elegant place to sample French-influenced English cuisine. With white table cloths and candles, it is proper, but not stiff. The restaurant is owned by the same people who own the **Capital Hotel**, but the menu is much more traditional and straightforward. £40–£50 for two.

27a Hays Mews W1, Tel. 01-499 3331. U: Green Park. Hours: Mon–Fri 1900–2300; Sat 1930–2300.

The Guinea Grill

Very good huge steaks — though quality can vary from night to night and prices are high. A couple can easily spend £80. Not to be confused with the **Guinea Restaurant** at the old address (30 Bruton Place), which is now owned by Young's Brewery, with lower prices and OK food.

26 Bruton Place W1, Tel. 01-629 5613. U: Green Park. Hours: Mon–Fri 1200–1430; Mon–Sat 1900–2300.

The Savoy Grill

Not far from **Simpson's**, the **Savoy Grill** can always be relied on to offer good British specialities every day, although the choice varies throughout the week. Tuesday lunchtime is a favourite meal, when a hearty *steak, kidney and oyster pudding* is on the menu. Unfortunately, it is seldom possible to arrange one's diary on the basis of a single dish. *Roast sirloin of beef* is on the dinner menu for both Thursday and Saturday. Good wine list. Prices are high — probably upwards of £70 for two. (M.C.)

Savoy Hotel, Strand WC2, Tel. 01-836 4343. U: Charing Cross/Embankment. Hours: Mon–Fri 1230 1430, 1800–2315; Sat 1800–2315.

Simpson's-in-the-Strand

This is where they still keep up the great British roast, complete with all the attendant ceremony — the great silver-plated trolleys on which the beef is wheeled around, for example, a much-imitated custom that was introduced way back in 1848. **Simpson's-in-the-Strand** has a long and venerable tradition. It started life in 1828 as a 'home for chess', but in 1848 re-opened as Simpson's Tavern and Divans. The **Simpson's** that we see today is the one that re-opened in the Edwardian era, after the old restaurant was demolished when the Strand was widened at the turn of the century.

Roasts are always available and come complete with all the trimmings (Yorkshire pudding with the roast beef, redcurrent jelly with the *saddle of lamb*); but there are equally tempting alternatives, not least the *steak, kidney and mushroom pie*. Prices include VAT and service, but not 'table money' of £1 per person — a euphemism for cover charge. In the old days it was customary (and still is at the Connaught) to tip a 50p coin to the chap who carves your helping of 'rare' or 'well-done' from the trolley.

Simpson's can be very touristy. If you don't mind that, it isn't as expensive as some places. £60 upwards for two. (M.C.)

100 Strand WC2, Tel. 01-836 9112. U: Charing Cross/Embankment. Hours: Mon–Sat 1200–1445; 1800–2145.

Tiddy Dol's Eating House
An atmospheric restaurant set in eight small eighteenth-century houses in historic Shepherd's Market. During the Christmas season they have a festive all-inclusive holiday meal with entertainment nearly every night. In the other eleven months Tiddy Dol's runs a not dissimilar *à la carte* evening programme, with costumed strolling entertainers, and disco dancing from 10.30, and an Olde English menu. In contrast to its many rivals, great attention is paid to the quality of food and wine. The wine list includes both 'superior' and 'undervalued' wines. You'll probably spend at least £50 for two — but don't forget that this includes the dancing and entertainment.

55 Shepherd Market W1, Tel. 01-499 2357. U: Green Park. Hours: Mon–Sun 1800–2300.

- **Carveries** (see *Fast Food*)

- **Breakfast and Sunday Lunch** (see *More Selections:* many of these restaurants serve other meals)

British Modern
- **Alastair Little** (see *Critic's choice*)
- **Clarke's** (see *Favourites*)

Frith's
This pretty little place calls itself 'new British' and has innovative renderings of traditional dishes and ingredients. In summer, there is extra seating in a lovely back garden. Set meals only make this a relatively inexpensive place to eat — a little over £20 per person.

14 Frith Street W1, Tel. 01-439 3370. U: Piccadilly Circus. Hours: Mon–Sat 1200–1430; 1800–2330.

Waltons
A fancy, high-priced restaurant that really specializes in its set menus. Come to think of it, we've never actually seen anyone eating *à la carte*. Still, the overplush decor and imaginative Anglo-French menu provides an amusing and relaxed setting for the boozy, rainy afternoon set menu lunch (£12–£16). *A la carte* for two with wine could easily cost upwards of £100.

121 Walton Street SW3, Tel. 01-584 0204. U: South Kensington. Hours: Mon–Sun 1230–1430; 1930–2300.

Chinese

London Chinese restaurants are not known for outstanding decor or smiling service, but many, particularly in Chinatown, serve excellent food. Set meals are good value.

- **Memories of China** (see *Critic's Choice*)
- **Chuen Cheng Ku** and **New World** (see *Favourites*)

Dumpling Inn

An under-rated Northern Chinese cuisine place with a very quiet relaxed atmosphere inside as you watch Chinatown go by outside. Dumplings and noodles fill you with warmth and well-being on a cold day. £15 per person.

Gerrard Street WC2, Tel. 01-437 2567. U: Piccadilly Circus. Hours: Mon–Sat 1200– 2330.

Fung Shing

With some hesitation, we'd say this is the best Cantonese restaurant we've enjoyed out of many good Chinatown restaurants. Pleasant surroundings, helpful staff. Try the *salt-baked chicken*. £22 per person.

15 Lisle Street WC2, Tel. 01-437 1539. U: Piccadilly Circus. Hours. daily 1200–2345.

The Lido

Another plain decor, wind-dried meat place. We prefer it to **Poon's**, because it is cheaper, more popular with Chinese and less popular with tourists. Keep walking up the stairs until you see a spare table. Late hours can be a real advantage. Service is very fast. £10 per person.

41 Gerrard Street W1, Tel. 01-437 4431. U: Piccadilly Circus. Hours: daily 1600–0400.

The Ming

A very pleasant, mainly Peking-style restaurant with a number of innovative 'sizzling' approaches to prawns, spare ribs and more unlikely dishes. Attention to detail in ingredients. About £20 per person.

35 Greek Street W1, Tel. 01-734 2721. U: Piccadilly Circus. Hours. daily 1200–1400.

Poon's

A place to try wind-dried meats — a Cantonese food preservation method that you won't see in many US restaurants. Decor is unexciting, but the menu is long and at this branch it's relatively inexpensive. About £15 per person.

4 Leicester Street WC2, Tel. 01-437 1528. U: Piccadilly Circus. Hours: daily 1200– 2330.

Tiger Lee

This Chinese seafood restaurant is comfortable and elegant, and the fish is fresh (the exotic varities are bred locally). One of the more expensive Chinese restaurants in town, but a frequent Michelin entry. £25 per person.

251 Old Brompton Road SW5, Tel. 01-370 2323. U: Earl's Court. Hours: daily 1800– 2315.

Far Eastern

Chiang Mai

Very authentic 'temple' of Thai cuisine designed to represent a Thai wooden stilt house. Relaxed feel helps with the digestion of very spicy and sometimes garlicky

Thai food. Has some northern specialties that you might not have tried before. £14 per person.

48 Frith Street W1, Tel. 01-437 7444. U: Piccadilly Circus. Hours: daily 1200–1500; 1800–2300.

Mandalay
London's only Burmese restaurant, and one of the very few outside Burma; so, cuisine-tryers, this is your big chance! Some say Burmese food resembles Thai food; others say it's an Indian-Chinese hybrid with curry and soup combinations. Try *coconut and seaweed cake* for dessert. The owners — a family — run the restaurant in the refurbished basement and ground floor of their house. £15 per person.

100 Greenwich South Street SE10, Tel. 01-691 0443. British Rail: Greenwich. Hours: Mon–Sun 1930–2215.

The Penang
Wood-panelled basement restaurant with friendly service; the cooking — a mixture of Malaysian and Chinese — is more innovative than most small Asian restaurants. £14 per person.

42 Hereford Road W2, Tel. 01-229 2982. U: Notting Hill Gate. Hours: daily 1800–2230.

Saigon
London now has several Vietnamese restaurants. If this is not the best, it is certainly the most romantic, especially upstairs. For the uninitiated, Vietnamese cooking is more herb-flavoured than Chinese, and makes more use of chillis, coriander and strong flavourings than that of the neighbouring Cantonese. £15 per person.

45 Frith Street W1, Tel. 01-437 7109. U: Piccadilly Circus. Hours: Mon–Sat 1200–2330.

Fish
If you want to try fish and chips, see our *Fast food* section; otherwise, London fish restaurants are not generally cheap. Americans should note that fish restaurants in London tend to be just that — with an emphasis on grilled plaice or baked Dover sole or oysters. Shellfish choices are expensive and less common — there is nothing that compares with Gulf seafood or Cajun cuisine. London has several famous old-fashioned fish and oyster restaurants that have long been commended to tourists as an Olde England experience — **Sheeky's**, **Bentley's**, **Scott's**. **Wheeler's** is now a chain. **Overton's** seems to be all tourists. All of these places have become touristy and expensive. If you just want to say you've been there, go — and enjoy the atmosphere. But we recommend **Wilton's** or **Green's** (see below) for those in search of the real thing.

Green's Champagne and Oyster Bar and Restaurant
Club-like atmosphere combines with an outdated but charming attempt 'not to let the side down' with modern styles of British cooking. Still, it's less stuffy than **Wilton's** (below), dress is smart casual, and many of the dishes aren't expensive: shepherd's pie, sausages, fish cakes and steamed puddings. Excellent oysters, fish and crab. You can nibble seafood snacks with your drink at the bar. £20 per person.

36 Duke Street SW1, Tel. 01-930 4566. U: Piccadilly Circus. Hours: Mon–Sat 1230–1445; 1830–2245; Sunday brunch 1130–1530.

Manzi's
An Italian-English fish restaurant with a cheerful checked tablecloth atmosphere

downstairs. Simple, good value, and well-loved by regulars. Have a drink in the tiny bar upstairs while you wait for your table. £15 per person.

1–2 Leicester Street WC2, Tel. 01-734 0224. U: Piccadilly Circus. Hours: Mon–Sat 1200–1430; 1730–2330; Sun 1800–2030.

La Pirogue
Very unusual wine bar that serves Mauritian seafood in relaxed surroundings with a friendly staff. Mauritian seafood cooking is spicy and strong, very closely related to the cooking of those parts of India from which many Mauritians' ancestors came. Out-of-the-way, but worth it. £15 per person.

131 Askew Road W12, Tel. 01-749 9030. U: Stamford Brook. Hours: Mon–Fri 1200–1500; Mon–Sat 1900–2230.

Wilton's
Charming Edwardian decor and old-fashioned service make you feel you are in a pre-war England time-warp. **Wilton's** is less self-publicizing than the places mentioned above, and requires jacket and tie — all of which makes for an atmosphere that is rather stiff and clubby, and so the mass tourist trade stays away. Oysters, fish and game are well prepared in traditional, unexciting ways. £22 per person.

55 Jermyn Street SW1. Tel. 01-629 9955. U: Piccadilly Circus. Hours: Mon–Fri 1230–1430; Mon–Sat 1830–2230.

French

La Bastide
The attitude is low-key, welcoming, pleasing. Although the *à la carte* menu looked delectable enough (next time I'll go for the *smoked mussels in pastry* with oyster sauce), we found the set menu excellent value at £13.90 for three courses, or £15.80 for four (the latter adds a handsome cheese board, which includes *chèvre* [goat's cheese]).

La Bastide is decorated — blissfully simply — in cream, pink and beige, with opulent carpets, linen tablecloths, and a cozy, serene atmosphere. Its elegance is quiet — no glitzy bizzy crowd here, or, if they are, they're not boisterous, which is more than one can say about other more desperately trendy places. *A la carte* £25 per person. (J.E.)

50 Greek Street W1, Tel. 01-734 3300. U: Tottenham Court Road or Leicester Square. Hours: 1230–1430; 1800–2330.

Au Bois St Jean
Lovely candle-lit basement restaurant in St John's Wood that provides a complimentary glass of Kir when you are seated at your table. Several fixed-price menus might be available. French soups and sauces are the main attraction. Set lunch £8.50. Set dinner £12.75–£15.

122 St John's Wood High Street NW8, Tel. 01-722 0400. U: St John's Wood. Hours: Mon–Fri, Sun 1200–1430; Mon–Sun 1900–2330.

Au Bon Actuel
Good traditional French food, near Kensington museums. Light atmosphere; eat outside in summer. £15 per person.

19 Elystan Street SW3, Tel. 01-589 3718. U: South Kensington. Hours: Mon–Fri 1230–1430; Mon–Sat 1900–2330.

Chez Gerard
There are two branches of this restaurant. The most charming is on Charlotte Street. The usual thin *steak frite* or thicker cuts of meat are served French-style on a wooden board with a bowl of French fries and a salad. Fish soup and other French bistro fare. £15 per person.

8 Charlotte Street W1, Tel. 01-636 4975. U: Goodge Street. Hours: Mon–Fri, Sun .1230–1430; daily 1830–2300.

Chez Moi
A little restaurant in leafy Holland Park, offering a very serious traditional gourmet set dinner for £16.50. *A la carte* is slightly more expensive, at about £20–£25 per person. Have a stroll around this pleasant neighbourhood.

1 Addison Avenue W11, Tel. 01-603 8267. U: Holland Park. Hours: Mon–Fri 12.30– 2.30. Mon–Sat 1900– 2330.

Chez Victor
Near the corner of Shaftesbury Avenue and Wardour Street is a small survivor. Enter, the memories will flood back — perhaps of simple little restaurants still recommended by Les Routiers; of Paris before tourist restaurants began to take over the Left Bank, or even of pre-nouvelle London, when Soho had more of these places and fewer ethnic restaurants. Chez Victor is a simple place in all respects. Some might think it could use a good refit: it still looks like a 1950s Paris bistro, with tarnished mirrors, an indifferent red paint job and simple cutlery on the clean white tablecloths. There is a yellowing picture of Marshal Foch on the wall (I hope it is not Marshal Pétain). Service is authentically Gallic — cold, proud, austere, stoic.

When the candles are lit, it all adds up to a certain romantic ambience, particularly if you, like me, are tired of formula eateries that try too hard to manufacture it. The menu is simple. Choices are printed on old dog-eared cards. Prices are simply erased and pencilled in as they change. All the typical bistro offerings — patés, escargots, escalope de veau — nothing very surprising. What's served here is real, solid French food — even the delicious apple and strawberry flans on display on the trolley.

I just wish London food was as cheap as similar places in France, where we've eaten about the same meals for less than £10 per person with wine. Chez Victor will cost you £18–£20 per person with a bottle. The wine list is well chosen, but again, not cheap. Just order the house white — it's one of the best I've had — for £7. Good for pre- or after-theatre.

45 Wardour Street W1, Tel. 01-437 6523. U: Piccadilly Circus. Hours: Mon–Sat 1200– 1430; 1800–2400.

Christian's
Tiny, one-man restaurant with a pleasant atmosphere in a converted Chiswick shop. Christian is the Belgian chef who has created the quintessential neighbourhood French restaurant. Soothing classical music plays while the chef cooks to order. £20 per person.

1 Station Parade, Burlington Lane W4, Tel. 01-995 0382. British Rail: Chiswick. Hours: Tues–Fri 1230–1400; Tues–Sat 1930–2200.

Gavvers and **Les Trois Plats**
Training grounds for the Roux brothers' restaurants, especially **Le Gavroche** (see *Critic's Choice*). Both have set meals only — but they provide a relatively inexpensive golden opportunity to sample very professional, critically acclaimed modern French

food. Set meal at **Gavvers**: £23, including a half bottle of wine. Set meal at **Les Trois Plats**: £23.

Gavvers: 61 Lower Sloane Street SW1, Tel. 01-730 5983. U: Sloane Square. Hours: Mon–Sat 1900–2300.

Les Trois Plats: 4 Sydney Street SW3, Tel. 01-352 3433. U: Sloane Square. Hours: Mon–Sat 1900–2300.

Au Jardin des Gourmets

A good place for pre- and after-theatre nouvelle French meals in the heart of Soho. Good house wines. £25 per person, but set meals are half this price.

5 Greek Street W1, Tel. 01-437 1816. U: Tottenham Court Road. Hours: Mon–Fri 1215–1430; Mon–Sat 1815–2315.

Le Metro

Very busy, great-value bistro restaurant started by the ex-chef from the highly-regarded **Capital Hotel Restaurant** next door. You can sample fine wines by the glass. Very handy for lunch after shopping at Harrods. £15.

28 Basil Street SW3, Tel. 01-589 6286. U: Knightsbridge. Hours: Mon–Sat 1200–1430; Mon–Fri 1730–2215.

Mon Plaisir

Very popular, very French café-restaurant that has not lost its authenticity despite the Covent Garden location. *Plat du jour* shown on a blackboard with very reasonable £8 set lunch prices. £15.

21 Monmouth Street WC2, Tel. 01-836 7243. U: Covent Garden. Hours: Mon–Fri 1200–1415; Mon–Sat 1800–2315.

Monsieur Thompson's

Pleasing traditional decor of mirrors and pink tablecloths. Set modern French menu is good value — have Saturday lunch here while visiting the Portobello Market. *A la carte* menu is pricey, £22 per person; £10.50 set lunch or £13.50 set dinner.

29 Kensington Park Road W11, Tel. 01-727 9957. U: Ladbroke Grove. Hours: Mon–Sat 1230–1430; 1930–2230.

Le Mont St Michel

Out of the way, neighbourhood French family-run restaurant with homey atmosphere and excellent classical French food in hearty portions. Service is slow but that's because everything is freshly prepared. Set meals are better value than *à la carte*. which can be £20–25 per person.

282 Uxbridge Road W12, Tel. 01-749 5412. U: Shepherds Bush. Hours: Mon–Sat 1200–2400.

Porte de la Cité

Smart, very French restaurant with blue and white wallpaper and good value set meals. Good place for a business lunch. Set meals £12–£16.

65 Theobalds Road WC1, Tel. 01-242 1154. U: Holborn. Hours: Mon–Fri 1200–1430; Mon–Sat 1800–2300.

Le Poulbot

Lunch-only French restaurant, with a Roux-trained chef. Downstairs each table has its own screen for private dining. A set four course meal is £24. Upstairs has set meals plus a glass of wine for about £10 per person.

45 Cheapside EC2, Tel. 01-236 4379. U: Mansion House. Hours: Mon–Fri 1200–1500.

La Poule au Pot
Very pretty French country bourgeois restaurant — decor of brass, copper and old oak. Open fire in winter. Old French favourite dishes like *lapin au moutarde* or *soupe à l'oignon.* House wine is charged by what you drink. Set lunch (£9.95) is outstanding value. £25.

231 Ebury Street SW1, Tel. 01-730 7763. U: Sloane Square. Hours: Mon–Fri 1230– 1430; Mon–Sat 1900–2315.

Le Routier
French bistro in Camden Lock with gingham tablecloths. Sit outside by Regent's Canal on pleasant days. £15 per person.

Camden Lock, Chalk Farm Road NW1, Tel. 01-485 0360. U: Camden Town. Hours: Mon–Sat 1230–1430; 1900–2245.

Thierry's
Romantic and comfortable Chelsea institution for many years. Good soufflés, steaks, quenelles; great profiteroles. Informal, and relaxed dress. £18 per person.

342 Kings Road SW3, Tel. 01-352 3365. U: Sloane Square. Hours: Mon–Sat 1230– 1430; 1930–2330.

German

Twin Brothers
London doesn't offer much in terms of German or Austrian cuisine. In most London German restaurants the accent is on the Oompah band, not the food. But one quiet little place that certainly offers a lot is the excellent value **Twin Brothers**.

It is not, strictly speaking, a German restaurant. *Bismarck herring, Wiener schnitzel* and *Holstein schnitzel* are on the menu, but so are *Dover sole, steak,* and the (highly recommendable) *beef Stroganoff.* Admittedly, these dishes are strongly-influenced by German seasonings and style, because the restaurant is owned and run by Helge and Detlef, two colourful German brothers. As one of those 'quiet little places' of which travellers are always in search, Twin Brothers has a perfect setting: a cosy panelled bistro whose walls are crowded with paintings. Like the food, it has a combined ambience of Old Europe and English clubland that somehow works. The menu is kept short and simple. Each main course selection is approximately £6 and served with a generous helping of potatoes and a bouquet of vegetables that are not only delicious but attractive. Dessert includes a scrumptious *apple cake* that can be served with cream or ice-cream. At the moment, only a choice of red or white house wine is available, but the brothers have applied for an extended licence.

Twin Brothers has been going for many years and has a large following who are enthusiastic about this London rarity — a pleasant little restaurant where a couple can have an elegant three course meal for a total of about £20–£25. My only complaint is that the restaurant is erratic about its opening times and can sometimes close unexpectedly. Call and reserve a table before you go.

51 Kensington Church Street W8, Tel. 01-937 4152. U: High Street Kensington. Hours: Mon–Sat 1200–1500; 1830–2200.

Cosmo
Another time-travelling location: a Central European café-restaurant, offering

mostly German food like herrings, sauerbraten and delicious Viennese cakes, but with an inexpensive if eccentric variety of dishes from other countries to choose from. In either the restaurant or the coffee bar next door you can watch the aging Hampstead Slavic and Germanic clientele. Were they once Generals, Counts, Viennese Jewish bankers? Cosmo features as a meeting point in several minor spy novels. Restaurant £12; coffee bar £7 per person.

5 Northways Parade, off Finchley Road NW3, Tel. 01-722 1398. U: Finchley Road. Restaurant hours: 1200–2300; coffee bar 2030–2300.

Greek
Lots of Brits go to the Greek islands on holiday, and London has a bigger Cypriot population than Nicosia, so there is a big demand for dishes like kleftiko, souvlakia and dolmades. Menus tend to be similar and quality is generally above what you'll find in some of the holiday places. Soho and the Charlotte Street area have many Green restaurants. If you're hungry, order the *mezze* – usually a large selection of house specialities. In most places it's very good value.

- **Kleftiko** (see *Favourites*)

Beotys
Last time we went to Beotys, the place seemed so like a slightly-faded elegant restaurant of the 1950s that we thought we were in another time warp, but the service was almost faultless, and their efforts at anglicizing and internationalizing their menu seemed endearing rather than annoying. Food is basically sound and the now renovated restaurant is a quiet oasis in Covent Garden to have a pre- or after-theatre or opera meal. £15 per person.

79 St Martin's Lane WC2, Tel. 01-836 8768. U: Leicester Square. Hours: Mon–Sat 1200–1445; 1730–2330.

Tsiakkos
A well-known secret, this wonderful little family-run restaurant is preserved by its slightly out of the way location. Without a doubt the best value *mezze* in town at £8.00 for a giant meal with delicious hummus, sausages, kebab, moussaka, dolmades, salad, olives, bean stew and kleftiko. Other dishes are good and inexpensive. £10 per person.

5a Marylands Road W9, Tel. 01-286 7896. U: Royal Oak. Hours: Mon–Sat 1730–2300.

White Tower
This restaurant is old-fashioned too — the oldest Greek restaurant in London. The service is charming and professional, the menu is unusual (written by a literary critic) and the French-influenced Greek food is some of the best in town. House wine is good but most of the list is expensive. £22 per person.

1 Percy Street W1, Tel. 01-636 8141. U: Tottenham Court Road. Hours: Mon–Fri 1230–1430; 1830–2230.

Hungarian
- **The Gay Hussar** (see *Favourites*)

Indian

Eating Indian: guide and recommendation
If you're at all interested in food, and notice restaurants while you're in London, you'll undoubtedly be struck by how many of these are Indian. Almost every street has at least one, and often more, Indian restaurants.

For many foreign visitors, particularly those from the suburbs or small towns, Indian food probably evokes little or nothing. But for the English, whose involvement in the sub-continent spanned nearly 200 years, eating Indian has now become as habitual as stopping for a pizza or a hamburger is for the average American. This is in part because the Indian restaurants are open later than most others except the Chinese. And it is also because of the good value: a delicious, exotic meal, elegantly served, will often cost less than at an ordinary English restaurant.

But because Indian restaurants are so common and taken for granted, you're unlikely to have them recommended to you as the answer to a request for somewhere good to eat. It would be a shame to miss them entirely. There is little that you won't recognize as some variation on chicken, lamb, shrimp or beef, and if you don't have a local contact to interpret the menu for you, make use of these suggestions to guide you between the restaurants and help you to make sense of what to order.

Indian restaurants can basically be divided into three types. There is the curry house, distinguishable by its name, which will contain the word 'curry' somewhere, or by its flock wallpaper and generally garish decoration. A second type is the new breed of Indian restaurant, done in pastel shades or Indian fabrics, which offers dishes with more of a European influence, and creates more daring combinations of ingredients. The word 'tandoori' will often feature in its name, but both varieties of restaurant will still offer *tandoori* or *tikka*, the staple of North Indian cooking, which is meat marinated in herbs and cooked in a *tandoor*, an Indian oven which cooks quickly and at such a high heat as to seal the meat juices inside and give a crisp outer skin. *Nan*, a puffy, chewy Indian bread also cooked in the *tandoor* usually accompanies the tandoori chicken, lamb or prawn.

The third type of restaurant is often distinguished by references to 'South Indian' or 'vegetarian', and offers strictly vegetarian dishes and features vegetable curries, rice pancakes with coconut chutney, or rice sponge cakes with vegetable sauces and other potato, chick pea and sauce combinations. Even very worldly vegetarians will find these dishes a new taste sensation. Southern Indian cooking is generally hotter and uses yogurt and coconut to cool. There are few restaurants serving exclusively South Indian cooking, but to get the idea just order a *korma* cooked with cream or *ceylon* cooked with coconut.

Other cultures have also left their mark on Indian cuisine. The Portuguese, who ruled Goa, are probably responsible for the rare fish dishes. The Moghuls left the *pilaus* — rice dishes with chicken, mutton and prawn — and the *biryanis* — rice flavoured with saffron and containing meat, fish or vegetables and served with a sauce. The Persian influence can also be traced in dishes flavoured with sweet and sour sauce and lentils.

Indians don't generally eat their meal according to the conventional order of appetizer, main meal and vegetables, but the menus, bowing to English tradition, are organized according to that convention. Since some of the starters are just smaller versions of full meals listed below in the menu, it pays to try something that is not. *Samosas* are triangular-shaped packets of dough filled with vegetables or meat and fried, somewhat like a Chinese egg roll. *Bhajis* are fried onions mixed in a spiced flour paste and deep fired. Other lighter and less oily starters are *dal* (lentil soup), an Indian speciality, or *mulligatawny soup*, a lightly curried chicken and rice soup which signifies the true melding of Indian and English cuisine.

Indian foods blend up to a dozen different spices in each dish, but it is the chilli alone which determines the heat it gives off. Every restaurant offers a range of dishes from mild to spicy, but you can ask the chef to adjust any of them to your taste.

At the classier Indian places like the **Bombay Brasserie** or the **Red Fort**, many choose to order a three-course meal as you would in an English restaurant. Otherwise, when a couple or a group of people go to an ordinary restaurant it is common to order several dishes and share — as you would in a Chinese restaurant. If you are eating Indian for the first time, try at least one of the types of bread, a tandoori, and a pilau or biryani. Ask for yogurt or chutney with the meal to cool you off if you accidentally order something too hot.

A number of restaurants have good-value lunch buffets where you can sample a little of everything. To answer a frequent question: no chopsticks; nor will you be expected to eat with bread and hands as Indians do — just a knife and fork. Most restaurants have wine, but beer goes better with Indian food. (L.M.V.)

Elegant, expensive and highly rated
• **The Bombay Brasserie** (see *Favourites*)

Lal Quila
If you want to experience sophisticated well-prepared 'new wave' Indian food and can't get in at the **Bombay Brasserie**, this is the next best place, though not quite so luxurious. Elegant enough, though, in surroundings and service. £20 per person.

117 Tottenham Court Road W1, Tel. 01-387 4570. U: Warren Street. Hours: Mon–Sun 1200–1445; 1800–2315.

Last Days of the Raj
Another subscriber favourite, though not one of ours. But our reason is trivial — they bumped us when we were ten minutes late. Beautifully decorated to theme, and elegantly-dressed waiters. This restaurant is credited with starting the 'new wave' of delicate, subtly-flavoured gourmet Indian food that sprang up about a decade ago. £18 per person.

22 Drury Lane WC2, Tel. 01-836 5705. U: Covent Garden. Hours: Mon–Sat 1200–1430; 1730–2330.

The Red Fort
We include this restaurant mainly because so many visitors enjoy and appreciate the elegant service and luxurious atmosphere. The food is good, but nothing extraordinary in our humble opinion. £25 per person.

77 Dean Street W1, Tel. 01-437 2525. U: Piccadilly Circus. Hours: Mon–Sun 1200–1430; 1800–2330.

Other tandoori restaurants with good food and a special atmosphere
• **Khan's** (see *Favourites*)

The India Club
Cheap, eccentric, Strand institution with good food and pictures of Indian revolutionaries on the plain walls. BYOB. £10 per person.

143 Strand WC2, Tel. 01-836 0650. U: Aldwych. Hours: Mon–Sat 1200–1430; 1800–2200.

Kensington Tandoori
Set in a posh area but more like your friendly neighbourhood Indian restaurant. Glass dividers give a feeling of privacy in this helpful place with excellent tandoori cooking. A good place to try Indian food for the first time. £12 per person.

1 Abingdon Road W8, Tel. 01-937 6182. U: High Street Kensington. Hours: daily 1200–2345.

The Khyber
Head for the corner of Westbourne Grove and Queensway if you can't decide where else to go. The Khyber has special dishes and a good-value £5.50 lunch buffet. Nearby

are the equally good **Al Khayam**, and **Gandhi Cottage** restaurants, but the local institution is the inimitable **Khan's** (see *Favourites*). All have similar hours, menus and prices. £10 per person.

56 Westbourne Grove W2, Tel. 01-727 4385. U: Queensway/Bayswater. Hours: Mon–Sun 1200–1500; 1800–2400.

Mumtaz
Quietly atmospheric Indian restaurant beloved by many visitors for the location near Regents Park. Take a walk here after their £11.50 Sunday lunch buffet. £18 per person.

4 Park Road NW1, Tel. 01-723 0549. U: Baker Street. Hours: daily 1200–1500; 1800–2300.

The Veeraswamy
Claimed, at 62, to be the oldest Indian restaurant in London. Beautifully-costumed waiters. No longer top rank, but a wonderful multi-choice all-you-can-eat buffet lunch for only £9.50 including coffee and dessert. £16 per person.

99 Regent Street W1, Tel. 01-734 1401. U: Piccadilly Circus. Hours: Mon–Sun 1200–1430; Mon–Sat 1800–2330.

Indian vegetarian

Mandeer
Wonders done with strict vegan Indian cooking according to Ayurvedic principles. £10 per person.

21 Hanway Place W1, Tel. 01-323 0660. U: Tottenham Court Road. Hours: Mon–Sat 1200–1430; 1800–2215.

Sabras
Plain, six table, southern Indian vegetarian in competition with **Woodlands** (below) for the title. £9 per person.

263 High Road NW10, Tel. 01-459 0340. U: Willesden Green. Hours: Tues–Fri 1230–1500; 1800–2130; Sat, Sun 1230–2200.

Woodlands
Thought to be the best Indian vegetarian in town. £10 per person.

77 Marylebone Lane W1, Tel. 01-486 3862. U: Bond Street. Hours: Mon–Sun 1200–1500; 1800–2330.

Irish

Minogue's
Irish-Americans might enjoy this happy 'Irish cafe-bar' which does innovative, well-prepared versions of many dishes normally thought unsophisticated, like Irish stew. Live music, whiskey, Guinness and plenty of Irish good cheer in this always crowded, popular spot. About £10 per person.

80 Liverpool Road N1, Tel. 01-359 4554. U: Angel. Hours: Mon–Sat 1200–1500; 1830–2400.

Italian
London has a large number of run-of-the-mill Italian restaurants in which food standards are above average and service is smooth and polished in the Italian way, but the menu tends to be virtually identical and not very innovative. These places are an enjoyable evening out, but there's little to say about them.

Few London Italian restaurants are genuinely bad. Some of the central London cafés are bland and a few trattorias are expensive for what they are. Places like the Spaghetti House chain and most of the new pasta bars are OK, but there can be too much pasta and too little sauce. (For pizza and pasta places, see **Fast Food**.) We list a few Italian restaurants which offer something special.

- **San Frediano** (see *Favourites*)
- **La Barca** (see *Favourites*)

Bertorelli's

The main Covent Garden Bertorelli's is now reputed to be the only one still owned by a member of the family. The rest have been sold off to a conglomerate and are no relation in any sense of the word. Bright new grey, white and blue decor and a new chef makes this London institution worth a visit, especially for lunch. Their lighter Italian dishes are not nearly as heavy as your shopping bags. £15 per person.

44a Floral Street WC2, Tel. 01-836 1868. U: Covent Garden. Hours: daily 1200–2345.

Trattoo

Elegant light, airy Italian restaurant with mirrors and greenery. Order innovative, well prepared pasta dishes as a main course at lunch or from the standard but good menu anytime. £15–20 per person.

2 Abingdon Road, W8, Tel. 01-937 4448. U: High Street Kensington, Hours: Mon–Sun 12–14.45; 19.00–23.00.

San Lorenzo

Pretty, charming place that has the famous and the fashionable among its devotees. My wife and I once celebrated an anniversary there. At the next table was a pop star with a punk haircut and a dirty fringed jacket; his companion was dressed like Princess Diana. Eating is as good as the people watching, but dress up and pretend to be famous. £22 per person.

22 Beauchamp Place SW3, Tel. 01-584 1074. U: South Kensington. Hours: Mon–Sat 1230–1500; 1930–2330.

Japanese

Some of London's Japanese restaurants are outrageously expensive, but many have good-value set lunches.

Ajimura

Nestled in Covent Garden, Ajimura does not have the pretty, formal setting of other higher-priced and very authentic Japanese restaurants (If that's what you're after, try **Wakabe**, 31 College Crescent NW3, Swiss Cottage tube, Tel: 01-722 3854 — wonderful!). Instead, the atmosphere of this small popular place is casual, the staff and clientele young, the air not quite as hushed. But the food is *very* good and reasonably priced, and it's the perfect place for a quick refreshing lunch or an easy dinner, where quality is guaranteed (and after stepping about the Covent Garden environs, that is a godsend!). There's a sushi/sashimi bar, and good vegetarian and other set meals. And don't forget the *sake*. You're expected to choose your own bowl to drink it from, incidentally. It's bad luck to have the waiter or waitress do it for you. Enjoy the bizarre mural of frogs and rabbits doing odd things . . . Two of you can do very well for under £20. (J.E.)

51–53 Shelton Street WC2, Tel. 01-240 0178. U: Covent Garden. Hours: Mon–Fri 1200–1500; Mon–Sun 1800–2300.

Ikkyu
Unusual restaurant where you get good-sized portions of a style called 'Japanese country cooking'. Good for vegetarians, and good value for all at £12 per person.

67 Tottenham Court Road W1, Tel. 01-636 9280. U: Tottenham Court Road. Hours: Mon–Fri 1230–1430; 1800–2315; Sun 1900–2215.

Jewish

Bloom's
Book your table for a Sunday lunch at the most famous kosher restaurant in Great Britain — even if you're not Jewish. This is one of the famous 'London experiences', and has become rather gimmicky; but there's still a unique, noisy atmosphere and very filling East European kosher food, washed down by Israeli kosher wine. If you want to savour this guidebook London experience to the full, visit the nearby **Brick Lane Market** on a Sunday first. £15 per person.

90 Whitechapel High Street E1, Tel. 01-247 6001. U: Aldgate East. Hours: Sun–Thurs 1130–2130; Fri 1130–1400 or 1500.

Latin American

Paulo's
Another London neighbourhood curiosity, this is a Brazilian self-service buffet (including Bahian specialities), open only in the evenings. Charming family-run place, sometimes with live music. Wine, beer and cocktails now available, but you can BYOB. £12 per person.

30 Greyhound Road W6, Tel. 01-385 9264. U: Barons Court. Hours: Mon–Sat 1800–2230.

Lebanese and middle Eastern
- **Phoenicia** (see *Favourites*)

- **Caravanserai** (see *Favourites*)

Le Petit Prince
Friendly little North African restaurant in Kentish Town, serving inexpensive couscous with chicken, vegetables, sausage and other accompaniments. Unusual and great value (diners are frequently offered seconds), plus a free cup of tea. £6 per person. Book.

5 Holmes Road NW5, Tel. 01-267 0752. U: Kentish Town. Hours: Tues–Fri 1200–1430; Mon–Sun 1900–2330.

Polish and Russian
After the war, Britain permitted many refugee Poles who served in the wartime RAF and Polish units of the British army to settle in Britain. This large and influential community was recently augmented by a further influx of refugees from General Jaruzelski's regime. Their rich, heavy cuisine is warm and filling on a London winter's day, as is that of the less-numerous Russians. The welcome is generally warm, whether you speak the language or not.

Daquise
Handy for the museums in South Kensington. If you're not looking for a heavy meal, you can go here for morning coffee or afternoon tea, with delicious Polish cakes and pastries. Warm up on a cold day with a lunch of borsch, stuffed cabbage and veal cutlets with beetroot garnishes for an incredibly cheap £4.

20 Thurloe Street SW7, Tel. 01-589 6117. U: South Kensington. Hours: daily 1000–2245.

Luba's Bistro
This Russian restaurant may be more about fun than serious eating (another Russian restaurant, **Borscht 'n Tears**, is even less serious). Stroganoff, pancakes with sour cream or stuffed with cream cheeses, and a few well-cooked non-Russian specialities. Discounts offered before 8 pm; choose a later sitting so you won't be hurried. Inexpensive (about £12 per head), partly because it's BYOB.

6 Yeoman's Row SW3, Tel. 01-589 2950. U: Knightsbridge. Hours: Mon–Sat 1200–1500; 1800–2345.

Nikita's
Claims to be London's most authentic Russian restaurant, though there is an emphasis on fun here too. You can knock back one of several flavours of vodka (including lemon and pepper), but no one will complain if you order wine. Restaurant is in a red and green basement with the intimate dining alcoves you read about in Russian novels. £20 per person.

65 Ifield Road SW10, Tel. 01-352 6326. U: West Brompton. Hours: Mon–Sat 1930–2300.

Scandinavian
● **Anna's Place** (see *Favourites*)

The Causerie
This is, in fact, Claridges international restaurant, but we are here concerned only with the fantastic all-you-can-eat lunchtime smörgåsbord that costs only £10.50–£13.50 — a real bargain, considering what's on offer, and including a drink (the higher price is for spirits). Must book.

Claridges Hotel, Brook Street W1, Tel. 01-629 8860. U: Bond Street. Hours: Mon–Fri 1200–1430.

Spanish
● **El Bodegon** (see *Favourites*)

Rebato's
Main attraction here is the giant tapas bar. A huge selection of the little snacks costing £1.50–£3.50 each should be washed down Spanish-style with a glass of wine. Another worthwhile London experience, though slightly out of the way.

169 Lambeth Road SW8, Tel. 01-735 6388. U: Vauxhall. Hours: Mon–Fri 1200–1430; Mon–Sat 1800–2315.

More selections

For breakfast
A good British breakfast — eggs, bacon, sausage, toast, possibly with kippers, grilled tomato, mushrooms or one of a number of 'exotic' dishes — is one of the great treats of these islands. You'll find it in two types: the formally-served, finely-prepared breakfast served in the major hotels, and the big, greasy but good version found in 'caffs' and little restaurants. The difference is more a matter of style and presentation than quality — you can get good or awful breakfasts in both places.
    Curiously, Britons still find it odd to eat breakfast 'out', and they don't do it unless they're travelling away from home or work in an early morning job. Consequently, breakfast remains mostly a hotel and workman's phenomenon, and few restaurants

serve it. If you're not a big breakfaster, the many continental patisseries and small cafés offer rolls, pastries and coffee.

Here are some breakfast spots you may enjoy.

Formal

Brown's Hotel
Many of our subscribers have thought **Brown's** formal breakfast with many selections to be the finest in town. Book ahead.

Albemarle Street/Dover Street W1, Tel. 01-493 6020. U: Green Park.

Connaught Hotel
Most tables are reserved for residents, so book a breakfast that is probably the equal of **Brown's** (above).

Carlos Place W1, Tel. 01-499 7070. U: Bond Street.

Cheaper

The Fox and Anchor
Gigantic breakfasts served on pyrex plates with a colourful mix of early morning East Enders, journalists and City types in this dark Art Nouveau period pub. Book.

115 Charterhouse Street EC1, Tel. 01-253 4838. U: Farrington Road. Breakfast hours: Mon–Fri 0600–1015.

The Muffin Man
Englishy little place which serves a good hearty breakfast. Also good for tea, with excellent cakes.

12 Wright's Lane W8, Tel. 01-937 6652. U: Kensington High Street. Hours: Mon–Sat 0815–1700.

The Quality Chop House
Another inexpensive East End breakfast institution, popular with journalists. Sit at long tables and enjoy the Victorian atmosphere.

94 Farringdon Road EC1, Tel. 01-837 5093. U: Farringdon Road. Breakfast hours: Mon–Fri 0630–1000.

See also *Cafés* and *Tea Rooms* and *Patisseries*

Sunday lunch
Sunday lunch roast is more of a tradition in England than the American 'brunch'. Properly prepared and served, this is a London experience you shouldn't miss. You might prefer brunch or something more exotic, so here also are a few other selections in several categories.

Traditional English

Mrs Beeton's
No set lunch, but a homey place with homey English-style cooking. Local chefs work in rotation, so the menu's always changing. Good reputation for puddings (desserts). Enquire about menu and price when you book.

58 Hill Rise, Richmond, Tel. 01-940 9561. U: Richmond.

Drakes
Offers the choice of an excellent roast set lunch or imaginative *à la carte* variations.

Decor simple — a duck theme. The only drawback is that the place is too well known, and therefore attracts fellow tourists. Book. £15 per person Sunday lunch.

2a Pond Place SW3, Tel. 01-584 4555. U: South Kensington, then No 14 bus.

Reed's

A good first choice. Quiet, relaxed dining room with typically English decor. Wonderful quenelles and some unusual dishes available from the *à la carte* menu, and a superb English cheese board. The set Sunday lunch is very good value at £14.50 including starter, choice of roast, vegetables and dessert. House wine is £6.95. Must book.

152 Old Brompton Road SW5, Tel. 01-373 2445. U: Gloucester Road.

Pollyanna's

Simple place with very good value Sunday lunch (only £9.95). During the week this is an Anglo-French bistro, but on Sundays they serve the traditional roast with basic starters (pea soup, prawn cocktails, etc) and simple (some think stodgy) desserts. Good wine and brandy list. Two drawbacks — spartan seating and location in Battersea (take BR from Victoria). Book.

2 Battersea Rise SW11, Tel. 01-228 0316. British Rail: Clapham Junction.

Hotels

Try a silver service set lunch in one of the major hotels, for example, the **Dorchester Grill** (£17), or **The Ritz** (£20).

Pubs

Many pubs now serve a good-value Sunday lunch. One of the best is the **Red Lion** (£11.95), Waverton Street W1, Tel. 01-499 1307, U: Green Park, but phone to check if it's still available. Other pubs serve traditional Sunday lunches for as little as £2.95.

Brunch

Le Caprice

Serves an American-style Sunday brunch rather than English Sunday lunch, but wide-ranging choices often include traditional favourites, especially salmon. A good all-round restaurant that can be difficult to book.

Arlington House, Arlington Street SW1, Tel. 01-629 2239. U: Green Park.

The exotic

Mumtaz

Atmospheric Indian restaurant with an all-you-can-eat £11.50 buffet. See *Indian*.

Chuen Cheng Ku

A Chinatown *dim sum* experience. See *Favourites*.

Sunday in the country

Sir Charles Napier

About an hour and a half from London, in the Chilterns. They serve a generous traditional lunch for £12. A nice piece of Olde England with — for a change — few tourists in sight. Excellent wine list (it's a French restaurant during the week). Car essential. Visit one of the many National Trust houses afterwards. Must book.

Sprigg's Alley, Chinnor. Tel. (0240) 263011.

Waterside Inn
Another Roux brothers' three-star Michelin. French food served in a stunning Thameside location. Watch the ducks, boats and punts go by. Go for the *Menu Gastronomique* at £19.50 (or else £40 per person, or more). Sunday lunch served from 1200–1400 from Easter to October.

Ferry Road, Bray, Berkshire, Tel. (0628) 20691 (taxi from Windsor or Heathrow).

Vegetarian

Cranks
The best known is the cafe in Covent Garden; there are eight other branches with similar prices. For wine and candle-light go to the Marshall Street branch. The new Adelaide Street branch is the most trendy. All serve breakfast.

11 The Market, Covent Garden WC2, Tel. 01-379 6508. 8 Marshall Street, W1, Tel. 01-437 9431; Adelaide Street, Tel. 01-836 0660; 17–18 Great Newport Street, WC2, Tel. 01-836 5236. U: Covent Garden. Hours: Mon–Sat 0900–2000.

East West Restaurant
Macrobiotic restaurant with lots of stir-fry vegetables, a different ethnic lunch each Wednesday and a seafood and fish supper every Thursday. Desserts contain no honey, sugar or dairy products. Price £6.

188 Old Street EC1, Tel. 01-608 0300. U: Old Street. Hours: Mon–Thurs 1100–2200; Fri 1100–2030; Sat 1100–1500.

Manna
Another well-used vegetarian restaurant. Seems to attract TV personalities — they must have heard that they are sure to find some of the finest vegetarian dishes in London here. If *arami seaweed salad* (£1.65) or a large helping of *nut roast* or *lasagne* (£3.95) appeals to you, you will enjoy it too.

4 Erskine Road NW3, Tel. 01-722 8028. U: Chalk Farm. Hours: daily 1830–2300.

Slenders
Near St Paul's cathedral. Some of the best vegetarian food around, with nut, bean and vegetable burgers, vegetable stews and salads. £6.

41 Cathedral Place EC4, Tel. 01-236 5974. U: St Paul's. Hours: Mon–Fri 0800–1800.

See also *Indian Vegetarian; Japanese*

Vegetarian Take-aways
If you need a quick and delicious vegetarian take-away meal while touring or shopping, try the following:

French Franks
Authentic French bread sandwiches, filled croissants and pizza slices.

97 High Holborn WC1.

Food for Thought
Delicious fresh meals like spinach lasagne and stir-fry vegetables. Eat in or takeaway.

31 Neal Street WC2. Hours: Mon–Fri 1200–1700.

Wholemeals
Good for a sandwich or pitta bread, salad, homemade soup and cakes.

64a Fleet Street WC2.

Stocking up
Should you want to stock up on good food, try the **Neal's Yard** complex (Covent Garden WC2), with its wholefood warehouse, dairy, flour mill, apothecary and bakery. (L.M.V)

Before and after theatre
The timing of most entertainment events (starting times between 7 and 8pm) creates a problem for the hungry and those in search of a full evening of dinner and theatre. Many of the restaurants in the theatre district (Soho and Covent Garden) and the major hotels do special pre- and after-theatre meals. These deals, and what's on offer, change frequently, so check the ads or call and ask. If you're hungry after the theatre and don't know where to go, head for nearby Soho and walk around **Romilly, Frith, Greek** and adjacent streets, or go into Chinatown, where many restaurants are open for orders till at least 11pm. Here are our selections:

- **Lido** (see *Chinese*)
- **Beoty's** (see *Greek*)
- **Chez Victor** (see *French*)
- **Manzi's** (see *Fish*)
- **Joe Allen's** (see *Fast Food*)
- **Rules** (see *British*)

Delicatessens and prepared food to take home

Acquired taste
Patés, terrines and microwavables.

9 Battersea Rise SW11. BR: Clapham Junction.

Le Gourmet Gascon
Many French delicacies, terrines and bisques, unobtainable elsewhere.

3 Hillgate Street W8. U: Notting Hill Gate.

Harrods Food Hall
More for looking than buying, but the only place to find some things.

Knightsbridge SW1. U: Knightsbridge

Justin de Blank (Provisions)
Pricey, but good for baked goods, sausages and exotic microwavables.

42 Elizabeth Street SW1. U: Sloane Square. Other locations.

Lidgates
A fascinating old-fashioned butchers with some prepared dishes.

10 Holland Park Avenue. U: Holland Park.

Marks and Spencer
For excellent prepared foods, sandwiches and non-staple groceries at reasonable prices.
Marble Arch W1 (main branch). U: Marble Arch.

Mr Christian's
The proprietor is a noted chef and descendant of Fletcher. His excellent deli makes good sandwiches and take-home delicacies, particularly on Saturdays — the best food in the Portobello Market.
Elgin Crescent W11. U: Ladbroke Grove.

Partridges
Interesting food and groceries from around the world.
132 Sloane Street SW1. U: Sloane Square.

Paxton and Whitfield
Pricey, but some of the world's best cheeses.
39 Jermyn Street SW1. U: Piccadilly Circus.

Taffgoods
Some of the cheapest salmon in town.
128 Wardour Street W1. U: Tottenham Court Road.

Taking tea in style
Afternoon tea is as British as crooking your little finger — and just as superfluous. There is no reason why healthy, able-bodied people should sit down to another meal a mere two hours after finishing lunch, unless it's to revel in the sheer, blissful indolence of doing so. Afternoon tea should be a luxury, a treat, slightly wicked and ever so indulgent, taken at a time when you least expect it. Happily we can report that the traditional English tea is pottering along nicely, although standards, my dears, do seem to be slipping. Even in the grandest hotels a necktie is no longer obligatory and — oh come back, romance — the only person wearing a hat was me.

Fortnum & Mason
Fortnum & Mason has two venues suitable for afternoon tea: the **Fountain Restaurant** on the ground (first) floor, and the more elaborate **St James' Restaurant** upstairs. Queues were forming at the Fountain on the day we arrived, so we opted for St James', which was only a quarter full. We rattled around the enormous wallpapered room like passengers at Paddington station during a railroad strike, and still the service was slow. My companion had already finished her — albeit delicious — anchovy toast by the time our stern-faced waitress informed us they were out of toasted brioches. The dainty French Provençal-style tables were attractive to look at, but not so comfortable to eat off — too tall in relation to the low-slung sofas — so try a chair instead.
   F & M offered a varied but expensive *à la carte* menu — tea specialities, in addition to the absent brioches, included cinnamon toast, toasted croissants or buttered crumpets. The sardine and watercress sandwiches were inviting, but I opted for an open-faced Danish. It was prettily presented — smoked salmon garnished with prawns and lemon — but contrived to be both pricey and bland. There's a comprehensive selection of Fortnum's own teas, and my friend reported her *Mille Feuilles* the best she's ever tasted. My chocolate sponge, however, was only slightly

more up-market than a Mr Kipling's, and a major disappointment. The **Fountain Restaurant** might be a better bet after all . . .

181 Piccadilly W1, Tel. 01-734 8040. U: Green Park.

Harrods

Queues form early here, and as the restaurant doesn't always open promptly at teatime, you should expect at least half an hour's delay. Velvet chairs in the outer lounge are thoughtfully provided to cushion the wait. The lines thin out around four o'clock, but by quarter past the food has thinned out as well — snapped up by the greedy Sloane Rangers who obviously have the routine off pat. Once inside, there are crisp pastel tablecloths and a Victorian view through the windows. If you're eating alone no one forces you to share a table. The Grand Buffet Tea is mounted under the Georgian Room's filigree ceiling — a dazzling display of goodies. Quivering coffee mousse embellished with a chocolate Harrods logo, glacé peaches on a thin pastry shell; I counted at least 25 different varieties of pastry or cake, and everyone just helps themselves. **Harrods** serves no sandwiches and the only savoury snacks are slices of bread and butter. Each table, however, is supplied with individual portions of jam and cream; scones are available at the buffet. Tea is from tea bags and thought to be Harrods own label, or there's orange juice for the kids. If you skip lunch and have an incredibly sweet tooth, the Grand Buffet can work out terrific value for money.

Knightsbridge SW1, Tel. 01-730 1234. U: Knightsbridge.

Liberty's

A smooth glide in the wood-panelled lift to the fourth floor, a quick goggle at the Persian carpets and then into the restaurant at the back of the store. It is best to arrive around 4pm at this demure little dining room; if you get there earlier you might find yourself having to share a table — there are only thirteen of them! Each table is covered by a Liberty-print cloth draped to the floor. The furniture is high-quality repro, and ferns grace the windowsills — in all, a 'feminine' atmosphere, though there were a surprising number of men. **Liberty's** seems to be popular with people who work in the area as well as tourists; purple carrier bags sporting the Liberty logo were much in evidence.

The cream tea was inexpensive but somewhat disappointing — two scones, jam and a pot of Devonshire clotted cream. My scones were too crumbly and the jam too smooth; they had run out of China tea and I had to settle for Indian. My companion was unhappy with her selection as well, so we decided to order all over again. The *à la carte* menu featured Danish pastries and assorted sandwiches; she opted for a cream éclair and found it quite tasty — fresh and filling with a shiny covering of chocolate. I spied tall glasses of a frothy mixture which reversed my opinion of **Liberty's** for ever — a heavenly lemon syllabub, tart and light as air. The aftertaste was one of warm honeyed brandy — delicious. As it had been left over from lunch, the waitress gave me a discount on the price.

Perhaps pot luck is the best way at **Liberty's** — they often put unsold lunchtime food on display, and you might find something wonderful instead of an inferior cream tea.

Regent Street W1, Tel. 01-734 1234. U: Oxford Circus.

The Ritz Hotel

Tea at the **Ritz** is still an institution, and a very popular one. There were several well-heeled people waiting for tables when we arrived, but the delay is not a long one. The pink and gold Palm Court lies three steps above the foyer, a rococo terrace giving one the impression of being on stage. Under the watchful gaze of two Art Nouveau cherubs, the players acted their parts beautifully — retired sergeant major types apparently intent on the *Financial Times* were scattered amid the smart white suits worn only by people who send their laundry out. I felt crumpled by comparison, although not ill at ease. Reports of shoddy service seem to have been unfounded, and the food was very good. Finger sandwiches included a welcome cream cheese and chives portion, and the egg was smothered in mayonnaise, the way I like it. A common problem seems to be stale bread, although when dealing with tiny sandwiches perhaps it's understandable.

Scones were on the menu, but none was in sight; instead we were treated to several unusual desserts. The chef obviously has a love for sweet and sour combinations — whole, fresh grapes laying atop a custard 'boat', or gateau with raspberries, honey and cream, a hint of alcohol lingering on the tongue. There were also thickly-iced petit fours. This was the only restaurant visited to provide a 'slop bowl' (in keeping with the genteel reputation of the **Ritz**), tastefully appointed in blue and white and handy for depositing the grounds of used tea. Although the portions were not overly generous, and the set tea as a whole rather pricey, the experience is a pleasant one, and the **Ritz** is certainly the place for people-watching. Smoking, however, is discouraged.

Piccadilly W1, Tel. 01-493 8181. U: Green Park.

The Savoy Hotel

Jeans are definitely out of order at the **Savoy**, but rules of discretion do apply — 'A gentleman can be elegant without wearing a suit,' said the coat-tailed man at reception, so if you come in a T-shirt, make sure it's silk. Women are allowed more licence; I spied everything from jumpsuit to pearls. The **Savoy** is one of the more expensive places in London for tea, and the quality of service, food and general ambience can vary enormously. On one occasion the captain-suited waiter seemed so remote as to be virtually non-existent; on another he served the bite-sized sandwiches (including cucumber embellished with cress) with both style and a wonderful sense of propriety. The atmosphere can seem stiff and conversation-haltingly formal, or it can envelop the diner in a romantic haze as warm as the sun setting over the Thames outside. Pastries, however, are always fresh, and you are encouraged to take seconds on the sandwiches. The velvet settees lining the walls are comfortable and elegant, and the ladies' loo is not to be missed. Try to make a day when the long-haired lady harpist is performing languidly in a corner; the mellow mood is incomparable. (M.E.Z.)

The Strand WC2, Tel. 01-836 4343. U: Charing Cross/Embankment.

For less formal tea locales, see *Tea Rooms* and *Patisseries* in *Fast Food*.

Fast food and budget restaurants

Fast food and budget restaurants are becoming a necessity of modern life in London, where the cost of eating out is far higher than it should be. The trouble is, most modern fast food joints are so ugly. They're gradually defacing central London. You can't live with them and you can't live without them. We'll define fast food as a carry-out, or a quick light meal, usually no more than one course. It's the kind of food you look for when you just want to fill a small hole in a hurry.

British fast food

Prior to the 1960s, things were pretty limited because Britons seldom ate out. Outdoor dining was still considered by some as slightly shocking, as was a glimpse of stocking in olden days. Office workers might crowd into tiny little bars where they bought sandwiches — slim fillings between thin white buttered slices. There were the greasy cafés. The Wimpy chain served 'hamburgers' so awful it was necessary to drown them in runny, vinegary ketchup in order to make them edible at all. There were Kardomahs, Lyons corner houses and tea rooms for the ladies. In the evening there were few alternatives to the local fish and chip shop.

Things have now improved enormously, thanks to the British discovery of foreign food during holiday-packages, and as a result of a massive tourist invasion of Britain itself. Both locals and tourists began to demand quality and variety as American chains moved in to transform the scene. Chinese and Indian restaurants came out of the East End and began to proliferate; Cypriots set up kebab houses; even Wimpy began to imitate McDonalds. But perhaps the biggest British fast food expansion has been of the type often referred to as 'pub grub'.

Pub food
Nothing in London guidebooks is so over-rated as the pub lunch. While some pub food is exceptionally good and good value, a lot of it is mediocre or even just plain awful. Out in the country it's getting better and better, but in London pub food has peaked and the city's pubs are now bucking a general British trend towards improved culinary quality. As the number of pubs serving food has increased, more and more comes from brewery-owned pubs with a tourist, transient or simply undiscerning clientele. You may have better luck with freehouses, but a lot of them don't care either.

Over the years I've eaten in a number of London pubs and developed a few rules to cope with the uncertainties.

First, a pub that is running a 'restaurant', or sets aside a restaurant area, is usually better, though more expensive, than a bar that serves food informally.

Second, I avoid eating in a pub that only serves sandwiches — these are usually not very good, once you pry open the cellophane.

Third, in an unfamiliar pub you're better off with salads, cold meats or a ploughman's lunch of bread and cheese than the hot dishes. Britain's cheeses are so good it's hard to go wrong.

Fourth, if you must order a hot meal, stick to the British choices like meat pies, bangers (sausages), shepherd's pie (beef and mashed potatoes) etc. Cheap copies of foreign foods like lasagne (often runny) or curry (very hot to disguise stale food) may disappoint.

For specific recommendations, see *Pubs*.

Sandwich bars and bakeries
You'll find many of these around areas with a lot of clerical staff, like Covent Garden. Much better than they used to be, but change takes time — a lot of what's on offer is the old-fashioned thin sandwich. Nowadays sandwich bars are becoming more health conscious and serving a wider choice of bread and fillings. If you decide to join the queue, be careful to specify your preference. Rolls are often better quality than bread.

In my opinion, most British bakery cakes are not as good as they look. I've had a particularly bad time with the brownies. Bakeries usually have a take-away lunch counter. Their meat pies and Cornish Pasties (meat and veg filling in a pastry crust) are usually fresh and good, but chips are often soggy-stale, with the pulpiness of long-frozen, pre-cut fries. Try a bag of British crisps (potato chips) instead. Among the best brands is Golden Wonder.

Blooms
Kosher. See *A Pleasant Meal Out (Jewish)*.

90 Whitechapel High Street E1. U: Aldgate East.

Cordon Brown
Upmarket sandwich bar.

32 Bedford Street WC2. U: Covent Garden.

French Franks Café Croissanterie
A not-bad sandwich bar chain.

97 High Holborn and other locations. U: Holborn.

De Swarte's
Good sandwiches. Friendly service.

50a Bedford Street WC2. U: Covent Garden.

Paul Tregeser
Better-than-average bakery chain.

Fish and chips
Tourists inevitably want to sample this famous British dish. Unfortunately, most of the 'chippies' in the city centre now cater to a tourist market that doesn't know the real thing from the fake (fried up fresh from the freezer rather than fresh from Billingsgate and the vegetable market). The best fish and chip shops are in the north, where brightly-lit shops fry up lots of warmth and well-being at pub closing time on cold winter nights. They're more innovative too: I know of one in Aberdeen that sells 'T-bone steak suppers' (a T-bone and chips, salted and vinegared in a brown paper bag).

Some of this atmosphere can be found in 'chippies' in working-class areas of London, but grease and good cheer are not necessarily guarantees of quality. Also note that many shops now offer local favourites like saveloys (a kind of sausage), hamburgers, bangers, roast chicken and Jamaica patty (a spicy veg pie) with chips. These can be of variable quality. Your best bet is to stick to fish — probably cod or haddock. Real British chips are deliciously bad for you — fresh, fat and crisp, and no relation to anything ever even contemplated by Arthur Treacher's, the American chain.

Geales
A pleasant, inexpensive fish and chip restaurant. Licensed, and will even serve half-bottles of wine. No take-away, but **Costas Fish Restaurant** a street away is almost as good and you can carry out. Under £10.

2 Farmer Street W8, Tel. 01-727 7969. U: Notting Hill Gate. Hours: Mon–Sat 1200–1500; 1800–2300.

Seashell
Big and gimmicky, but rated by some as the best in town. Licensed. Take-aways too.

49 Lisson Grove NW1, Tel. 01-723 8703. U: Marylebone. Hours: Tues–Sat 1200–1400; 1715–2230.

Department store restaurants coffee shops and cafeterias
Most department stores now offer some kind of food for on-premises consumption. **Marks and Spencer** is the main exception, but they do offer a big range of carry-out food of extraordinary quality and at fairly reasonable prices.

British Home Stores and Littlewoods
Always have cafeterias with edible but unexciting standard British fare. Cheap, but watch how many items you pick up: it can add up. Both have branches on Oxford Street and in other locations.

Oxford Street W1. U: Oxford Circus (both); Marble Arch (Littlewoods).

Fortnum & Mason
The Fountain was recently redecorated to modern taste. They serve excellent light meals and salads. I've always craved their milkshakes, but the price is now £1.80 and still climbing. You may have to queue for this restaurant or the also mostly-inexpensive **Patio and Buttery**; you can't book.

181 Piccadilly W1. U: Green Park.

Harrods
The Georgian Room has an atmospheric though noisy lunch carvery buffet. The *Green Man* in the basement has good pub food. The little food bars in the food hall can suddenly change theme and prices, but recently the coffee bar has been offering a good value £1.25 coffee with delicious Danish.

Knightsbridge SW1. U: Knightsbridge.

John Lewis
Boasts a foodcentre-type restaurant where you can choose from one of several counters — breakfast, quiche and salads, sandwiches, seafoods, etc — and eat in a central seating area with individual tables and chairs. Also has a small coffee shop. Moderate prices, but don't look for the 'never knowingly undersold' philosophy here.

Oxford Street W1. U: Bond Street/Oxford Circus.

Peter Jones
This Sloane Square store, part of the John Lewis empire, has a relaxed green-decor restaurant. Views over the square are spectacular, food is quality but prices are not cheap. The coffee shop in the floor above has similar views and better prices.

Sloane Square SW3. U: Sloane Square.

Bargain restaurants
Few 'bargain' restaurants will meet your expectations for a night out. Most of London's cheaper places have an obvious flaw somewhere — atmosphere, food or service. You can still have a good time, but don't forget that a majority of restaurants, even top-rated places, have good-value set lunches and, less commonly, set dinners, that are true bargains. You can even go to the Michelin 3-star **Le Gavroche** for £20 each if you book the lunchtime set menu. (*A la carte* you'd probably spend at least in excess of £60 each.) In fact, two people looking for a decent evening with a three course meal and wine will be lucky to find much under £12.50 per person at *à la carte* rates in central London.

Here are a few pleasant, less-expensive options:

- **Chez Gerrard** (see *French*)
- **Chinatown Chinese Restaurants** (particularly the set menus for two or more persons)
- **Cosmo** (see *Pleasant Meal Out — German*)
- **Geales** (see *Fish and Chips*)
- **Khan's** (see *Favourites*)
- **Paulo's** (see *Pleasant Meal Out — Latin American*)
- **Le Petit Prince** (see *Pleasant Meal Out — Lebanese and Middle Eastern*)
- **Pheonicia** (bargain lunch only — see *Favourites*)
- **Le Routier** (see *French*)

- **Tsiakkos** (see *Pleasant Meal Out — Greek*)

- **Twin Brothers** (see *Pleasant Meal Out — German*)

- **Westbourne Grove Indian Restaurants** (see *Pleasant Meal Out — Indian*) and many other Indian restaurants

Plus:

Bistro Vino
A chain of inexpensive bistros that provides OK French food and international dishes at inexpensive prices.

303 Brompton Road SW3 (and other locations), Tel. 01-589 7898. Hours vary. U: South Kensington.

Le Bistingo
Decent bistro food and good value £6.75 set meal. Open late.

Old Compton Street W1 (and other locations), Tel. 01-437 0784. Hours vary. U: Piccadilly.

The Footstool Restaurant Gallery
In Smith's Square, behind Westminster Abbey, you will see a seventeenth-century church, **St John's** (famous for its concerts, often broadcast live). Strange as it may seem, aim for the crypt, descend the few spiral stone steps, and you will find yourself being welcomed into a bright underground eatery. A fine example of English Baroque architecture, the church and crypt have been protected by its Grade I listing. The original brickwork arches are well lit and small tables huddle around the pillars. Pink tablecloths and fresh pink carnations add colour to what would otherwise be stark surroundings.

At lunch time you have the choice of a cold counter (crisp salads, game pie, quiches and cheese boards with the most beautiful granary bread) or an *à la carte* menu. Everything is fresh and well presented. Recitals are sometimes held in the restaurant, and what better way to unwind from the pace of life above than good food, a glass of wine and classical music in such surroundings as these. You may also find yourself rubbing shoulders with some familiar faces. Regular clientele include ministers from the House of Commons, the Westminster Boys Choir and an occasional Royal. (A.B.)

St John's, Smith Square SW1, Tel. 01-222 2779. U: Westminster. Hours: lunch 1130– 1500 (cold counter); 1200–1415 (à la carte); dinner 1730–late (but only when a concert is on).

The Galleon
One of the few remaining old-fashioned dining rooms that serves good filling plain-style meals. Usually crowded out with old ladies. Unlicensed, but you can BYOB.

35 Pembridge Road W11, Tel. 01-727 9620. U: Notting Hill Gate. Hours: Mon–Sat 1130–2200.

Porters
Gimmicky ('the London home of the Earl of Bradford'), but air-conditioned in summer and they do serve classic English meat pies.

Henrietta Street WC2, Tel. 01-836 6466. U: Covent Garden/Charing Cross. Hours: daily 1200–1500; Mon–Sat 1730–2230.

Charlotte Restaurant
Light meals or ample portions of Germanic food, two minutes from West Hampstead tube.

221 West End Lane NW6, Tel. 01-794 6476. U: West Hampstead. Hours: 0730–1130; 1200–1600; 1800–2300.

Coffee shops and tourist 'fast' restaurants

Funnily enough, there used to be more of these. In the past few years the pancake chains like Texas, Kentucky and Tennessee have gone the way of the earlier Golden Egg group. The trend has been towards more specialized fast food joints — hamburgers, pizzas, ribs — but many of the former sites are now occupied by the London semi-monopoly **Garfunkels**. This chain is undoubtedly better than its predecessors. It offers a variety of quick dishes — hamburgers, ribs, chicken — but the best thing about it is its *massive* salad bars. Salad bars are now featured by several of the pizza chains. So you might compare prices because **Garfunkels'** rates and the surliness of its staff, who often speak little English, seem to be increasing as the number of branches grows.

Useful coffee shops:

● **Strand Palace Hotel**, The Strand WC2, U: Charing Cross.

● **Waldorf Hotel Brasserie**, Aldwych WC2, U: Aldwych.

● **Peter Jones**, Sloane Square SW3, U: Sloane Square. Great views of the square.

Cafés

The plain old cheap British 'caff' is of interest for two reasons only. One is breakfast, which can be so good that you forget about the greasy formica or the peculiar smell of milky coffee and cigarette smoke. The other is sociological — there is no doubt that you see a whole side of life generally hidden from view.

Some better than average cafes:

Blue Sky Restaurant
High standard plain cooking.

106 Westbourne Grove WC2. U: Notting Hill Gate.

Diana's Diner
Cheerful. Good home-cooked food. Very popular.

39 Endell Street WC2. U: Covent Garden.

Gaby's Continental Bar
Middle Eastern café with photos of the dishes on offer.

30 Charing Cross Road WC2. U: Charing Cross.

Peter's Restaurant
London taxi-drivers' favourite. Good breakfasts.

59 Pimlico Road SW1. U: Sloane Square.

Stockpot
A good cheap place to eat near Piccadilly Circus. A branch at 6 Basil Street provides the same service for Harrods shoppers who've spent it all before they got to the Georgian Room. There is also a branch in James Street, handy for Oxford Street shoppers.

40 Panton Street SW1. U: Piccadilly Circus.

Meat restaurants
I take the view that central London's steak restaurant chains (**Aberdeen, Angus,** etc) are really fast food joints, because they serve meals almost too quickly and efficiently. In the red-plush luxury, you can run up a pretty good bill in a short time, because almost every item is charged. If you are meat-hungry and want a quick meal, you'd be better off going to one of the carveries.

Carveries
The **Cumberland, Strand Palace** and **Regent Palace** hotels, all owned by Trusthouse Forte, have all-you-can-eat carvery buffets of beef, pork and lamb, edible vegetables and desserts and good cheeses for a set price of only £10.75.

Cumberland Hotel, Marble Arch W1, Tel. 01-262 1234. Strand Palace Hotel, Strand WC2, Tel. 01-836 8080. Regent Palace Hotel, Piccadilly Circus W1, Tel. 01-734 7000.

Tea rooms
The old-fashioned unlicensed tea room, the respectable haunt of the respectable lady shopper, has all but died out. Nowadays, tea is taken in hotels, department stores and continental-style patisseries (for a rundown of the hotels and stores, see *Taking Tea in Style*). Along with tea, the tea shoppe usually sells light meals. The one remaining **J. O. Lyons Corner House** at 450 Strand has nothing much to recommend it, but some people like it out of nostalgia.

Tea Time
A pleasant reminder of the old-time tea shoppe, out at Clapham Common.

21 The Pavement SW4, Tel. 01-622 4944. (Hours: Mon–Sat 0930–1900; Sun 1000–1900).

Other outer parts of London like Richmond and Hampstead still have a few real tea shoppes. Especially notable:

Lascelles
Closer to the centre, but of course packed with tourists.

2 Marlborough Court, Carnaby Street W1, U: Oxford Circus.

Maids of Honour
The brightest gem, next to Kew Gardens, and home of the famous Maids of Honour cakes.

288 Kew Road. U: Richmond.

Rituals
Homey little place with good cream tea.

45 High St, Wimbledon Common SW19. U: Wimbledon.

Coffee houses
Unlike coffee shops, coffee houses sell coffee and sometimes pastries and light meals.

Monmouth Coffee House
Sells bargain exotic beans in the front. In the back you can sit at wooden tables in alcoves, read the newspapers and sample brands like Papua New Guinea, plus chocolate.

27 Monmouth Street WC2. U: Covent Garden.

Garbanzo
Jazz-music themed coffee bar.

411 City Road EC1. U: Angel.

Continental-style patisseries
These provide a pleasant informal (though not particularly British) place to have coffee or tea with a pastry. Some also have light meal menus.

Maison Bertaux
Plain 120-year old French patisserie with many regular fans.

28 Greek Street W1. U: Leicester Square.

Maison Sagne
Relaxed atmosphere of Old Europe. Omelettes and light meals.

105 Marylebone High Street. U: Baker Street.

Maison Bouquillon
Beautiful tasty croissants, cakes and pastries in the take-away and the next-door café.

41 Moscow Road W2. U: Bayswater/Queensway.

Patisserie Française, Maison Pechon
Busy, noisy little café with bread and chocolate; good quiche.

127 Queensway W2. U: Bayswater/Queensway.

International fast food

American restaurants
America seems to have invented fast food, and American theme restaurants often deliver simple quality inexpensive dishes. A number of London's best value American restaurants are controlled by Chicago-born entrepreneur Bob Payton.

Joe Allen
Not fast, but fashionable Covent Garden restaurant that is becoming pricier.

31 Exeter Street WC2. U: Covent Garden.

Smolensky's Balloon
Open 12-midnight with excellent food and affordable steaks. Licensed. Children welcome — even offers babysitting on Saturdays.

1 Dover Street W1, Tel. 01-491 1199. U: Green Park.

Henry J Bean's
Formula Bob Payton place with burgers, chicken, etc.

195 King's Road SW3. Tel. 01-352 9255. U: Sloane Square.

Chicago Meatpackers
Like a general suburban restaurant across from the shopping mall.

96 Charing Cross Road WC2, Tel. 01-379 3277. U: Leicester Square.

Vegetarian
Regular fast food is of a type that is anathema to many vegetarians, but London has

many quick service restaurants and carry outs that cater for them. (See *More Selections: Vegetarian*).

Hamburgers

During the last decade American chains have revolutionized the British idea of the hamburger. Previously, a 'hamburger' was exactly that, and as likely to contain the cheaper parts of pig as those of cattle. Rumours used to circulate about the Wimpy chain's sources of supply. To this day you will hear that the majority of London restaurant burgers came from one place — the butchers Pyke-Biggs.

In the 1970s, first **McDonalds**, then **Burger King** and **Wendy's** moved into London in a big way. Faced with competition not only in quality and price but in cleanliness and upkeep, **Wimpy** had to make drastic changes. Out went the greasy formica, thin milk shakes and hammy-tasting burgers; in came a slick new chain of McDonalds imitations.

Wimpy is now no better nor worse (depending on your point of view) than the American chain it imitates. I rather like their toasted buns and French fries. In fact, you'll find that most hamburger chains here compare very similarly in taste and price to those in the US. **McDonalds** became embroiled in a controversy several years back about importing its own potatoes. It claimed that British tatties did not meet its standards.

Everybody has their own preference in fast food chains. My own is for **Burger King**, but when I'm in the US I try to find a real hamburger place, if I have the time. Where can you find good hamburgers in London?

Countless books will send you to the **Hard Rock Café** on Piccadilly (U: Green Park). This is fine if you are under eighteen and like long queues and ear-shattering music, shared tables and all the stops pulled out for the gimmicks. Their burgers are good, it's true, but it's hard to taste them when your ears are being blasted. I prefer the **Texas Lone Star Saloon** at 145 Gloucester Road SW7 (U: Gloucester Road), with authentic burgers and pretty reasonable chilli. **Joe Allen** (see above) does the best job in Covent Garden but ask – it's not on the menu. Avoid 'hamburgers' served from street trolleys or off greasy spoons. Many of these come straight out of cans.

Other Good Hamburgers

- **Ed's Easy Diner** 12 Moor Street W1 U. Leicester Square.

- **Wolfe's** 25 Basil Street SW3 U: Knightsbridge.

- **Parson's** 311 Fulham Road SW10 U: South Kensington, then No 14 bus.

- **Tootsie's** Branches at 120 Holland Park Avenue W11 (U: Holland Park); Notting Hill Gate (U: Notting Hill Gate); Queensway (U: Bayswater); 140 Fulham Road (U: South Kensington, then No 14 bus).

Pizza

Again, US chains like **Pizza Hut** are dominant. Generally, British and US chain pizza is bland and unexciting. By far the best is **Pizza Express**. Their pizza is thin crusted and served in small, manageable sizes. They have an interesting and romantic flagship at **Kettners** in Soho. But pizza just isn't as good as many places in Italy or the US.

Pizza Condotti

Our favourite. Light, airy decor and relaxed surroundings. Fresh, crispy pizzas. A very pleasant, inexpensive place to linger over lunch.

4 Mill Street W1, Tel. 01-499 1308. U: Oxford Circus. Hours: Mon–Sat 1130–2400.

Lorelei
Just a cafe, but reputedly the Italians' favourite. BYOB.

21 Bateman Street W1, Tel. 01-734 0954. U: Tottenham Court Road. Hours: Mon–Sat 1200–2300.

We must, however, admit to a bias towards thin-crusted pizza. If you like thick-crusted, go to two places run by Americans: **L.S. Grunt's Pizza**, 12 Maiden Lane WC2, U: Charing Cross, or **Chicago Pizza Pie Factory**, 17 Hanover Square W1, U: Oxford Circus (another Bob Payton place).

Pasta
Pasta bars are now common around Covent Garden and Soho. Some are on an all-you-can-eat basis. Quality is generally pretty fair, but beware of too much pasta and too little sauce.

Fatso's Pasta Joint
All you can eat for £2.60 from Sunday to Thursday in the heart of Soho.

13 Old Compton Street WC2. U: Leicester Square. Hours: Sun–Thurs 1200–2300; Fri, Sat 1200–0100.

Pasta Prego
1a Beauchamp Place SW3. U: Knightsbridge.

Pollo
Expect a lunchtime queue for this genuine Italian cafe that out-pastas them all with London's best bargain: a huge plate for £2.50.

20 Old Compton Street W1. U: Leicester Square.

Dutch Pancakes
Choose between a simple or a savoury — with fillings like ham, bacon, cheese and over 100 variations at **My Old Dutch** open 12.00 to 22.30 Mon–Sat at 131 High Holborn WC1. U: Holborn or 221 King's Road SW3. U: Sloane Square.

Chinese
If you want Chinese food to go (better known here as take-away), it's better to order it in a Chinese restaurant than from a Chinese take-away, because quality is usually better. However, there is a fairly good take-away in Chinatown, **The Phoenix**, in the middle of Gerrard Street. Don't forget that peculiar Chinese form of fast food, *dim sum*, is available from many places around Chinatown during the early afternoon. The best places to go are **New World**, Gerrard Place, and **Chuen Cheng Ku**, on Wardour Street. A very good place for a cheap filling snack in Chinatown is **Kai Kee Restaurant** on Wardour Street (U: Piccadilly Circus or Leicester Square).

Indian
Curries don't always lend themselves to outdoor eating, but some Indian foods, like delicious tandoori chicken, do. Again, it's best to buy from a restaurant, but there are a few good take-aways, like the **Curry Hut** at Portobello Green, Portobello Road (U: Ladbroke Grove). **Anwar's** is a friendly self-service at 64 Grafton Way W1 (U: Warren Street). **Curri Express** is handy to tourists at 17 Swallow Street, near Piccadilly Circus. Many Indian grocers sell *samosas*, which they will heat up for you. Give them a try — they're probably about the most common exotic snack in London. *Samosas* are basically little fried or baked triangular pies with spicy meat or vegetable fillings.

Malaysian
London's first quality **Satay Ria** outlet has opened near the corner of Queensway and Westbourne Grove (U: Bayswater). The Singapore-based chain has successfully commercialized Malaysia's national dish of chicken, lamb or beef charcoaled on wooden skewers and dipped in peanut sauce. It's delicious even here, but better as a snack than a meal. At 269 Portobello Road, in the Market, is **Makan**, a wonderful Malaysian carry-out with more filling dishes like *Nasi Goreng* and *Ayam Goreng* (U: Ladbroke Grove). And it might be worth mentioning a **Thai** food stall which can be found some market days near the corner of Portobello Road and Elgin Crescent.

German
Fancy the German hot dog (*Heisse Wurst*) with bread and mustard? Visit **Jurgen Klatt's German Sausage Stall** in the Portobello Market (U: Notting Hill Gate/Ladbroke Grove), or the **Wurst Max** at the corner of Bayswater and Queensway (U: Queensway). The **German Food Centre** in Knightsbridge is useful for take homes.

Middle Eastern and Greek
Kebab shops first sprang up during the Arab invasions of the seventies and are now more common than fish and chips in central London. In restaurant form, they are among the cheapest places in town to have a sit-down meal. Most just dispense the popular sandwiches-in-a-pitta as take-aways. Doner kebab, shish or even just salad in pitta bread is preferable, I think, to most of the hamburgers on offer.

With the fall in the price of oil, there are fewer Arabs now, but you can still find plenty of Middle Eastern take-away foods — along Queensway and Edgware Road. At 118 Edgware Road is **Arabic Takeaway** (U: Edgware Road), with delicious kebabs, fellafels, hommous and salads. Good versions of fellafel and other Levantine delicacies are well prepared by **Pitta the Great**, under the Westway on Portobello Road (U: Ladbroke Grove). My favourite 'local' takeaway kebab shop is **Alpha** on Ladbroke Grove; I can't think of any better or more generous kebab shop anywhere in London.

8   *Pubs and bars*

No traveller to London should miss the opportunity to visit a few pubs. Not all will fit your preconceptions or live up to your expectations, because they come in all shapes, sizes, atmospheres and themes — such as 'The Sherlock Holmes' or 'The Gilbert & Sullivan' — and not a few have names that merit further investigation, like 'The Slug and Lettuce'. Some are the 'territory' of a specific group of patrons — business pubs, gay pubs, straight pubs, yuppie pubs, drag pubs, you name it. Most attract a somewhat mixed bag of people and in most you will be at least tolerated or ignored, if not welcomed.

Foreign visitors will find British pubs to be rather different from 'bars' abroad. Though you may not find skittles, darts, yard-long glasses, wood panels or an open fire (country pubs more often live up to this image), generally the London pub is brightly lit, music may or may not be too loud and, most of the time, the atmosphere is fairly low-key and wholesome.

The grand opportunity pubs present is to be a 'fly on the wall'. Sit and anonymously eavesdrop on a slice of local London while you consume your brew. Get a close-up on the millions of private little worlds that make up perhaps the most private metropolitan city on earth. Or you might strike up a conversation and be admitted for an even closer look, or — more likely — not. But there are not many other places where tourists and locals can mingle shoulder to shoulder in a common pursuit.

Of course, the more famous and popular places get besieged by visitors in high summer. Some publicans say their regular clientele disappears in June and doesn't come back until September. I must admit I like the summer, particularly in those pubs with a garden or a patio, where you can stand or sit outside on a cool summer's evening with sleeves rolled up and pint in hand.

Tips

Pub hours
Even though pubs may now remain open from 1100 to 2300 (except for Sundays, when they may only open from 1200–1500 and 1900–2200), some have chosen to keep traditional mid-afternoon closing hours. Shortly before closing time you may hear a bell or a shout of 'Last orders!' from the landlord, which usually means you have ten minutes to order your last drink. Another bell may ring when the bar closes, and when you hear 'Drink up!' it means you have a few minutes to finish; the landlord wants to lock up for the night.

Pubs
Pubs are primarily in the business of serving beer. If you want wine you'll do better in a **wine bar**. Most pubs sell no more than a few types of cheap wine by the glass. Fancy mixed drinks are more readily available in American bars or cocktail bars. Britons prefer their spirits straight, or with water, soda or tonic. Ice, once rare, is now more common, but most mixed American cocktails are not familiar to British pub barmen — except in some trendy places. Soft drinks and canned fruit juices and packets of peanuts or other nibbles are often available.

Beer
Despite widespread adoption of the metric system, beer is still ordered by the pint or half-pint glass. Ask for lager (light yellow brew similar to continental or American beers) or try bitter — a brown ale that is the traditional British drink. (If you go up to Scotland, ask for 'export' instead of bitter). Many visitors say they didn't care for it the first time, but it grows on you. The best bitters are 'real ale', made in the traditional way, and now even the brewery chain pubs usually sell at least one. Some pubs now offer a selection of foreign beers, particularly Australian and American.

Food
Pub food is very cheap and convenient, but unfortunately much is now bland, standardized fare from centralized caterers. See *Fast Food: Pubs* for general advice. In the selections below we indicate pubs that have a good standard of food. Mostly it's served at lunchtime only.

Customs
If you meet one or more fellow drinkers in a pub and become friendly, it is customary to order a 'round' — buy everyone in the group a drink — rather than go 'Dutch treat'. They should reciprocate. Better take your turn early, before too many new friends arrive!

Which pub?
Most pubs are now 'tied' — owned by one of the major breweries such as Courage. Naturally, your choice of beer is usually limited to their own products and a few uncompetitive foreign beers. Freehouses are a small independently-owned minority of pubs; if you want to sample a variety of beers, you should head for one of these establishments. They aren't necessarily more atmospheric — many of London's more historic houses are strictly brewery outlets — and unless you're a connoisseur, you may not care.

For good beer and usually good surroundings, look for outlets affiliated with the two remaining London independents, **Fullers** or **Youngs**. Alternatively, the **& Firkin** chain (example: The Frog & Firkin) is a small chain controlled by entrepreneur David Bruce that offers a selection from small breweries and beers brewed on the premises. Some of London's most interesting and historic pubs are in the East End. After all, this is the oldest part of town, even if it is the grimiest. If you prefer a lighter charm, riverside Hammersmith, Chiswick and Richmond have several pleasant houses with good beer and Thames views.

Selections

Here are a few London Traveletter selections from the many hundreds available. You could try going on a 'pub crawl' (spend an evening in several pubs) and make your own discoveries. Remember, meals are often served at lunchtime only.

The following pubs are historic, atmospheric, or interesting in some other way.

East End, the City and Fleet Street

Prospect of Whitby

The East End is the oldest part of town. As you might expect, some of London's most atmospheric pubs are found here, particularly along the river. Probably the most famous of London's riverside pubs, the **Prospect of Whitby**, displays a board listing the 22 sovereigns under whom it has survived, the earliest being Henry VIII (1509–47). The name is not as old as the pub, dating back to 1830 when a ship called *The Prospect* used to dock outside to unload its coal and stone from Yorkshire. Long before that it was the Devil's Tavern, where diarist Samuel Pepys used to dine in a room once used for cockfighting, and Judge Jefferys ('the hanging judge') used to relax blithely on the porch, watching the struggle of the poor wretches he'd condemned to death as they hung from Execution Dock until three tides had washed over them.

Artists Gustave Doré and James Whistler loved the view from here, and England's greatest Victorian painter, Joseph Turner, used to paint sunsets from the same spot. You can sit with a pint of Watneys and admire them today. A long wooden bar dominates the room, with cushioned casks for seating, and attractive alcoves. Good food and a Thames-side view that's unsurpassed. There's a trapdoor in the lower floor through which smugglers are said to have unloaded their duty-free tobacco. It might be a bit crude to say that this pub can be something of a tourist trap for coach parties. (J.W.)

Wapping Wall E1. U: Wapping.

Dirty Dick's

Dirty Dick's cavernous upstairs at least justifies the pub's name (derived from a slovenly seventeenth-century landlord who let the place go to seed after his bride-to-be died on their wedding day, and who paid a local church to ring a bell on his birthday until the end of his life). During the week it's a typical City pub, catering mostly for business types, but at evenings and weekends it's thronged with tourists and has succumbed to modern ways with the installation downstairs of a video jukebox. Wide selection of beers: Courage, Charrington's, Watneys and Green King.

204 Bishop's Gate St EC2. U: Liverpool Street.

The Grapes

The view downriver from **The Grapes** is of **Cuckold's Point**, marking the limit, according to legend, of the land paid off by King John to a local miller who had returned home unexpectedly and caught the King with his wife. True or not, the view is magnificent. Whistler did an etching of it, and Charles Dickens was a frequent customer, renaming it Six Jolly Fellowship Porters in his book *Our Mutual Friend*.

The pub's Dickens Room leads off the balcony behind which the bar offers tasty snacks and Ind Coope and Friary Meux beers. Upstairs is a seafood restaurant. 'The tavern,' wrote Dickens, 'was of a dropsical appearance, with not a straight line or hardly a straight floor'. Alice M. West's painting, *Saturday Night at The Grapes*, which hangs in the bar, depicts some of this and was shown at the Royal Academy in 1949. Saturday nights are still lively here, with an old piano much in use.

76 Narrow Street E14. BR: Stepney East.

The Hand & Shears
Up to the middle of the last century, the **Hand & Shears** was the main stopping place for all the French and Flemish clothing trade representatives when they came to London for the annual St Bartholomew's Fair every August. This sixteenth-century pub has changed little, except for its customers, who are now a mixture of local printers, city analysts, and porters and traders from the nearby Smithfield meat market, who, especially at lunchtime, crowd the central bar and numerous panelled rooms surrounding it. Hanging lanterns, framed cartoons and prints on the walls.

1 Middle Street EC1. U: St Paul's.

Williamson's Tavern
A pair of wrought iron gates presented by William III and Mary to the Lord Mayor of London guard the approach to the cul-de-sac on which stands **Williamson's Tavern**, a former Mansion House and Lord Mayor's residence. Like many other pubs, it claims to be the oldest in the city, and a table in the restaurant marks what is said to be the 'exact centre' of London. Before its transformation into a pub in the eighteenth century, it was home to Sir John Falstaff, and long before that it stood on the site of some Roman villa. Tiles from that era, unearthed during rebuilding earlier this century, are now incorporated into the pub's fireplace.

Bow Lane EC1. U: Mansion House.

The Hoop & Grapes
Charrington Brewers recently spent more than a million pounds restoring and propping up the original timbers of this seventeenth-century pub. The 1670 frontage, interior panelling and Jacobean staircase are understandably its pride and glory, and its former role as a vintner's is revealed by its large and sprawling cellars. Its location, right on the dividing line of two ancient parishes — St Mary's, Whitchapel, and St Botolph's, Aldgate — is marked with a 1782 boundary plate in the window jamb. Drinking here must be confined to a six-day week, as the pub has no Sunday licence.

High Street, Aldgate EC3. U: Aldgate.

The Cock
Alfred Lord Tennyson once dined here with Edward (Omar Khayyam) Fitzgerald, but the pub had already been immortalized by diarist Samuel Pepys 200 years earlier, when he wrote that he went 'by water to the Temple and then to the Cock alehouse and drank and ate a lobster and sang and made merry'. Other historians have recorded that Pepys used to dine there with his attractive friend Mrs Knipp, much to the chagrin of Mrs Pepys. It was known for its rum punches in those days, but the sign today boasts: 'Famous for food since 1549'. Once called the Cock and Bottle, the pub was originally on the other (northern) side of Fleet Street, and was closed briefly because of the Great Plague in 1665. Thackeray, Dickens and Tennyson were all customers during the last century, probably before it was moved across the street in 1887, along with its James I chimney-piece and carved sign attributed to the celebrated sculptor Grinling Gibbons. (J.W.)

22 Fleet Street EC4. U: Blackfriars.

The Black Friar
First built in the seventeenth century, and rebuilt in this one, this pub by Blackfriars Bridge is ironically best known today for the Edwardian style of about 80 years ago. Decorated by noted artist Henry Poole in Art Nouveau style, it features bas-relief friezes of Dominican monks and the ancient monastery that gave the area its name. It's a mish-mash of marble, mosaics and mirrors, and popular with Fleet Street employees and those from *The Observer* on nearby St Andrews Hill.

Bass and other beers and a wide range of home-cooked food are served at reasonable prices. There's an unusually large space outside the pub for tables, and on summer days drinkers have an unsurpassed view of traffic pouring off the bridge. Some of the signs on the walls were obviously meant for a different era: Haste is Slow; Industry is All; Silence is Golden; and Finery is Foolery.

174 Queen Victoria St EC4. U: Blackfriars.

Ye Olde Mitre
In 1547, in the days when the Bishops of Ely were absolute lords over their own patch of land in London, the **Olde Mitre** was built for people working in their place, and although the building is not the same one, it's pretty similar. Small, oak-panelled rooms with jugs hanging from beams, antique furniture and vases of bright flowers recall Shakespeare's day.

Ely Place EC1. U: Chancery Lane

Ye Olde Cheshire Cheese
Very well known, with good food, sawdust on the floor and an open fire. Touristy, but probably worth a visit for the atmosphere. Wine.

Wine Office Court, 145 Fleet Street EC4. U: Temple.

The Fox and Anchor
See *Eating Out: Breakfasts*

South of the river
East and south of the river are some of London's best riverview pubs.

The Anchor
This Southwark pub (built in 1750, rebuilt after a fire in 1676, renovated in the 1960s) used to play host to William Shakespeare and (much later) Samuel Johnson and has rooms named after them. The good doctor, who was compiling his dictionary nearby, used to quaff a particular porter brewed specially by nearby Barclay Perkins for the Empress of Russia, and averred it was his favourite drink.

Nobody's quite sure how long there's been an inn on the site, but historians speculate that this was the 'little alehouse on the Bankside' to which Samuel Pepys retired in 1666 to watch London ablaze in the Great Fire. The Press Gang (not journalists, but 'recruiters' for the Navy) operated out of here, spiriting away many a poor wretch who'd unwarily downed a pint too many. Across the street was the old Clink prison, its name still commemorated in contemporary slang, and doubtless the jailers found the tavern a handy place in which to relax.

Courage beer, good food, and plenty of atmosphere (rambling corridors, smoke-stained wine barrels, secret rooms, double doors, etc) — at least until the tourist buses disgorge the daily hordes. (J.W.)

1 Bankside SE1. U: London Bridge.

The Angel
With several hundred pubs going out of business in each of the last few years, and

nine out of ten of the others declaring that only the sale of food makes them profitable, the **Angel**, with its vast menu of snacks, salads, sandwiches and an upstairs restaurant, would seem to be safe for a long time to come, especially as the old dockland area all around is all set for renovation. A riverside pub whose balcony is built on timber piles over the water, it has, according to the *Good Pub Guide*, 'perhaps the finest Thames view', looking northwards to Tower Bridge and downriver to the Pool of London. Courage is the brewery, and past customers include Captain Cook and Samuel Pepys.

Bermondsey Wall East SE16. U: London Bridge.

The Mayflower

Before Captain Christopher Jones set sail for America in 1620, he moored his ship *The Mayflower* at Bermondsey by a hostelry already 60 years old and called the Spread Eagle & Crown. That pub has, unsurprisingly, been renamed after his ship, and is now something of a tourist Mecca.

It's a comfortable place, with low beamed ceilings and a terrace hanging over the river; it offers both bar snacks and full meals in an upstairs restaurant called **Pilgrims** (there's also a **New Settler Bar**). Damaged during the wartime air raids, it was restored in seventeenth-century style to 'incorporate some of the great history of the ship for which the inn is named and the adventurous spirit of those who sailed in her'.

Rotherhithe Street SE16. U: Surrey Docks.

The Anchor Tap

Behind the murky waters of Thames Upper Pool, just below Tower Bridge, sits the **Anchor Tap**. A sinister spectre haunts its cellar. Proprietor John Warrender recently encountered it. One night in the cellar, John was changing some beer cylinders. A sharp drop in temperature caused him to shiver. Sensing he was not alone, John turned and saw a figure pass slowly through the wall opposite. On another evening, John was clearing up the aptly-named **Crypt Room**, adjacent to the downstairs bar. A lamp hangs from the ceiling. 'Suddenly it began spinning wildly,' says John. 'Seconds later, the bulb exploded.' Barmaid Debbie was given a nasty shock when stacking glasses in the upstairs bar at closing time. She watched, terrified, as those on the top shelf were thrown to the floor. 'There was broken glass everywhere,' she says.

Who is the frantic phantom? John believes he was once the pub manager who hanged himself in the cellar many years ago. Nicknamed Charlie, he obviously still regards the pub as his territory. Best not sit too near the upstairs bar when you drink here!

Looking every inch the haunted pub, with its high ceilings, narrow staircases and ancient mirrored walls, the **Anchor Tap** offers the ghost hunter a warm welcome. Both bars have adjacent rooms, including a **Family Room** and the infamous **Crypt Room**. All are splendidly decorated with fine ornaments and fascinating prints. Being a Samuel Smith House, a wide range of real ales is available along with the usual wines and spirits. Food is served seven days a week. The menu runs from cheeseburgers to rainbow trout — all with French fries and salad. (B.R.)

28 Horsleydown Lane SE1. U: Tower Hill.

The George Inn

Away from the bustle of Borough High Street, in its own courtyard, stands this majestic 400-year-old Southwark pub, London's only surviving galleried coaching inn, harbouring a full contingent of ghosts.

Sitting in a ground-floor bar, with its square-latticed windows overlooking the courtyard, it's easy to imagine those far-off days when Shakespeare drank here. Bare floorboards, low beams, oak and elm tables — all create a grand atmosphere. A splendid central staircase leads up to the dining rooms. Food is available seven days a week, and an imaginative menu includes poached Scotch salmon steak, vegetarian pancake, and venison with red wine sauce and croutons. Fine real ales, wines and spirits are served at the bars.

77 Borough High St SE1. U: London Bridge.

Covent Garden and Holborn

The Sherlock Holmes

What true fan of Sir Arthur Conan Doyle's famous detective could resist this pub just off Trafalgar Square? Only a pane of glass separates diners from his authentic-looking room with its Victorian furniture, globe, sporting prints, racks of Meerschaum pipes and canned tobacco, old-fashioned chiming clock, sofa strewn with century-old newspapers, and a violin. Holmes' deerstalker hat and coat hang from a peg, a bearskin rug covers the floor in front of the fireplace, and a lifesize bust of the sleuth himself stands cheek by jowl with a stuffed mastiff head in the corner. Sir Arthur himself used to drink here when it was the Northumberland Arms, and mentions it in *The Hound of the Baskervilles*. The downstairs bar is lined with framed engravings from books and posters from various Holmesian productions, as well as T-shirts and carrier bags bearing the pub's sign displaying an intense-looking Sherlock perusing a letter. Whitbread, Flowers and other beers as well as bar food, which can be eaten outside if it isn't raining.

10 Northumberland St WC2. U: Charing Cross.

The Lamb & Flag

If you can squeeze into this always-crowded pub, you may enjoy a Dickensian inn with good food and real ale. Bar food is simple, with a good selection of cheeses.

Rose Street WC2. U: Leicester Square.

The Princess Louise

Old-fashioned decor, good variety of ales and edible food.

208 High Holborn WC1. U: Holborn.

The Gilbert & Sullivan

Photographs of the famous Victorian lyricist and his composer partner adorn the interiors, but the pictures, photos and posters are devoted more to the productions than the partners, an upstairs wine-and-cocktail lounge being called **Mikado's**, and plush sofas, soft lighting and hanging baskets of flowers everywhere. It's all very cosy, belying the trilingual 'Welcome to a traditional English pub' in the doorway. ('Traditional' usually meaning something rather tattier than this.) (J.W.)

23 Wellington Street W2. U: Covent Garden.

Bloomsbury

Bloomsbury pubs attract many drinkers from London University and the publishing industry, who contribute to an academic ambience.

The Museum Tavern

Everybody knows that Karl Marx used to while away a lot of his time in the British Museum/Library, and everybody assumes that he was at least an occasional denizen of the **Museum Tavern** across the street, but as he died in 1882, nobody is left alive to tell the tale. Equally flimsy evidence points to another customer having been Virginia Woolf, most of whose Bloomsbury crowd lived in adjoining streets and squares.

Certainly the old-fashioned benches and cast-iron tables, Victorian antique mirrors and exterior gas lamps are authentic enough, and it's one of those rare pubs that stays open outside traditional licensing hours to operate as a café, serving afternoon tea between 3.45 and 5pm on weekdays. Good bar food, choice of real ale, and even space for children in the eating areas.

The convenience of the pub is just as much appreciated by today's users of the Library as ever it was: the wait between requesting books and their arrival is usually just long enough to pop over for what the British call 'a quick one'. (J.W.)

Great Russell Street WC1. U: Tottenham Court Road.

The Friend at Hand Tavern
Very atmospheric, with summer outdoor seating.

Herbrand Street WC1. U: Russell Square.

The Lamb
A cosy place with cut-glass bar screens, old sepia photographs, Youngs bitter and a decent standard of pub food.

94 Lamb's Conduit WC1. U: Holborn.

Mayfair, Marylebone and Bayswater
Mayfair and areas adjoining Hyde Park have many atmospheric pubs.

The Red Lion
Mayfair's **Red Lion** is one of the more expensive pubs, but it is classy enough to warrant it, being somewhat reminiscent of an upper-class country pub complete with tree-shaded barrels in the quiet cul-de-sac outside. The name comes from the insignia adopted by John of Gaunt (1340–1399), son of Edward III and father of Henry IV. The pub was once a farmhouse and the paintings, prints and antique carriage lamps are reminders of this. Watneys, Ruddles and other beers available, as well as first-class food served morning and evening, and a separate restaurant.

Waverton Street W1. U: Hyde Park Corner.

The Swan
When Hyde Park was a royal hunting preserve, and Marble Arch in the countryside, the Tyburn Gallows were the focus of an afternoon's outing — particularly if the crowd could watch someone being hanged. The Floral Tea Gardens was a popular stopping-off point then, and on the same site today stands **The Swan**, opposite the park.

You can still get afternoon tea on the premises, but in all other respects it's a typical pub with John Bull and Yorkshire Bitter among the beers, and a large food buffet which sometimes includes a whole turkey. (The swan, by the way, was an emblem of innocence in medieval times, and the badge [silver swan surmounted by the image of the Virgin] was adopted by the Cleeves family — the best known member of which was the unfortunate Anne, fourth wife of Henry VIII.)

66 Bayswater Road W2. U: Marble Arch.

The Guinea
This used to be the famous **Guinea Grill** until the lease ran out and they had to move a few doors down. The Grill's steaks are famed, but expect to spend at least £30 a head. Youngs have taken over and still provides plenty of Olde English atmosphere — prints, built-in leatherette seats and panels — but the food here is simpler and much cheaper.

30 Bruton Place W1. U: Bond Street.

The Bunch of Grapes
You can get oysters in the quiet little dining area of this old-fashioned pub, or in the separate restaurant.
Shepherd Market W1. U: Green Park.

The Audley
Heavy Victorian ornamentation and mahogany panelling, but relaxed atmosphere and good food.
41 Mount Street W1. U: Bond Street.

Kensington
Notting Hill and the central Campden Hill areas of Kensington have plenty of agreeable public houses

The Windsor Castle
Has won several 'favourite pub' contests because it oozes atmosphere from its dark panelling, wood partitions and cosy winter log fires. In summer you can sit outside on the big tree-shaded terrace. Good bar food.
114 Campden Hill Road W8. U: Notting Hill Gate.

The Ladbroke Arms
Inside, it's old-fashioned and cosy, but in the summer you can sit outside on park benches and watch the comings and goings at the Notting Hill police station across the street. Good food.
Ladbroke Road W11. U: Holland Park.

Frog & Firkin
Everybody should try one of the '& Firkin' chain's outlets. This one is a kind of 'piano pub' with a resident pianist, wide selection of beers and regular neighbourhood clientele.
41 Tavistock Crescent. W11. U: Westbourne Park.

Victoria
Recently this has become more of a wine bar area, but at least one pub merits investigation.

The Slug and Lettuce
The name alone makes this pub worth a visit — the place is actually nothing special, but, almost ironically, they serve good pub grub. Both lunch and dinner.
11 Warwick Way SW1. U: Victoria.

Chelsea and Belgravia
Chelsea is a charming neighbourhood. Both this area and Belgravia have a number of Englishy upmarket pubs. Along the Kings Road you'll find younger, flashier places.

The Antelope
Once a hang-out of the painter Augustus John, but few artists today could afford to live in the area, and most of the clientele are Sloane Rangers and tourists. Good lunch food counter and plenty of relaxed old-fashioned atmosphere.
22 Eaton Terrace Square SW1. U: Sloane Square.

The Cross Keys

Good lunches at this pub with high ceilings and military prints. The real attraction is its location, in a famed Chelsea neighbourhood next to the Cheyne Walk Gardens by the Thames.

Lawrence Street SW3. U: Sloane Square.

The Grenadier

The **Grenadier** is London's most famous haunted pub. Nearly 200 years ago it served as the Officer's Mess for the Duke of Wellington's Regiment. Gambling was the main pastime. Caught cheating at cards, one officer was flogged, hurled down the cellar stairs, and left to die. He never left the premises. Many have caught sight of his vanishing figure on the cellar stairs and in the bedrooms. Debbie Mace, the Holding Manager, believes the ghostly guardsman delights in turning on the cellar beer taps and playing with the light switches.

The **Grenadier** is in a mews behind Hyde Park Corner. Very much a traditional British pub, it also enjoys a military ambience. Sabres, muskets and pistols hang from the ceiling; the walls sport prints of guardsmen through the ages and, naturally, news cuttings from the world's press concerning the ghost. The restaurant has two candle-lit rooms and meals are available seven days a week. The menu is upmarket English and Continental, including turtle soup and frogs' legs. Wide selection of drinks from Watneys ale to Dom Perignon. (B.R.)

18 Wilton Row, Belgrave Square SW1. U: Hyde Park Corner.

The World's End

In the days when the old Kings Road through Chelsea was literally 'the king's road', and commoners had to request permission to travel along it — or settle for the route by boat up the Thames — the **World's End** was a cosy tavern surrounded by tea gardens in which Restoration dramatist William Congreve was a familiar habitué. He refers to the tavern, in fact, in his comedy *Love for Love*. In recent times it has become a popular Chelsea Bohemian haunt.

459 Kings Road SW10. U: Sloane Square.

Hampstead

Hampstead was once a spa town, and has a long tradition of pubs with literary, historic and artistic associations.

The Holly Bush

The portrait painter George Romney used to live on one of the prettiest streets in Hampstead, and the **Holly Bush** has stood since 1802 on the side of what had been his stables. Surely he'd have patronized it if he'd still been alive . . . but, anyway, it named a room for him and in most essentials the pub looks much as it must have done when it was built, with sloping ceiling, gas lamps, panelled walls and glass partitions. There's a selection of beers, good home-cooked food, and seats for outside drinking in the adjoining alley. Another celebrated painter, John Constable, is buried in the nearby churchyard.

Holly Mount NW3. U: Hampstead.

Jack Straw's Castle

The modern building replaces one destroyed in World War II and is situated at almost the highest point in London (437 ft above sea level), and almost opposite where the thrice-yearly fairs take place on the heath. It is not a castle but does commemorate a certain Jack Sraw (thought to have been Jack Rackstraw), co-leader with Wat Tyler of the 1381 Peasants' Revolt, who lived in a hut nearby. The pair of them led a raggle-taggle army from Kent to London, capturing Richmond Castle *en route*, but were eventually captured and executed.

An inn has stood on this site for at least three centuries. Highwayman Dick Turpin is said to have hidden his horse behind an earlier hostelry, and Dickens, recommending the previous pub to a friend, wrote: 'I know a good 'ouse where we can have a red chop for dinner and a glass of good wine — although even today that is hardly a rarity!

North End Way NW3. U: Hampstead.

Spaniard's Inn

The original pub was built in 1630 across the road from the old toll house. Very atmospheric, with open fires and little oak-panelled alcove rooms. Good value food. Famed for the incident in 1780 when the innkeeper kept mobs from burning down nearby Kenwood House by getting them thoroughly soused. Sit outside in the attractive garden in summer.

Spaniards Lane NW3. U: Hampstead.

West London waterside pubs

Some of London's most atmospheric drinking is found at riverside pubs on the upper Thames. At Strand-on-the-Green and Hammersmith Mall, there is a selection.

The City Barge

Named after the Lord Mayor's official barge, 136 ft long and towed by horses to Hampton Court after the Lord Mayor had embarked here, the **City Barge** dates back to 1484. It was rebuilt after bomb damage in World War II, but with its copper-topped tables, antiques, beamed ceiling and brassware, as well as the pan used to mull beer (with a touch of ginger) for several centuries, it's very much an old-style pub, although there's a new bar at the back with darts and a one-armed bandit. Courage beer and snacks. There are seats outside on the canal towpath, and others inside; the ones around the fireplace are raised because flooding is not unknown after particularly rainy days. Pay a visit to the **Bull's Head** and the **Bell & Crown** as well.

Strand on the Green W4. U: Kew Bridge.

The Dove

The main highway in the time of Charles I was the river, and it was at **The Dove** that riverside meetings between Charles and Nell Gwynn used to take place. Its sign is a dove bearing a branch to the Ark through parted clouds. It was here, on the partly vine-covered terrace, that the celebrated landscapist J. M. Turner sat and painted sunsets over the Thames; James Thomson, author of *Rule Britannia*, lived in an upstairs room in 1725; authors Captain Frederick Marryat and Samuel Taylor Coleridge also dropped by to imbibe. Set in a row of Georgian houses, **The Dove** is just as attractive inside, with low beams, bare floorboards and ancient furnishings, and outside a fine view of Hammersmith Bridge. A London magazine recently alleged that Ernest Hemingway liked the place, describing it as 'a pub to get high in, to talk in and meet Englishmen — if you like them'.

19 Upper Mall W6. U: Stamford Brook.

The Old Ship

Sit out on the terrace and enjoy the views of the Thames. Lunchtime meals and Ruddles Yorkshire County beer.

25 Upper Mall W6. U: Stamford Brook.

Richmond and Twickenham

Further down river, Richmond and Twickenham, on opposite sides of the Thames, have a number of charming riverside pubs with good food and atmosphere. Particularly notable are the **Rose of York** (U: Richmond) and **The White Swan**, Twickenham. Even further away, but worth the trip, is:

The London Apprentice

The **London Apprentice** stands right opposite the exact spot where the Romans first crossed the Thames. It has always had a close association with the river, its cellars being a storing place for smuggled goods landed at nearby All Saints Church and transported to the inn via an underground passage. Until 1739 it was open 24 hours a day for travellers, and at least two kings (Henry VIII and Charles II) have been among its customers. Lunchtime and evening buffet snacks can be eaten overlooking the river, and the famous Henry VIII's Room restaurant specializes in Dover sole (Reservations: 01-560 1915). (J.W.)

62 Church Street. BR: Twickenham.

Wine and champagne bars

London's wine bars are funny creatures. Most haven't been around all that long, and new ones sprout up as old ones die. Some have the characteristics of a pub, some of a restaurant. And many aren't worth very much, charging exorbitant prices for less-than-minimum measures of execrable house wines, or soggy quiche. Most take on the ambience of the surrounding neighbourhood, so for a good personal sampling you should hit the City business quarter places after work, in addition to any in Hampstead, Chelsea or other areas you fancy, for a spectrum of flavours.

At their best, wine bars are pleasant, affordable places to eat bistro-type meals and try obscure vintages by the glass, or, if you like, by the bottle. (J.E.)

Draycott's

Slightly faded in its pale green/dark wood setting, but that gives it an easier, established feeling rather unusual for the Kensington area. Almost half-pub, half-wine bar. The wine list is pleasant, though not for the connoisseur, with prices ranging from £6–£12.

114 Draycott Avenue SW3. U: South Kensington.

Julie's Bar

We've had several recommendations for this bar, and a good place it is. Green and wood, with stained glass and plants everywhere — and lots of people on two floors. Too many, at certain times — not the place for a calm and quiet chat.

137 Portland Road W11. U: Holland Park.

Grabowsky's

For City boys, with Filofax and oversized glasses, posing at **Grabowsky's** is an evening's activity. It's been called an art gallery and wine bar in one, but I wouldn't think hard on that. It comes complete with piano, a good selection of French wines, seven non-vintage and four vintage champagnes, track lighting, white walls and floors, and the most horrendous garish papier-maché framed 'paintings' you ever saw.

84 Sloane Avenue SW3. U: South Kensington.

The Champagne Exchange

One of the new Yuppie bubbly-bars sprouting up. The decor is cool banker's grey (how appropriate), food prints adorn the walls, and there's a white marble banquette. Tables are at the back. There is definitely a feeling of money. The dinner, heavy on the smoked stuff, is moderately priced, considering the locale, for the high flyer's pre-theatre tipple, or at least worth an adventurous peek. A regular there advised me that happy hour or late evening was the perfect time to see the place at its best.

17c Curzon Street W1. U: Green Park.

Kettners Champagne Bar
Bollinger, Perrier-Jouet, Mumm, Moët, Roederer and Pommeroy and *Taittinger* and more are available — by the glass or bottle — with a reasonable pizza.
29 Romilly Street W1. U: Piccadilly Circus.

Some other suggestions
- **Gordon's**
  47 Villiers Street WC2. U: Charing Cross (see *Restaurant Favourites*)
- **Vats**
  51 Lamb's Conduit Street WC1. U: Holborn
- **Solange's Wine Bar**
  11 St Martin's Court WC2. U: Leicester Square
- **Drinks**
  21 Abingdon Road W8. U: Kensington High Street
- **The Ebury**
  139 Ebury Street SW1. U: Victoria

American cocktail bars
Since pubs are mainly in the business of selling beer and cider, or spirits with a dash of tonic, soda or water, you often have to look to a specific American or cocktail bar if you want something like a *Tom Collins*, *Screwdriver* or a *Black Russian*. Trendy wine bar and pub barmen elsewhere may know how to make them, but don't count on it. Mostly, you find cocktails in hotel 'cocktail bars'.

The American Bar
Famous WW2 US officers' hangout. Savoy Hotel, Strand WC2. U: Charing Cross.

The Cocktail Bar
Dorchester Hotel, Park Lane W1. U: Hyde Park Corner.

Trader Vic's
London Hilton, Park Lane W1. U: Hyde Park Corner.

Athenaeum
Athenaeum Hotel, 116 Piccadilly W1. U: Green Park. Along with the renowned selection of Scottish malt whiskies, they know cocktails.

Jules
85 Jermyn Street SW1. U: Piccadilly Circus.

Muswells
28 Paddington Street W1. U: Baker Street, and other locations. Inexpensive American bar-restaurant chain.

9 *Entertainment and events*

Despite the famous sixties' idea of 'swinging London', the city is not a late night town. The public transport system closes down between midnight and 1 am. Pubs are obliged by law to sell no more pints and send their customers home well before the midnight hour. Only clubs and restaurants may serve alcohol afterwards. Nightclubs tend towards the exclusive or the sleazy. Dullsville?

No, not at all. The city is always brimming with entertainments of all kinds for all tastes. Pick up a thick copy of one of London's major weekly entertainment-listing magazines. Plenty is going on in unlikely places like pubs. Much of the city's folk, rock and jazz takes place there, and many support fringe theatres of all kinds. London is the world capital for theatre. The **National Film Theatre** and the many repertory, classic and general cinemas provide a wide choice for film lovers. Two opera companies and at least three ballet companies thrive. Major singing stars give concerts on world tour. Classical music performances have several important daily venues.

It's just that most of it happens before midnight. Afterward, people tend to drift off to informal parties at home. Nevertheless, determined nightbirds can, with a little effort, find plenty to amuse them into the small hours.

Don't forget that 'entertainment' is best defined in a broad sense. Just sitting on a bench, walking down a street, people-watching, listening to buskers and enjoying the atmosphere of London's parks and streets may be as entertaining as an evening out.

The areas around **Leicester Square, Piccadilly Circus** and connecting streets are the best place for an evening stroll, with plenty of bright lights and street performers of all kinds.

The entertainment scene is constantly changing: all we can do here is point you in the direction of some of the more interesting venues. Once in London, it's easy to find out more about the current cultural feast.

Where to find out about entertainment events in London

London has three major weekly entertainment magazines: *What's On, Time Out* and *City Limits.*

What's On (60p)

The most oriented towards tourists and people of middle age and upwards. It also seems to be the most unashamedly commercial rather than critical. Many listings are repeated week after week, though it's hardly staid. A recent caption beneath a stripper's photo read: 'An evening out can lead to many things, but most of the clubs provide an extremely good floor show and plenty of laughter and gaiety to keep everyone happy'.

Time Out (90p)

True to its name, **Time Out** is more timely, though the front part of the magazine is often taken up with interesting articles not directly relevant to London. The music and film listings and paragraph reviews can be cleverly written and very comprehensive. In earlier years, **Time Out** was heavily concerned with the young left political scene. A section headed Agit/Prop (mainly about political demonstrations) was prominent and this point of view flavoured all review opinions. The magazine has now grown up with the yuppies, and has a much broader market outlook, although still oriented toward the 18–40 age group. Many politically-concerned readers have been lost to **City Limits.**

City Limits (85p)

Much of the perspective of the old **Time Out**. Some say this magazine has better coverage of gay events. Otherwise, unless you're young, left and really interested in London politics, stick with **Time Out.**

Other sources

The **Evening Standard** is the best daily paper for entertainment and sports information. **New Musical Express** and **Melody Maker** provide more information about rock and jazz gigs. Outside London, some newsagents (particularly at railway stations) carry the above magazines. The national newspapers, particularly **The Sunday Times** and **The Observer**, have weekly listings for film, theatre and classical concerts, and these are available (sometimes weeks later) in many public libraries abroad. Those abroad interested in the current theatre scene can obtain some fairly up-to-date information from the offices of the **British Tourist Authority**, or the theatre-ticket agents listed below often send out print-out lists.

And you can, of course, subscribe to our newsletter, **London Traveletter,** which features a detailed monthly pull-out London theatre listing!

Please keep in mind that most shows are either short, limited-run affairs, or subject to quick closure, so re-checks may be necessary. In compiling our theatre pages, we've been told that bookings are being taken to a date two months ahead, only to find out a week later that the show is abruptly closing. Refunds are seldom a problem, but it's extremely frustrating and disappointing to arrive for a non-event.

Tips: getting tickets

There's always at least one London show that's sold out. For several years it was *Cats*, but tickets for this very unusual musical are now much easier to get. Last year's prize for the most heavily-booked London show easily goes to Andrew Lloyd Webber's *The Phantom of the Opera*. At the time of this writing, it is still booked solid for months ahead. At certain times of the year all popular shows can be difficult to book. And unless you know the right people, or want to fork out the big money, or take your luck in the lottery process, tickets for major events like the **Wimbledon** semis and final can be almost impossible. But sometimes just buying ordinary tickets can be a confusing process.

So let's talk about tickets. What are the major methods of obtaining them?

1. Direct

Go to the box office of the theatre or event. Aside from half-price or sponsor tickets (see below), this simple method is usually the cheapest. No commission, scalper's fees, service charge or porter's tips. You'll get a chance to look at the theatre's seating plan, and there are fewer mix-ups than with other methods. Two obvious disadvantages: first, you can only get what's available for a particular date — few theatres hold back tickets for sale at a higher price (for example, *Cats* tickets have been easier to obtain from agencies than from the New London Theatre); second, more time, trouble and effort are involved in actually going to the box office during opening hours. Many theatres now have a phone number for credit card bookings. Most theatres don't impose an additional charge for this service, but many are increasingly turning to centralized companies that do. Ask.

2. Telephone booking agencies

These credit card agencies now handle all kinds of bookings, even NCP parking spaces, and some restaurant reservations. Generally, there is a 15 per cent charge, but for some theatres and events there is none. Their 24-hour service may be useful to some people phoning from overseas.
The best known services: **Ticketmaster** 01-379 4444, **First Call** 01-240 7200.

3. Returns

Go to or call the theatre or the major booking agencies on the day you want. Returned tickets are more numerous than you might think, because tour companies and other block-bookers regularly return a number of unsold seats. For some major sold-out events like *Cats*, returns are an institution that produces available tickets each day. The big agencies have many of their own issues returned to them. For example, *Phantom* procedure was: join the queue outside the theatre at 10am each morning and just before the performance. **Keith Prowse's** spokesman said 'Ring any of our branches for *Phantom* returns at 12 each day — but we seldom have any'. Of course, single seat and matinee returns are the easiest to find. Theatre or big agency returns usually cost no more than their original price.

4. Half-price

These are available at the **Society of West End Theatre (SWET) Ticket Booth** at Leicester Square. During the summer months, huge queues build up before noon (for matinees) and 2.30 (for evening performances) and stretch round the square. Tickets for some, but not all, performances are offered for half-price plus £1 service charge. Beware of the compulsion to see anything that's still available once you get to the head of the queue.

Some theatres also sell half-price tickets just before the show. The **National Theatre** sells a limited number of 'day seats' for all performances after 10am on the day, and all remaining tickets are sold at much-reduced standby prices two hours before the show.

5. Big agencies
Keith Prowse (Tel: 01-741 9999) has branches in central London and the major hotels. **Edwards and Edwards** (Tel: 01-379 5822) has a main office at 156 Shaftesbury Avenue, and several other branches. There are a number of smaller agencies some of which also 'scalp' hard to find tickets. Even on ordinary tickets, most big and small agencies charge a hefty commission — up to 30 per cent on top of the ticket fee. So, it's usually cheaper to buy direct from the theatre; but if the box office is sold out, call the agencies: sometimes they have returns or access to other supplies of available tickets.

6. US-based agents
These include the US offices of **Keith Prowse** (800 223 4446) and **Edwards and Edwards** (212 944 0290). Travel agents and tour planners should know about **Group Sales Box Office** (800 223 7565). Two smaller and friendly but efficient booking organizations are **Maggie Brewer's London Theatre and More** (800 231 0629 then 255, or [Texas only] 800 392 4900 then 255) and **London Stages** (818 881 8433). Bookings can usually be confirmed the same day and commissions are similar to those charged in London. For Americans, using a US agency is most useful for those who are on a tight schedule or who want to reserve hard-to-get seats in advance. It's possibly cheaper than phoning London, and less trouble than writing. Conventions and high summer surges of tourists can make all kinds of tickets scarce at certain times. Americans please note: if a new London show attracts much publicity in the States, you should probably book in advance to avoid disappointment.

7. Scalpers (or 'Touts')
There are two types. Legitimate, upfront ticket scalpers buy tickets in advance from a variety of sources and resell them at high prices. Examples: *Phantom* £65–£140; *Les Miserables* or *Chess* £50–60. One of them told me, 'We need at least three hours notice, but we can obtain nearly any ticket any day'. Big events like **Wimbledon** are a speciality: going price for the men's finals £500–£700; men's semi-finals £400–£550. (Sexism is clearly in evidence here: women's semis were only about £360, and finals £450.) Some include a champagne lunch in the price. **Seatfinders** (see below) offered 'Debenture Holder's Seats' with access to the lounge and a reserved place in the car park for £650. These agencies can also find tickets for major sports, concerts and other events. I don't want to recommend any of them, but here are a few of the better known, high-profile scalpers: **Dial-a-Ticket** Tel: 01-930 8331; **Obtainables** Tel: 01-839 5363; **Seatfinders** Tel: 01-828 1678. Another type is represented by the small-time scalpers who advertise in *Time Out*, *The Guardian* and a number of other papers. Be careful. Prices are considerably lower, but reliability is much more suspect. You can also find them at the gates of theatres or events, or hanging out on Shaftesbury Avenue. Buy at your own risk — tickets could well be forgeries.

8. Sponsors
Do you work for a big company that is a sponsor or a client of major arts sponsors like big banks, the oil companies or the big eight accounting firms? One reason for seat shortages is that company sponsorship has massively increased in recent years. In return, these sponsors often obtain a certain number of seats. If they can't be used for business entertainment, the tickets are given to employees. We've heard of several people who simply rang up public affairs offices, identified themselves as employees of clients, or clients, and obtained free seats.

N.B. A final word about the theatre. If you're going to see a lot, £1.95 spent on a **Stubs Directory** (available at Tourist Information Offices and some bookstores) is a good investment. It contains the seating plans of most London theatres. You can ask for the best seats by specific row and number when you book your ticket.

Theatre

London now promotes itself as the 'theatre capital of the world', and, if not *quite* true, that is pretty close to the truth. With 40–50 West End theatres live at any time, and more than 60 fringe and repertory venues, not many places could hope to compete with the sheer volume and variety on offer, not to mention quality. British actors have the advantage of working on a small island in which the entertainment industry is centred on London — there's no separate New York and Hollywood — and most of Britain's top actors get plenty of experience in theatre, film and television. Playwrights and directors have many venues for dramatic and comedy works, and they don't have to worry so often (as their New York counterparts do) about critics' notices closing a show. Though tourists buy about 30 per cent of West End tickets, prices are low enough to attract a broad and enthusiastic local audience. Here's what's on offer.

West End

London's equivalent of Broadway is often called 'West End' because most of the theatres are located in the West End. The dividing line between West End and fringe can be rather blurred, but, apart from geography, fringe productions may be identified by price, quality of actors and experimental nature. Some new productions are first tried out in fringe theatres or the thriving British provincial theatre and arts festivals. When a play is showing in the West End, it has reached the top — and also commands higher prices. By world standards, these are, however, cheap — now ranging between £5 and £15 depending on the view. Blockbuster, sold-out productions may charge more (for hints on ticket buying, see above).

There are too many West End theatres to discuss most of them here. Many theatres are Victorian or Edwardian in design, and a delight in themselves. Each has a history and personality of its own. And if the production bores you, most theatres have a bar. Unfortunately, most theatres are not open to non-playgoers for casual inspection, but tours of some are available (see below).

National Theatre

Britain's **National Theatre Company** stages very high-quality plays with many world-famous actors in its home in the **South Bank** — an arts complex which includes the **Royal Festival Hall** and the **National Film Theatre** as well as the ugly big concrete modernist box that houses the 'NT' itself. This same building also houses useful bars, restaurants, bookstalls and art exhibitions, though we think the riverside location is itself a redeeming feature. The upstairs terrace has a very serene view over the Thames and city lights on a summer evening. Down below is a charming tree-lined river walk where from time to time there is something of a 'left bank' atmosphere, with book and print stalls.

For a pre-theatre meal, we much prefer the licensed self-service restaurant at the **National Film Theatre** next door, with its excellent salad bar and reasonably-priced wine. The NT is divided into three separate venues — the **Olivier**, the **Lyttleton**, and the smaller, more experimental, studio theatre, the **Cottesloe**. Discounts are available (see *Tickets* above).
South Bank SE1. Tel: 01-928 2252. U: Waterloo

Barbican Centre

Opened only in 1982, the **Barbican Centre** is a big building in an even larger Barbican complex that is almost Pentagon-like in its labyrinthine size and complexity. The main **Barbican Theatre** is the London home of the **Royal Shakespeare Company**. It has what is possibly the most advanced theatre design in the world: each row has its own side door and no one is further than 65 seats from the stage. The small **Barbican Pit** is a highly experimental studio theatre. You have to take the lift to get to its deep

basement location, and you could be forgiven for thinking you're entering a bomb shelter. There are two self-service restaurants and the **Cut Above** carvery. Our favourite is the small salad-oriented one on the mezzanine.
Silk Street EC2. Tel: 01-638 8891. U: Barbican or Moorgate

Mermaid
A small, well-designed modern theatre. Excellent light meals are served upstairs pre-peformance.
Puddle Dock EC4. Tel: 01-236 5568. U: Blackfriars

Old Vic
Once the home of the National Theatre, the charming Victorian interiors have been faithfully restored by the new owner, Canadian 'Honest Ed' Mirvisch.
Waterloo Road SE1. Tel: 01-928 7616. U: Waterloo

Palladium
This famous locale hosts mass-market spectaculars and variety shows — the kind of old-time entertainment enjoyed by Britain's royal family in the annual Royal Command Performance.
8 Argyll Street W1. Tel: 01-437 7373. U: Oxford Circus

Fringe
As we said above, it's sometimes hard to draw a line between West End and fringe — London's equivalent of off-Broadway. Fringe productions are sometimes lower quality than the West End, but not always — especially at those theatres mentioned below. Prices are often lower, productions less lavish and seating less salubrious — but you may have the opportunity to see a highly-experimental play that will later suddenly transfer to the West End and become a hit. Productions are not always well publicized: check *Time Out* and other magazines and newspapers.
    These are some of the more important locales:

Royal Court
Some people would say this old charmer on Sloane Square is not fringe, but it certainly serves the fringe ideal of presenting excellent new writing for short periods. Successful productions often transfer to the West End.
Sloane Square SW1. Tel: 01-730 5174. U: Sloane Square

Bush
Uncomfortable theatre, though famous for high-quality experimental plays, often from abroad.
Shepherds Bush Green. Tel: 01-743 3388. U: Shepherds Bush

Riverside Studios
This complex often presents plays with highly politically controversial themes.
Crisp Road W6. Tel: 01-748 3354. U: Hammersmith

Donmar Warehouse
A studio-type venue in rapidly-developing Covent Garden that often presents music- and dance-oriented productions.
41 Earlham Street WC2. Tel: 01-240 8230. U: Leicester Square

Hampstead
Similar in importance and prestige to the Royal Court, though in a modern complex that suffers from street noise.
Swiss Cottage Centre. Tel: 01-722 9301. U: Swiss Cottage

Lyric Hammersmith
Big name stars often appear in very serious productions that are somehow cheaper to stage in this modernized theatre.
King Street W6. Tel: 01-741 2311. U: Hammersmith

Young Vic
Studio-type, uncomfortable theatre-in-the-round presents plays that are too uncomfortably serious for its more famous older brother up the road.
The Cut SE1. Tel: 01-928 6363. U: Waterloo

Pub theatres
Few people know how much quality theatre is presented for love rather than money in tiny upstairs rooms of pubs by aspiring actors and actresses. Attending a pub theatre has a unique quality — perhaps a bar meal beforehand (if available), see a short performance, then have a pint afterwards with the players. Tickets are inexpensive. Some can be booked through the **Fringe Theatre Box Office** (see *Fringe*). More information can be obtained from **Pub Theatre Network**, 169 Battersea Park Road SW11, Tel. (01) 622 4553.
Some of the better known are:

Gate
Prince Albert pub, 11 Pembridge Road W11, Tel. 01-229 0707. Near many Notting Hill Gate restaurants. U: Notting Hill Gate.

Cafe Theatre
37 Charing Cross Road WC2. Tiny theatre above a pub in the heart of tourist London.

Old Red Lion
St John Street EC1. Room above a pub in trendy Islington.

Orange Tree
45 Kew Road, Richmond, Tel. 01-940 3633. Little, locally-supported pub opposite Richmond Station, with real ale on tap downstairs.

Open air

Open Air Theatre
Regents Park, Tel. 01-486 2431. This unusual theatre, similar to New York's 'Shakespeare in the Park', puts on popular Shakespeare and a musical on alternate summer evenings (June 1–September 10). Food available.

Tours of London theatres — Stage by Stage
Stage by Stage is a specialist in behind-the-scenes tours of London's theatres and famous productions like *Cats* and *Phantom*. The idea is the brainchild of actress Barbara Kinghorn, who recognized that many of us are curious about what happens before house lights go down and the curtain comes up, and that she was in a position to know. At the time, Barbara was 'resting' between acting jobs, and giving tours seemed ideal. As luck would have it, both the backstage business and the acting career took off simultaneously, so now the work is shared with other actor friends. Basically, her very personal guides explain how the theatre works, from props and costumes to lighting and sound. The history and architectural detail of each particular theatre is also revealed.
Stage by Stage, 59 Fairfax Road NW6, Book on Tel. 01-379 5822. Different London theatres can be visited, at a cost of £5 per tour. A few theatres require tickets to that evening's performance, which the company can also arrange. On Sundays, when London theatres are dark, walking tours of several nearby theatres are available.

Theatre trips out of town
Outer parts of London have good theatres that make an outing. You might want to go out earlier in the day, have a look around the attractions, a meal and a wander before the show. Or do the same, and take in a Saturday matinee.

Richmond
The **Theatre on the Green** (Tel: 01-940 0088) has West End previews, often with all-star casts. Have a look round the charming residential area around the Green, and the riverside and its pubs are not far away. Or visit the *Orange Tree* theatre above a pub opposite Richmond station (Tel: 01-940 3633).

Greenwich
The **Greenwich Theatre** has good repertory and classical productions. Crooms Hill. Tel: (01) 858 7755. BR: Greenwich.

Guildford
The **Yvonne Arnaud Theatre**, 40 minutes away from Waterloo Station by train, is a big 'feeder' to the London West End. On one recent date, five West End plays had started there. Top off a visit to this charming town with good, compact shopping, restaurants and historic buildings with a play at this waterside venue. Box office: (0483) 60191.

Films

Few cities can equal London in the range and number of films on offer, but those film fans who haven't been to London in a number of years will probably be disappointed in the current scene. Ten years ago, there were many more repertory cinemas, film clubs and opportunities to see some of the world's more obscure but excellent avant-garde experimental work. Video, high ticket prices and redevelopment of urban cinemas have killed off many of London's more interesting theatre venues like the **Paris Pullman**. Nevertheless, London remains an important film centre — but you need to know where to look.

The big cinemas around **Leicester Square** host the British premières of (mostly) American films and international block-busters. Shortly afterwards, these are exhibited in central London and outer areas, primarily by the major chains — **Odeon** and **Cannon**. Americans will generally find American films to be three to five months behind US releases. High-quality British, American and Continental films often spend a long time at the **Odeon Haymarket**, **Cannon Shaftesbury Avenue** or the **Curzon Mayfair** before going on more general release, but many small artistic successes have a short run at one of the small independent cinemas before becoming available for general release. Chains dominate the British film industry and this makes chances of success for quality, low-budget films small. London affords an opportunity to see many of these films, which are never shown in large parts of Britain and America unless later by local film societies. Every year in November, the city stages its own Film Festival.

Regular seat prices are high by world standards (£5 and more is not unusual for a seat at a new release). But, like film theatres in other countries, London cinemas often have cheap £2 evenings and lower matinee prices. Some independent cinemas are clubs, which require a yearly membership fee (30p–60p). This fee may also admit you to other memberships.

The **National Film Theatre** and some repertory theatres have programmes that change daily, or almost daily, so it's very important to check times and changes.

Some of the more important venues

The National Film Theatre
The NFT is situated on the South Bank beside the **National Theatre** and the **Royal Festival Hall** (U: Waterloo). The programme changes daily, with different features appearing simultaneously in its two cinemas. This allows a tremendously-varied diet of film, from early silents and art films to recent Chevy Chase comedies and James Bond. There is some emphasis on British cinema — enabling American visitors to catch some movies that neither come to US movie houses nor appear on American television — but no one type of film seems to predominate. Another reason for the NFT's popularity is that many old movies don't seem to fit on television. The NFT is just about always packed out whenever the widescreen epic *Lawrence of Arabia* is shown.

You have to be a member to buy a performance ticket, but foreign visitors can get a temporary monthly membership for £3.30 or weekly membership for 70p. Admission tickets to most films are £2.50. The NFT has a very pleasant little licensed restaurant and bar (though it can be crowded). Weekly London entertainment magazines usually carry details of current NFT performances.
South Bank SE1. Tel: 01-928 3232. U: Waterloo

Barbican Centre
Major releases and independent films are interspersed with classics and repertory theme programmes in the film theatre of this giant modern art complex.
Silk Street EC2. Tel: 01-638 8891. U: Barbican or Moorgate

ICA
A unique arts complex, set in John Nash's elegant Regency Carlton Terrace on The Mall. Cinema, art gallery, bar, theatre and café restaurant (recommended for light meals). The cinema has a good programme of new, cult and avant-garde and repertory classics. Worth the day membership of 50p just to enjoy the complex.
Nash House, The Mall SW1. Tel: 01-930 0493. U: Charing Cross

Independents and repertory

Renoir
Brunswick Square WC1. Tel: 01-837 8402. Frequently shows French and Continental films.

Screen
Baker Street 96 Baker Street NW1, Tel: 01-935 2772; **on the Green** Islington Green N1, Tel: 01-226 3520; **on the Hill** 230 Haverstock Hill NW3, Tel: 01-435 3366. Show quality recent and repertory films.

Gate
Notting Hill Gate W11. Tel: 01-727 4043. Shows many quality British films.

Lumerie
St Martin's Lane WC2. Tel: 01-836 0691.

Co-op
42 Gloucester Avenue NW1. Tel: 01-586 8516.

Everyman
Hollybush Vale NW3. Tel: 01-435 1525.

Phoenix
High Road East, Finchley N2. Tel: 01-883 2233.

Rio
Kingsland High Street E8. Tel: 01-254 6677.

Ritzy
Brixton Road SW2. Tel: 01-737 2121.

Riverside Studios
Crisp Road W6. Tel: 01-748 3354.

Scala
275–277 Pentonville Road N2. Tel: 01-278 0051.

Opera

Opera has become very fashionable in London during the last few years, and tickets are getting harder to obtain.

The Royal Opera at Covent Garden
The dressiest, snobbiest and most expensive (£43 a ticket — and more), but it does attract world-class superstars like Domingo and Pavarotti. Operas are presented in the original language in the traditional, formal atmosphere, though a few productions are surprisingly innovative. Discount standby tickets are available for some performances after 10am on the day, but availability may be strictly limited. If you're going to be just passing through London, it may be worthwhile to book far in advance. Even if you're not an opera fan, you might want to dress up and enjoy the splendid surroundings.
Bow Street WC2. Tel: 01-240 1066

English National Opera
Opera-going novices are more likely to enjoy the **English National Opera**. The distinctive feature of the ENO (as it's called) is that all productions are sung in English. After years of wondering what the fuss over opera was all about, I am now on the verge of becoming an opera fan. English makes all the difference, though purists will say that translation destroys the beauty and meaning of the original work. For me, it makes opera an accessible new discovery.

The use of the English language does not diminish the skill, creativity or innovation of the opera performers, directors and designers. It seems to enhance these qualities to a much expanded and very appreciative audience. Sets and costumes can be just as lavish, as in a recent performance of *Aida* — where the monumental Egyptian backgrounds were straight out of Cecil B. De Mille.

The ENO lives at the **Coliseum**, a huge and magnificent old theatre in St Martin's Lane (the heart of the theatre district). A good seat (dress circle) usually costs about £14 (another advantage of the ENO is that it's cheaper than the Royal Opera and *much* cheaper than the Metropolitan in New York). Avoid the cheapest balcony and upper circle seats — they can be cramped, hot and uncomfortable.
The Coliseum, 31 St Martin's Lane WC2. Tel: 01-836 3161. CC 01-240 5258

Sadler's Wells
Now mostly used for dance, but operas and touring companies sometimes perform in this theatre.
Rosebery Avenue EC1. Tel: 01-278 8916

D'Oyly Carte
The famous operetta company has been re-formed, but they are mostly away on
tour.
No permanent home as yet. Info on Tel: 01-405 2092

Dance

London has at least three highly-regarded ballet companies, plus the **London
Contemporary Dance Theatre** and a host of smaller fringe companies. During the
summer, these companies tour, and you may be as likely to see a prestigious visiting
company. See the weekly entertainment magazines for listings of the many small
dance events.

The Royal Ballet
Alternate performances with the **Royal Opera** at the Covent Garden **Royal Opera
House**. Classics have been the mainstay of this company, with interpretations by
top-class performers, choreographers and directors in very elegant surroundings.
Criticism that this company sticks with the tried and true have brought about more
innovation and contemporary works in recent years. Touring and experimental
companies also occasionally perform at the Opera House, especially in the summer.
Another Royal company, Sadler's Wells Royal Ballet, performs at Sadler's Wells
(below) when not touring.
Bow Street WC2. Tel: 01-240 1066

Ballet Rambert
A modern, innovative company over 50 years old. Performs regularly at **Sadler's
Wells**, but is frequently away touring.
Sadler's Wells Theatre, Roseberry Avenue EC1. Tel: 01-278 8916

The Festival Ballet
Like the Royal Ballet, mainly performs the classics, but at lower prices in the less
opulent **Royal Festival Hall** (again, when it is not touring).
South Bank SE1. Tel: 01-928 3191 or 928 8800

London Contemporary Dance Theatre
Performs modern and experimental dance.
Sadler's Wells (as above).

Fringe companies
These perform at locations like the **ICA, Donmar Warehouse, Riverside Studios** and
local arts centres.

Classical music

Classical music-lovers should plan ahead and come during the summer, when not
only London's major music venues but a host of spectacular events are available (see
Summer musical events). But London is a major world centre for classical artists at
any time. Locals and touring performers play to very enthusiastic audiences. In
addition, many London churches have excellent church music. Each Sunday a page
in the Arts Section of the *Sunday Times* provides a listing of classical concerts and
recitals. Again, listings are also available in the weekly entertainments magazines.

The South Bank Centre
Part of the South Bank arts complex, and known throughout the world for the superb
acoustics of the three halls, built in 1951 for the Festival of Britain. The largest is the

Festival Hall, for full symphony concerts. The **Queen Elizabeth Hall** is much smaller, and the little **Purcell Room** houses chamber groups, recitals, readings and lectures. Ample restaurant, bar and shop facilities, but again we prefer the little self-service restaurant next door at the **National Film Theatre** — especially on warm summer evenings when you can sit outdoors at candle-lit tables.
South Bank SE1. Tel: 01-928 3191 or 928 8800. U: Waterloo

The Barbican Centre
The new home of the **London Symphony Orchestra** has a controversial design and, some say, unsatisfactory acoustics that are still not perfect, but many people enjoy concerts in the hall of this huge complex (see *Theatres*).
Silk Street EC2. Tel: 01-638 8891. U: Barbican or Moorgate

Wigmore Hall
The place where many artists make their London debut in a splendid Victorian building with excellent acoustics.
36 Wigmore Street W1. Tel: 01-935 2141. U: Bond Street

St John's, Smith Square
A splendid Baroque church converted to a mostly chamber music hall. Downstairs in the crypt is the excellent and cheap **Footstool Restaurant**. Near Westminster Abbey and the Houses of Parliament.
Smith Square W1. Tel: 01-222 1061. U: Westminster

Nightlife and clubs

Before going any further, you should be aware of the following factors:

● London has some high-quality nightclubs, but most of the best have strictly-enforced membership policies. Overseas visitors should try applying in advance for temporary membership.

● A number of the heavily-advertised places are clip-joints or 'Gentlemen's Clubs'. Much of the clientele consists of lonely businessmen paying extortionate prices to sit and sip champagne with fast-drinking, fast-disappearing hostesses.

● Like many cities, London's discos are heavily dominated by the 18 to 40 age group. In some places you may feel old if you're over 30.

● Some places operate 'dress codes' at the door. These can vary. Some reject people in evening dress because they're not 'interesting' enough. Casual smart or perhaps 'casual elegant' are the safest looks to get you into most discos and nightclubs.

● Many venues may have a different style — both music and lifestyle — on different nights of the week, so it pays to check with them or with the listings in magazines like *Time Out*.

● Because much of London's public transport closes down between midnight and 1am, you'll probably have to take a taxi home, so don't spend all your money.

● Nightlife is a fast-changing scene, both in terms of the reputation of various clubs and their very existence. The clubs mentioned below are better known and established than many, but by the time you read this, even they may be on the way 'out'. Phone before you go.

Private clubs (exclusive)

Annabel's
Probably London's most exclusive and (even more likely) most expensive club. A gossip columnist's dream: a lot of 'top' people take their non-spouse lovers here. A very discreet, sedate place to see and be seen. It is something of an achievement to be admitted without being accompanied by a member. If you are an overseas visitor, try applying (with your passport) at least a week in advance for a three-week temporary membership.
44 Berkeley Square W1. Tel: 01-629 3558. U: Bond Street. Mon–Sat 2030–0400

Private clubs (less exclusive)

Legends
Once a show-biz hangout, but now mostly an international clientele in this Hollywood-style nightspot.
27 Old Burlington Street W1. Tel: 01-437 9933. Mon–Sat 2230–0300

Tramp
Go for a voyeuristic look-around if invited to see this young club-disco scene. Now easier to get in.
40 Jermyn Street W1. Tel: 01-734 3174. Mon–Sat 2230–0400

The Hippodrome
One of two London nightclubs belonging to entrepreneur Peter Stringfellow. If you're young and stylishly-dressed, they'll probably let you in. Might be worth a visit for the lavish (well, frankly, glitzy!) high-tech decor with laser shows, giant videos, several bars and a disco floor. Expensive drinks charges — presumably you pay for the cost of the expensive surroundings.
Cranbourn Street WC2. Tel: 01-437 4311. Mon–Sat 2130–0330

Stringfellows
The Hippodrome's more up-market, fussier sister-club. Harder to get into, basic requirement is more expensive, stylish dress. Also flashy (boasts a spectacular light show) and shamelessly vulgar. Today's version of swinging 60s London.
16–18 Upper St Martin's Lane WC2. Tel: 01-240 5534. Mon–Sat 2000–0330

Discos
Most Londoners are neither chic enough nor rich enough to hang out in fashionable private clubs. Discos have been, and continue to be, the meaning of nightlife for many young people. Many of the better discos are 'clubs' (selective about who they let in); others impose a cover charge. Like clubs, discos constantly change in popularity, clientele and reputation. These are some of the most enduring rather than the most chic or trendy. Phone first — some nights are private parties.

Cafe des Artistes
Smoky dungeons filled with people from all walks of life eating pizzas and hamburgers and listening to varied music.
66 Fulham Road SW10. Tel: 01-352 6200. 2030–0200

Empire Ballroom
Huge disco, popular with the very young and tourist clientele.
Leicester Square WC2. Tel: 01-437 1446. U: Leicester Square. 2000–0200

Gulliver's
This spot has been around for years. Oriented towards nostalgia and American food and soul music.
11 Down Street W1. Tel: 01-499 0760. U: Green Park. 2100–0330

Limelight
Sister to The Hippodrome and Stringfellows, but a disco rather than a membership club. Air-conditioned, with a sushi bar, dance floor and good acoustics. One of the higher-class non-membership places.
136 Shaftesbury Aven W1. Tel: 01-434 1761. U: Leicester Square. 2100–0330

Maximus
This used to be down-at-heel, now it's a trendy place. Good laser show, funky music. Popularity and central location, rather than snobbishness, can make it hard to get into. Cover charge.
14 Leicester Square WC2. Tel: 01-734 4111. U: Leicester Square. 2000–0300

The Park
Upmarket, ultra-modern disco with restaurant catering to a rather older crowd than usual.
38 Kensington High St W8. Tel: 01-938 1078. U: High Street Kensington. 2100–0330

Samantha's
A London institution that has endured since its 1960s heyday. A number of the clientele seem to have been coming since then too . . .
3 New Burlington St W1. Tel: 01-734 6249. U: Green Park. 2030–0330

Wag Club
Trendy, hip place, with an eclectic selection of music from current styles.
35 Wardour Street W1. Tel: 01-437 5534. U: Piccadilly Circus. 2030–0330

Floor and strip shows
By popular demand, here are some male-oriented 'girlie' type places. Personally, I'd advise you to save your money (very hard to do once they've got you in the door) — but to each his (if not her) own.

Raymond's Revue Bar
Pretty much a straightforward lavish strip show, rather than a haunt of B-girls. Three people I know (male and female) thought it was 'good for a laugh', because it's somewhat self-mocking. Two or three shows each evening.
Brewer Street W1. Tel: 01-734 1593. U: Piccadilly Circus

Eve
Cabaret, dancing, drinks and restaurant. 'Charming multi-lingual female dining and dancing companions.' You get the idea?
189 Regent Street W1. Tel: 01-734 1585. U: Piccadilly Circus

The Stork Club
Glittery cabaret show with food and drink.
99 Regent Street W1. Tel: 01-734 3686. U: Piccadilly Circus

Gaslight Club
Similar to Eve, above.
4 Duke of York Street W1. Tel: 01-930 4950. U: Piccadilly Circus

Dine and dance restaurants
For some unfathomable reason, London lacks the cafés with music which you can find on the Continent — lively with people of all ages and in good spirits, where couples drift in, in the evenings, without booking, have a meal or a drink or two, and get up and dance. Nevertheless, London has a few places for those over 40 who don't like flashy discos or girlie floor shows and may find dinner dancing more to their liking. Falling somewhere between the formality of West End hotels and the informality of Continental cafés-with-music are restaurants — all run by Italians, incidentally — where you can enjoy good food, dance until 2 or 3 in the morning and not ruin yourself into the bargain.

The River Restaurant
Famous for the past 50 years for its dinner dances. It offers a view of the River Thames, the food is recommendable and there is live music into the 'small hours' — i.e. as long as there are guests on their feet and dancing. Some nights are relatively quiet.
Savoy Hotel. Strand WC2. Tel: 01-836 4343

The Ritz Hotel
More conservative with their dinner dances here, confining them to Friday and Saturday nights, with dancing to live music from a quartet.
Piccadilly W1. Tel: 01-493 8181

Concordia Notte
Although this white-washed, arched, Roman-style downstairs restaurant near Paddington Station attracts a share of film and television personalities because a romantic quartet, alternating with two guitarists, provides music for dancing every night, it is not expensive in London terms — a night out for two can cost less than £50.
29–31 Craven Road W2. Tel: 01-402 4985. U: Paddington. 2030–0200

Barbarella 1
Barbarella 2
Run by notably charming Neapolitan twin brothers, the two **Barbarellas** are lively, romantic and colourful, with the dance floor (dancing to disco) encased in glass so that the music doesn't overwhelm the diners. A popular late-night rendezvous for up-and-coming showbiz people, the food (mainly Italian) is excellent and varied, and the bill under £60 for two.
428 Fulham Road SW6. Tel: 01-385 9434
43 Thurloe Street SW7. Tel: 01-584 2000. Mon–Sat 1930–0300 (last orders 1am)

Villa dei Cesari
Dine and dance beside the river to pop tunes and eat good Italian food.
135 Grosvenor Road SW1. Tel: 01-828 7453

Royal Roof
Middle-of-the-road music on top of the Royal Garden Hotel.
Royal Garden Hotel. Kensington High Street W8. Tel: 01-937 8000

Elephant on the River
Very similar to and rivalling the Villa dei Cesari.
129 Grosvenor Road SW1. Tel: 01-834 1621

Tea dancing
One of London's truly nostalgic experiences. The Ritz has, unfortunately, stopped its highly regarded Sunday afternoon tea dances, but two excellent venues remain.

Take a partner and ballroom dance to between-the-wars music and later easy-listening tunes. Or just face the music and enjoy your tea. At both it's best to book.

Café de Paris
3 Coventry Street W1. Tel: 01-437 2036. Wed, Sat, Sun 1500–1745. £2.80 admission.

Waldorf Hotel
Aldwych WC2 Tel: 01-836 2400. Fri, Sat, Sun 1530–1830. £9.50 set price.

Old time music hall

Players' Theatre
One of the few places where the tradition of old time music hall (similar to US vaudeville) has been kept vibrantly alive is the **Players' Theatre**, a London club behind Charing Cross station — a locale that formerly housed the famous **Gatti's Under-the-Arches Music Hall.**

Although **Players'** is a club with over 6000 members, anyone can join as a 'temporary member' for a week. A visit is worthwhile just to see the theatre itself, which the club strives to maintain in keeping with Victorian taste — original red-plush spendour and large round drink tables interspersed in each spacious row of auditorium seats. Two old-fashioned bars dispense a variety of drink and old-fashioned food: 'Members and guests may remain in the bar at the back of the auditorium during the show'. A charming traditional 'supper room', open before and after each performance, looks a bit like **Rules** (see *Restaurants*) and its menu includes old English favourites like steak and kidney pie at £3.95, mixed grill at £6.75, or a three course set dinner featuring roast beef and Yorkshire pudding.

It sounds touristy, but it's not. On the night I went, most of the audience were regular members and their guests. As always, it was MC'd by 'The Chairman' Dominic Le Feu — a jolly but dignified white-haired and goateed character in grey tails. And, as it has for the last 50 years, the show opened with a toast to 'the Queen' — who turned out to be Victoria. Everyone in the audience gets song sheets; the show always begins with a chorus of *Covent Garden in the Morning and Oh, the Fairies.*

Singers and comedians are costumed from a vast collection of authentic Victoriana that has been amassed over the years. Songs are interspersed with two intervals and The Chairman's own monologues, in which he invites questions and comments from the audience — always managing to respond with a put-down or a piece of self-mockery. Overseas visitors are asked to make themselves known and The Chairman responds to them in accordance with Victorian tradition.

Performances: Tues–Sat 2030; Sun 2000. Theatre opens 1800 (Sun 1845). Dinner from 1830; last orders 2315; bar closes midnight. Box office open from 1000. Temporary membership £6 (good for one week's entrance). Annual membership £17.50. Each guest £5.
Villiers Street WC2 Tel: 01-839 1134. U: Embankment or Charing Cross (May still be at a temporary home at Duchess Theatre Katharine Street WC1 — check)

Jazz clubs

Ronnie Scott's
Not cheap, but top-notch acts change frequently, and the famous jazz club atmosphere makes for one of London's best evenings out. A 'we're all friends here' ambience has been promoted from the beginning by the legendary Scott, well known for his between sets bad puns and excellent tenor sax solos. The food is pretty

unexciting, but you may not notice, and by the end of the evening you may even forget the expensive cover charge, too.
47 Frith Street W1. Tel: 01-439 0747 for reservations. U: Leicester Square

100 Club
If you can't afford Ronnie Scott's, try this club on a jazz-oriented night. Also a friendly place with poor food. Cover charge, but both this and the bar are cheaper than Ronnie Scott's.
100 Oxford Street W1. Tel: 01-636 0933 (call beforehand — some nights are rock or reggae). U: Tottenham Court Road

Inexpensive restaurants with entertainment

Terraza Est
Opera singing at the 'Spaghetti Opera', with good-value set Italian meals.
109 Fleet Street EC1. Tel. 01-353 2680 U: Blackfriars

Break for the Border
Tex-Mex food. Loud C&W bands.
5 Goslet Yard, W1. Tel. 01-437 8595. U: Tottenham Court Road

Jazz Café
Wine bar with good live and recorded jazz.
56 Newington Green N16. Tel: 01-359 4936. Bus 73 or 141

The following pizza places also have good live jazz:

Pizza Express
10 Dean St W1. Tel: 01-437 9595

Kettner's
24 Romilly St W1. Tel: 01-437 6437

Pizza on the Park
11 Knightsbridge SW1. Tel: 01-235 5550

Tourist nightclubs
These offer some kind of atmospheric 'English' evening. *Tiddy Dol's* is in a class of its own, and several businesspeople I know consider it a good wholesome place to entertain foreign customers who *don't* want the £100 bucket of champagne and hostess-type place. For the rest of the selections, suspend your critical faculties (with the help of plenty of 'grog' or mead) and go and enjoy yourself.

Tiddy Dol's
See *Restaurants*

The Old Palace
Elizabethan banquet in a real Tudor palace. Price includes transport by coach.
Hatfield House, Herts. Tel: 01-837 3111

Shakespeare's Feast
Entertainment by jugglers and the like during six-course banquet in town.
Blackfriars Lane EC4. Tel: 01-408 1001. U: Blackfriars

1520 AD Tudor Rooms
Similar to the above two entries.
17 Swallow Street W1. Tel: 01-340 3978. U: Green Park

Comedy clubs
Foreign visitors may not always understand British humour — but laughter is contagious!

The Comedy Store
Two shows on Friday and Saturday night.
28a Leicester Square WC2. Tel: 01:839 6665. U: Leicester Square

Jongleurs
Good-quality cabaret and good food.
Lavender Gardens SW11. Tel: 01-585 0955. BR: Clapham Junction

Many pubs also feature comedy acts. See the weekly entertainment magazines for listings.

Music pubs and small clubs
Much of London's rock, folk and jazz music scene (as well as fringe theatre and comedy) is to be found in pubs. Many musicians get their start in such places, playing for next-to-nothing to an audience that may pay nothing more than higher beer prices. On a good convivial evening, the atmosphere can be special, and makes for a cheap, memorable, intimate evening out. Many pub and small club music listings appear in the entertainment magazines. Check before you go.

Bull's Head
Riverside pub with nightly jazz. Sometimes also at lunchtime with food and a river walk afterwards.
Barnes Bridge SW13. Tel: 01-876 5241

Caernarvon Castle
Established rock place near Camden Lock.
7 Chalk Farm Road NW1. Tel: 01–485 7858

Cock Tavern
Well-known folk club-pub.
27 Great Portland Street W1. Tel: 01-737 0107

Greyhound
Rock.
175 Fulham Palace Road W6. Tel: 01-385 0526

Half Moon
A riverside pub popular for modern jazz and 60s rock.
93 Lower Richmond Road SW15. Tel: 01-788 2387

Hare & Hounds
Country and R&B.
181 Upper Street N1. Tel: 01-326 2992

King's Head Islington
Attractive pub with folk and rock band as well as theatre.
115 Upper Street N1. Tel: 01-226 1916

Oporto
Modern jazz.
168 High Holborn WC1. Tel: 01-474 4609

Pied Bull
Jazz and folk.
1 Liverpool Road N1. Tel: 01-226 8180

Tunnel Club
Modern and African jazz.
338 Tunnel Avenue SE10. Tel: 01-858 0895

Casinos

Many visitors are surprised to learn that gaming Las Vegas or Monte Carlo style is legal in Britain so long as you do it in a 'club'. What is a 'club'? The definition can be very elastic, from the very exclusive to the easy-membership place owned by one of the big betting shop chains. With regulations tightening up and ownership in flux, we'd prefer not to recommend any casinos. The **Ritz**, **Crockfords**, the **International**, and **Aspinall's** are the most famous. The **Playboy Club Casino** has lost its license. Ask at your hotel or call the betting shop chains (casinos are not allowed to advertise). All casinos require membership at least 48 hours in advance.

The gay scene

Like 'straight' nightlife, much revolves around pubs and clubs, and just as often, the scene is always changing. To find out the latest, check the gay sections in the weekly entertainment magazines, or phone **01-837 7324** for the **Gay Switchboard**, a 24-hour advice and information service. **LL&GC** (London Lesbian and Gay Centre) is open evenings at 67 Cowcross Street EC1, Tel: 01-608 1471, U: Farringdon. Earl's Court is an area with many gay bars and activities.

Gay clubs

Club Copa
Gay men's drinking club with light meals and disco. Inexpensive membership fee.
180 Earl's Court Road SW5. Tel: 01-373 3407. U: Earl's Court

Heaven
Aims to be a flashy gay men's version of certain enormous straight clubs. Probably London's most famous and popular gay disco and club. No membership fee. Tues–Sat 2200–0300 except Thursday.
Underneath the Arches. Villiers Street WC2. Tel: 01-839 3852. U: Charing Cross

Spats
Non-stereotyped bar and disco.
37 Oxford Street W1. Tel: 01-437 7945. U: Tottenham Court Road

Gay restaurants

The Locomotion
Light meals in diner and bar. Some vegetarian meals. Green chrome and pink meeting place for the gay community.
18 Bear Street WC2. Tel: 01-839 3252. U: Leicester Square

Gay pubs

The Bell
Young, mixed and busy.
239 Pentonville Road N1. U: King's Cross.

Bolton's
Big Victorian pub on three floors. Mostly male.
216 Old Brompton Road SW5. U: Earl's Court

Brief Encounter
Smart-looking crowded men's bar.
St Martin's Lane WC2. U: Charing Cross

The Fallen Angel
Mixed popular pub with vegetarian food. Women only Tuesday and Saturday.
65 Graham Street N1. U: Angel

King's Arms
Central friendly gay men's pub.
23 Poland Street W1. U: Oxford Circus

The Duke of Wellington
Friendly, with live entertainment. Mixed.
119 Balls Pond Road N1. U: Highbury then bus

Sports

Both newspapers and weekly entertainment magazines have extensive coverage of
sports events. Major venues are:

Athletics

Crystal Palace
Ledrington Road SE19. Tel: 01-778 0131. The major location. Smaller venues are:

Battersea Park
Albert Bridge SW11. Tel: 01-622 2263

West London
Du Cane Road W12. Tel: 01-749 5505

Cricket

Lords
St John's Wood NW8. Tel: 01-266 2099

Oval
Kennington Oval SE11. Tel: 01-735 4911

Where the famous Test Matches are played. But these can last for days. If you have
little knowledge of the game, you're better off at a one-day trophy or cup. Or watch a
local 'village' team.

Football (soccer)

Matches are held at leading club grounds during most of the year, but especially in
the winter. Call one of these clubs for details:

Chelsea (Tel: 01-385 5545)

Fulham (Tel: 01-736 6561)

West Ham (Tel: 01-472 2740)

Golf
Most courses are private, but visitors can often pay a green fee. This is usually preferable to public courses, which are very crowded. Because visitor policies are always changing, we'd prefer not to recommend a course and then see policies quickly changed after a deluge of visitors. If you belong to a club at home, it helps to bring a letter of introduction.

Horse racing
For general daily recorded information, ring **(0898) 500 300.**

Ascot
Flat and jump racing. Trains from Waterloo.

Epsom
Flat racing. Trains from Victoria

Kempton
Steeplechasing and flat racing. Trains from Waterloo.

Sandown Park
Steeplechasing and flat racing. Trains from Waterloo and Esher.

Rugby (union)
The big matches are at **Twickenham**, across the river from Richmond. Trains from Waterloo. Great atmosphere at match and surrounding pubs. Season is October–April.

Swimming
Open-air swimming is available at the **Serpentine** in **Hyde Park**, and in **Hampstead Heath**. Most boroughs have indoor municipal pools. (See also *Activities: Baths.*) My local favourite is:

Kensington Sports Centre
Walmer Road W11. Tel: 01-727 9747. U: Ladbroke Grove

Tennis
Tournaments are on at several London locations throughout spring and summer. For this and Wimbledon information call the **All England Lawn Tennis Association** on **01-946 2244,** and see *Events* (below). If you want to play, there are hundreds of municipal courts, or you may be able, as a visitor, to get temporary membership in one of the many indoor clubs. It doesn't hurt to ask, but we would endanger the privilege if we mentioned any names.

Special summer musical events

Glyndebourne
Tickets to this summer opera season held in idyllic lakeside settings at Lewes, Sussex, are virtually impossible to obtain. Most go to members of the Society (15-year waiting list) or company sponsors. Phone **(0273) 812321** early in the year to find out the date when telephone bookings begin. Later, call the box office **(0273) 541111** to check for returns. May–August.

Kenwood and Marble Hill House
Provides something of the experience of Glyndebourne with concert music and lakeside picnicking in Hampstead Heath. 10,000 tickets available for each of the 13

summer Saturday evening performances. A similar concert series is now held at Marble Hill House in Twickenham. (Info on 01-734 1877 bookings from **English Heritage** 01-379 4444)

The Proms

The famous concerts at the Royal Albert Hall from late July to September. To go to the famous last night, you now have to attend five previous concerts. Otherwise, watch it on TV for a true British experience. Season and individual tickets from **Proms Box Office, Royal Albert Hall, London SW7**. Tel: 01-589 8212.

Annual London and Nearby Events

(and how to get tickets)

Many people time their visits to coincide with London's big events like **Wimbledon**, royal ceremonies, the **Chelsea Flower Show** or **Crufts**. This can be doubly rewarding, but don't assume that tickets will be available. Some events are no problem, but others need advance planning, acquaintance with the right people or an awful lot of money (for the telephone numbers of the scalpers see *Getting Tickets* at the beginning of this section). Precise dates change each year, so we've given only the months. Foreign visitors may also be able to get tickets and general information from **British Tourist Authority** offices abroad.

Annual **Gun Salutes** take place on 6 February, 21 April, 2 June, 10 June and 4 August at Hyde Park and the Tower of London (if the date falls on a Sunday, the event is held on the next day). The **Ceremony of the Keys**, locking the main gate of the Tower of London, takes place nightly at 2150 hours. Passes are free of charge. Send a stamped, self-addressed envelope or reply coupons in advance to **The Resident Governor, Queen's House, HM The Tower of London, EC3N 4AB**.

January

The International Boat Show

Held at Earl's Court. For a small admission fee, payable at the door, the public is allowed to roam around glamorous yachts and spiffy little dinghies and see demonstrations. Usually early in the month.

The sales

London's big after-Christmas sales, the best bargain time of the year, continue at London department stores and shops. **Harrods** is usually the last to start, around the beginning of the second week.

February

Crufts

One of the world's largest and most important dog shows. Over 117 different breeds are shown in four days of events, exhibitions and competitions. Since 1892 this show has attracted dog trainers and fanciers from all over the globe. Tickets are available at the door at Earl's Court, but advance and reserve main ring seats can be obtained from **Crufts Dog Show**, 1 Clarges Street W1, Tel: 01-493 6651. They can also give information about hotel discounts for Crufts visitors. Usually mid-month.

March or April

Chelsea Antiques Fair

Visitors as well as dealers are welcome at this very high-quality fair held in the **Old Town Hall**, Chelsea SW3. A small admission fee allows an enjoyable browse. Usually about ten days from mid- to late March. A season of antique fairs all over Britain starts in spring and lasts through to midsummer.

Ideal Home Exhibition
The general public flocks to this massive exhibition at Earl's Court. Surprisingly, a number of American subscribers have enjoyed it as an opportunity to see new ideas in home life on this side of the pond. Mid-March.

Oxford–Cambridge Boat Race
Visitors often confuse this rowing race with the **Henley Regatta**, which takes place in the summer and the similar **Head of the River Race**, held a week before. This event is much more low-key, although it is avidly watched by many people. Anyone can watch from a bank of the Thames. Usually the day before Easter.

Easter
London is no longer the capital of a church-going country, and you don't see much Easter finery. A fun, informal **Easter Parade** has become a tradition in Battersea Park. Live music, dancing and events on boats in the Thames.

London Marathon
The Marathon is fun for the runners, but is not yet much of a festival. Usually mid-April.

May

The Chelsea Flower Show
An amazing event in which the national passion for gardening comes into full flower. Crowd demands on the many display tents have led the show's organizer, the **Royal Horticultural Society**, to impose limits. The first two days are for members only. The last two days are for the general public, but it is now thought unlikely that any tickets will be available at the gate. Apply early to the Society at Vincent Square SW1, Tel: 01-834 4333. The society welcomes members regardless of nationality. Rates (at last notice) were £14 single member, £24 for two plus £5 enrolment fee. Member tickets to the show were £8 for member days and £5 for general public days. Non-member tickets £14 (Thursday) and £10 (Friday). Usually late May.

Football Association Cup
Held at Wembley Stadium. Almost impossible to get tickets.

Arts festivals
Take place in Brighton and Bath.

Glyndebourne Opera
Festival until the end of August (see *Special Summer Music Events*).

June

Royal ceremonies: Trooping the Colour; Beating the Retreat
Colourful ceremony on horseback, celebrating the Queen's birthday (two months late). You need to apply for tickets by 1 March to **Brigade Major, Trooping the Colour**, Household Division Horseguards, Whitehall SW1A 2AX. Selection is by ballot (limited to two per application). If unsuccessful, you get tickets for the rehearsals on one of two Saturdays before. Or you can watch from TV's excellent vantage point. Usually first or second Saturday of June. Tickets for **Beating the Retreat** (colourful military ceremonies held a week or two before) are available at the end of April from the **Premiere Agency**, 18 Bridge Street SW1, Tel: 01-839 6815.

Royal Ascot and Epsom Derby
These are society horse race meets, at which, aside from some expensive tours, the finery can only be viewed from the grandstand. Grandstand tickets are usually not difficult to come by in advance. A limited number of tickets to the Ascot Royal Enclosure are available to the US and other Embassies for their nationals. More information on **Ascot (0990) 22211** or **Epsom (03727) 26311**.

Royal Henley Regatta
Another big event of the society 'season' takes place at Henley-on-Thames, 60 miles from London, where expensively-dressed people gather to watch the boat races. Tourists are generally unwelcome in the enclosures, though several expensive tours go there. Ticket information: **The Secretary, Regatta, Henley, Oxfordshire RG9 2LY**, Tel: (0491) 572153.

Wimbledon
The world's most famous tennis tournament takes place from *about* June 20 to July 4. The obvious and cheap way to get Centre Court or Court Number 1 tickets is by public ballot. You apply to the **All England Lawn Tennis and Croquet Club**, P.O. Box 98, London SW19, Tel: 01-946 2244, between October 1 and December (enclosing a stamped self-addressed envelope or reply coupons) for the next year's tournament. Or you can get them in advance through the US offices listed in *Getting Tickets* at the beginning of this section. Ticket holders who must leave early may drop their tickets into special boxes and these are then resold at £1 each. If you're unlucky at getting advance tickets, you can queue outside for a ticket to enter the grounds and see matches on any of the courts where there are spare seats (or room to stand). Sometimes you can see jolly good matches, as well as enjoy the atmosphere at the pavilions. Scalpers sell tickets to the finals and semi-finals for hundreds of pounds.

Summer sales
London's stores' other big sales begin in mid-June and last into July, with **Harrods** usually starting around the beginning of the second week.

Arts festivals
Aldeburgh and Greenwich.

July

The Royal Tournament
Annual show of military bands and acrobatics. Tickets usually available, but advance information can be had from BTA offices abroad; or write to **The Royal Tournament**, Horseguard Parade, Whitehall SW1A 2AX, Tel: 01-930 4288.

Arts festivals
City of London, Cambridge, Chichester, Chester, Cheltenham and King's Lynn.

Henry Wood Promenade Concerts (the Proms)
At the Royal Albert Hall until September (see *Special Summer Music Events*).

August

Edinburgh Festival
Admittedly, not near London — but as the British capital is fairly quiet in August, visitors should consider taking a trip to Scotland's capital and Europe's largest arts festival and fringe, with a dazzling array of shows, exhibitions and events.

Notting Hill Carnival
On the last weekend in August, festivities with colourful floats, costumes, food and events are staged by London's West Indian community.

September–October

Chelsea Craft Fair
Very high-quality crafts fair at the Chelsea **Old Town Hall**. For more information, contact **The Crafts Council**, 8 Waterloo Place, London SW1 Tel: 01-930 3107.

November

Guy Fawkes Day
5 November. Contact the **Tourist Board** for details of firework displays. Tel: 01-730 3488.

State Opening of Parliament
You can't see the impressive ceremony inside parliament (except on TV), but you can watch the Queen's procession and coaches *en route*. Ring **01-219 3107** to find out this year's date.

London to Brighton Veteran Car Run
Various festivities, especially in Brighton. First Sunday in November.

Lord Mayor's Show
Watch the coaches and the pageantry through City streets and along the Strand. Second Saturday in November.

December

Christmas
Festivities in several locales. There are ceremonies for the lighting up of the Christmas tree in Trafalgar Square, and the Regent and Oxford Street Christmas lights. Christmas carollers in Trafalgar Square, Westminster Abbey and many churches. Foreign visitors should also investigate the many Christmas or New Year breaks available from London and country hotels.

New Year
Celebrations in Trafalgar Square — mostly for the young.

10　*Going shopping*

There are few things you can't buy in London if you're willing to search, browse and ask. Even if not in stock, a number of legendary stores and shops (especially **Harrods**) can find it, or have it made for you, if the price is right. London shoppers will encounter the same basic difficulty as sightseers: there is no centralized area, and so a search for a particular item can involve several expensive taxi trips or exhausting tube journeys across town. Do your research first: use the telephone and narrow down the number of appropriate stores, shops or markets. Or take the easy option: pick a likely department store, area or street and spend most of your time there. Our chapter incorporates both these approaches, plus some suggestions for gifts and souvenirs, to help you enjoy your shopping time.

Five things foreign visitors should consider

1. Getting a discount: VAT sales tax
Sales tax on goods and services (including hotel and restaurant meals) is a hefty 15 per cent Value Added Tax, commonly known as VAT. If you are resident in the United States or Canada, or any other country outside the EEC, and are planning to leave the UK within three months, you can usually avoid paying the tax on goods you take or send home. All major stores and most shops of any size are well-versed in helping foreign visitors with this effective 15 per cent discount — the Personal Export Scheme. It can be done in two ways:

Over the Counter
The retailer furnishes a form and a self-addressed envelope. You take the goods with you. On departure, you must appear at a special customs counter beyond passport control with the goods. The form is sent back to the retailer, who sends you a refund cheque.

This cumbersome procedure is fraught with problems. Firstly, some shops refuse to operate this scheme unless your purchases total over a certain amount. Secondly, you can't check your purchases in with your bags, since they must be presented *after* passport control; so you are limited by airline hand baggage regulations. Thirdly, refund cheques are in sterling, so you may have to pay your local bank a hefty commission to change small cheques into dollars or other home currency.

There are two variations on this method which simplify the process a little. Some shops operate special arrangements with companies like **Tourist Tax Free Shopping**, which refund the purchaser in his own currency. Or, refund cheques can be sent to **New York Foreign Exchange**, 26 Broadway, New York NY10004, to get a cheque in US dollars with a minimal service charge.

Direct export
When dealing with a large (or reputable smaller) shop, you can make arrangements to pay only the discounted price (minus 15 per cent) and have the goods shipped direct to your home or other recipients abroad. The only disadvantages of this method are the shipping charges and the time you must wait for the goods when you get home, where duties may be higher because exemption limits may not apply. It might be cheaper and less trouble just to pay the VAT and take your purchase home in your luggage.

Tip
Take your passport with you when shopping, in case you do want to take advantage of the VAT discount. If the shop is willing, always pick up the documentation. Then choose whether it's worth all the hassle when you pack to go home. It's no skin off anybody's nose if you decide not to bother to reclaim the VAT.

2. Shipping home
Have you considered how you are going to get your purchases home?

Carry it with you
If you've got the space and are within accompanying baggage limits (check with your airline), then this is the least troublesome way. The purchase is there when you get home and you can check it through customs yourself without any shipping or agent fees.

Pack it and mail it yourself
Surface rates for small items aren't too bad. It's a good idea to buy regulation-sized boxes from post offices.

Have the retailer pack it and post it
As long as the retailer is reputable (both for honesty and careful packing), and shipping charges are moderate, you may prefer to have him send it direct to you. You will thus avoid the VAT and the hassle of packing and posting it yourself or paying someone else to do it. Surface mail to North America usually takes 6–8 weeks, but charges are moderate. Air mail is fairly expensive. If they plan to ship by any other method, ask whether you will have to pay a port agent to clear the item through home customs for you; this can add a hefty hidden charge.

Let your hotel handle it
Some head porters at major hotels are very knowledgeable and will pack and ship your purchases for a small charge *and* a nice tip.

Use an air courier
The major air couriers **Federal Express, DHL** and **Purolator** all have London offices. This is a very expensive method, but some people prefer to pay the price and get the goods within three days, without the delays and problems of international mail.

Packers and shippers
Several London companies specialize in packing and shipping. Look in the Yellow Pages under Shipping Companies or Shipping and Forwarding. Consult your hotel and read the newspaper ads. For large, bulky or heavy purchases, they'll probably recommend you to 'share-a-container' — you pay only for the space taken up — but shipment does not take place until a port destination container is filled. Shipment to US ports can take anything from two weeks to three months. Ask about port clearance charges at home which can add to the total. You usually save some of the fee by picking up the goods at the port of entry.

One of our writers uses a Kent firm, **Harrison Lennon & Hoy**, and swears by their reliability and skill in packing and their reasonable rates. For a small charge they will pick up anywhere in the London area, and provide a friendly, old-fashioned service. Address: 17 Mason Hill, Bromley, Kent BR2 9HY, Tel: 01-460 8535.

Excess baggage
The airlines usually charge 1 per cent of the first class fare for each kilo overweight. The **London Baggage Company**, 262 Vauxhall Bridge road, Tel: 01-828 2400 or (0293) 502 197 offers passengers an inexpensive alternative — usually about one fourth the airline rate — for air shipment to the USA.

Temporary storage
Companies like **Harrisons** and the **London Baggage Company** (above) also have temporary storage facilities. Check with them, and with the 'left luggage' facilities at the railway stations.

3. Return customs — US and Canada
Returning *US citizens* and residents are *each* allowed to bring back up to $400 worth of merchandise, duty free — provided they haven't been out of the country for less than 48 hours and haven't claimed the same exemption within the past 30 days. As part of the quota, only one litre of wine or liquor, 100 cigars and 200 cigarettes can be brought in duty free. Only one bottle of perfume can be brought in per person, if it is trademarked in the US. Antiques (defined as anything over 100 years old) can be brought back free of duty, but be sure to get a certificate from the dealer. Remember, people in the same party can pool their purchases to avoid duty. For more information, call **Customs Adviser, US Embassy**, Tel: 01-499 9000.

Residents returning to *Canada* after an absence of 7 days can claim up to $300 in Canadian funds for each calendar year abroad, plus 40 ounces of alcohol, 50 cigars and 200 cigarettes. For more information, call **Canadian High Commission**, Tel: 01-629 9492.

4. Clothing and measurements
British, American and European sizes can be different. Britain is switching over to the European metric system, but many measures are still imperial.

Men's suits
British and American sizes are the same, but American men may find the next size up to be more comfortable. The European equivalents (in brackets) are:

34 (44); 36 (46); 38 (48); 40 (50); 42 (52); 44 (54); 46 (56)

Men's shirts
Again the same, but British 'tall' shirts are rare. The European equivalents (in brackets) are:

(36) 14; (37) 14.5; (38) 15; (39) 15.5; (40) 16; (41) 16.5; (42) 17; (43) 17.5.

Men's shoes
The British equivalent is about one size smaller (i.e. a US 7 is a British 6) — but of course you'll have to try them on.

Women's dresses, coats, skirts, blouses and sweaters

British	9	10	11	12	13	14	15	16	17	18	19	20
American		7	8	9	10	11	12	13	14	15	16	17	18
Eur (French)	39	40	41	42	43	44	45	46	47	48	49	50

Women's shoes
You can use the table below — but it's a bad idea to buy without trying on.

American	4.5	5.5	6.5	7.5	8.5	9.5	10.5
British	3	4	5	6	7	8	9
European	35	36	37	38	39	40	41

5. A special note on the annual sales
To take advantage of London's best bargain periods, time your visit for the **last week in December to mid-January** (a bit later if you're interested in **Harrods'** sale), or the **last week in June to mid-July**. These dates are approximate. Those who want to be sure should phone the stores before making their travel arrangements. At these sales, discounts of 30–50 per cent are common on all kinds of merchandise. Not all stores have good sales. Among the best are: **Harrods, Harvey Nichols, Jaeger, Aquascutum** and **Selfridges**.

Tip
False pricing is illegal. You can check a bargain by looking at the price tag. Under the law, the original price must be displayed, though it might have a pen mark through it, along with the sale price. If it isn't, you know the item has been brought in specially for the sale (often marked Special Purchase).

Shopping tips

- We can't stress enough: if you're looking for a particular purchase, research first and narrow down your choice of shops, or pick a likely shopping street or area.

- For moderate-priced clothes, china, shoes, records and accessories, the easiest approach is to concentrate time and effort on **Oxford Street**, where most of the less expensive (and not a few of the more expensive) department stores, clothing and shoe shops are located or have branches.

- **John Lewis** is a quality but unexciting department chain owned by partner-employees. Their motto is 'never knowingly undersold'. For brand-name cutlery, china, duvets or perhaps hosiery (their own Jonelle brand), prices are very competitive.

- **Marks & Spencer** is the best place to buy good-quality, reasonably-priced sweaters and other woollens. Choice, once limited to solids and plain patterns, has expanded greatly in recent years, especially at their flagship store at Marble Arch.

- Check the price of brand-name china, silver or glassware in the department stores before buying in a smaller shop, particularly in central London.

- **Reject China Shops** discounts are now mostly based on volume sales and seconds from top brands rather than imperfections (often imperceptible anyway). Not always the cheapest, but close. Consider also a day trip to **Rochester** (see *Day Trips*). **Chinacraft** has a wide selection with not necessarily much more expensive prices.

- The best shopping prices are during the **January Sales** (after Christmas) and **Summer Sales** (mid-June–July). The earlier you go, the better the 'find' bargains. **Harrods** and **Liberty's** have some outstanding values.

- Many **tourist-oriented shops** now have **branches** in popular day-trip towns like Windsor and Bath. Shopping may be less frantic, but prices aren't that different.

- Department stores and shops in less-popular British towns and cities may sell woollens and brand-name goods at more affordable local prices. Local antique shops and art galleries may be more amenable to bargaining. They don't have London's huge volume of visitors who stay for long periods of time.

- You can avoid the exchange commission on cash or travellers' cheques if you use your credit cards — though it's a gamble if the rate becomes less favourable before the merchant turns in the charge.

- **Carnaby Street** is now a big tourist trap — a place of historic (1967) curiosity, souvenir shops and chain stores rather than fashion boutiques.

- Foreign visitors shouldn't miss the 15 per cent VAT discount — take your passport with you — and read *Five things foreign visitors should consider* at the beginning of this section.

- The mark-up on **postcards, souvenirs** and **soft drinks** in the central tourist area around Piccadilly Circus is outrageous. Cokes that sell for 25p elsewhere fetch 45p or 50p. Postcards that cost 20p at the post office are sold for as much as 50p. Buy cards and souvenirs away from main tourist areas.

- **Museum shops** have become more dynamic and enterprising. Some sell fascinating facsimiles of exhibits.

- For an unusual gift to take home, consider crafts from the craft centres or one of the national craft shops; old jewellery or bric-a-brac from one of the street markets; or one of the London Transport Museum Shop's fascinating old poster reproductions.

- When touring in the country, check your itinerary to see whether you're going to be near a factory outlet (for example, woollens in **Bradford**, china in **Stoke-on-Trent**) for lower prices.

- Watch your budget by separating window shopping for pleasure from serious purchase shopping. The same item you see in elegant, glorious and expensive Burlington Arcade, Jermyn Street or Bond Street might just be selling for quite a bit less in a department store.

Department and major stores

Department stores aren't necessarily the cheapest places to buy things, but they do provide an accessible place to check prices. When you are looking for brand-name china, glass or other popular wares, you might do well to price them in department stores, where prices are exposed to the mass public and therefore more competitive. Smaller shops can often be either a bargain or dramatically over-priced for tourists. At least three London department stores — **Harrods, Liberty's** and **Selfridges** — are world-famous tourist attractions in their own right. **Harrods** is entertaining for its very enormity and wide coverage. **Selfridges** is less elegant, though similarly vast. **Liberty's** handsome timbered interiors make it one of the world's most beautiful department stores, as well as the home of a quality style of fabric design.

Major stores

Aquascutum
Like Burberry's, **Aquascutum** is also on Regent Street and famous for its raincoats, whose price is now on a par with the competition. They sell a similar tweed and wool traditional look, but are more fashion-conscious. In the past they have left the distinct impression that, like Jaeger, they are for small-boned people. I now know a few more amply-proportioned satisfied customers. *Mon–Sat 0900–1730, Thur 0900–1900.*
100 Regent Street W1. Tel: 01-734 6090. U: Piccadilly Circus

BHS
Known as 'Home and Colonial' in the days of Empire, then British Home Stores, this chain began as something similar to Woolworths. Now it aims to be a quality mid-range retailer where clothing is affordable and mass-merchandisable. They still fall short of the high standards set in this area by Marks & Spencer as a home department store catering to Mr and Mrs Average Briton. Until recently, BHS has been of little interest to visitors, but we may see more changes now that the chain has been acquired by the Habitat group. *Mon–Sat 0900–1730.*
252 Oxford Street W1. Tel: 01-629 2011. U: Oxford Circus.
99 Kensington High St W8. Tel: 01-937 0919. U: High Street Kensington

Burberry's
Famous for the legendary raincoats, which have become an indisputable international status symbol. And there's the famous Burberry Look — hat, silk scarf, tan coat, sweater and plaid skirt, or corduroy trousers (supposedly what the aristocracy wears). Most people you see in the full 'look' turn out to be American or Japanese; wait till you get home to be admired. The Regent Street and Haymarket stores are not exciting places to shop — you can buy Burberrys and similar clothing in other major stores, so compare quality and prices. Their sales are also unremarkable. Basically sells variations on its own classic tradition. *Mon–Sat 0900–1730; Thur 0900–1900.*
165 Regent Street W1. Tel: 01-734 4060, and 18 Haymarket SW1. Tel: 01-930 3343. U: Piccadilly Circus

C&A
Want something inexpensive to replace the swimsuit, plain blouse, kid's clothing item that you've lost or ruined but need during your trip? Something reasonably fashionable that'll do, but not dear enough to make you care if it's dragged in and out of a suitcase or gets coffee spilled on it? This is the place — but look at Marks & Spencer first and compare prices. *Mon–Sat 0930–1800; Wed 0930–2000.*
505 Oxford Street W1. Tel: 01-629 7272. U: Marble Arch

Conran Shop
This new version of the former Conran's is becoming a tourist attraction in itself. One reason is the location — the beautifully-restored Art Deco Michelin building. The other is the range of well-designed, individualized furniture, carpets, housewares, glassware, fabrics and kitchen items by Jasper Conran and other top designers. The shop is part of the design empire of his father Sir Terence, and some of the standard **Habitat** merchandise is also on sale. The complex includes an oyster bar and bookshop, and **Whittards**, the famous Chelsea coffee and tea merchants, have moved into the basement. Stunningly presented. *Mon–Sat 0930–1800.*
81 Fulham Road SW1. Tel: 01-589 7401

Debenhams
Dazzling chain flagship store, with a little bit of everything. Many well-known labels and brands are on offer. Not the favourite store of anyone I know, perhaps because it tries too hard. Still, might be worth a visit for the range. *Mon–Wed, Fri, Sat 0930–1800; Thur 0930–1930.*
Oxford Street W1. Tel: 01-580 3000. U: Oxford Circus

Dickens & Jones
Dickens & Jones is a House of Fraser store. For those not in the know, this company used to belong to the late Sir Hugh Fraser, who managed to buy and standardize many family-owned department stores across the country (ruin them, said many critics). Now this, together with Harrods and 100 other stores in the chain, are owned by the Al-Fayeds, an Egyptian merchant family.

According to their plans, Dickens & Jones is to become the name and focal point for women's fashion in the chain, though fashion-conscious males will also be made welcome. Some household departments are being phased out. To attract the customers back and please the tourists, the store has been refitted in a traditional style. Regular patrons hope that prices will continue to be affordable. *Mon–Wed, Fri, Sat 0900–1730; Thur 0930–1900.*
244 Regent Street W1. Tel: 01-734 7070. U: Oxford Circus.

Fortnum and Mason
Fortnum and Mason is best known for its ground-floor food store selling luxurious super Englishy marmalades, jams, biscuits, teas, patés, and food specialities of all kinds. Emphasis is on beautifully-packaged food and wine as gifts or expensive souvenirs, rather than to take home to eat. The **Fountain Restaurant** is a favourite of mine for its delicious pastries and milkshakes. Downstairs and upstairs are departments selling antique furniture, elegant china, accessories, and women's wear. A confident impression is left that royalty and aristocracy shop here. They must have their needs delivered — all the customers I've seen are tourists, eager to live the legend. And why not? The staff in long-tails make it all quite believable. *Mon–Sat 0930–1730.*
181 Piccadilly W1. Tel: 01-734 8040. U: Piccadilly Circus

Harrods
Harrods is not always the most expensive, but it's far from the cheapest. There seems to be a certain premium for the status conferred by a Harrods purchase. People have been known to store cheap furniture with Harrods' delivery service for a month, just so neighbours could see it arrive in a green Harrods delivery van. Though it's true Harrods either has or can find just about anything a shopper could want, most of what's on offer is good quality and at least moderate to expensive in price.

If you want to be a Harrods man or woman, you'll find it all here — five restaurants, clothes, travel agent, Persian carpets, pets, china, glass, wines, hairdressers, theatre tickets, even a bank where many frequent American tourists keep a permanent

account. My two favourites are the pleasant well-stocked bookshop and the vast vaulted food hall, with every edible you can think of (do they really sell alligator meat *every* day?). Harrods is now being restored to former Edwardian glories by the current owners, the Egyptian Al-Fayed brothers. Avoid Saturdays — it's one big madhouse. The domed **Georgian Room**, though also vast, is a good place for an elegant set price roast lunch (no alligator). Harrods is a particularly easy and helpful store to arrange export of your purchases. Their sales usually start a week or two later than most of their competitors (usually beginning of the second week in July and several days into January) and offer good value — if you go early enough. *Open Mon–Fri 0900–1700; Wed 0930–1900; Sat 0900–1800.*
Knightsbridge SW1. Tel: 01-730 1234. U: Knightsbridge

Harvey Nichols
Next door to Harrods is this expensive, high-fashion and classic line department store. If you've just emerged from its neighbour, you'll quickly notice a change in atmosphere — smaller, quieter, more selective and elegant. For women especially, the store is a place to see a varied collection of designer fashion from a range of different houses under one roof. Also well known for glassware, oriental rugs, duvets and leather accessories. Not the place to look for a bargain. *Mon–Sat 0930–1800; Wed 0930–1900.*
Knightsbridge SW1. Tel: 01-235 5000. U: Knightsbridge

Jaeger
Usually more stylish men's and women's clothes than Aquascutum or Burberry's. Those who want the traditional English look in wool, but with more innovation and panache, will enjoy **Jaeger**. The men's clothes have a strong Italian influence, with a slim-fitting cut. The main Regent Street branch has a ground-floor designer boutique. *Mon–Sat 0930–1730; Thur 0930–1900.*
200 Regent Street W1. Tel: 01-734 8211. U: Piccadilly Circus

John Lewis; Peter Jones
These two stores are part of a national chain best known for its motto 'never knowingly undersold', which means that if you find goods bought at these stores for sale at lower prices elsewhere, they will refund the difference. They are also known for the fact that all sales people who stay long enough can become partners in the business.
The focus is on middle-market British homeowners rather than tourists, but the famous motto makes the store a must for the cost-conscious who are looking for a standard brand name or value for money in china, glassware, kitchenware, hosiery, luggage, linen, good children's clothes or beautifully-designed duvet covers. The stores also provide a good price guide for name or type shopping. Their own-brand Jonelle clothes are durable and good value, though often bland and unexceptional. Personnel seem to be either enthusiastic and knowledgeable, or totally indifferent. Have they been made partners yet? *Mon–Sat 0900–1730; Thur 0900–2030.*
Oxford Street W1. Tel: 01-629 7711. U: Oxford Circus; Sloane Square SW3. Tel: 01-730 3434. U: Sloane Square.

Liberty's
You want a souvenir or gift that reeks of England, yet is not cheap or tacky? Buy a Liberty-print tie, handkerchief or scarf in London's most beautiful department store well, not a complete department store — you can't buy a washing machine or shower-head). Emphasis is firmly on the famous Liberty's school of design, derived from the Victorian arts and crafts and Art Nouveau movements: soft colours and finest cotton floral prints in women's clothes and materials; delicately-made

glassware and china; well-tailored woollen men's suits; carpets and beautifully-crafted furniture. Quality is very high and prices tend in the expected direction, though you will find glass, pottery and fabric bargains in the basement. The two annual sales are excellent — scarves have been sold at 70 per cent off. And it costs nothing to wander through the store's civilized oak-panelled, dome-ceilinged splendours. Don't miss the antique furniture on the top floor, or the scent department. *Open Mon–Fri 0900–1730; Thur 0900–1900; Sat 0930–1730.* **Regent Street W1. Tel: 01-734 1234. U: Oxford Circus**

Littlewoods
Littlewoods has a larger range of low to moderately-priced clothing than most mid-range price chains. Their reputation has been pretty downmarket — somewhere between Woolworths and BHS — and despite improvements they are still not the equal of BHS, still less Marks & Spencer. *Mon–Fri 0930–1730; Thur 0930–1930; Sat 0900–1800.*
207 Oxford Street W1. Tel: 01-434 4301. U: Marble Arch

Marks & Spencer
A British institution: Margaret Thatcher and an astounding 70 per cent of the British buy their underwear at 'Marks' or 'M & S'. If you've ever noticed how British holidaymakers all seem to dress alike, it's probably because they all shopped at **Marks & Spencer**. What is the secret? The short answer is a reputation for high quality standards, developed through careful control and enlightened management with generous benefits for dedicated staff.

In the last ten years this 250-store chain has been slowly improving both the range and design of its clothing, as well as expanding other lines like food, books and fabrics. You still won't find high fashion, but you will no longer find unvarying solid styles and plain patterns. Woollens and knitwear are often stylish, understated, durable and very good value for money — there's probably no better place for the quality classic sweater. Foreign visitors looking for comfortable, attractive, moderately-priced clothing may find what's on offer more interesting than the locals do — after all, not everybody abroad wears it! My brother in Texas loves their patterned cotton sweaters — perfect for an English summer or a cool South Texas winter. And if you're renting a flat in London or just going on a picnic, it's hard to beat Marks' groceries, well-selected wines and prepared food.

The store does have one idiosyncrasy: you can't try clothes on (though no one seems to object if you quickly slip on a sweater for size). Instead, they have an enlightened returns policy: they'll refund your money for whatever reason — wrong size, colour, flaws or change of mind.

There are several branches in London, but go to the big, mad, Marble Arch branch for the largest range. No credit cards accepted (except their own). *Mon–Sat 0900–1730; Tues 0930–1730* (Marble Arch: *Mon–Fri 0900–2000; Sat 0900–1800*).
458 Oxford Street W1. Tel: 01-935 8954. U: Marble Arch

Selfridges
Among Londoners, **Selfridges** is known for its huge colonnaded front and spectacular window shows at Christmas time. Henry Gordon Selfridge, an American promoter and showman, founded the store in 1909, using marketing techniques he learned at Marshall Field in Chicago. Today Selfridges is owned by Sears Holdings — not the American chain, but a British company that controls a number of shop chains, including the **Miss Selfridge** fashion chain.

Inside it's vast, barn-like and unextraordinary. The store feels like a poor relation of Harrods, trying to match quantity and variety, but not quality. The own-brand clothing and other wares are not terrifically innovative or exciting, but prices overall do not seem to match Harrods' levels. If you want to buy several items from one big

shop, you'll probably find Selfridges more accessible, convenient and slightly cheaper than Harrods, though lacking Harrods' charm, status and personality. *Open Mon–Fri 0930–1730; Thur 0930–1900; Sat 0930–1700.*
Oxford Street W1. Tel: 01-629 1234. U: Bond Street

Simpsons
A rare survivor, the family-owned London department store. Best known for the classic look of its own DAKS brand, for which it has its own small cult of repeat customers. In recent years they have tried to introduce some trendier designs to attract more of the younger set. Good for a look similar to Burberry's in traditional menswear. Less famous and sometimes cheaper. *Mon–Sat 0930–1730; Thur 0930–1900.*
203 Piccadilly W1. Tel: 01-734 2002. U: Piccadilly Circus

Woolworths
Nicknamed 'Woolies' in Britain, this is nevertheless a familiar store to visitors from all over the world. Here, as elsewhere, it is the cheap place to go for basic necessities: confectionery, stationery, toys, plants, tools, records, housewares and children's clothes. Like other downmarket stores, it is now trying to brighten up and modernize. *Hours vary.*
Many locations

Street markets

London is famous for street markets, especially **Portobello Road, Camden Lock, Camden Passage, Church Street, Petticoat Lane, Brick Lane** and **Bermondsey**. We find that too many visitors have too high expectations. Occasionally a real bargain is found — usually a suddenly-discovered heart's desire — amid the bric-a-brac and junk stalls, or in an antique dealer's store where they don't let anyone get the better of them. Sure, it's fun to find a bargain, but that shouldn't be your main reason for going. Go to at least one street market while you're here to enjoy part of the spirit of London.

Talk to the clever stall holders and listen to their patter. Watch tourists being happily taken in. Marvel at the strangely-designed accessories and everyday objects of 50–100 years ago. Then have a sausage from a stall or a 'cuppa' in a neighbourhood café. Markets are good places to find unique gifts or a one-of-a-kind treasure to take home, but think twice about whether you really want a Victorian glass display box with two stuffed curiosity mice in dinner jackets playing violins.

Market days
Because I live near the Portobello Market, I can't stress enough the need to pay careful attention to limited market days. Too many times I have met disappointed tourists looking for the Portobello Market on a Thursday afternoon when even most of the fruit and vegetable stalls are shut.

Portobello
Only on **Saturday** (though fruit and vegetable stalls are there most of the week **except** Thursday afternoons and Sundays).

Bermondsey
Friday – best go very early. Serious buyers arrive as early as 4.30am.

Camden Lock
Saturday and **Sunday**.

Camden Passage

Wednesday and **Saturday**. Wednesdays are more serious, Saturdays have more atmosphere, plus you can combine with nearby **Chapel Street** on that day only.

Petticoat Lane; Brick Lane; Columbia Road

Only on **Sunday** morning, and all within walking distance.

Which market?

The easiest choice is just to go to **Portobello Road** — Europe's largest and one of the most varied. But it's neither the cheapest nor, probably, the most genuine. Early-morning **Bermondsey** is more serious and professional, but you do have to get up early. More bargains than anywhere else, but being knowledgeable helps.

Camden Lock is the most oriented towards youth, trends and fashion, and has some useful amenities like the **Le Routier** café and a pleasant location on the canal — a base for walking or a highly-recommended boat trip to Little Venice. **Camden Passage** is mostly not cheap, but there are some very high-quality stalls. **Church Street** is good around **Alfie's Market**, junky in other parts. **Petticoat Lane** is mostly clothing and modern junk, but not without atmosphere. **Brick Lane** is junky though very atmospheric. **Covent Garden** has very beautiful crafts, but most customers seem to be tourists.

The biggest

Portobello Road

The famous **Portobello Antique Market** won its name in the 1960s. Now a lot of the antique traders have moved to pastures new and let their premises to a plethora of small stall-holders. There are still items of good value to be found in this, Europe's largest street market. But there are also a great many reproductions and copies, so make sure you're buying what you think you're buying.

The antiques market runs along **Portobello Road**, through the intersection with Westbourne Grove, to the Elgin Crescent junction, with most of the stalls concentrated in arcades at the latter end. From here on the market changes to its fascinating North End of vegetable stands, hawkers and ethnic diversity.

Shops and indoor stalls generally sell higher-quality antiques than the outdoor traders, who deal mostly with junk and bric-a-brac. Those interested in furniture and paintings should also browse along the more sedate part of **Westbourne Grove**, which cuts across Portobello Road about halfway down the hill, where there are more expensive but more interesting antique furniture shops.

Down near the flyover you shouldn't miss the interesting collection of artisans and designers at **Portobello Green**. Here you can find stained glass, funky jewellery, designer dresses, knitwear, ceramics and leatherwear for sale in a tiny but attractive shopping centre. One of the most interesting shops is **Necklace Maker**, which has thousands of beads — antique, modern and semi-precious.

The whole **Portobello Market** is at its best on Saturday mornings and afternoons. Most of the rest of the week the North End shops are busy, but there are few street traders other than the vegetable stall-holders. If you can't go on Saturday, it is still worthwhile visiting the market during weekdays when Portobello's everyday street culture in the northern part is buzzing and most of the non-antique shops in the heart of the market stay open (except Thursday afternoon and Sundays).

To get a good look at the whole, we suggest you take the tube to **Notting Hill Gate** on a Saturday morning, walk down **Portobello Road** through the length of the market, then follow **Thorpe Close** to the **Ladbroke Grove** tube station.

Fun but touristy

Covent Garden
Is it even necessary to mention this 'market'? Most visitors will go there regardless, although many Londoners would consider it too tourist-oriented to fit their concept of a market. Nowadays, people forget that **Covent Garden** was once London's major fruit and vegetable market. In 1974 it moved to a location on the South Bank. After much controversy, a plan for renovating the derelict piazza buildings and the area was put into action, and has become one of Britain's most successful urban projects. The central market eventually re-opened in 1980 as a kind of high-class shopping mall with street stalls, and the whole area soon attracted hordes of tourists and speciality shoppers.

In 1987 the adjacent **Jubilee Market** formally re-opened, giving space to stall holders, who may also be found on the fringes. Stalls in the main building are very craft-oriented, except on Mondays. Antiques are more often found in the **Jubilee Market** building, especially on Monday, which is 'antique day'. Some Londoners I know won't even go to Covent Garden any more, but we've bought quality handmade jewellery, cutlery and knitwear there, and several friends have found some exceptional old prints and maps for less than £10. Nearby streets provide the opportunity to shop for many fine and speciality items. Where else would you find a shop selling only gifts from New Zealand?

The **Theatre Museum**, the **London Transport Museum** and the many pubs, restaurants and wine bars are among other attractions, though be aware that much in the area is becoming over-trendy and over-priced. *Open Mon–Sun 0900–1700.* U: **Covent Garden.**

Fun and fashionable

Camden Lock
In and around *Camden Town*, a whole series of markets centre on an area near a lock on the Canal on Saturdays and Sundays 0800–1800. This proximity to the canal, with its walks and boat trips, to Regent's Park and to a growing number of specialized shops, wine bars and unusual attractions like the **Camley Street Urban Wildlife Reserve**, makes this market one of the most enjoyable to visit.

Antiques aren't the main feature — an area up **Camden High Street** is specially reserved for them — but the main emphasis at the Lock is on modern crafts: pottery, stained glass, pine furniture, printed fabrics and young and old fashions. Nearby stall areas specialize in collectables, junk and books. Can be combined with several local attractions. U: **Camden Town.**

Mostly serious

Bermondsey (or New Caledonian) Market
Known as a serious antique dealers' market, which preserves professional status by early morning hours (0500–1500 Fridays only), **Bermondsey** actually welcomes retail customers and tourists. If you're a serious antiques hunter, you should go well before 0800, as this is the best market to find quality antiques at — sometimes — bargain prices. Be aware, though, that there are two drawbacks. First, the market is in South London, and getting there is not easy, particularly early on Friday. If you go by tube (after it starts running) you still have three quarters of a mile to walk from either **Borough** or **London Bridge** underground stations. Second, though safe in the daytime, the area is unsalubrious, and Bermondsey lacks the ambience of many less-professional markets. **Bermondsey Street SE1**, at the corner with **Long Lane.**

Camden Passage
Mostly an upmarket, fairly expensive series of specialist shops and stalls, with some bric-a-brac. The way in which the market snakes down a narrow alleyway gives it a

particular charm and makes the market both unique and fun to visit. **Camden Passage** is especially good for clocks, prints and orientalia. A different perspective is offered by nearby **Chapel Street** Saturday general market. For serious antique collectors, however, the best time to go is on Wednesday mornings, the other market day. The surrounding area is trendy, rapidly-gentrifying Islington — not Camden at all. **U: Angel.**

Church Street

This smaller market centres on **Alfie's** indoor antique market of more than 150 stalls. Open most of the week 0900–1630 (except Sunday and Monday), the atmosphere is less hectic than the one-day opportunities, and traders seem pleasanter and more relaxed. **Alfie's** is especially good for Art Deco and porcelain in the modern price range. On Saturdays, **Church Street** and adjoining streets are transformed into a vast market with second-hand goods, fruit and vegetables. A few additional antique stalls appear, including good-value oriental carpets and doll dealers. The immediate neighbourhood is unremarkable, but you are near the canal, Regent's Park, Madam Tussaud's and the famous **Seashell** fish and chip shop. **U: Edgware Road.**

East end Sunday markets

Sundays in London are traditionally quiet, but going to the Sunday morning East End markets is another tradition you might enjoy. You also get a glimpse of East End life that many tourists miss. **Petticoat Lane**, **Brick Lane** (clothes and junk) and **Columbia Road** (plants and gardening tools) are all within walking distance. Go early and visit all three. Afterwards, it's traditional to have lunch at **Blooms**, the famous Jewish restaurant (see *Restaurants*), or, now, one of the many inexpensive Indian restaurants. **U: Liverpool Street.**

Street by street shopping

Here are a few major streets in London considered vital for the shopper — short cuts if you haven't the inclination, time or energy to traipse in and out of every emporium.

Beauchamp Place

(Pronounced Bee-cham) This small street off Brompton Road teems with small design boutiques of the famous and trendy, along with a **Reject China Shop** and a host of speciality shops and restaurants.

Bond Street

Both **New Bond** and **Old Bond**: the names conjure up *nouveau* luxury and old money and elegance, elegance, elegance. The whole street, which truly does combine the New with the Old, runs from Oxford Street on one end to Piccadilly on the other (**U: Bond Street** or **Piccadilly Circus**). The designers here are all — **Boucheron, Aigner, Cartier, Hermes, Lauren, Sulka** . . . If you're wealthy enough to disregard the price-tags and are seduced by trademarks, then ignore me and send the servants with a list. Otherwise, consider a few shops worth taking note of and take care in the others, where you could find the same thing in any other big city, for less.

New Bond Street

Church's at 163 (Tel: 01-499 9449) has the reputation for beautiful classic ready-to-wear men's shoes, comfortable and well-made. At 15 is **Georg Jensen** (Tel: 01-499 6541), world-renowned for the sleekest, most beautifully-designed Scandinavian silver jewellery and tableware. Expensive, but true quality. Everything is handmade, with emphasis on line, shape and balance. You're wearing a piece of sculpture around your neck, and using a masterpiece to spoon your sorbet.

Check **Sotheby's** (34–35, Tel: 01-493 8080) for the week's auctions. Despite their reputation for world-record sales, they've lots of auctions for smaller and far more accessible items, from Japanese prints to vintage clothes to tiny works of art by the unknown. You'd be surprised what you can pick up for little. The **Bond Street Antique Centre** at 124 is a small warren of stalls for high-priced but good-quality antique jewellery and *objets d'art*. Of course, famed **Asprey's** at 165 (Tel: 01-493 6767) has to be the most luxurious and varied-in-taste gift shop in England. If they don't have it, you can get it made, but oh, what prices for their gold, silver and gems!

For good cashmeres try **Bill**, a pretty wood-panelled shop at 93 (Tel: 01-629 2837). And **Fenwick's** at 63 is a moderately-priced department store that is big on accessories and dresses for the under-40 woman.

Old Bond Street
At 23, **Truefitt & Hill** (Tel: 01-493 2961) has to be the most distinguished men's hairdressers around (see *Practical Matters; Hairdressers*). **Rayne** (15–16) outfits the Queen, her mother, and other women looking for quality shoes in elegant styles at reasonable cost. **Tiffany** has recently moved in at 25 (Tel: 01-409 2790), with the same window-wit and inexpensive fun to fabulously-priced jewellery as the shop in New York.

Brompton Street
(**U: Knightsbridge**) A few upmarket clothing shops, such as **Jaeger** and **Austin Reed**, as well as **Rosenthal** for china; however, its best landmark is, of course, **Harrods**, *the* shopping emporium, and possibly the world's largest store, with over 200 departments.

Burlington Arcade
Lying parallel to **Old Bond Street** (between **Burlington Gardens** and **Piccadilly Circus**), this arcade houses half a dozen shops that are a must. **James Drew** at 3 (Tel: 01-493 0714) has pure English classic clothes for women, from ruffled or 'pie-crust'-collared blouses, sensible hats to silk pyjamas as worn by Lauren Bacall in *Sweet Bird of Youth*. **S Fisher**, 22–23 for men, 32–33 for women (Tel: 01-493 4180), has gorgeous cashmere, with silk and wool waistcoats hard to find elsewhere. They even carry another rarity — 10-ply cashmere!

The Pen Shop at 27 (Tel: 01-493 9021) is the for gracious and refined scribbler, with international pens, some very rare. They also do repairs and have just the right nib for your hand. **N Peal** (Tel: 01-493 5378) is a gem of a place, as natives well know, with the largest selection of cashmere in England. No boring beige-and-black-only place, Peal's have very *updated* classics, and their long fluid robes and capes made of the stuff are out of this world. Not cheap, as might be expected, but you won't care.

The **Irish Linen Co**, 35–36 (Tel: 01-493 8949), is the only privately-owned shop left in London selling the ultimate fabric in bed-linen, handkerchiefs, tableclothes and towels — great variety of sizes, beautiful embroidery and superb quality of cloth. **Penhaligon**, 55 (Tel: 01-629 1416), has one of its five shops here.

Jermyn Street
Yet another historically-hallowed strip of shopping, situated between Haymarket and St James's Street (**U: Piccadilly** or **Green Park**). It tends towards the male interests, with superb ready-to-wear hats (**Bates** at 21a, Tel: 01-734 2722); pipes (**Asley's** at 104a — *the* place since 1860); bespoke shoes (**Trickers** at 67, less expensive than **Lobb**), and accessories (**Alfred Dunhill** at 30 Duke Street). Above all, for shirts try **Turnbull & Asser** at 71 or **Hilditch & Key** at 87.

If you're hungry, follow the smell wafting along the street from possibly the finest cheese shop in England, 200-year old **Paxton & Whitfield** at 93 (everything began, one suspects, 200 years ago!). 89 is the home of scented **Floris**, and 39c of **Czech & Speake** for superior colognes and oils (see *Women: Perfume and Beauty* below).

King's Road

Once a path of glory in the flip Carnaby Street/Swinging Sixties days, but now a hodge-podge of young and disposable boutiques and wine bars. Exceptions are two antique emporiums of great fun: **Antiquarius** (135–141, Tel: 01-351 5353), where you could spend half a day (unless you got saturated earlier) and buy everything under the sun, and **Chenil Galleries** (181–183), smaller and more informal, but no junk there either — just accessible quality. If junk is what you want, the **Chelsea Antique Market** at 245–253 is stuffed full of it. Otherwise, if leather, old jeans and young labels like *Die For It* and *Just Sex* are for you, then you're in the right place.

Oxford Street

Millions of people teem down **Oxford Street** (which, for practical purposes, runs from Tottenham Court Road tube to Marble Arch tube), and on any given day it can feel as if every llast one of them decided to choose the same day *you* decided to go. However, the street is mostly a collection of chain-store branches, banks and a handful of screamingly-atmosphered video and boutique shops. There are a few notables, all down the left side as you venture east from Marble Arch: **Marks & Spencer, Selfridges, Debenhams** and **John Lewis** (see *Major stores*, above, for further info). At the end, across from Tottenham Court Road tube, is the noisy **Virgin Megastore**, for those English and international soundtracks you couldn't live without. Bring aspirin and headphones, but the prices are fair.

Piccadilly Circus

The Circus has regressed over the past years from a beautiful symbol of the capital to a circle of hawkers, tacky cafés and cheap souvenir shops. The slick shopping complex, **The Trocadero**, doesn't help.

Piccadilly

Of the four streets leading off the Circus, however, **Piccadilly** has the most distinguished appearance, with hints of past dignity. From Piccadilly Circus tube to Green Park tube, a few shops are definitely worthwhile: **Fortnum & Mason** at 181 (Tel: 01-734 8040); **Hatchards** (books) at 187, and **Swaine Adeney Briggs & Sons** (leather) at 185.

Regent Street

Running, for our purposes, from **Oxford Circus** to **Piccadilly Circus** in a gracious curve, **Regent Street** has plenty to offer. At 100 is *Aquascutum* (Tel: 01-734 6090) for popular raincoats and tweed jackets for men and women. **Austin Reed** at 103 (Tel: 01-734 6789) is where the fashionable but conservative person can feel confident of quality. **Garrard** the Crown Jeweller is at 112 (Tel: 01-734 7020), and **Burberry** (*the* raincoat!) at 165.

On towards Oxford Circus, **Mappin & Webb** at 170 (Tel: 01-734 0906) has expensive and gorgeous '30s silver, as well as modern pieces. They're the silver supplier to the Queen and other crowns, and their silver plate is guaranteed not to need recoating for 30 years.

Hamley's at 200 (Tel: 01-734 3161) is supposedly the largest toy store in the world, and certainly exhausting enough. **Liberty's** at 210 hardly needs introducing — it's one of England's traditions (see *Major stores*). If you must stoop to cliché, you can buy everything in the **Wedgwood** line – and much of it *is* pretty — at 266 (Tel: 01-734 5656).

Savile Row

Situated between Regent Street and New Bond Street (**U: Bond Street**), the tailors of **Savile Row** have been justly renowned for centuries: their reputations have spread the 'English suit' throughout the world (in Japan, the word for suit is 'Se-bi-ro'). For the finest in bespoke suits, but expensive. See *Men's bespoke.*

Sloane Street
Angled between **Knightsbridge** and **King's Road** is this stamping ground of the Sloane Ranger — the British equivalent of the preppie. The shops are excellent and the street wide and (compared with other major shopping streets) fairly uncrowded. At the Knightsbridge end is what is, to my mind, London's most civilized department store: **Harvey Nichols** (see its own entry, above, under *Major stores*).

Further down the street you'll run into **Joseph Pour la Maison** (his clothing is nearby) for fabrics, home accessories and furniture from sophisticated designer showcases, and a handful of chic Japanese designers, such as **Kenzo** at 17 (Tel: 01-235 1991), with his brilliantly-coloured clothes for both sexes, or the more eclectically-styled **Issey Miyake** at 21 (Tel: 01-245 9891).

Max Mara at 42 (Tel: 01-235 7941) has extremely-wearable and beautifully-tailored outfits for the career woman, while **Sloane Pearls** at 49 will sell her pearls set in lovely jewellery or rejuvenate her old strands by mixing in gold, lapis and other semi-precious rocks.

Courtenay's at 188 (Tel: 01-235 5601) is a tiny elegant shop with a split personality, one half subdued but luxurious lingerie, the other country clothes in neutral colours — moderately priced and timeless. At the other end is the **General Trading Company** (144, Tel: 01-730 0411) with everything for the well-bred Sloane home, and **Peter Jones** department store (see *Major stores*).

South Molton Street
South Molton Street is just off Oxford Street near the Bond Street tube station. There is a lot of movement in this small strip of street — shops come and shops go, lately with curious irregularity. With few exceptions, however, its reputation for upmarket clothing remains. In contrast to the slightly more distingué and sedate, a-few-years-older customer of Bond Street, South Molton's are yuppier and more trendy, though still slaves to the fashion scene. Here are a few highlights.

Down on your left, **Katherine Hamnett** 49, Tel: 01-629 0287), one of England's favourite young-style designers, has opened a tiny branch. Despite the cool-mood atmosphere — dashy brush-stroked walls, grey floors and pillars in the middle of everything — Hamnett-followers pick through racks of cotton and gabardine sportywear separates in neutrals: black, navy, beige, white and red. She's the designer, you may remember, who resuscitated the message T-shirt ('Frankie Says Relax').

At 58 is **Molton Brown's** (Tel: 01-629 1872), a hair salon-beauty-shop which is well-reputed, with reason. In a few small floors you can get your hair beautifully snipped and coiffed (often without an appointment), have your face done (£7.50 a make-over, which is ludicrously cheap) and browse for high-quality paints, powders and potions.

The **City Bag Store** (Tel: 01-499 2549), next door, is the only place in the UK to find the 'le sport sac' line of baggage/handbags; they have an enormous selection as well. They also carry the Enny line of handbags and satchels, which are the best in the world for sleek quality and durability.

Now, to **Browns** (Tel: 01-491 7833), where designers' wares converge under one emporium roof — five connecting rooms, in fact, with one devoted to men's wear. Heaven help you if you're not young, rich and less than 112 pounds dripping wet. Alaia, Donnar Karan, Thierry Mugler, Byblos, Maud Frizon shoes, Missoni, Gaultier, Montana, Romer Gigli and more are here, as are a handful of lesser-known English designers at (slightly) less-frightening prices. Like other shops here, you'll find the minimalist pale wood floors and sparse decor. However, Brown's is somewhat more warm and comfortable. The same cannot be said for the highly fashioned-trained but indifferent young staff.

St James's Street
A small street between Piccadilly and Pall Mall (**U: Green Park**) that is home to a handful of historically-famous quality shops, nestled around the odd gas-light and antiquated alleys. At 3 is **Berry Bros. & Rudd**, Wine and Spirit Merchants (Tel: 01-839 9033), purveyors since 1690 of superb wines to kings, dandies and any other imbiber. The unchanged dark wood interiors, expert staff and reasonable prices make it a joy to patronize.

At 19, **Robert Lewis Cigars** (Tel: 01-930 3787) will store your supplies for you until needed, as they have for Churchill and others for the past 200 years. **D. R. Harris & Co Ltd** at 29 is an apothecary of the same vintage, which has the royal warrant as chemist to the Queen Mother. Among the old wood cases and gold-lettered glass you'll find popular creations of theirs not to be found elsewhere, such as the *Pick Me Up*, a peculiar 120-year-old formula which claims to revive the dead, and *Crystal Eye Drops*, used by Broadway beauties as well as West End thespians.

At **Lock & Co** at 6 (Tel: 01-930 8874), the 'conformateur' gizmo (the only one still in existence) will 'print out' the shape of your head for an exact hat fit. Statistics are stored for future reference, along with those of the Duke of Wellington and other luminaries. Service is impeccable, materials likewise, and prices are no higher than those of any good department store, which is a nice surprise, since you couldn't find better quality anywhere. 'Lock's is a part of a man's upbringing,' they tell me. A worthy habit. From head to foot: **J Lobb** at 9 (Tel: 01-930 3664/5) has been the *only* place, to thousands of fanatically-loyal customers, for bespoke shoes and boots.

Recover from your exertions at the **Ritz Hotel**, around the corner near the tube, with a therapeutic cream tea — a slice of heaven, indeed.

Walton Street
Just a short walk from Harrods (**U: Knightsbridge**) is this street with a reputation for stylish little shops — but take along a few grains of salt as you browse. Pass by the cutesy needlepoint and nursery furniture shops, and the scattered clutch of interior decorators. At the end of the street you'll find two gems: **Merola** (178), for good (albeit expensive) Art Deco jewellery pieces, and, at 94, **Walton Street Stationery** (Tel: 01-589 0777) for the most beautiful writing stock, some handmade, you could imagine. They also carry inks in rich and unusual colours which suit the most fragile pens. (J.E.)

Where to buy?

Antiques
London is easily the antiques capital of the world. An 'antique' is defined by Customs as anything over 100 years old, but as more people have taken up the collecting craze, virtually anything nowadays can be an 'antique' — at least pre-World War II. Later objects are often called 'collectables'. Unless you're very knowledgeable, you need to face up to several unpleasant truths.

- There are no real bargains in London for the unknowledgeable, only buys that may later turn out to be lucky.

- There are many fakes and later reproductions in circulation.

- Except for some small items, it's difficult to be a serious collector for 'investment purposes' unless you can spend at least several hundred pounds with ease.

- You cannot hope to win price-wise even with most reputable dealers.

- If you want to make a large purchase, bring along someone knowledgeable, or at the very least consult **Miller's** (£12.95).

- Check to see whether the dealer belongs to LAPADA (London and Provincial Antique Dealers Association) or BADA (British Antique Dealers Association). Many reputable (especially small) dealers aren't, but membership can be some indication of reputability.

- Reputable dealers will answer questions if asked, but don't expect them to give out information you haven't asked for.

- With many dealers, sadly, an American accent bumps up the price. View, then send an English friend back to negotiate.

- If you haven't much to spend, buying bric-a-brac and Victorian prints and curiosities in street and indoor markets may prove more satisfying than visiting dealers and galleries (that is, if you really intend to buy).

- That said, if you see something you really want and you really can afford it — buy it. This is the only good reason for buying any antique. Popular tastes and trends change, but you may not see the object of your desire again.

Covered antique markets

If you're on a budget, or just want enjoyable browsing, do your antique shopping in street and outdoor markets (see *Street markets*, above). Hundreds of dealers and a vast range of antiques, bric-a-brac and (we have to say it) junk are accessible in one spot. Markets are mostly only one or two days a week, but indoor covered markets are open 5–6 days a week, *with hours similar to normal shops*. Street and indoor markets usually have permanent antique shops clustered in the same vicinity, but stall dealers change frequently, so you'll just have to investigate each for yourself.

Alfies
Pleasant, open all week, part of Church Street market.
13–15 Church Street NW8. Tel: 01-723 6066

Antiquarius
Probably the best and most interesting for most visitors from the standpoint of size, range and affordability. Entertaining dealers — many have a real 'act' or line of patter.
135 King's Road SW3. Tel: 01-351 5353

Bond Street Antique Centre
About 40 dealers. Not generally as expensive as Bond Street shops, if that's saying anything.
124 New Bond Street W1. Tel: 01-252 5353

Chelsea Antique Market
Especially memorabilia, records and books.
245 King's Road SW3. Tel: 01-352 5689

Grays Antique Market
Big market, smart, but perhaps too tourist-oriented.
58 Davies Street and 1–7 Davies Mews W1. Tel: 01-629 7034

Dealers

London has so many antique shops that it's impossible to do justice with a selection here. If you like browsing, the areas around the markets hold the majority of shops — but not all are open every day and some are for (mainly overseas) dealers only. The biggest concentrations are on **Kensington Church Street W8**, on and around **Portobello Road** and **Westbourne Grove W11**, **Bond Street W1**, **Camden Passage N1** and scattered around **Chelsea** and **St James's** areas. Here are a few of the more interesting.

The Gallery of Antique Costume and Textiles
A truly unusual shop. Only three years old, it's the kind of treat that London is —
decreasingly — famous for: a one-of-a-kind place in an old-fashioned setting, with
knowledgeable, labour-of-love (as well as profit) staff. It has a marvellous international collection of clothing and textiles ranging from the 1600s to the 1930s. They
provide an exceptional service to decorators and other trades-people associated
with interior design, and provide materials for magazines and even films. They'll also
sell to the average customer looking for something special for the home.
2 Church Street NW8. Tel: 01-723 9981

Maggs Brothers Ltd
Autographed letters and historical documents make an unusual present to bring
back from London. Hinda Rose, this firm's authority on documents, warns 'Within the
next 20–30 years most of the letters will be bought up by libraries and corporations.
This is the right time to buy. There are so many collectors now that, if you wait, the
market will actually dry up.' Many are surprisingly cheap: T. S. Eliot £60, Field
Marshal Montgomery £45, Virginia Woolf £45. Queen Victoria costs £185, George
Washington £2400. You can walk in and request to view the documents, but it's best
to write to the address below, enclosing postage, and request a catalogue with
current prices, and an appointment. (G.M.)
50 Berkeley Square W1. Tel: 01-493 7160

Adams Antiques
Fine Georgian furniture.
47 Chalk Farm Road NW1. Tel: 01-267 9241

Arthur Middleton
Scientific instruments.
12 New Row WC2. Tel: 01-836 7042

Blunderbuss
Militaria.
29 Thayer Street W1. Tel: 01-486 2444

Crick
Antique lighting.
166 Kensington Church St W8. Tel: 01-229 1338

David Black
Oriental carpets.
96 Portland Road W11. Tel: 01-727 2566

The Galleries
A trade centre where the public can sometimes buy at trade prices.
157 Tower Bridge Rd SE1. Tel: 01-407 5371

Howard Philips
Glassware.
11a Henrietta Place W1. Tel: 01-580 9844

Hotspur
Fine Georgian Furniture.
14 Lowndes Street SW1 Tel: 01-235 1918

Strike One
Clocks.
51 Camden Passage N1. Tel: 01-226 9709

Tradition
Toy soldiers.
5a Shepherd Street W1. Tel: 01-493 7452

Antique prints and maps
In recent years, prints and maps have soared in value. London is, of course, one of the great print markets of the world. In many of the street markets and old bookstores you can still find a selection for £5–£20, which may not be collector's items, but will handsomely decorate your home or office or make a unique gift. Occasionally a cheap type of print will come into vogue and make a good investment. Nowadays you usually have to pay a bit more for any print likely to have 'potential'. If you have investment in mind, be sure to buy only those in good condition. **Christie's** print room director told one of our writers, 'Condition is everything'.

Look around the street and indoor markets, **Cecil Court WC1**, and the **Covent Garden** area. Some of these shops are particularly interesting:

Arthur Ackermann
(Sporting — £200 plus)
3 Old Bond Street W1. Tel: 01-493 3288

Cartographia Ltd
(Maps — generally £10–£200)
Bury Place WC1. Tel: 01-404 4050

Chelsea Rare Books
313 King's Road SW3. Tel: 01-351 0950

Lacy Gallery
(Military)
38 Ledbury Road W11. Tel: 01-229 9105

Map House
(Maps)
54 Beauchamp Place SW3. Tel: 01-589 4325

Paul Mason
(Marine — £200 plus)
149 Sloane Street SW1. Tel: 01-730 3683

The Parker Gallery
(Topographical)
12a Berkeley Street W1. Tel: 01-499 5906

Art and antique auctions anyone can attend
Why are so many people intimidated by the image of London's four major auction houses — **Christie's**, **Bonhams**, **Phillips** and **Sotheby's**? Anyone can attend most of the sales. And all four have accessible counters where you can take items for identification or valuation without an appointment and free of charge.

A calendar of sale dates for the year can generally be obtained from any branch of the auction house concerned. Weekly dates and times for London appear in Monday's *Daily Telegraph* and other publications. However, if you are a collector interested in a particular area, it may pay you to subscribe to a catalogue service. Catalogues give estimated prices — not infallible, but helpful. Then you won't miss *the* sale, even as an absent bidder. For the occasional or one-time buyer, simply telephone or write to the address given in the advertisement of the sale in which you're interested. They will either send you a catalogue with invoice, or may ask you to send a cheque for the amount in question.

How to browse, spectate or bid

Browsing
Let's take **Christie's** as an example. There are enquiry desks in the hall, and catalogues, but as a browser, simply go up the stairs and look for a room with an auction in progress. No one will object if you stand by the door or take a seat. People come and go. Then look for rooms with exhibits on view for future sales. If you want to know prices, simply ask if the item has been catalogued.

Buying
Bidding: if you've never been to a London auction and have heard all those stories of scratching your nose and ending up with a Matisse and no money to pay for it, take courage. But if itchy and you must scratch, ask the person next to you to oblige. Nevertheless, a spokesman at **Christie's** says, 'It's never happened. You are in no danger of bidding unintentionally. We have a system. Intending buyers register beforehand and are given a paddle with a number on it.' All bidders use different signs — from a wink, a nod, to holding up a newspaper — but when the last bid is made, the buyer raises his paddle.

If you get into the act impulsively and have not registered, then just hold your hand up high. If the hammer comes down on your call, an attendant will approach you with a sheet for details to be filled in. Everything happens at great speed, so be prepared.

Payment is more complicated. It depends on whether you are known to the particular auction house. There is a Buyer's Premium of 10 per cent of the hammer price (adjusted for VAT as necessary). But Conditions of Sale should be examined before buying in any saleroom.

Most salerooms do not accept credit cards. Cash or sterling bankers drafts are acceptable, but ordinary cheques have to be cleared, unless previous arrangements have been made. Belinda Mitchell Innes of **Bonhams** offers a useful tip: 'Visit the Accounts Department before the actual sale if in doubt'.

Buyers are also expected to remove their purchases as quickly as possible. *Liability for insurance is immediate upon purchase.* Examining the article carefully either before bidding starts or on viewing days is advisable, as there is no redress afterwards if fault is found. Read the Conditions of Sale in the catalogue carefully.

Bidding by proxy
Auction houses will bid on your behalf. As your bid is confidential, so are those of others. If you're after something you can't live without, ignore the estimated catalogue price and name your maximum figure, otherwise you may lose the race before it starts. It doesn't necessarily mean you will actually pay that much. If bidders are few and disinterested, you may well get your heart's desire below the estimated price — depending on the reserve price — if there is one. It is maddening, however, to be pipped by a few pounds. (A.L.)

Addresses

Bonhams
(Chelsea Auction Rooms)
New Chelsea Galleries. 65–69 Lots Road SW10 0RN. Tel: 01-351 7111

Bonhams
(Montpelier Galleries)
Montpelier Street SW7 1HH. Tel: 01-584 9161. Telex: 916477 BONHAM G

Christie's (South Kensington) Ltd
85 Old Brompton Road SW7 3LD. Tel: 01-581 7611

Christie, Manson & Woods Ltd
8 King Street SW1Y 6QR. Tel: 01: 839 9060. Telex: 916429. Fax: 01-839 1611

Phillips Marylebone
Hayes Place, Lisson Grove NE1. Tel: 01-723 2647

Phillips West 2
10 Salem Road W2 4BU. Tel: 01-221 5303

Phillips
**Blenstock House, 7 Blenheim Street W1Y 0AS. Tel: 01-629 6602. Telex: 298855 BLEN
G**

Sotheby's
**34–35 New Bond Street W1A 2AA and Bloomfield Place (off New Bond Street). Tel:
01-493 8080. Telex: 24454 SBLON. For details of a number of regional locations call
the number above.**

Books

Book browsing is one of London's great pleasures. Visitors from overseas discover a
whole new world of titles, subjects and shops. The antiquarian and second-hand
trade is not what it once was: there is still plenty of interest, but don't expect great
bargains or an *84 Charing Cross Road* relationship. An exception is the discounted
hardback remainders often found even in good book shops. Remainders aren't
necessarily bad — it just may be that not enough people shared your particular
interest.

New books

Compendium
Here you'll find many books from small presses not found elsewhere, crammed on
two floors and on high shelves. A good general bookstore, though the atmosphere is
redolent of the 60s, with many books, pamphlets and magazines on politics,
anarchism and alternative living. Another Camden Market attraction open all week.
234 Camden High Street NW1. Tel: 01-485 8944

Dillons
Of the two giant London bookshops, we much prefer **Dillons**, though it's not what it
was ten years ago. **Dillons** is better organized and the staff more courteous and
knowledgeable. They acknowledge the modern world enough to take several
international credit cards. Best for academic books — though critics allege all width
and no depth.
82 Gower Street WC1. Tel: 01-636 1577

Elgin Bookshop
A pleasant-browse general bookshop in the Portobello Market.
Elgin Crescent W11. Tel: 01-229 2186

Foyle's
The World's Largest Bookstore (or at least a close contender) is a London institution worth a visit, but not a pleasant place to browse. Organization is chaotic and the staff can be unhelpful and uninterested. Infuriatingly, they insist that you leave your book with a sales person while you go to a caged cashier, sometimes on another floor, to pay and collect a receipt, which you must then present to get your purchase. Visa and American Express cards are now accepted.
119 Charing Cross Rd WC2. Tel: 01-437 5660

Hatchards
A famous and also pleasant place to browse when not too crowded. Stocks many serious titles, unlike some London shops.
187 Piccadilly W1. Tel: 01-437 3924

Waterstones
For browsing we now particularly recommend the new go-ahead **Waterstones** chain: the shops are beautifully presented, the atmosphere relaxed and uncluttered and, uniquely, they have an interested, all-graduate staff. Combine that with a wide selection and long opening hours (Mon–Fri 0930–1930; Sat 1030–1900; sometimes Sundays) and you'll understand why I always head there first.
121 Charing Cross Rd WC2. Tel: 01-434 4291; 193 Kensington High St W9. 99 Old Brompton Road SW3

Harrods
And don't forget the excellent book department for both browsers and buyers at **Harrods.**

Specialist books

Arts Bibliographic
Art specialist.
37 Great Russell Street WC1. Tel: 01-636 5320

Books for Cooks
A cookbook shop with (of course) a café and excellent personal service.
4 Blenheim Crescent W11. Tel: 01-221 1992

Shipley
Another art specialist.
70 Charing Cross Road WC2. Tel: 01-836 4872

The Travel Bookshop
A must for those interested in travel (and most visitors are). Big range of modern and antique travel books in an attractive shop.
13 Blenheim Crescent W11. Tel: 01-229 5260

Zwemmer's
Famous art book shop.
24 Lichfield Street WC2. Tel: 01-836 4710

Other specialists

Atlantis
(Occult)
49a Museum Street WC1. Tel: 01-405 2120

The Cinema Bookshop
13 Great Russell Street WC1. Tel: 01-637 0206

Forbidden Planet
(Science fiction and fantasy)
71 New Oxford Street WC2. Tel: 01-836 4179

French's Theatre Bookshop
52 Fitzroy Street W1. Tel: 01-387 9373

Gay's The Word
66 Marchmont Street WC1. Tel: 01-278 7654

Mowbray's
(Religious)
28 Margaret Street W1. Tel: 01-580 2812

Probstain & Co Oriental Booksellers
41 Great Russell Street WC1. Tel: 01-636 1096

Silver Moon
(Feminist)
68 Charing Cross Road WC2. Tel: 01-836 7906

There are many other specialist shops. A good place is around **Cecil Court**, just off Charing Cross Road.

Second-hand books

Skoob Books
London's biggest and best selection of reasonably-priced second-hand books.
15 Sicilian Avenue WC1. Tel: 01-404 3063

Modern maps

Stanford
Claims to be the world's largest stockist of maps, including the famous detailed Ordnance Survey maps, very useful to walkers in Britain.
12 Long Acre WC2. Tel: 01-836 1321

Antiquarian books

Bernard Quarich
Very expensive, top market, top editions. One-to-one relationship with clients.
5–8 Lower John Street W1. Tel: 01-734 2983

Henry Southeran
Large-roomed, atmospheric shop. Not specialists, but emphasis on English literature, travel, natural history and 'Edwardian general'.
2–5 Sackville Street W1. Tel: 01–734 1150

G Heywood Hill
Small shop with English first editions and illustrators.
10 Curzon Street W1. Tel: 01-629 0647

Quinto/Francis Edwards
Friendly. Good search service.
48a Charing Cross Road WC2. Tel: 01-379 7669

Zwemmers
Art and architecture.
24 Lichfield Street WC2. Tel: 01-836 4710

China and glassware
A big 'Made in Britain' purchase that many visitors want to make.

Reject China Shops
The obvious choice, which, despite the name, is now about discounting-through-volume buying. Most of the imperfections are sold only at sale time. Many big names and over a thousand patterns are available at varying prices that depend on popularity, but overall prices are usually among, if not the, lowest. Two of the Beauchamp Place (near Harrods) shops specialize in crystal and earthenware. The corner shop (with Brompton Road) is mainly china.
33–35 Beauchamp Place SW3 (three shops). Tel: 01-581 0737

Chinacraft
Like the Reject China Shop, this nearby rival is heavily geared to selling to an export tourist market on Beauchamp Place and at other outlets. **Chinacraft** claims to stock just about every pattern in existence, as well as glass and cutlery.
1&3 Beauchamp Place SW3. Tel: 01-225 1696; 499 Oxford Street W1. 50 Brompton Road SW1, and other locations

Waterford/Wedgwood
A kind of upmarket factory outlet at *Oxford Circus* and an even bigger one on Piccadilly, with very good discounts at sale time. **Tel: 01-734 4737**
    If all this mass-merchandising puts you off, price china and glassware in the department stores — **Harrods**, **Selfridges** and (especially for value) **John Lewis**. For more individualized, expensive porcelain and glass figures and china at non-bargain prices, try **Garrard**, the famous crown jeweller, at 112 Regent Street W1 (Tel: 01-734 7020), or **Thomas Goode**, the elegant, snobbish, Mayfair place to buy both the best china and china you could get cheaper elsewhere (19 South Audley Street W1, Tel: 01-499 2823). **Liberty's** department store has some find china and glassware in the basement, as well as a few craft bargains. For other designer glassware and ceramics, see *Crafts*.
Oxford Circus W1 and 173 Piccadilly W1. Tel: 01-629 2614

Women's clothes, jewellery, accessories and cosmetics
General
London has all the respected international couturiers you could find in New York or Paris or Milan (Chanel, St Laurent, Armani, Valentino, etc), of course, but I shall assume that you are not shopping in London for these, but for things you could find *only* in London. An exception is **Ralph Lauren**, whose clothes, while being American in nature, have tended to go for the country English look — even outdoing the English, at times! Although veering sometimes towards the desperately Brideshead mood, his shop at 143 New Bond Street W1 (Tel: 01-491 4967) does carry all three of his lines — corresponding to price tags as well — and the dressing rooms are the height of civilized luxury.
    Aquascutum (100 Regent Street W1, Tel: 01-734 6090) and **Burberry** (165 Regent Street, Tel: 01-734 4060 and 18 Haymarket, Tel: 01-930 3343), for trenchcoats, should be considered twice a year at sales times. The **Beauchamp Place Shop** (55 Beauchamp Place, Tel: 01-589 4118) represents a small handful of British and international designers, for very coordinated clothing in the British look. Prices between the modest and somewhat maniacal. For the truly trendy designer look, often in the seasons's neutrals, go to **Browns** (23–27 South Molton Street, Tel: 01-493

4232), an emporium of extremely well-chosen, upmarket and up-to-the-minute top designers within five interconnecting shops. Yes, expensive. Montana, Conran, Donna Karan, Alaia, Missoni and the rest — who prefer you young and lithe. **Hyper-Hyper** (26–40 Kensington High Street W8, Tel: 01-937 6501) houses the creations of over 70 up-and-coming young British designers — for both men and women.

Courtenay House (22–24 Brook Street W1, Tel: 01-629 0542, and 188 Sloane Street SW3, Tel: 01-235 5601) is a dignified little place carrying smart English country clothes, again in easy neutral colours and natural fabrics. The items are of classic — and that need not mean dull — quality. Very smart and very upper-class.

The first floor of **Harrods** (Knightsbridge SW1, Tel: 01-734 1243) is entirely fashion for women, a one-stop shop with many important designers — famous and not-so — gathered together. More of a price range than people might suspect, but it gets crowded, so go early in the day and bring plenty of patience and energy. The selection at **Harvey Nichols** (Knightsbridge SW1, Tel: 01-235 5000) across the street is smaller, but so is the store, yet four of its six floors are devoted to clothes. Everything is fashionable and there is the best of everyone, including the younger designers. There is a shopping service and colour consultant.

Bruce Oldfield's Shop (27 Beauchamp Place SW3, Tel: 01-584 1363) is full of very feminine dresses, from flirty and sumptuous couture evening gowns to ready-to-wear day things. Accent is on what a fabric can do. Prices are crazy. **September** (2 Portobello Green, Portobello Road W10. Tel: 01-960 3274) has limited lines in a very distinctive art deco look made from silk and other natural fabrics at reasonable prices. **Margaret Howell** (25 St Christopher Place W1, Tel: 01-935 8588) has been known for ages among the young well-heeled(ish) sporty set for pretty and very wearable clothes in three or four colours each season, so that everything can be coordinated. More pleats than ruffles.

Marks & Spencer (173 Oxford Street W1, Tel: 01-437 7722, and branches) carry sweaters of all kinds which are very good value, especially the Arran-style pullovers in pure wool. You can always say you were in Ireland for the day to scoop one up, and nobody will know the difference. **N Peal** (37–38, 54 Burlington Arcade W1), on the other hand, has the largest selection of cashmeres in the country, in lots of styles and colours, from the perennial-in-cut to the very fashionable. Scarves to dressing-gowns (the ultimate luxury). A must.

Paddy Campbell (8 Gees Court W1, Tel: 01-493 5646 and Beauchamp Place) is a pretty, tiny wood-and-white shop which carries linen and cotton separates, all moderately- priced and beautifully made. She designs a limited number of pieces per season and, with the exception of the odd 50s' tone creeping in on one or two, all last nicely for several of them. **S Fisher** (22–23, 32–33 Burlington Arcade W1, Tel: 01-493 4180) also carry cashmere sweaters and other items in classic-to-current styles, and are also known for having the very luxurious (and unusual) 4-, 6- and even 10-ply yarn. **Simpsons** (203 Piccadilly W1, Tel: 01-734 2002) carry their own renowned DAKS label, as well as other established and rather sensible (though not staid) designers, many of whom are British.

Speaking of famous names, **Laura Ashley**, the famous line of floral print dresses and fabrics, is at 256 Regent Street W1 (Tel: 01-734 5824, and branches), and **Benetton** is at 225 Oxford Street W1 (Tel: 01-439 6311), and also 111, 257, 328 and 443, as well as many other branches.

Nicole Farhi (25–26 St Christopher's Place W1 and Hampstead High Street NW3, Tel: 01-909 1727) is a very popular designer for the sophisticated career woman. Her emphasis is on cut and quality, and although her pieces are fairly expensive, her more casual separates are quite reasonable. Her smart stuff will look good for season after season, and her cut is terrific. Neutrals again — taupe, navy, that sort of thing.

Jade (22 Hampstead High Street NW3, Tel: 01-794 3889) is a small corner place specializing in simple silks — taffeta, crêpe de Chine, Charmeuse — brightly-coloured separates, a few pretty patterns. Hong Kong makers keep prices pretty low, though not as low as they used to be. For 20–50 age group. **Droopy & Brown** (16 St Christopher Place W1, Tel: 01-935 3198) is a split-personality place: tailored circle skirts in rich corduroys hang side by side with Laura-Ashley type dresses with over-romantic cut (some are beautifully feminine, however, and not stickily ana-chronistic!). They do expensive rustly balldresses; stick to the day ones. Fairly moderate prices, nice staff. **Long Tall Sally** (21 Chiltern Street W1, Tel: 01-487 3370) is a good place for tall women. Let's not forget the **Constant Sales Shop** (56 Fulham Road SW3, Tel: 01-589 1458) with bargains on end-of-season designer clothes.

Lingerie

Bradley's (83–85 Knightsbridge SW1, Tel: 01-235 2902) have a wide selection of lingerie, from polyester to tartan wool to silk. Prices like everyone else. Large shop, varied quality, so pick and choose. Downstairs is the underwear, with a huge choice of size, and everything adapted to the larger figure (generally not the case with other shops). Bras up to 46FF ready-made, and mastectomy concerns well catered for. **Rigby & Peller** (2 Hans Road SW3, Tel: 01-589 9293) are corsetiers to the royals, with a wide range of sizes for us mortals. **Night Owls** (78 Fulham Road SW3, Tel: 01-584 2451) has a more confectionery tone, carrying pretty dressing gowns and pyjamas and bright silk underwear.

Keturah Brown (85 Regents Park Road NW1, Tel: 01-586 0512) is a shoe-box sized shop with feminine nightdresses in silk and lace for reasonable prices. Regular sizes only — i.e. small and medium. Conventional styles and colours, with little touches like silk buttons and ties. **Courtenay's** (22–24 Brook Street W1, Tel: 01-629 0542, and 188 Sloane Street, Tel: 01-235 5601) again for continental as well as terribly British underthings. Lots of detail, hand-work and pretty embroidery. With few exceptions, most pieces more elegant than vampish, with pleats and yokes and dropped waists and the like. Expensive, but worth a look, and lovely quality.

A Reger is a Reger is . . . **Janet Reger** (2 Beauchamp Place SW3, Tel: 01-584 9360) is still the doyenne of gorgeous elegant-to-Hollywood-style lingerie. Breathtaking and expensive stuff. Knickers may not be worth the price (£30 and up), but her nightdresses (to sleep and seduce in) could be — she shapes, ruches, waists, pleats, tucks, gathers, drapes and generally swooshes her richly-coloured silks into goddesses' gowns. Well-conceived (nothing trampy!), well-made and much lusted after. Broad size and style range; durable, and washable, so I'm told, though I'd be wary of trying.

Knickerbox kiosks (one at 189 Regent Street, Tel: 01-439 8430, another at Waterloo tube stations, and others) sell pretty silk underwear for £8, just for contrast, as well as a few other titbits in Chameuse to cotton. Nice presents. Bras pretty and good value.

Antique clothes

Antiquarius (135 Kings Road, Tel: 01-351 5353) has niches of clothing among its warren of stalls, from 20s to 60s, all in beautiful shape. From Victorian nightdresses to heavily-beaded frippery, with varying prices. No changing rooms, but stall-holders can be of great help in sizing you. Definitely worth a look, as this is not junk-shop stuff. **Annies** (10 Camden Passage N1, Tel: 01-359 0796), carries lower-priced pretties in good condition. Her choice is small; regulars browse periodically. **Cobwebs** (60 Islington Park Street N1, Tel: 01-359 8090) is another to try.

Sale or return clothes

Don't sneer. Wonderful designer's things, near new, are cast-offs from guilt-ridden fashion slaves who feel more virtuous for getting a few pence back — to spend on the next season's must-haves. At **Designs** (60 Rosslyn Hill, Hampstead NW3, Tel: 01-435 0100) the gracious owner offers nearly new *and* new Big Names, such as Max Mara, Valentino, St Laurent and Oldfield. Everything in pristine condition and well-organized. Prices are good, and nothing stays longer than six weeks, and all only one season old. Regulars come from all over, and frequently, with reason. **The Dresser** (39–41 Sussex Place W2, Tel: 01-724 7212), **Frock Exchange** (450 Fulham Road SW6, Tel: 01-381 2937) and **Pandora** (16–22 Cheval Place SW7, Tel: 01-589 5289) are three others to try.

Shoes

Beware, slender-footed foreigners: you'll have trouble here. English women have smaller and wider feet, and it is they who are catered for. With the exception of bespoke firms and a few men's shoe places, the painful truth is that the British are not known for their shoes. Much of the making is Irish or Italian. However, quality chains such as **Russell & Bromley**, **Bally** and (especially) **Rayne** are notable exceptions. Way up the (expensive) scale, you can try **Manolo Blahnik** (48–51 Old Church Street SW3, Tel: 01-352 8622) for stylish and, in his words, 'sense of humour'-ed shoes. Often shown in Vogue. **Charles Jourdan** (39–43 Brompton Road SW3, Tel: 01-581 3333) is fashionable and **Johnny Moke** (396 King's Road SW3, Tel: 01-351 2232) trendy. Are you 'narrow' people still reading? Try **Crispins** (28–30 Chiltern Street W1, Tel: 01-486 8924), and for long sizes too. Most designs are low-heeled, and of good quality, at reasonable prices. Always crowded, incidentally.

Bespoke shoes

Prices for a pair of handmade shoes start at around £300 and can climb skyward for, say, a pair of detailed knee-high boots. They'll be made from the ground up — literally — from a wooden last (a 3-D model of your foot) to the last lick of polish. But you'll never have to walk a mile in anyone else's shoes — yours will last a lifetime, and be pampered by personal service for every minute of it. Bespoke shoes are primarily a male domain, alas, but there are two good ones which will serve women: **Henry Maxwell** (11 Savile Row W1, Tel: 01-734 9714) and **John Lobb** (9 St James's Street SW1, Tel: 01-930 3664).

Hats

The Hat Shop (58 Neal Street WC2, Tel: 01-836 6718) is a tiny place with a large choice of berets, caps, straw-saucer things, the odd cloche, you name it. Not couture, but nice quality and reasonable prices. **James Locke** (6 St James's, Tel: 01-930 8874), better known for men's bespoke hats since the year dot, will make you a beautiful creation at prices that will, surprisingly, not surprise you into a faint. **Herbert Johnson** (30 New Bond Street W1, Tel: 01-408 1174) has hats for Ascot or for funerals, and is rather expensive. **Kirsten Woodward** (26 Portobello Green W10, Tel: 01-930 0090) is a big name in women's millinery, and her styles are nicely feminine and not too outré, unlike those who would have you wearing fruit and parrots.

Handbags

Henry's (185 Brompton Road SW3, Tel: 01-589 2011, and Golders Green High Road) has a good selection of bags to briefcases, although they tend to be on the expensive side. **The City Bag Store** (434 Strand WC2, Tel: 01-379 7762, and 73 South Molton Street, Tel. 01-499 2549) is the only place in the UK stocking the Le Sac line, and they stock an enviable selection of the revered Enny bags, at possibly a few pounds less than elsewhere. Good choice — from parachute material to a £200 Enny briefcase-type.

Bespoke clothes

Amy and Grace Li (18 Pembroke Mews W11, Tel: 01-938 2323) are a pair of talented sisters who will whip up a pretty dress in feminine and rich fabrics, as will **Emma Willis** (Tel: 01-736 3026) who travels with fabric samples and sketches. **David Chambers** (Tel: 01-499 1674) specializes in women's suits at around £500, of Savile Row quality. **Karen Beeley** at **Image d'Or** (7 Pond Place SW3, Tel: 01-225 1232) can create works of art from either her ideas or yours, at a reasonable price.

Jewellery

Cartier, Bulgari and other international names are here, mostly on **Bond Street**, though you can find them anywhere. My top two favourites aren't exactly British, either, but they are unusual and special. **Aalto** (8 Ganton Street W1, Tel: 01-439 8320) is (pardon the pun) a gem of a place. You'll find select Scandinavian silver jewellery here from the 50s and 60s — all hand-crafted, of course, and of the most superb quality imaginable — by Georg Jensen, David Anderson, Hans Hansen and other craftspeople revered in their countries and by those who *know*. It is not cheap, and shouldn't be: each piece is a sculpture. **Cobra and Bellamy** (149 Sloane Street SW3, Tel: 01-730 2823) has pretty costume jewellery from the 20s to the 60s, with some sterling and some 24-carat gold. Moderate prices, unusual things.

Liberty's (Regent Street W1, Tel: 01-734 1234) has a good line on ethnic pieces, and **André Bogart** (5 South Molton Street W1, Tel: 01- 429 4869) has simply-styled jewellery in 18-carat gold and streamlined mixed-metals that is not cheap, but beautiful. For the heavy of wallet there is always **Asprey's** (Bond Street) and **Mappin & Webb** (106 Regent Street W1), the standbys of the Empire.

Perfume and beauty

Joan Price's Face Place (31 Connaught Street W2, Tel: 01-723 6671) carries 18 brands of cosmetics; it's a relaxed place to choose from all of them, unlike the chaos at department stores, and you'll receive helpful advice from staff who care. **South Molton Drug Store** (64 South Molton Street W1, Tel: 01-493 4156) carries discounted lines by Arden, Revlon, Quant and Factor at terrific prices. Phone to save time. **The Body Shop** (32–34 Great Marlborough Street W1, Oxford Street and 50 other branches) carries make-up and toiletries in handy plastic bottles. Good quality stuff, and nothing, blessedly, tested on animals. Prices are kept low due to word-of-mouth over advertising.

Cosmetics à la Carte (19 Motcomb Street SW1, Tel: 01-235 0596) will reproduce any shade of anything you're out of or cannot find. They also carry 116 shades of lipstick and 130 eye shadows. Good skin care range and personal service by assistants who know their work. **Culpepper** (9 Flask Walk NW3, Tel: 01-794 7263, and branches) carries herbs, spices, exotic vingegars, potpourris, pillows, oils, soaps and colognes — as English as Harrods. Catalogue, export and no products tested on animals either. Lovely smelling place.

Floris (89 Jermyn Street, Tel: 01-930 2885) is also an English tradition. Perfumes and bath things in very English scents for both sexes, as generations have discovered to their delight. Other accoutrements for bath and vanity table as well, of varying prices. **Penhaligon** (41 Wellington Street, Tel: 01-836 2150) is a beautiful old Victorian shop of rich dark wood, burgundy and gold, which has sold to the renowned and the royal for a couple of centuries. Beautifully-orchestrated scents, silver-topped bottles and brushes, expensive vanity boxes, and all sorts of things to delight. **Les Senteurs** (227 Ebury Street SW1, Tel: 01-730 2322) carries the most gorgeous perfumes from France, all of which couldn't be found outside that country. Respected Annick Goutal's line is here, as well as Molinard and other products of exclusive French boutiques. This place is a must: although pricey, it's unusual and lovely. (J.E.)

Men's clothes and shoes

London is one of the few cities in which bespoke tailoring rather than ready-to-wear reigns at the top end of the market. American menswear retailers don't understand this fact of British life. Hence, frequent complaints about London's ready-to-wear suits not being up to the standard of the quality American counterpart. Maybe so. Certainly there's not a lot to cheer about at the bottom end of the market. In the mid-range, there are now quite a few continental-flavoured lines with slimmer, more tapered cuts. In fact, many suits on the rack are now direct imports from Italy, West Germany and other countries.

Men's fashion and designers have become increasingly important in London, though much of the famous stuff is high-priced and too daring or outrageous for most of us. The big chains, especially, have become more fashion conscious and affordable stores like **Next** have interested more men in dressing in something other than tweed and Marks & Spencer casuals.

Still, most visitors come in search of more traditional, classic British looks. With these factors in mind, we've selected the stores below.

If you don't know how much you want to spend, begin by pricing the clothes at **Austin Reed**, both off-the-peg and their own made-to-measure service, which, using their own in-house tailoring, is relatively inexpensive — a two-piece suit can cost less than £200. I have a beautiful classic wool suit from their top Chester Barrie line that I bought ten years ago and it still looks good. The big store at 103 Regent Street (Tel: 01-734 6789) is comprehensive, with even a classic women's department, a barber and a restaurant.

Aquascutum (100 Regent Street W1, Tel: 01-734 6090), **Simpsons** (203 Piccadilly W1, Tel: 01-734 2003) and **Moss Brothers** (88 Regent Street W1, Tel: 01-494 0666) are also places where you can still find value-for-money quality suits and other clothing among more expensive choices. Mostly traditional — though fashion is getting more emphasis. **Simpsons** and **Moss Brothers**, like **Austin Reed**, are also known for their made-to-measure service. **Moss Brothers** is also famous for evening-wear hire. They have recently opened **The Suit Company** (Tel: 01-727 1556), a chain of suit shops selling design-name lines at reduced prices.

Jaeger (200 Regent Street W1, Tel: 01-734 8211) is more stylish than the above-mentioned shops, but their clothes look best on the slightly built. If you like the fashionable look in suits and don't mind paying for it, the Italian **Cerruti** (76 New Bond Street W1, Tel: 01-493 2278) is the place for you.

Harrods and **Liberty's** have good men's departments. **Harrods** has a big range, but prices for the same lines found elsewhere can be very uncompetitive. **Liberty's** menswear has a knack of being trendy and stylish without being too flamboyant. Over the last few years their men's knitwear has been particularly outstanding. (For more details on these two shops see *Major stores*).

Harvey Nichols (see *Major stores*), **Browns** and **HyperHyper** (see *Women's clothes*) are places where you can see a wide choice of designer collections for both men and women. **Bazaar** (4 South Molton Street W1, Tel: 01-629 1708) has quality fashion design at affordable prices.

Let's not forget that many Savile Row tailors sell off-the-peg suits, trousers and shirts. For the standard-sized, this offers the traditional tailored look at much lower prices. Two of the best are **Tommy Nutter** and **Gieves & Hawkes** (see *Bespoke*), with some less than £300. **Blades** (see *Bespoke*), is not a Savile Row old-timer, but the value is good.

I'm high myself (not sure about mighty) and one of the few places big and tall men can find quality in their size is at **High & Mighty** (177 Brompton Road SW3, Tel: 01-589 7454). I wish style and selection were as interesting. If you're headed for or working in a hot climate, one of the few places in town you can find lightweight suits, and a wide selection for tall and big men too, is at **Airey & Wheeler** (129 Regent Street W1, Tel: 01-734 8616). **The Trouser House** (8 New Bond Street W1, Tel: 01-493 8931) has high-quality Scandinavian-designed and manufactured clothes — mostly trousers. **T M Lewin & Sons** (106 Jermyn Street SW1, Tel: 01-930 4291), the famous maker and seller of elite ties for regiments, schools and clubs, won't sell you an Eton or other restricted ties unless you can demonstrate your right to wear it.

Next (54 Kensington High Street W8, Tel: 01-938 4211) sells traditional and fashionable men's clothes at reasonable prices. The best-looking, best-quality suits, coats and jackets in the less-expensive category can be had from **Marks & Spencer** (see *Major stores*). **Top Man** (Oxford Circus W1, Tel: 01-636 7700) has some useful jeans and casuals at affordable prices and more big sizes than other chain stores.

Shoes
London is not the best place in the world to buy inexpensive, durable men's shoes. If you're willing to spend quite a bit more, there are several renowned shops and high-class shoe and bootmakers (see *Bespoke*). Good men's shoe departments can be found at **Harrods, Selfridges, Austin Reed** and **Moss Brothers. Church & Company** (163 New Bond Street W1, Tel: 01-499 9449) are world famous for quality shoes. **Alan MacAfee** (100 New Bond Street W1, Tel: 01-629 7975) is another famous, durable quality make.

Hats and umbrellas
These shops are worth a look for their olde-worlde atmosphere, even if you don't plan to buy anything: **Bates** (21a Jermyn Street W1, Tel: 01-734 2722); **James Locke** (6 St James Street W1, Tel: 01-930 8874) — since 1696, and claims to have invented the bowler, and **James Smith & Sons** (53 New Oxford Street WC1, Tel: 01-836 4731), who easily win the contest for London's most interesting old-fashioned shop front, and sell quality umbrellas and canes.

Bespoke tailoring and shoemaking
Many of us cherish a secret ambition to have a suit made on Savile Row, the famous street (along with adjoining streets) housing Britain's top tailors. As you might expect, a bespoke (made to order) suit is very expensive. A three-piece wool suit can be over £1000, a tweed jacket £600, but the shops do vary quite a bit in their quotes. And there are endless squabbles about which is the best . . .

What good Savile Row tailoring can do is construct a suit appropriate to you alone. If you decide to take the plunge, consider where you will wear the suit, as well as your preferred colours, fabrics and styles. All this information will help the tailor-craftsman make a suit that will flatter you with a perfect fit, in all senses of the word. And if the price still sounds high, have a look at the ready-to-wear racks most of them now feature. The standard-sized will be able to get a next-best-thing at a reasonable price.

Note that some tailors require more than one fitting, and this isn't Hong Kong: a good suit, shirt or pair of shoes takes time.

Gieves & Hawkes (1 Savile Row W1, Tel: 01-434 2001) is a conservative firm with many military customers (including Wellington and Captain Bligh) still on its ledgers. Probably the most famous, well known for excellent service. **Huntsman** (11 Savile Row W1, Tel: 01-734 7441) is expensive but also renowned for good service, atmosphere and quality suits. With customers like Elton John, **Tommy Nutter** (19 Savile Row W1, Tel: 01-734 0831) is more innovative than most traditional Savile Row designers. He can still offer you the classic suit, but with as much style as you want to put into it. Some good value clothing in ready-to-wear. You might check prices at **Blades** (8 Burlington Gardens W1, Tel: 01-734 8911) — generally not as high as their neighbours' for similar quality. **Turnbull & Asser** (71 Jermyn Street SW1, Tel: 01-930 0502) is the best and most famous of several Jermyn Street shirtmakers.

The smell of hand-treated leather is very like that of **John Lobb** (9 St James's Street SW1, Tel: 01-930 3664) — rich, mellow and old-fashioned. Bootmakers to Prince Charles, Lobb employ 27 craftsmen, many of whom have worked for the firm for decades. First-time visitors should allow three to four months before the shoes are finished; subsequent visitors require only the same number of weeks, as each individual's lasts are stored carefully in the basement for up to fifteen years. Shoes from £325 to £500; boots £800. **Poulson & Skone** (53 Jermyn Street SW1, Tel: 01-493 9621) used to be a family business, but now share premises with **New & Lingwood**, the shirtmakers. They have a large American and military market, with shoes starting at £400 and riding boots at £700; two fittings preferred. **Trickers** (67 Jermyn Street SW1, Tel: 01-930 6395) take five months to deliver, with fittings at the half-way point, and sell their first pair of shoes for £240, subsequent pairs at £190.

Crafts, gifts and unusual items
Covent Garden and surrounding streets are the best place to look, though not necessarily the cheapest.

General

Crafts Council Shop
Provides a shop sampling of many London craftsmen, with knowledgeable service. £10–£1000.
Victoria & Albert Museum, Cromwell Road SW7. Tel: 01-589 5070

Design Centre
A good selection of British modern design cards, jewellery, glass, housewares and small gifts, with a constantly-changing stock. Conveniently located for tourists.
28 Haymarket SW1. Tel: 01-839 8000

Contemporary Applied Arts
A showcase for constantly-changing exhibits, and a shop selling well-designed modern jewellery, glassware, ceramics, rugs and other items.
43 Earlham Street WC2. Tel: 01-836 6993

Craftsmen Potters Shop
Cooperative with a range of ceramics and prices.
7 Marshall Street W1. Tel: 01-437 7605

Stained Glass Shop
Sells tools as well as stained glass at reasonable prices. Call for opening times.
62 Fairfield Street SW18. Tel: 01-874 8822

Coleridge
Contemporary designer glass. Friendly service and wide price range.
192 Piccadilly W1. Tel: 01-437 0106

Endell Street Place
Display space for varied craftsmen of all kinds in Covent Garden.
27 Endell Street WC2. Tel: 01-240 1060

The Glasshouse
One of several glass shops where you can watch the craftsmen at work.
65 Long Acre WC2. Tel: 01-836 9785

Naturally British
A sometimes quality, sometimes cutesy shop, selling a wide range of British gifts.
13 New Row WC2. Tel: 01-240 0551

The Doll's House
Crafted dolls and houses in Victorian antique styles.
Unit 29, The Market, Covent Garden WC2. Tel: 01-379 7243

Liberty's Basement
Often a selection of good bargains as well as pricier items from British craftsmen. (See below: *Less expensive gifts*)
Regent Street W1. Tel: 01-734 1234

The Irish Shop
Specializes in handcrafted Irish products. A good place to find names like Arran, Bellek and Waterford in all their variety, as well as linens, souvenirs and curios.
11 Duke Street W1. Tel: 01-935 1366

The Scotch House
Mainly woollens and clothes, but they do stock a range of (mainly) tasteful Scottish gifts — including that old standby, the tartan tie or scarf. Not cheap.
Brompton Road SW1. Tel: 01-581 2151

Welsh Craft Centre
Crafts, gifts, quilts and slate carvings from Wales.
34 Piccadilly W1. Tel: 01-409 0969

The Candle Shop
Various shapes, colours, sizes and fragrances (some are perfumed). Some look like fruits, vegetables or politicians. Also kits to make your own. Inexpensive.
Unit 30, The Market, Covent Garden WC2. Tel: 01-836 9815

Portobello Green
Under the Westway along **Portobello Road**, enter a small designer crafts and gifts shopping centre that's not to be missed. Of special interest is the **Necklace Maker.**
Thorpe Close W10.

Expensive gifts

Asprey
See *Street by street: Bond Street*

Alfred Dunhill
The old, gentleman's gift shop now has more modernized minimalist decor, though prices are anything but minimal. A small, smart range of exclusive luggage, sport and tobacco goods.
30 Duke Street SW1. Tel: 01-499 9566

See also *Jewellers: Garrard, Mappin & Webb*; and *Major stores: Harrods, Harvey Nichols* and *Liberty's.*

Less-expensive and moderately-priced gifts

Gift shops of all kind abound in the Covent Garden area. Here are some suggestions for elsewhere:

F.Fwd (Fast Forward)
Much of the stock is inexpensive to moderately-priced modern and high-tech design versions of usual gift shop items. Some expensive stock, but many purchases under £10.
14a Newburgh Street W1. Tel: 01-439 0091

The General Trading Company
A kind of household gift department store with many affordable, tasteful small items, though some offerings are none of these. Worth a look for size, range and Sloane Square location.
144 Sloane Street SW1. Tel: 01-730 0411

Graham and Green
Near the Portobello Market and a handy place to find very clever craft, household and bric-a-brac items that don't stray too far into the cutesy.
4 and **7 Elgin Crescent W11. Tel: 01-727 4594**

Hinkley & Greaves
Very bizarre gift shop with peculiar ideas and tastes. Famous for 'time bomb alarm clocks', and 'magic' gloves and socks that stretch to any size.
25 Pembridge Road W11. Tel: 01-221 9291

Liberty's Basement
Visit the basement of London's most beautiful and charming department store for a wonderful selection of gift items — many obtained from individual craftsmen — for as little as £3–£4. Jewellery, ceramics, fancy boxes, lacquers, woods, Venetian glassware, bottles and delicate earrings. Good buys in Chinese and Japanese bowls and other small orientalia. Near Christmas time, tree ornaments also make interesting buys.
Regent Street W1. Tel: 01-734 1234

Foreign crafts

Australian Gift Shop
More of a fun souvenir shop than a serious craft shop, but they usually stock some interesting Aboriginal art work.
115 Strand WC2. Tel: 01-836 2292

Bizarre Bazaar
This shop in the Portobello Market has an incredibly eclectic collection of mostly inexpensive oriental items: masks, papier mâché, mobiles and many other small curiosities. Worth at least a browse is you're in the area.
251 Portobello Road W11. Tel: 01-221 9489

Ganesha
A kind of small, upmarket oriental Woolworths with splendid little novelties in a tiny shop off Fulham Road. Unlike Woolworths, all items have been carefully and tastefully selected. Masks, puppets, silks, parasols, unusual and highly-decorated cooking utensils, and wall hangings from China, India and South-east Asia. You won't see many of the goodies anywhere else because they've never been exported to other places. A good place to find a 'cheap but extraordinary' gift from £1 to £20.
6 Park Walk SW10. Tel: 01-352 8972

The Greek Shop
Handicrafts, inexpensive clothing, costume jewellery, dolls and curiosities from Greece.
6 Newburgh Street W1. Tel: 01-437 1197

Kikapu African Crafts
Mostly East African carvings, baskets, exotic jewellery.
38 King Street WC2. Tel: 01-240 6098

Kiwi Fruits
Very high-quality, reasonably-priced New Zealand gifts and crafts: woollens, wood carvings, jades and pottery.
25 Bedfordbury Road WC2. Tel: 01-240 1423

Magpie
One of the better-quality, if not the best, Chinese gift and craft shops. Silks, chests, furniture, prints and many small moderately-priced items. A bit out of the way: for that reason less expensive than some more centrally-located shops.
82 Westbourne Grove W2. Tel: 01-229 1691

The Russian Shop
If you've been to Russia, you'll recognize this as a big Beriozka (tourist) shop, selling the usual range of wooden dolls, lacquered boxes and other craft items. Prices are not high, because they're after hard currency here too.
99 Strand WC2. Tel: 01-497 9104

Také
Some very high-quality Japanese crafts on sale — many items come from provincial craftsmen. Hand-painted silk screens, lamps, tea sets and porcelain.
45–46 Chalk Farm Road NW1. Tel: 01-267 3937

Tumi
All kinds of jewellery, wall-hangings, knitwear, carvings, pottery, musical instruments and unusual handicrafts from the Andean countries, Mexico and Central America. Most items relatively inexpensive.
23 Chalk Farm Road NW1. Tel: 01-485 8152

Unique and unusual specialist shops

Anything Left-Handed
Regarded as a godsend by some left-handed people, and parents of left-handed children, this is the only left-handed shop in town. Scissors, kitchen tools and many other specially-designed items. Half the business is mail order. Catalogue available.
65 Beak Street W1. Tel: 01-437 3910

Cartoon Gallery
This gallery run by cartoonists sell original cartoons for as little as £10. Even cheaper, and very useful for tourists, are cartoon postcards (20p), drawn by these artists and not available anywhere else.
83 Lambs Conduit St WC1. Tel: 01-242 5335

Davenports Magic Shop
Old established magic and joke shop
7 Charing Cross Underground Shopping Arcade, Strand WC2. Tel: 01-836 0408

David Godfrey's Old Newspaper Shop
Stock of antique papers provides gift ideas. Give someone a real paper from the day they were born, or a framed front-page story on a world event.
37 Kinnerton Street SW1. Tel: 01-235 7788

Dodo Old Advertising
Ever wondered where those old ads for Weetabix, Horlicks and the London and N.E. Railway that hang in your local bar come from? There's a good chance that they passed through **Dodo**, an almost unrivalled Notting Hill shop that specializes in selling old advertisements of all kinds. Antique posters are primarily in the £8 to £150 range, biscuit tins cost £9 to £40, and there are bar statues, standup showcards, miniatures and some lovely pictorial chocolate and cigar boxes for less than £25. Old labels cost as little as £1.
    It's hard not to be struck by some of the vintage ads. What was thought to be vulgar

in its day has acquired, with time, the charm of a vanished simplicity, innocence and naïvety. I was sorely tempted to buy a yellowing French circus poster for my little son. Saturdays only (700–1600) or by appointment.
286 Westbourne Grove W11. Tel: 01-229 3132

Eaton's Shell Shop
Beautiful seashells.
30 Neal Street WC2. Tel: 01-379 6254

Frontiers
Many travellers come back from East of Suez with some very amazing exotic jewellery and stories about how they traded a lighter, ballpoint pen or 'only $2.95' for it . . . or maybe they stopped off in **Frontiers**, a small elegant shop near Portobello Market. **Frontiers** carries all kinds of tribal beads, necklaces, bracelets and adornments from the world's more remote and primitive areas — especially Nepal, the Indian hills, Yemen, Thailand, Afghanistan and Ethiopia.
39 Pembridge Road W11. Tel: 01-727 6132

Get Stuffed
Sells real stuffed animals of all kinds. They emphasize that they never kill animals to stuff — they buy carcases from parks and zoos. Perhaps a mole (£10) for a friend with a very bizarre sense of humour?
105 Essex Road N1. Tel: 01-226 1364

The Light Fantastic Gallery
Sells holograms
Unit 48, The Market, Covent Garden WC2. Tel: 01-836 6423

Mysteries
A peculiar shop run by very unusual people, who not only sell Tarot cards and crystal balls, but will 'read' you in the shop. Or you can buy a gift certificate to allow a friend to be 'read'.
11 Monmouth Street WC2. Tel: 01-240 3688

The Vintage Magazine Shop
Not just magazines, but posters and all kinds of movie ephemera from the past few decades.
39 Brewer Street W1. Tel: 01-439 8525

Medicines, films, cosmetics, scents and perfumes
Boots (many locations, **Underwoods** (several locations) and other chemist chains can provide for most needs at competitive prices. Many small chemist shops now have next-day set-rate film development per roll (regardless of the number of snaps). **Bliss** at 50 Willesden Lane NW6 (Tel: 01-624 8000) is no longer a 24-hour chemist, but is now the druggist with the longest hours (open 0900–0200) — and a long way from central London. For more selections, see *Women: Perfume and beauty.*

Jewellery and silver
New British jewellery mostly comes in four kinds: costume, craft, less-expensive retail, and fashionable expensive. Costume jewellery can be found everywhere. Craft jewellers have stalls at many of the markets — **Covent Garden** and **Camden Lock** are particularly good places to buy from stall holders who exhibit their own designs. **Portobello Green** is another good spot (see *Unique and unusual shops*).
Those who are interested in commercial jewellery or in search of a possible bargain might take an interest in the shops around **Hatton Garden** and **Clerkenwell**

Road in EC1. It's a trade sales area, but many shops are willing to deal with the public, and several workshops undertake repairs.

For the generic gold chain or ring, prices are competitive at major high street chains like **Samuels** or **Ratners**. London has several world-renowned jewellers or branches of famed international shops in **Mayfair**. Prices are out-of-sight, but they can suddenly be a 'bargain' to the Japanese or whoever else's currency is riding high. (See also *Women's jewellery*.)

Silver is, of course, often sold with jewellery. Many shops sell modern as well as antique pieces, but you'll do just as well in most cases to explore the **Silver Vaults'** many dealers' stands (Chancery Lane WC2, Tel: 01-242 3844; Hours Mon–Fri 0900–1730; Sat to 1230). Unless you just want a new English pewter tankard or the like (in which case head for the High Street chains), go to 'the vaults' first and get a good idea of prices.

Those who want first-class service and professional advice will have to pay for it at **Aspreys** or other **Bond Street** establishments. With similar prices, and high quality and professional services, **S J Phillips** is probably the best silver shop in the top range.

Aspreys
165 New Bond Street W1. Tel: 01-493 6767

Cartier
175 New Bond Street W1. Tel: 01-493 6962

Clerkenwell Workshops
Craftsmen and repairs.
37 Clerkenwell Close EC1. Tel: 01-251 4821

David Joseph
Among the more interesting and affordable shops in the Hatton Garden area.
33 Clerkenwell Road EC1. Tel: 01-250 1462

Garrard
Among the most relaxed and approachable of the expensive stores. They don't seem to mind browsers, even though they're supposed to be the crown jewellers. Beautiful porcelain and antique silver.
112 Regent Street W1. Tel: 01-734 7020

London Diamond Centre
Visitors can go on a tour to see how stones are cut and prepared, then select from a wide variety of settings (or leave). Works as well as in Amsterdam and Rio.
10 Hanover Street W1. Tel: 01-629 5511

Mappin & Webb
Really an upmarket chain, and usually more affordable than some of the others mentioned here.
170 Regent Street W1. Tel: 01-734 3801

Mineral Stones
Another interesting, affordable Hatton Garden shop.
98 Hatton Garden EC1. Tel: 01-405 0197

S J Phillips
139 New Bond Street W1. Tel: 01-629 6261

Necklace Maker
Unit 25, Portobello Green W10. Tel: 01-968 5599

Linens

You may need to look no further than the department stores, which often have excellent ranges, with outstanding values at sales time. **Liberty's** and **Harrods** have good reputations at the middle to top end of the market. Americans should ask whether sheets will fit American-sized beds, which can be slightly different. **Harvey Nichols** makes a big point of stocking American sizes. For less-expensive good-quality duvet covers, and attractive hard-wearing sheets, go to **John Lewis**.

Irish Linen is particularly famed and the **Irish Shop** (see *Crafts and gifts*) and other 'Irish' shops sell it at moderate prices. **Givan's Irish Linen Shop** (207 King's Road SW3, Tel: 01-352 6352) has a higher price range and quality. Some stock is prettily embroidered. Embroidered and monogrammed bedlinen and nightwear are the specialities of **The Monogrammed Linen Shop** (169 Walton Street SW3, Tel: 01-589 4033).

The **White House** (51 New Bond Street W1, Tel: 01-629 3521) is renowned as an expensive linen shop. Prices are stratospheric, but there appears to be no disdain for those customers who want to buy only their fine and famous handkerchiefs. The nearby chic continental shop **Frette** (98 New Bond Street W1, Tel: 01-629 5517) is less friendly, and how many of us have £2000 to spend on satin sheets? **Lunn Antiques** (86 New King's Road SW6, Tel: 01-736 4638) has antique clothing and old linen. **The Linen Cupboard** (21 Great Castle Street W1, Tel: 01-629 4062) has some good-value deals on an interesting stock in linen and bedding.

Museum and gallery shops

Sometimes it seems as if the only difference between what you see in London's shops and what you can at home is the stamp 'London' across the item. Much-improved museum shops are now a notable exception, and most are a far cry from the days in which they sold cards, prints and junk. Many now sell tasteful, finely-crafted replicas of their display items. The Duke of Atholl recently formed a new company to make these 'fakes' for museums. Their vastly-improved bookshops are often well-stocked and sell prints and posters you can't find elsewhere. So, for the unusual gift to take home, don't bypass the museum or gallery shop. (For addresses and other details, see *Museums*)

Bethnal Green Museum of Childhood
Copies of dolls and other Victorian childhood nostalgia.

British Museum Shop
Many well-crafted reproductions available for as little as £10, but sculptures can cost hundreds. Good book selection.

London Transport Museum
An excellent range of between-the-wars and Victorian transport poster repro-ductions. Also T-shirts and other ephemera featuring the famous Underground map.

National Gallery and National Portrait Gallery
Of course, great prints and cards (though no scale forgeries!). Calendars and diaries make nice gifts.

National Postal Museum
Of course, a great place to buy stamps!

Pollock's Toy Museum
Part museum and part shop, where you can still find old-fashioned toys.

Royal Academy of Arts Gift Shop
Open even where there's no exhibition. Designer T-shirts and accessories. Gifts for budding artists.

Science and Natural History Museums
Books and small items make good gifts for kids.

Tate Gallery
Of course, very good prints. The Clore Wing has a small shop selling Turner books and prints.

Victoria and Albert Museum
As you might expect, the museum's decorative arts emphasis makes this one of the better museum shops, with pottery, jewellery and fabrics by modern British craftsmen. Some photographic prints are exceptional.

Sports equipment and clothing

Lillywhite's
Six floors of sporting goods and sportswear. Good, knowledgeable staff. British-oriented sports items — rugby jerseys, cricket bats, golf accessories — make good gifts for foreign visitors to take home or send from a useful export department.
Piccadilly Circus SW1. Tel: 01-930 3181

Stamps
London is still the stamp collector's Mecca, and British stamps can make an interesting and attractive present to bring home. The **Strand** is the centre of the stamp business. **Stanley Gibbons** at 399 Strand (Tel: 01-836 8444) claims to be the world's largest stamp dealer.

Toys and games

Hamley's
Claimed to be the 'world's biggest toy store', and true or not it has five floors of goodies, enough to boggle the mind not only with choice, but also with, surprisingly, organization and quiet. Instead of screaming manic children, there are stares of awe and smiles. Hamley's insist that all children can play with the toys on the floor — and they do. **Hamley's** was started in 1760, and on an average day (not Christmas!) over 18,000 people walk through their doors. They are not the cheapest, but they must be doing something right!
188 Regent Street W1. Tel: 01-734 3161

Beatties
Models of all kinds.
202 High Holborn WC1. Tel: 01-405 6285

Bethnal Green Museum of Childhood
Has a shop that sells some replica traditional toys.
Bethnal Green. Tel: 01-980 2415

Children's Book Centre
One of the largest selection of children's books in London.
237 Kensington High Street W8. Tel: 01-937 7497

Early Learning Centre
Interesting selection of bright and fun, but still educational, toys for younger children.
225 Kensington High Street W8. Tel: 01-437 0419

Eric Snook
Very imaginative.
Unit 21, The Market, Covent Garden. Tel: 01-379 7681

Galt Toys
Famous well-designed wooden toys and the fabulous **Brio** wooden trains. Also has small shop in **Liberty's**.
84 Fortisgreen Road N10. Tel: 01-444 0282

The Kite & Balloon Co
Enormous range of kites and balloons — they even print personalized balloons.
160 Eardley Road SW16. Tel: 01-679 8844

Pollock's Toy Museum
See *Museums* for lots of info.

Tiger Tiger
Lovely toys of all kinds.
219 King's Road SW10. Tel: 01-352 8080

Virgin Games Centre
For games.
100 Oxford Street W1. Tel: 01-637 7911

Woollens and knitwear
Knitwear of all kinds is probably the most popular purchase the foreign visitor brings back from Britain. Wool or knit chain shops are everywhere in central London. Most of their cheap merchandise is below par in quality and above in price, aimed at a tourist clientele. Make up your mind whether you want to pay high prices for superb quality or moderate prices for good quality. There's no point in buying very cheap knitwear — it just doesn't last.

Good quality at a moderate price
You can't do better than **Marks & Spencer** (for more details, see *Major stores*). No brand names other than their own, but the range of colour and design on offer has been greatly expanded in recent years, particularly in the **Marble Arch** main store. **Westaway & Westaway** (65 Great Russell Street WC1, Tel: 01-405 4479) is the place to go for a greater variety in brand names and types at lower prices than most other shops. Conveniently located across the street from the British Museum.

Fine quality but more expensive
Of course, stores like **Harrods, Burberry** and **Harvey Nichols** all have fine cashmeres and other high-quality woollens, but have a look at **The Scotch House** (2 Brompton Road SW1, Tel: 01-581 2151, and other branches). The other major place to go is **Burlington Arcade** (Piccadilly W1), which has several top-quality knit shops.
The very chic go to **Joseph Tricot** (18 Sloane Street SW1, Tel: 01-235 2719), which is, of course, very expensive. But if you want good designer knitwear at high but not outrageous prices, try **Scottish Merchant** (16 New Row WC2, Tel: 01-836 2207). **Covent Garden** and other markets often have stalls run by new not-yet-recognized designers. In-the-know, shabby-genteel Londoners pick up second-hand cashmere and designer knits from **Oxfam** and other charity sales.

11 *Going to see the sights*

Whether this is your first trip to London or your fiftieth, the first and most important tip to remember is: you can't see everything. Those of us who've lived here for years still haven't. The second (and almost as important) is: London is not just a collection of notable sights, but a living, breathing metropolis made up of distinct areas, some say 'villages', with their own looks and special atmospheres. Much of the pleasure of visiting will come from just walking around their little streets and major roads; riding the double deckers, tubes and taxis, and talking to people in queues, shops and pubs. So, make little discoveries of your own and don't over-organize the seeing of sights, whether major or more unusual. The time you spare for walks, browsing or just sitting on a park bench may turn out to be the most memorable.

Having said that, the question naturally arises: which sights are worth seeing? We can't answer it for you except to say that it's a matter of personal interest and taste. You'll probably agree with us, but we think you should take this statement seriously. If you don't like art galleries or museums, but are a keen gardener, you shouldn't feel guilty. Spend the day at **Kew Gardens** rather than in the **British Museum** or the **Tate Gallery**.

On the other hand, London offers an incredible variety of experiences and chances to see art, places and life that you won't see elsewhere. If you don't know what you want to see, have a look at as many London sights as you feel up to visiting. And get out of town at least once to see something of the vast array of attractions and experiences within a comfortable day's excursion from London. In this section, we'll make our own suggestions to help you make up your mind, but remember, it's all up to you!

'Sights' clearly divide into categories. **Westminster Abbey, St Paul's Cathedral** and the **British Museum** are so famous and of such importance to the heritage of world civilization that most first-time visitors will feel they can't ignore them. Many other sights are notable places and buildings — the **River Thames, Piccadilly Circus, Trafalgar Square, Whitehall, Fleet Street**, etc — that people have heard about all their lives and want to see. Some of these 'place sights' merit closer investigation; a good impression of others may be gained with a passing glance from a bus. Museums and parks are clearly two more categories that would be of interest to most visitors. At the bottom of our list, but maybe at the top of yours (especially if you have children), are London's artificial 'tourist attractions', like **Madame Tussaud's** and the **Guinness World of Records** or the **London Dungeon**. But again, please feel free to disagree!

We hope you'll take a look beyond London, so we also include a section on day trips and further afield in Britain. Some sights come as but once a year 'events', or might be more correctly designated 'activities', so you might also want to take a look at the *Activities* section of this chapter and the *Events* section in the *Entertainment* chapter.

Sightseeing tips

- You can's see everything: make a decision about how you want to utilize your time.

- All first-time visitors should take a short bus tour of Central London to orient themselves and get an overview of the city's layout and major sights. The inexpensive (£6) **London Transport Tour** passes most of the important sights and goes through the major historic, cultural and shopping districts in about 1½ hours.

- Take along pen and paper and jot down a note about any shops, buildings or areas that catch your fancy. Decide for yourself what you'd like to go back to on your own: maybe everything, maybe nothing.

- Our recommendation is that these major sights, at the very least, merit a close inspection on foot: the **Tower of London, St Paul's Cathedral**, the **British Museum, Westminster Abbey** and **Parliament Square**.

- If your knowledge of British history or London is a bit sketchy, early stops might be made at the **Museum of London** or the **National Portrait Gallery** (both worth a visit on their own account anyway). The **Museum of London** is full of modern easy-to-follow exhibits that make the city come alive. The **National Portrait Gallery** will enable you to put famous faces with places and dates.

- First-timers might want to allocate at least a day out of their trips for general London sightseeing: say, a morning tour and then a return in the afternoon or later to anything that particularly interests you.

- An alternative to a bus tour, and cheaper but more time-consuming, is to ride the full length of the **15** or **52** bus routes (see *Getting oriented*).

- When doing your own sightseeing, you can make the best use of your time if you note which attractions are near to one another. For example, **Harrods**, the **Victoria and Albert Museum** and the **Science** and **Natural History Museums** are within walking distance of each other.

- Two weeks in Britain for the first time: how much time in London? A minimum of three days is necessary to really get much feel or enjoyment of the big city. Five days would be better.

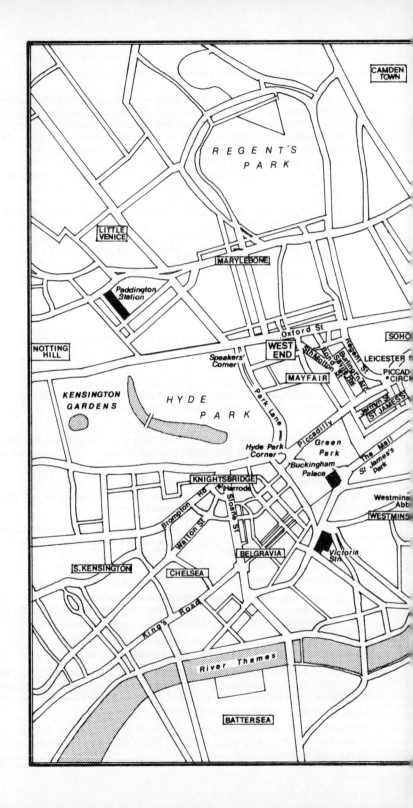

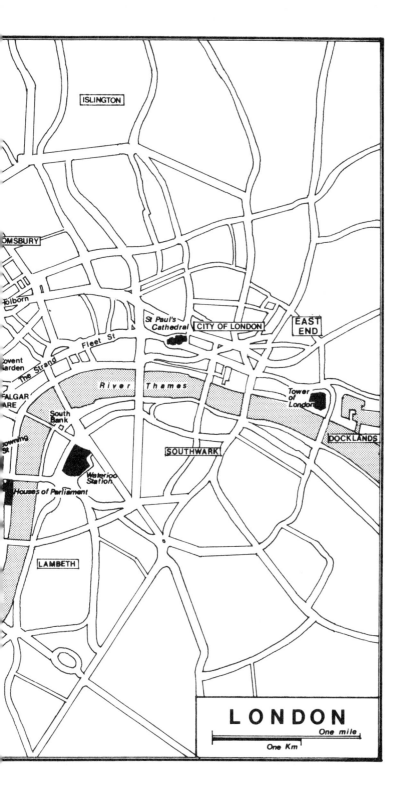

ISLINGTON

OMSBURY

Iolborn

ovent
arden

The Strand

Fleet St

St Paul's
Cathedral

CITY OF LONDON

EAST
END

FALGAR
ARE

River Thames

Tower
of
London

South
Bank

owning
St

SOUTHWARK

DOCKLANDS

Houses of Parliament

Waterloo
Station

LAMBETH

LONDON

One mile

One Km

- Take a boat trip on the Thames and walk along the river bank, especially between **Westminster Bridge** and **Waterloo Bridge**. The river is the city's too-obvious but nonetheless not-to-be-missed attraction. The canal trip between **Camden Lock** and **Little Venice** is also highly recommended.

- While you're here, don't just visit the sights, but take in the theatre, go to a pub for lunch, eat in an Indian restaurant, walk through Hyde Park or take one of the other walks we suggest.

- If the Royal family interest you, check *The Times* for the **Court Circular** to see if one of the royals will be opening a building, dedicating a school, etc. Go and join the crowd.

- Unless your time is very limited, try to take at least one day-trip to get out of noisy crowded, tourist-hustled London. Further on in Chapter 12, *London's Britain* we list many places you might fancy.

The major sights

Few people would dispute that the **Tower of London, St Paul's Cathedral**, the **British Museum, Westminster Abbey** and the **Houses of Parliament** are sights of major importance, not only to Britain's history, but also to the heritage of mankind, and the English-speaking world in particular. This obvious fact means that all are besieged by tourist hordes from April to October. In the mad rush some of the special ambience of each is lost. Nevertheless, if you haven't been before, go and brave the crowds and try to enjoy them anyway. But we also have one special recommendation: don't miss London's all-too obvious asset, the **River Thames**. A boat trip on the river and a walk along the banks will add something special to your trip.

The Tower of London and surroundings
Not really just a tower, of course, but a massive castle complex beside the Thames, where the Crown Jewels are protected in the **Jewel House**. Perhaps no other edifice in London has seen so much history through so many uses — fort, residence, political prison, place of execution, observatory, armoury and mint. If you haven't seen a castle before, this is a good place to start.

The **White Tower**, the central four-towered keep, dates back to its completion by William the Conqueror in about 1078. **St John's Chapel** on the second floor is the oldest church in London. A series of outer towers and walls were added or altered by almost every medieval monarch. The moat is now drained and kept as carefully-clipped lawns that beautifully offset the old stone walls, but the castle still provides an inspiration to the imagination and a special place to learn about medieval buildings and fortifications that have fallen into ruins elsewhere. Take note that parts of the castle have undergone renovation and restoration, especially in the late 1600s (by Christopher Wren) and later.

Expect long queues in summer, particularly for the Crown Jewels. If you can't stand the wait, don't despair: the jewels are worth seeing, but are not a life-changing experience! Most of the originals were lost during Cromwell's Commonwealth, and today's jewels are largely post-Restoration. The colourful **Yeomen of the Guard** (or **Beefeaters**) are more concerned with their role as tourist symbols of London than with keeping a stern eye on potential jewel snatchers. Most are affable and seem to enjoy their silly costumes while posing for more photos with tourists than you can take breaths in a day.

Although you'll see other soldiers (it is still a military installation), the Tower is today mostly given over to tourism. The fairly steep admission fee may or may not (depending on policy changes) also allow admission to the jewels and an ever-growing number of other attractions, including a **Herald's Museum** and an **Armoury**.

Unless you are very interested in gemology, genealogy or military equipment, simply walk along the battlements and take in the spirit and superb location of the place. Afterwards, stroll the pleasant riverside path beside the Thames and visit other nearby attractions (see below). You can easily spend a whole day in the area.

Other nearby attractions

Tower Bridge
Another well-known symbol of London, the entrance to this twin-towered medieval-looking drawbridge is situated between the **Tower** and **St Katherine's Dock** (see below). It costs nothing to walk across it and enjoy some fantastic views of the Thames boat traffic, the Tower and London's skyline. (If you look up river, the next bridge you can see is a bland-looking concrete and steel modern affair — the London Bridge of the rhyme disappeared centuries ago. Its immediate predecessor was bought and transported to Arizona by a developer who mistakenly thought he had acquired Tower Bridge!) The view from the top is even more astounding, but you have to pay an admission fee for it and to see the marvellous old operating mechanism. By the way, **Tower Bridge** dates from only 1894.

St Katherine's Dock
This nearby marina is mainly a mooring for pleasure craft. Stroll around, look at the **Historic Ship Collection** and the many boat shapes and sizes, and enjoy the shops and restaurants in the restored dock warehouses.

Hays Gallery
Across **Tower Bridge** and then a short walk away, behind the *HMS Belfast*, is this glass-domed building containing expensive shops and restaurants, as well as a large, pleasant pub with bar meals — **Horniman's**. Nearby are the **London Dungeon** and **Space Adventure** (see *Tourist attractions and activities: Children*).

Docklands Light Railway
For a different perspective on London, take this high-tech elevated trip across London's dockland. Return to **Tower Gateway Station** (13 minutes), near the Tower Hill underground station, or cross the river via an underground foot tunnel to visit historic **Greenwich**, and perhaps return to the Tower's own dock by boat.

Tower Dock
Catch a river boat from here to **Westminster Pier** (near the **Houses of Parliament**) or down river to **Greenwich**.

Tower of London: details
Tel: 01-709 0765
Admission: £4.50 adult, £2.00 children
Hours
Mon–Sat 0930–1745; Sun 1400–1745 Mar-Oct.
Mon–Sat 0930·1600; Sun CLOSED Nov–Feb.
Crown Jewels may be closed in February. Go early or between 1230–1400, when many tour groups are at lunch.
Food and Drink
Cafés are available on site, and more pubs and food can be found in nearby **St Katherine's Dock**. Pubs are nearby and just across the river.
Getting there
U: **Tower Hill**; and **15** bus; **river boat** from **Westminster** to **Tower Dock**; or on the **Docklands Light Railway**.

St Paul's Cathedral

St Paul's, rather than the nearby **Monument**, is the real symbol of the resurrection of the City of London after the Great Fire of 1666 and the genius of Sir Christopher Wren, its architect. This symbolic significance is so strong that Churchill kept firemen up on the Cathedral roof during the World War II blitz to prevent its destruction. The immediate area was bombed flat and bland, modern buildings now surround St Paul's. These, and the City skyscrapers behind it, have diminished some of the imposing dominance of Wren's bold design. Nevertheless, the Cathedral is still an impressive sight.

Impressive, rather than endearing or charming, is the word for St Paul's. Everything is on a massive scale. The twin front Italian towers and two tiers of classical columns give the impression that the building is even taller than it actually is. A walk around the outside is a long one, but you can clearly see the massive cruciform layout — considered radical by the clergy of the day. Inside, the Cathedral is so vast and cavernous that it copes with the demands of the summer tourist surge better than any other London attraction.

Like most Cathedrals, it is filled with memorials. Even some of these are enormous, especially that of the **Duke of Wellington**. **Nelson, Kitchener, Johnson, John Donne, Reynolds** and **Turner** are among the other famous people commemorated here. Americans will take particular interest in the *Jesus Chapel* in the apse, where there is a memorial to American service men who fell in World War II.

Admission is free, but there are now little admission charges to the *crypt*, the **Whispering Gallery** in the **dome**, and other parts of the Cathedral. If you have the time, go on the excellent guided tour that admits you to these places and tells the fascinating story of Wren's struggle against king, clergy and critics during the 35 years from 1675 to 1710. The story is too long to repeat here in full, but it tells how Wren, in order to implement his innovative plan, had to employ considerable craft and influence at court. For those who don't have time for the tour, the unspectacular, unspooky, well-lit **crypt** has an exhibition which relates the story as well.

Wren lived to see his masterpiece nearly complete. He is, appropriately, buried in his Cathedral, and the tablet above his grave reads (in Latin): 'Reader, if you would seek his monument, look around you'.

St Paul's Cathedral: details

Tel: 01-248 2705
Admission: Free, but there are charges to some parts.
Hours
0730–1800 year round; sightseeing 1000–1615 weekdays; 1100–1615 Saturdays; closed Sunday. Tours: 1100, 1130, 1400 and 1430 lasting 1½ hours.
Nearby
St Paul's is in the City business district — **Lloyd's**, the **Stock Exchange** and the **Bank of England** are nearby. Also close is the **Barbican Arts Complex**, within which is the highly-recommended **Museum of London**.
Getting there
U: **St Paul's**. The **15** bus stops in front.

The British Museum and British Library

One of the world's great treasure houses, the **British Museum** is as popular an attraction as **St Paul's, Westminster Abbey** or the **Tower**. Despite the name, most of the collection isn't actually British: this is officially a museum of classical antiquities and prints and drawings. And the collection is so vast that only a portion of it is on exhibition. In fact, for a while the collection seemed to have overwhelmed the curators to such an extent that there was little effort to introduce creative or modern methods of museum display. This huge, dusty, musty treasure trove induced visitor exhaustion in a very short time.

Fresh paint and new display methods have now been introduced, but the scale cannot be defeated. You still need to approach the collection carefully and selectively. Buy the excellent £1.50 colour guidebook and map at the entrance, and decide what you really want to see most. Alternatively (this may seem heretical), take a relatively quick walk through all the galleries with a note pad and pencil. Jot down the exhibits or display items that most catch your fancy or attention. Go and have a coffee in the **Coffee Shop** (or head for the nearby **Museum** pub — but that's hardly likely to put you in a cerebral mood . . .) and decide which exhibits to go back and see, then or later. Most people who try to attack the British Museum with a full day's visit will fail miserably . . .

There is indeed much to choose from. Many visitors will want to see the most famous major exhibits. Possibly the most renowned of these are the **Elgin Marbles** in the **Duveen Gallery**. These are over a hundred white statues and pieces of panel friezes from the Parthenon in Athens that were bought by Lord Elgin from the Sultan of Turkey in 1810. Though most of this sculpture is fragmented, chipped, armless and even headless, they are nonetheless impressive representations of the Greek gods and wars. Greece now says that the marbles were looted and is trying to reclaim them. You can understand why they want them back, but it is also important to know that the marbles caused a great stir and acquired a significance out of all proportion in Britain when they arrived in 1810 as the first major pieces of Greek sculpture anyone had seen. And if Britain returned the marbles, the precedent could lead to the virtual emptying of the museum.

Next door to the marbles is the complete reconstructed tomb façade of the **Nereid Monument**. Other rooms contain more pieces of tombs and other buildings, sometimes very substantial fragments. Coins, metals and fine glass help to give the British Museum one of the world's finest Greek and Roman collections.

Many people also think of the museum as the home of the mummies that come alive in all those Hollywood horror movies. The **Egyptian Collection**, with its renowned mummy room, is again one of the world's finest. But don't ignore the hundreds of immaculately-preserved tomb statuettes and other artefacts, nor the famous **Rosetta Stone**, a slab of black basalt whose multilingual inscriptions allowed scholars to decipher hieroglyphics.

The **Oriental Galleries** contain many ancient and delicate porcelains, bronzes, earthenware and prints.

The most British part of the museum consists of a few rooms illustrating the Roman period in Britain, with preserved mosaics, crockery and jewellery. There are also magnificent finds from the famed Anglo-Saxon royal ship burial at **Sutton Hoo**.

The enormous and immensely-valuable **Print and Drawing Collection** has no permanent exhibition of its **European Collection**. Special exhibitions of artists like **Dürer, Rembrandt, Rubens, Watteau** and **Turner** are put on in the special **Print Room**, and change about three times a year.

The collections of the **British National Library** are housed within the British Museum — although they are expected to move to Camden at some point in the future, when the new **British Library** building is completed. The most famous items on display are two of the four surviving copies of the **Magna Carta**, the **Lindisfarne Gospels**, the **Gutenberg Bible**, and Shakespeare's **First Folio**. The sketchbooks of many famous artists, first editions and illuminated manuscripts are also on display.

And yes, you can see the **Reading Room** of the British Museum, under whose magnificent dome Karl Marx laboured to write *Das Kapital*. Parties of visitors are quietly escorted into the room at five minutes to the hour from 1100–1600.

British Museum: details
Tel: 01-636 1555
Admission: Free
Hours: Mon–Sat 1000–1700; Sun 1430–1800

Facilities
Coffee shop serving light meals.
Museum shops sell books and excellent reproductions of museum artefacts.
Nearby
Have a look at the fascinating **Museum Tavern** across the street. Surrounding
Bloomsbury has some pretty Georgian parks and squares, as well as Edwardian grid
blocks housing the **University of London**, corporations and tourist hotels.
Getting there
Greet Russell Street WC1. U: **Tottenham Court Road.**

Westminster Abbey

The 'best-loved' religious building in the Western world, according to the pamphlet
handed out to visitors; so much so that the incredible flow of summer tourist traffic
makes it almost impossible to stop and admire the vast clutter of monuments and
graves of the great and near-great. Much better to go in winter, when a completely
different impression of this sacred spot is to be had.

The **Abbey** is thought to be sited on a place that was of religious significance even
in pagan times. Later legends tell of miracles, even of the appearance of St Peter. The
first known church was dedicated by Edward the Confessor in 1065. It has been a
church, an abbey, and a cathedral, and is now designated a 'Royal Particular'.

Above all, the Abbey is a shrine that intertwines the religious and the British nation.
All British kings and queens, except two, have been crowned, and many have been
buried or married, here. The **Coronation Chair**, with the ancient **Stone of Scone**, is
kept here. British military heroes, poets, churchmen and politicians are commemorated. Someone from outer space might conclude that the Abbey is the place where
the British practise ancestor worship; certainly one is left with the impression that
God is an Englishman, with maybe a touch of Scottish, Irish and Welsh blood.

Admission to the **nave** is free. To see the most fascinating parts and memorials,
you must pay a £1.30 admission fee. Further on, there is an optional additional charge
to see the **Pyx Chamber**, the **Norman Undercroft** and a small museum. The inclusive
tour is excellent and well worth whatever price they happen to be charging by the
time you read this book.

Westminster Abbey: details

Tel: 01-222 5152
Admission: The nave is free. £1.80 to go beyond.
Hours
Mon–Fri 0900–1545; Sat 0900–1400, 1500–1645.
Services all day Sunday.
Nearby
Parliament Square, Houses of Parliament, Whitehall and **St James' Park.**
Getting there
U: **Westminster**

Houses of Parliament and Big Ben

Unless you can get a pass from an MP, it's very difficult to see much of the interiors of
these massive magnificent neo-gothic buildings (the **Houses** date from 1844; **Big Ben**
only from 1858). Nevertheless, we include them here because they are the world-
famous symbols of London and Britain. Have a walk round the outer fences or admire
them from across the Thames.

It is, of course, possible to queue for either the **House of Commons** or the **House of
Lords** on weekdays when Parliament is in session, but seating is usually limited and
you're in for a long wait. From late July to November, for a week in May and at
Christmas, Parliament is in recess, and you'll be out of luck. When Parliament is in
session, queues usually start to form about 1400. Visitors are admitted to the

Commons from about 1615. *Tip*: for a shorter wait, join the queue at about 1830. Parliamentary business begins late and ends late in the evening. *Hint*: the **Lords** is usually easier to see, and is prettier than the **Commons**, even if the benches are emptier and more of the occupants are asleep. For more information on the **Commons** Tel: 01-219 3000; on the **Lords** Tel: 01-219 3107

The River Thames

The obvious is always in danger of being over-looked, but visitors who fail to enjoy the **River Thames** miss something of the essence of London. Even today, when there's little commercial traffic, and the tidal floods have been stemmed by the new *Thames Barrier*, the river remains the central focal point and fact of the city's past, present and future heritage. The city's newest development area, the **Docklands**, is situated on the river, and flats and houses with a river view are sought-after. Why? Because there's something about flowing water that appeals to human beings, deep down. Combined with the majestic riverside sights of London — **Parliament** and **Big Ben**, the **South Bank**, pubs, warehouses, bridges, the skyline of **St Paul's** and many different buildings, river barges, tugs and pleasure boats — how could you bear to miss it?

Boat trips

Boats embark from **Westminster Pier, Charing Cross** and **Tower Hill Pier** at the **Tower of London**. A number of small companies operate cruise services from approximately 1000 to 1700–1800 (schedules depend on the tides). For more information you can phone the **Tourist Board's Riverboat Information** (Tel: 01-730 4812). **Westminster Passenger Services** operates trips downriver to **Tower** and **Greenwich** (Tel: 01-930 4097), or upriver to **Kew, Richmond** and **Hampton Court** (Tel: 01-930 4721). The new **Thames Line Riverbus** system offers a quick (25 min) service between **Charing Cross Pier** and **West India Dock** and points in between (Info on Tel: 01-376 3676). This same number provides info on the **London City Airport Riverbus**, with services to **Dockland Airport** and **Greenwich**. More piers and services are scheduled to open upstream in Chelsea and on the South Bank.

Every visitor to London should take at least one river trip, either way, from **Westminster Pier** to **Tower Hill** (next to the **Tower of London**). But we strongly recommend a trip all the way to **Greenwich**. You can come back on the futuristic **Docklands Light Railway** (13 minutes from **Island Gardens**, through a below-the-Thames tunnel from **Greenwich**, to **Tower Gateway**). But London is at its most majestic when approached from Greenwich: **Tower Bridge** and the London skyline get closer and closer, then you pass under the bridge. Unfortunately, the last boats return from Greenwich not much later than 1600, so check times. A number of other options, including dinner and lunch cruises, are also available (with **Catamaran Cruises** Tel: 01-839 3572).

Beyond Greenwich is an amazing feat of modern engineering — the **Thames Barrier** — which controls the tidal floods that once periodically threatened sections of the city. There is now a **Visitor Centre** (Tel: 01-854 1373) at the Barrier, which looks like a series of sail boats (or miniature Sydney Opera Houses). The Barrier is best seen from boat tours from Greenwich or Westminster Pier (morning and afternoon: Tel: 01-930 3373).

River Walks

You should be able to walk alongside the Thames all the way from the **Tower** to **Richmond**. You can't do so yet, and it's a crying shame. Plans for this facility have been proposed, but large sections of riverside walkway are still occupied by warehouses, private riverfronts and, at one point, the House of Commons riverside terraces (Members Only). In the meantime, you can take advantage of the sections that are open to enjoy stunning views and pleasant walks.

North Bank of the Thames to Westminster Bridge
1. St Katherine's Dock — Tower Pier
A pleasant, shaded, but short walkway in front of the **Tower of London** and the **Tower Hotel**, divided by a passage under **Tower Bridge** with its own excellent views.
2. Tower Pier — Houses of Parliament
The first third of this walk runs parallel to the river along **Lower** and **Upper Thames Street**. The river is mostly hidden from view and access is mostly private. So you might start again at **Blackfriars Bridge**, where a wonderful long sweep of river walkway begins, continues for a mile and passes permanently-moored ships, **Cleopatra's Needle** (the famous obelisk brought back from Egypt), and two river passenger boat piers. Magnificent views of the **South Bank**. Climb up the steps to **Westminster Underground Station** and **Parliament Square**.

South Bank of the Thames to Westminster Bridge
1. Tower Bridge — Blackfriars Bridge
Cross over at **Tower Bridge**. When construction finishes, you should be able to go down to the river here. At the time of writing the path to the **HMS Belfast Jetty** provides the first access to the river walkway. Visit the famous battleship or continue on to the new **Hay's Gallery**, a development of offices and ships with a spectacular high-tech curved roof. Pause at **Horniman's** pub or continue along the river walkway with the views of the **Tower** and the skyline of the City. Climb up onto **London Bridge**, the site of the long-gone medieval bridge of the rhyme.

Cross over the High Street to **Southwark Cathedral**, a little-known piece of medieval London. Just beyond is **Clink Street**, site of the old prison, whose name gave us the phrase 'in the clink'. Along **Bankside**, you'll find **The Anchor**, the pub which claims to have London's finest riverside views. Continue on **Upper Ground** to **Blackfriar's Bridge**, to the point where a beautiful tree-shaded river walk stretches away to just below **Westminster Bridge**, with views of the **North Bank** and **Big Ben** just down river. In summer, there is something of a Left Bank atmosphere around the **National Film Theatre**, with bookstalls, strings of coloured lights and outdoor drinking and dining. Walk down the **Albert Embankment** to **Westminster Bridge** and view the **Houses of Parliament**.

A short evening walk
Look across to the **South Bank** from the **Embankment**, then cross the river on the **Hungerford Foot Bridge**. From the bridge you can look up river to the lighted dome of **St Paul's** and across to the flashing, multi-coloured **wind sculpture** behind the South Bank complex. Continue across and enjoy a drink at the **National Film Theatre**, then walk down the **Albert Embankment** to **Westminster Bridge** to enjoy the views of **Parliament** and other illuminated buildings.

Further up river
On the **North Bank** you have to walk around the **Houses of Parliament** to get back to a very pleasant riverfront, the **Victoria Tower Gardens**. From there it is possible to walk all the way to Chelsea's **Cheyne Walk**, a charming area of pubs and famous houses, past the **Tate Gallery**, **Dolphin Square** and **Ranelagh Gardens**, though this is an approximately two-mile stretch and some of the enjoyment is lessened by the heavy traffic on the riverside road.

On the **South Bank**, there is a spectacular vantage point for the **Houses of Parliament**, on the **Albert Embankment**, in front of **St Thomas' Hospital**. Beyond **Lambeth Bridge** it is only a short walk before access to the river is limited; much of the surroundings consist of disused docks and modern blocks. Up river, there is another pleasant stretch in **Battersea Park**. Further up the North Bank, there is an interesting stretch of river walkway in **Bishop's Park**, in Fulham. But a really glorious stretch runs beside **Hammersmith — Chiswick Malls**.

Go to **Hammersmith Station**. Head south on the west side of **Hammersmith Bridge Road** under the flyover, to the lower mall. Here, beside the Victorian **Hammersmith Bridge**, you'll find houses fronting the river and a couple of charming riverside pubs. Just beyond the bridge, behind you, is **Riverside Studios** and a café. Continue west along the upper mall river walk with its gardens, willows, boat clubs and sweeping views of a great bend in the Thames. In one or two spots access to the river is blocked by a few Georgian houses. Soon you'll come to **The Dove**, a highly-recommendable historic riverfront pub. A ways beyond is **The Old Ship**. Both have good food, ale and views of boats on the Thames. You might want to continue along Chiswick's riverfront, then walk up to **Hogarth's House** and **Chiswick House**. Alternatively, walk to **Barnes** on the opposite bank. Your destination should be the High Street and village green.

Further up river in **Kew Bridge**, in **Richmond**, and across the river in **Twickenham** are pleasant riverside walks and pubs with plenty of ambience, in close proximity to several famous great houses. The truly energetic can walk, on different sides of the river, all the way from **Putney** to **Oxford**.

Visitors to **Hampton Court**, especially those staying in the area, might enjoy a river walk in **Surrey**. Take the train from **Waterloo** to **Hampton Court Station**. Almost directly opposite the station is a **tow path** at **Molesey Lock**, where you can begin a five-mile walk along the Thames to **The Weir**. Another mile will bring you to **The Swan**. Both pubs have good atmosphere, good food and beer. Even if you don't go all the way, you can see plenty of houseboats, river craft, locks, weirs, rowers and swans. Other pubs are nearby *en route* for the less energetic.

Places and buildings

Some very notable 'sights' are just places that have become world famous for a variety of reasons. Most visitors feel they want to have 'seen' them (though we can't think of any that merit the 'and die'). Many can be covered by a quick glance from a passing bus. Or, you may want to hang about and feed the pigeons. Some buildings are barred to visitors, or are open for only very limited hours and with lots of restrictions, but their exteriors may be enough to excite your imagination and stir your curiosity.

Place sights
More information about historic neighbourhoods and shopping streets is provided in the *Getting oriented* and *Shopping* sections. For your convenience, here is a listing of streets, squares and terraces you may want to see.

Piccadilly Circus
See *Getting oriented*.

Trafalgar Square
The tourist authorities consider feeding the pigeons in Trafalgar Square to be so important an attraction that they were gravely embarrassed when they temporarily had to ban the activity during renovations. If you want to do it, there are plenty of photo vendors eager to sell you a photo of yourself and the plump greedy little creatures. Personally, we think Trafalgar Square is worth a long look because no other place in London is so evocative of London's nineteenth-century grandeur as the capital of an empire.

Nelson, of course, still stands majestically atop his column, looking down the impressive vista to the south, along **Whitehall** toward the shadowy gothic towers of Parliament. Although we, on the ground, are afforded no such view, the impression is still mighty, especially from the north side of the square in front of the classic columns of the **National Gallery**.

On the west side is **Canada House,** with colourful provincial flags aflutter, and the **Admiralty Arch** (if you're feeling grandiose, have a taxi drive you through the arch and down the grand **Mall** to **Buckingham Palace**). On the east side is **South Africa House,** the embassy of that troubled former dominion, with a 24-hour demonstration and a number of Bobbies at the door. In fact, the square is a favourite place for peaceful public demonstrations of all kinds, so you might want to check the papers — either to avoid or to participate! On New Year's Eve the square is the scene of a raucous celebration similar to New Year in New York's Times Square.

Leicester Square
See *Getting oriented.*

Oxford Circus
Like Piccadilly, now an intersection (Oxford and Regent Street) rather than a true 'circus'. Nothing special, but at the centre of London's main shopping area. For **Oxford Street** and **Regent Street** see *Getting oriented.*

Marble Arch
Originally meant to be the gate to Buckingham Palace, this miniature Arc de Triomphe now sits forlornly on a traffic island off the north-east corner of **Hyde Park**. The arch is unspectacular and 'Marble Arch' is now better known as a neighbourhood, a tube station, and the location of Britain's flagship **Marks and Spencer** store.

Speaker's Corner
Not a proper geographical location, but marked on maps as the north-east corner of **Hyde Park,** opposite **Marble Arch.** On Sundays, you can see a variety of orators exercising their right of free speech as crowds drift around them. Some are witty professionals who come every Sunday and enjoy exchanges with the audience; others are deadly-boring religious or political fanatics.

Hyde Park Corner
The traffic swirls at high speed around the island where stands **Wellington's Monument,** another imitation Arc de Triomphe (every city has to have at least one, and London has two — see **Marble Arch**). Considered to be one of the blackest spots for drivers. Best seen from the top deck of a bus.

Belgrave Square
An elegant Regency square in the centre of an area of colonnaded houses and embassies. This posh square, along with neighbouring Georgian terraces and streets, may represent the ideal of 'London' for the foreign visitor.

Grosvenor Square
Famous for the **American Embassy,** whose roof-front eagle dominates the whole scene, and a statue of **Franklin Roosevelt.**

Bloomsbury Square
Along with **Tavistock, Bedford** and **Russell Square, Bloomsbury Square** helps to give style and grace to a neighbourhood dominated by the **British Museum** and geometric low-rise buildings from Georgian and Edwardian times.

Berkeley Square
Where 'the nightingale sang' — a charming square of green in smart Mayfair.

Soho Square
This square is partially fronted by Georgian houses. With these, trees, and a small pavilion in the centre, it has a special ambience of its own.

Bond Street
Often contrasted with 'downmarket' Oxford Street. Both the **Old** and **New** sections of this Mayfair street contain some of the city's most expensive shops, like **Gucci** and **Asprey's**.

The Mall
Long, triumphal, straight street leading from **Admiralty Arch** to **Buckingham Palace**. On one side is **St James's Park**, London's prettiest park, and on the other is John Nash's **Carlton House Terrace**. Ride the length in a London taxi or stroll it on a Sunday when it is barred to traffic.

Park Lane
Runs along the east side of **Hyde Park**. Still considered a smart address, though traffic and noise have diminished its former elegance.

Downing Street
You can't see much of the famed Prime Minister's residence at **Number 10**, nor the Chancellor's next door at **Number 11**, because the police have barricaded both ends of this tiny street. You can have a quick glance while walking down **Whitehall**.

Whitehall
This name properly refers to the street between **Trafalgar Square** and **Parliament**, but is more well known as the designation of the major government buildings along the street and of the British government and Civil Service. An interesting and not too exhausting stroll.

Charing Cross Road
Leading from the intersection of **Tottenham Court Road** to **Trafalgar Square**, this is the famed locale of many London bookshops, including the vast collections of **Foyle's**, and not forgetting the famous **84** (now *not* a bookshop). Good for a long walk and a browse. North to south is downhill and less exhausting.

Fleet Street
See *Getting oriented*.

Sloane Square
Centre of a trendy shopping and posh residential area that is home to Sloane Rangers — young upper-class people or aspirants with conservative lifestyles approximate to America's preppies.

King's Road
This long street leads from Sloane Square through the heart of once avant-garde, once trendy, now very upmarket **Chelsea**. A place to be seen both in 1960s Swinging London and 1970s punk-rock era. If you look hard you may still catch a glimpse of London's dwindling army of flamboyant, but now not so outrageous, punks. **King's Road** is an exhausting walk, unless you like shopping in boutiques or are on your way to visit some of Chelsea's charming residential neighbourhoods and pubs, like the area around **Cheyne Walk**.

Buildings
For those who want to enjoy or learn about architecture, London is a delightful mix of styles and revivals. Most of the central area is Georgian, Victorian and modern, though during the Edwardian era a style of Baroque revival captured the fancy of builders and property developers, who grafted graceful curving façades onto the tops and sides of many new red brick houses in Knightsbridge, Chelsea and

Belgravia. This followed the well-known Victorian passion for a Gothic revival, whose buildings still fool many tourists. Very little remains of the medieval, Tudor and Jacobean (Stuart) era buildings that once covered the City, Holborn, Covent Garden and the East End. With a few other exceptions, the **Tower of London, St Paul's, Westminster Abbey** and a number of churches are the major survivors of pre-1700 London. Fires, floods, bombs and constant urban redevelopment have changed the face of the city.

Palaces, houses and churches are shown in separate sections.

Especially worth a visit

The Banqueting House

London's principal early Stuart landmark (some would say their memorial), the **Banqueting House** is all that remains of the **Royal Palace of Whitehall**, otherwise destroyed by fire in 1698. The classical exterior may appear to be much like other Palladian London buildings, but it was actually far ahead of its time when it was designed by the distinguished architect Inigo Jones in 1619–22.

Inside, there is a return to the Baroque: the interior is a celebration of Stuart fantasies about the divine rights of kings. An immense panelled ceiling, installed during the reign of Charles I, depicts James I as a wise saint. The symbolism was not lost on Cromwell and the Parliamentarians of 1649. At his execution, Charles I was required to step onto the scaffold from a demolished Banqueting House window. Open Mon–Sat 1000–1700; Sun 1400–1700. **Whitehall U: Westminster**

The Guildhall

This beautifully-restored fifteenth-century civic function hall, just off **Gresham Street** EC2, is one of the few remnants of medieval London to survive. Much of the stonework is original, along with a window and undercroft. The magnificent **Great Hall** still conveys this atmosphere.

Within its walls a whole series of heresy and treason trials took place in the sixteenth century. The most famous of these were those of **Lady Jane Grey** and her husband, Archbishop Dudley, and **Lord Cranmer** in 1553. When civic functions are not being staged, the Guildhall and its valuable art gallery are open Mon–Sat 1000–1700; Sun 1400–1700 from May to September. Admission free. **U: St Paul's**

Inns of Court

The ancient and restored enclosures of these four inns (membership is required for a barrister to practise law in England) have a kind of tranquil otherworldliness that dates back 500 years. Like many other structures in this part of London, they have been badly hit by fires and bombs, and substantially rebuilt and modified over time. The inns still provide accommodation for lawyers, and most of the premises are off-limits. It is usually possible at least to stroll through their squares and gardens.

Lincoln's Inn is the prettiest. The **Tudor Old Hall** dates back to 1490, the **Chapel** to 1623. Check with the **Porter's Lodge** (Tel: 01-405 6360) in New Square, off Carey Street, to join a morning tour. You can see the magnificent Elizabethan **Middle Temple Hall** (Middle Temple Lane, off Fleet Street) from 1030–1200 and 1500–1630 (1000–1600 on Saturdays) except in August, when it is closed. Parts of **Inner Temple Hall** date back to the fourteenth century, though it was extensively rebuilt after war damage. **Temple Church** is open from 0930–1600 daily, except in August and September — it was founded by the Knights Templar, and has a unique circular nave. **Gray's Inn** (Gray's Inn Road) was badly damaged during the war, though the quadrangles are still worth a wander. For a tour, phone the Librarian (Tel: 01-405 8164, Ext 143).

Other recommended notable buildings and monuments

Albert Memorial and Royal Albert Hall
This extravagantly-ornamented icon-like fantasy tower in **Kensington Gardens** was erected in 1872. Once ridiculed, it is now revered by some as a monument to high Victoriana, as well as to the Prince Consort after whom it was named. The **Royal Albert Hall** stands across the street and contrasts the monument with a vaguely Renaissance design adorned with a Minton pottery frieze. **U: High Street Kensington**, then buses C1, 9, 52, 73.

Apothecaries' Hall
Preserved 1688 building. Interior visits by arrangement only. 12 Blackfriars Lane EC4. Tel: 01-236 1189. **U: Blackfriars**.

Bank of England
Classical nineteenth-century façade by John Soane. Visitors are not allowed beyond the entrance but in late 1988 a new museum opened, complete with interactive videos. Tel: 01-601 4444. Mon–Fri 1000–1800. **Threadneedle Street. U: Bank**.

Chelsea Royal Hospital
Vast and beautiful creation of Sir Christopher Wren and, later, Robert Adam. Now a home for old soldiers. The inhabitants wear the distinctive uniforms of the Chelsea Pensioners. The **Great Hall, Chapel** and **Council Chamber** are open to visitors. Hours: Tel: 01-730 0161. **U: Sloane Square**.

Greenwich Buildings
The **Royal Naval College** (1696–1715) is a splendid achievement by Christopher Wren and later architects. Inside the **Painted Hall** is a ceiling depicting the victory of William and Mary, and the age of peace under Queen Anne. The **National Maritime Museum** is housed in the Palladian **Queen's House** by Inigo Jones (1616–1635), and in adjoining wings. Further up the hill is Wren's **Royal Observatory. BR: Greenwich**.

Leadenhall Market
Charming old-fashioned city Victorian arcade missed by many tourists. **U: Bank**.

Lloyds
The famous insurance house now lives in one of London's few post-modernist structures. The architect was Richard Rogers, of Pompidou-fame. Visitors can observe from a gallery or visit the coffee house. Hours: Mon–Fri 1000–1430. **Lime Street EC3. Tel: 01-623 7100**.

County Hall
This massive 1920s neo-Renaissance building sits on the opposite bank of the Thames from Parliament. Until the Greater London Council was abolished in 1986, it housed the city government. Currently the home of the Inner London Education Authority and the Residuary Body which took over from the Greater London Council. As of writing, Parliament had not yet decided what to do with it. We include it only because you may wonder what this big building is. **U: Westminster**.

The Monument
A free-standing column 202 feet high commemorating the Great Fire of 1666. Since 1671 the exhausting climb (311 steps) has provided the determined with fine views from the top. **U: Monument**.

The Old Bailey
Here, and at the **Bow Street Magistrates Court** and the **Royal Courts of Justice**, you can see bewigged English justice at work. Except for some rather detailed fraud cases tried here, the Old Bailey is the most dramatic and interesting because it is the Central Criminal Court. The present building dates from only 1907. The **Public Gallery** is open Mon–Fri 1030–1300 and 1400–1600. Entrance in **Newgate Street. U: St Paul's.**

Prince Henry's Room
Claims to be London's oldest surviving domestic house (1610). Fine Jacobean panelling and mementos of the diarist Samuel Pepys. **Fleet Street U: Temple.**

Royal Courts of Justice (Law Courts)
Victorian Gothic architecture at its most enthusiastic, by George Street (completed 1882). The idea was that courtrooms should be housed in a cathedral. You can sit in on trials, but only civil cases are tried here, so you may not find the proceedings as interesting as at the **Old Bailey** (above). **The Strand U: Temple.**

Saint Pancras Station
London's most architecturally-interesting railway station, designed by Sir George Gilbert Scott at the height of the Gothic revival (completed 1874). **U: King's Cross.**

Scotland Yard
The headquarters of the Metropolitan Police are now housed in a modern (1967) glass and concrete structure named New Scotland Yard. The old Victorian building has been renamed. **Victoria Street. U: St James Park.**

Staple Inn
This big half-timbered building is much restored. Nevertheless, you can get a good idea of what Tudor London looked like. **High Holborn. U: Chancery Lane.**

Stock Exchange
Like its Wall Street counterpart, the London Stock Exchange is now housed in a modern building with a public gallery where you can watch options trading and see an exhibition. Open Mon–Fri 0945–1530. **Old Broad Street. U: Bank.**

Westminster Hall
Visitors are occasionally admitted when Parliament is not in session; otherwise you must accompany an MP to see the splendid hammer-beam ceiling of this last remaining portion of the Westminster Palace, first constructed in 1097. The first English law courts were housed here, within the Houses of Parliament complex. **Parliament Square. U: Westminster.**

Churches and ecclesiastical buildings

London is studded with steeples, though many churches are no longer in use. In the old days London was more densely inhabited, and parishes were smaller. Twentieth-century London is less crowded and England is a less religious country (one recent survey showed only 10 per cent of the population to be regular churchgoers). Now many are being converted into discos, demolished, or even reconsecrated as mosques or Sikh temples.

Of some 50 churches designed by the famed architect Sir Christopher Wren after the Great Fire, only 24 survive. Still, church buildings have lasted better than some other structures, and many provide a fascinating glimpse into the past. The selection below is based on architectural and historical interest — but you should also just wander into a local church, if the door is open, in one of London's historic neighbourhoods and make your own discoveries. For more selections, especially if you'd like to attend a service, see the section *Activities*.

Especially recommended

St Paul's Cathedral
(see *Major sights*)

Westminster Abbey
(see *Major sights*)

Southwark Cathedral
Some of our subscribers have said that they prefer out-of-the-way Southwark Cathedral to Westminster Abbey and St Paul's. They consider it a find — a truly Gothic church dating from the thirteenth century which was designated a cathedral only in 1897. The Cathedral is rich in medieval atmosphere and monuments from then and up to the present day. And you have space to breathe and enjoy. Not many tourists venture this far — though it is, in fact, only just south of the river across London Bridge. As an added interest, a street market is nearby. Open daily. **U: London Bridge.**

Westminster Cathedral
Unlike the Abbey of the same name, Westminster Cathedral is Roman Catholic and the seat of the current Catholic Archbishop of Westminster, Cardinal Basil Hume. Also unlike most London churches, the design and decor is wonderfully Byzantine, rejoicing in colourful mosaics and 100 different kinds of marble from all over the world. Although opened in 1903, the Cathedral is, unfortunately, still not finished. Those who fail to be charmed might still enjoy the great view from the Cathedral's 273-foot observation tower, especially since there's a lift (elevator). Open daily 1000–1600. **Victoria Street. U: Victoria.**

St Martin-in-the-Fields
In 1722–24 James Gibbs designed and built a classical church with a high steeple that has been copied all over the world. Today it is famed for its status as a royal parish church, for its choir and church music, the social activism of some of its vicars and, more recently, for church commercial enterprise. The crypt is now a pleasant restaurant and brass-rubbing centre. Many royals and famous people have been christened here. Beautifully gilded cream ceiling. Open daily. **Trafalgar Square. U: Charing Cross.**

St Bartholomew the Great
One of the oldest existing churches in town, if not *the* oldest, dating from 1130 — and most of the structure is pre-Reformation. Open daily. **West Smithfield EC1. U: St Paul's.**

St Margaret's
The official church of the House of Commons, next door to Westminster Abbey. Lots of Tudor charm. Open daily. **Parliament Square. U: Westminster.**

Lambeth Palace
The official residence of the Archbishop of Canterbury. Much of it was rebuilt in the nineteenth-century Gothic revival, but the crypt and some parts date back to the thirteenth century. We've heard good things from subscribers who have managed to get a place on the occasional conducted tours by writing to the Palace Secretary, Mary Cryer. Not generally open to the public. Beside the Palace is the church of **St**

Mary at Lambeth, long associated with the Tradescant family, now the **Museum of Garden History**. **Lambeth Palace Road. U: Lambeth North.**

Fulham Palace
The bishops of London lived in Fulham Palace from 1570 to 1973. The partly-Tudor building is currently leased to the borough council, who sponsor tours on some Sunday afternoons. Call them on 01-736 5821 to find out the times of their next tour. Even if you can't make one of these rare tours, go and enjoy the very pleasant grounds and river frontage in nearby Bishop's Park. **U: Putney Bridge.**

St Paul's Church
Fronting the Piazza in Covent Garden, this church is also known as the 'actors' church', since many famous theatre people have worshipped here since it first opened in 1638. Plaques and monuments inside commemorate many actors, actresses, directors and playwrights. Open daily. **U: Covent Garden.**

Some outstanding Wren churches

St James's, Piccadilly
A simple, but beautiful, Wren church; the most accessible to visitors, in the heart of tourist London. It has to be said that most of the church has been restored after blitz devastation. No longer the home of the **London Brass Rubbing Centre** (moved to St Martin-in-the-Fields), but there's a useful café for light meals Monday to Saturday. Lunchtime concerts. Interesting congregation combines social activism with High Church ritual. **Piccadilly. U: Piccadilly.**

St Clement Danes
The official church of the RAF, on an island in the Strand. Again, the interior is mainly a faithful reconstruction after bomb damage. Rumoured to be the origin of the 'Oranges and Lemons' rhyme. **Strand WC2. U: Temple.**

St Lawrence Jewry
Easily visited with the **Guildhall** next door. **Gresham Street EC2. U: St Paul's.**

St Bride
A painstakingly-restored parish church that has had many famous worshippers. **Fleet Street EC4. U: Blackfriars.**

St Mary-le-Bow
Famous for the bells that define as 'Cockney' anyone born within hearing. Built on an earlier church site with a still-visible Norman crypt. **Cheapside EC3. U: St Paul's.**

St Mary-at-Hill
Probably had the best-preserved interior of the surviving Wren churches until a recent fire. Located on a little street that retains a medieval impression despite modern buildings. **Lovat Lane EC3. U: Monument.**

St Mary Abchurch
The prettiest Wren church, according to some. Lovely restored painted dome and fine seventeenth-century woodcarving. **Abchurch Yard EC4. U: Bank.**

Museums and public galleries

Overseas visitors who expect all of Britain to be a museum are wrong, but perhaps tourist promoters are catching up with the idea: on average a new museum of some kind opens every two weeks in Britain. Some of these are more commercial tourist attractions than serious endeavours, and London is getting its share of these, which is a pity because London has so much worthwhile to offer.

Four — the **British Museum**, the **Tate Gallery**, the **National Gallery** and the **Victoria and Albert Museum** — are among the very top museums and galleries in the world. Two — the **Museum of London** and the **National Portrait Gallery** — should not be missed by any London visitor who really wants to understand the city. Beyond these, London has a number of small-but-quality museums and galleries and a number of 'curiosity' specialized museums you might want to visit if you can spare the time. We list our favourite seven, to which we hope you will pay particular attention.

In addition, we have noted several 'tourist attractions', the most famous of which is **Madame Tussaud's**, which, unlike many, more touristy, guides, we do not consider a 'must'.

Tip Bear in mind that even the most fascinating museums can induce fatigue if you try to see too much too quickly. When it strikes, you won't enjoy your visit as much, and you won't remember what you have seen. Study a museum plan in advance and limit yourself, or have a quick walk through, if possible, and then go back to those exhibits which most appeal. Try to intersperse museum-going days with more active outdoor days. London usually has more than its quota of grey days, even in summer: a perfect time to adjust your plans for museum-going and keep your fingers crossed for a brighter and clearer tomorrow!

Major museums and galleries

The British Museum
(see *Major sights*)

The Tate Gallery
People we know are about evenly divided between those who like the Tate best and those who prefer the **National Gallery**. For me, it's no contest. The National Gallery may have a better location, and its afficionados say it has a finer, more varied, and bigger collection — but that is just the problem. The collection is so vast that much of it is in store or on loan because there isn't space to display it all. Perhaps I'll change my mind when the controversial new extension is opened and relieves the problem.

But then again, so. The Tate has an especially fine collection of **Turner**, my favourite artist, and other British masters. My bias is here declared, though I also like the Tate for its location on the river in an until-recently slightly rundown, but safe, area. This removal from the centre of the tourist rush, combined with its own idiosyncrasies, give it a certain personality that the National lacks.

A whole new wing, the **Clore Gallery**, is devoted to Turner. I don't much care for the design of the new annex — it looks like a collection of multi-coloured building blocks on the outside, and the beige walls inside are deadly-dull backgrounds for Turner's masterpieces — but Turner paintings, like the famous *Shipwreck*, would look good even hung on a barn wall.

Those who are (or even who are not) familiar with English painting should see the masterpieces by **Sir Joshua Reynolds** and **Thomas Gainsborough**. Gainsborough and **John Constable** both had an uncanny ability to capture a certain quality of the East Anglian countryside — a quality that is still, thank goodness, discernible in that region today.

Those in a satirical or black mood will enjoy the paintings of **William Hogarth**; particularly apposite, for visitors, is *O the Roast Beef of Olde England*.

Pre-Raphaelite and Modern British art is well represented with the works of **Sir Stanley Spencer**, **Graham Sutherland**, American-born **Sir Jacob Epstein**, **Augustus John**, **Barbara Hepworth**, **Henry Moore** and **Wyndham Lewis**. But the whole Impressionist and Modern Era is an outstanding feature of the Tate's collections:

Dali, Matisse, Giacometti, Modigliani, Munch, Manet and many more are all represented.

These are the Tate's specialities, though there is also a variety of paintings from different eras and schools. And, even in the Tate, the collection is so large that the paintings appear in rotation. I should add that the Tate has an excellent lunch-time restaurant and coffee bar. Or you might prefer to stroll a few blocks to the fun and romantic **Restaurant and Brasserie** at **Dolphin Square**.

I hope I've whetted your appetite for British painting and the Tate — but by all means visit the National Gallery as well.

Admission free. Hours: Mon–Sat 1000–1750; Sun 1400–1750. **Millbank SW1. Tel: 01-821 1313. U: Pimlico.**

The National Gallery

This neo-classical building at the top of **Trafalgar Square** houses one of the world's best collections of European painting. You shouldn't miss it, especially if your tastes run to late medieval, Renaissance and Old Masters. Some of the eighteenth-century English artists seen at the Tate are also represented here. Both southern and northern schools are well represented, but the collection of **Rembrandts** is thought to be especially fine.

Among the artists whose works are on display: **Leonardo da Vinci, Masolino, Michelangelo, Raphael, Piero della Francesca** (*The Baptism*), **Titian, Tintoretto, Bellini, Botticelli** (*Mars and Venus*), **Velasquez, Goya, El Greco, Rubens** (*Samson and Delilah*), **Constable, Turner, Reynolds, Watteau, Chardin** and a sizeable number of French Impressionists and early Modernists, like **Degas, Manet** and **Renoir**. The basement has a good restaurant and café.

Hours: Mon–Sat 1000–1800; Sun 1400–1800. Admission free. Tel: 01-839 3321. **U: Charing Cross.**

Victoria and Albert Museum (or V & A)

The fortunes of this museum of fine, applied and decorative arts have risen mightily in the last few years with the addition of new Japanese, Indian and Sculpture sections. The emphasis is still on European work, but the new additions have made the collection more cosmopolitan and the Victoria and Albert can now lay claim to world-class status — especially because there are not many collections much like it.

If you've heard of the works of the fine eighteenth- and nineteenth-century English furniture makers and interior designers, this is the place to learn more about them. Don't miss the series of set rooms to learn how people lived and why decoration was so important to them.

Aside from this, there are thousands of small, even tiny, items on exhibit, and famous costumes, embroideries, stained glass, sculptures, and paintings (especially English). Vast and exhausting, but very worthwhile. If you get worn out, take a break in the beautiful courtyard, complete with a fountain and singing birds.

Admission free, but with suggested (virtually compulsory) charge. Hours: Mon–Thur, Sat 1000–1750; Sun 1430–1750. **Cromwell Road. Tel: 01-589 6371. U: South Kensington.**

Two museums where you should make an early stop

The Museum of London

Why is it (I mutter to myself as I direct yet another house guest to this treasure trove) that people stumble around London in a daze, struggling to make sense of its size, scope, history and culture, when one trip to this informal establishment would make the picture clear? Maybe it's because the museum is off the beaten track, for it is. Maybe it's because the building is ugly, for it is; squat, square and purpose-built, the **Museum of London** looks like a prim schoolhouse compared with the faded grandeur of the V&A.

The interior, however, is a different matter. Since it was constructed as a museum, rather than taking over an existing space, displays are arranged to maximum effect. Movement is the keynote, and as rooms are chronological — from pre-historic London to the twentieth century — it's possible to whizz through the eras at a terrific rate. People rarely do, as it happens, usually getting side-tracked somewhere around the Tudors. It's easy to see why, and actually very pleasant. From the Georgian chamber with its piped-in music through to the swirl and colour of modern London, the later rooms are delightfully free of visitors. Which suits many of us absolutely fine.

The museum takes a sociological approach to history, weighing trivia and consequence with equal measure. While appreciating Elizabethan London, for instance, we begin to understand just why Hamlet's doublets are always made of velvet. Amidst models of vast woollen mills, we learn that wool was the great industry of the sixteenth century, and therefore easy to come by. Artists and nobility craved something unusual, preferably imported, hence the fashion for velvet, which Hamlet, of course, would have followed.

The eighteenth century is illustrated by Visitors' London. In a case cluttered with theatre playbills and artefacts is an extract from a tourist's diary. What did a visitor enjoy on a trip to London, circa 1710? The Tower of London, of course, and the Crown Jewels; the bookshops around St Paul's. In the evening he went to the theatre, the next night to a concert, followed by a visit to a coffee house. Some things never change. This radical approach to documentation is always simple, but never simplistic. It works particularly well in the 'boring bits' of London history, like roads, for instance.

The Great Fire is explained in a separate 'fire chamber'. Inside, all is dark and grim. Suddenly flames spring up, screams ring out and panic is not far off. The noise is deafening, just as it must have been in 1666.

The Roman period is even better demonstrated. Rather than a simulated event, we have the real thing. An explanation of the Roman walls which once surrounded Londinium appears on platforms suspended above a window. After reading it, take a look inside. There, in all its glory, stands a hunk of authentic Roman wall, perfectly framed in glass.

It is the nineteenth and twentieth centuries which are my favourites, and not just because of the diminished crowds. This is the place where ephemera runs riot — full of buttons and boxes and tin soldiers galore. The period before WW1 is evoked by old gambling counters from St James's Casino, 'Votes for Women' badges and photos of Emmeline Pankhurst. In amongst carousels and hobby horses we learn that Dickens called funfairs a 'three day fever, which cools the blood for six months afterwards'. Lacy cardboard cut-outs reveal that in 1875, 10,000 women were employed to create the newest fad, Valentine's cards, and that Whiteley's in Westbourne Grove was the first department store.

Admission free. Hours: Tues–Sat 1000–1800; Sun 1400–1800 closed Monday. **London Wall EC2Y 5HN. Tel: 01-600 3699. U: Barbican** (but you can disembark at **Moorgate** and take the covered walkway — scenic and weatherproof). Terraced restaurant. Be sure to leave time to visit the gift shop, with its unusual postcards and high-quality souvenirs. (M.E.Z.)

National Portrait Gallery
Does it matter what Henry VIII or Elizabeth I looked like? It does if you want to understand something of Britain's past. Faces help names, dates and events come alive. So much so that countless London tourist guides have rightly urged this as an early stop. And the gallery seems to capitalize on the idea by doing everything it can to make the portraits and their stories easy.

You start at the top of the building with the earliest images. The top storey holds mostly portraits of medieval and Reformation royalty. As you move down to the first floor there are more non-royal, non-aristocratic faces, including novelists and artists, through the Victorian period. The basement holds mainly twentieth-century faces. Many of the portraitists are famous too: **Holbein** (*Henry VIII*), **Branwell Brontë** (*Brontë Sisters*), **Nicholas Hilliard** (*Sir Walter Raleigh*), **John Hay** (*Samuel Pepys*), **Reynolds, Romney** and **Lawrence** are some of the artists almost as famous as their subjects.

This journey through time is supplemented by detailed explanatory handouts. One is even called *Six Famous Portraits in Fifteen Minutes*. Yes, it all does seem a bit like instant history, but you may appreciate both this and the convenient location — just behind the **National Gallery** on Trafalgar Square.

Admission free. Hours: Mon–Fri 1000–1700; Sat 1000–1800; Sun 1400–1800. **St Martin's Place WC2. Tel: 01-930 1552. U: Charing Cross** or **Leicester Square.**

Smaller (but quality) collections

These museums are important London attractions; some are world famous. Just because we didn't list them under *Majors* or *Early stops* doesn't mean we think them not worth a visit. On the contrary, we emphatically believe that every one of the museums below merits a visitor's time. The question is, of course, how much? And that is highly dependent on your own interests. To help you plan your visit, we give reasons why a visit might be worthwhile.

Courtauld Institute Galleries

On Woburn Square in Bloomsbury, hidden away up a lift (elevator) in an unlikely-looking building, is the serendiptious surprise of an intimate eight-room gallery with an eclectic collection of famous Old Masters and French Impressionists. The gallery was named after Samuel Courtauld, the textile manufacturer and art collector, who, with his friend Viscount Lee, founded the gallery as an extension of the University of London in 1932. With further bequests the collection has grown so that many items have to be rotated. At the end of 1989 it will move to Somerset House.

Reason for a visit
Many individual Impressionist and Old Master paintings are famous in themselves and give the Courtauld an importance out of all proportion to its size. **Manet's** *A Bar at the Folies Bergères* and **Cranach's** *Adam and Eve* are but two examples.

Admission £1.50. Hours: Mon–Sat 1000–1700; Sun 1400–1700. **Woburn Square WC1. Tel: 01-580 1015. U: Russell Square.**

Wallace Collection

This collection is set in **Hertford House**, an imposing Georgian mansion that was once the London home of the Dukes of Manchester, and was bequeathed to the nation by Lady Wallace in 1897. Her husband, Sir Richard Wallace, had continued a long family tradition of collecting fine paintings, armour, gold, china and furniture. Artists on display include **Rembrandt, Rubens, Van Dyck, Boucher, Fragonard, Watteau, Murillo** and **Velasquez** and the English painters **Gainsborough, Reynolds** and **Romney.**

Reason for a visit
As in the **Courtauld Institute** (above), the individual painters and paintings are so outstanding that it would be a pity to miss them, and there is the added, lingering ambience of the private home.

Admission free. Hours: Mon–Sat 1000–1700; Sun 1400–1700. **Manchester Square W1. Tel: 01-935 0687. U: Bond Street.**

Hayward Gallery
Like the **Royal Academy,** this London art institution has no permanent collection but holds world-class exhibitions. Check the press for details of the current exhibition.

Reason for a visit
World-class exhibitions are staged here.
   Admission charges and hours vary with exhibitions. Located in the **South Bank Arts Complex. Tel: 01-928 5708. U: Waterloo.**

Dulwich Picture Gallery
When you're tired of noisy, dirty, central London, take a nice (half day or so) trip to a green and pleasant bucolic suburb where Mrs Thatcher has bought her retirement home (will she ever use it?) and visit a fine collection of Old Masters. **Rubens, Rembrandt, Poussin, Canaletto** as well as **Hogarth, Ramsey** and **Gainsborough** in a newly-restored building originally designed by Sir John Soane.

Reason for a visit
Good paintings and a pleasant half day out.
   Admission £1.50. Hours: Tues–Sat 1000–1300; Tues–Sun 1400–1700. **College Road SE21. Tel: 01-693 5254. BR: West Dulwich.**

Kenwood
Good collection of Old Masters set in a Robert Adam mansion in Hampstead Heath (see *Great houses* for further details).

Queen's Gallery and Royal Mews
These two Buckingham Palace museums are included because they are big tourist draws as the only parts of the palace complex that admit tourists, and the Queen does have some fine pictures and coaches. The paintings are mostly Old Masters and royal portraits. These are changed twice a year because her collection is vast and space here is strictly limited. The **Royal Mews** has an impressive gateway and you can see the ornate gilded carriages still used on State occasions.

Reason for a visit
Worth going if you're interested in the royals or the current exhibition.
   Admission £1.10. Gallery Hours: Tues–Sat 1030–1700; Sun 1400–1700. Mews: Wed, Thurs 1400–1600. **Buckingham Palace Road. Tel: 01-930 4832. U: Victoria.**

Royal Academy of Arts
Home of the oldest arts academy in the country, set behind an imposing eighteenth-century façade.

Reason for a visit
Whether you want to visit or not will depend on whether the current major loan exhibition is of any particular interest to you. Certainly worth finding out — Royal Academy exhibitions often become famous in their own right and tour the world.
   Admission charges and hours vary with exhibitions. **Piccadilly W1. Tel: 01-734 9052. U: Piccadilly.**

Whitechapel Art Gallery
A purpose-built exhibition gallery constructed in 1901. Interesting temporary modern and contemporary exhibits. Out-of-the-way location in the East End.

Reason for a visit
Check to see whether the current exhibit is of interest.

Admission varies. Hours: Tues–Sun 1100–1700; Wed 1100–2000. **80–82 White-chapel High Street E1. Tel: 01-377 0107. U: Whitechapel.**

Three big scientific museums

The Natural History Museum
This giant, cavernous Victorian mock-Romanesque building always seems to be full of noisy schoolchildren, which somewhat mars the atmosphere of its huge number of quality exhibits. These include not only the usual skeletons and stuffed animals of all kinds, including a spectacular giant blue whale, but also modern push-button video screens.

Reason for a visit
This natural history museum is world-class and a very good place to interest children. But if you've seen similar museums in New York, Washington, the Continent or elsewhere, there's no particular reason to stray into this one.
Admission £2. Hours: Mon–Sat 1000–1800; Sun 1430–1800. **Cromwell Road SW7. Tel: 01-589 6323. U: South Kensington.**

The Science Museum
Like the Natural History Museum nearby, the **Science Museum** is vast and full of noisy school parties. The history of technology and how-things-work is helped along by push-button and visitor-participation do-it-yourself exhibits. Lots of gee-whizz technology and futuristic notions in the **Telecommunications Gallery** and the new **Space Gallery**, but some may prefer the working models of Victorian bathrooms and kitchens.

Reason for a visit
The scientifically-minded or curious can spend hours in the well-designed exhibits. Others should pick out those parts and exhibits that specifically interest and can't be seen in major museums elsewhere.
Admission £2. Hours: Mon–Sat 1000–1800; Sun 1430–1800. **Exhibition Road SW7. Tel: 01-589 3456. U: South Kensington.**

The Geological Museum
The history of the earth and geological science is profiled, but the gemstone exhibits are the main attraction.

Reason for a visit
If you're interested in gemstones you might want to visit the sparkling displays in this collection near the **Science Museum** in South Kensington.
Admission £2. Hours: Mon–Sat 1000–1800; Sun 1430–1800. **Exhibition Road SW7. Tel: 01-589 3444. U: South Kensington.**

London Traveletter's seven favourite small museums
These seven museums are favourites of ours which we recommend to everyone. Each has a different special quality that makes it memorable. Perhaps you'll disagree with our classification of **Highgate Cemetery** as a 'museum'. You could be right — but go and see, and I think you'll change your mind.

The Cabinet War Rooms
A rare opportunity to step back into the days of wartime Britain, when the wail of air raid sirens and the crunch of exploding bombs were the commonplace accompaniment to the Londoner's nightly routine, is offered by an underground visit to what is surely one of the capital's most unusual tourist attractions. Two floors below street level, and protected by 10 feet of solid concrete, lie Sir Winston Churchill's War

Rooms. From here he directed Britain's war operations from August 1939 until the Japanese surrrender in 1945.

Built for secrecy and safety in a converted network of corridors under government offices in Great George Street, Westminster, they were left almost intact when the war ended. Nineteen of the rooms are now on show, viewed through glass from a corridor. Although the rooms are necessarily adapted for visitors, there has been a deliberate effort to keep changes to the minimum. So, seeing the peeling beige paint and piles of paper and files, the visitor senses the unique wartime atmosphere, dingy and drab, and is left with the unmistakable impression that history was made here.

Churchill held over 100 meetings in the **Cabinet Room**, the first on display. Just along the corridor is the minute, bare, **Transatlantic Telephone Room** in which Churchill used to talk to President Roosevelt in the White House, and later to Truman. Interestingly, this 'hot line' was fitted with one of the first scrambler devices — though it was a rather primitive and insecure system until 1943.

On the table stands an emergency candle and the large tin Churchill used for cigar butts. The only other feature is a large clock with black hands for London time and red ones for Washington. The door bears a bathroom VACANT/ENGAGED sign: Churchill always locked himself inside while talking.

The **Map Room** was one of the most secret rooms of all, open only to a tiny carefully-selected group of Churchill's military advisers. They continuously manned the banks of telephones, keeping themselves abreast of the progress of the war minute by minute. The maps in use during the last months of the war are all still in place.

Churchill's small bedroom was, for me, the most impressive room of all. Actually, against all advice, he rarely slept there, hating to be confined underground even at the height of the raids. His narrow, uncomfortable-looking bed is covered by a faded blue quilt, with a candle on the table beside it. Even here, there is a map on the wall. It shows Britain's airports, barrage-balloon sites and torpedo defenses.

Also in the room is the large brown desk from which he made many of his famous broadcasts. Looking at it, you can almost hear the defiant voice which inspired such hope: *'We shall not flag or fail, whatever the cost may be'.* (G.T.)

Admission £2 adults, £1 children. Hours: Tues–Sun 1000–1750. Closed Monday. Entrance at **Clive Steps, King Charles Street SW1. Tel: 01-930 6961. U: Westminster.**

Sir John Soane's Museum

John Soane had a dream — to be a brilliant architect. Once this ambition was realized, John Soane had another dream — to live in a house which celebrated the 'poetry of architecture'. Soane realized this dream too, and the result is this museum in Lincoln's Inn Fields — a tribute to one man's vision, craftsmanship and wonderful sense of the absurd.

John Soane rose from modest beginnings to become the architect of the Bank of England. Along the way he acquired not only pictures but a passion for collecting, the objects of his desire being as unorthodox as he himself. Marble busts, model temples and the cornices of buildings reflect an over-riding interest in architecture, but the sarcophagus in the basement rescued from the Valley of the Kings can only serve as a testament to the man's personal style.

Deeply disappointed by the conduct of his two children (one son published a diatribe against his father's profession, a gesture never forgiven), Sir John ordained in his will that his collection would remain in this house forever, and went so far as to secure a private Act of Parliament in 1833 to ensure nothing was disturbed. For Soane designed his house not just to live in but as a setting for his works of art. Before his wife's death he had lived at Number 12 Lincoln's Inn, but in 1813 he moved to Number 13, retaining the first house and later acquiring the one next door to make a harmonious composition from all three.

Soane's 'poetry of architecture' was primarily a question of light and space. The

Library, for instance, painted vivid Pompeian red, contains mirrored friezes to enlarge and reflect the artefacts on display. Mirrors can be seen throughout the house — on desks, around window-panes and in far-flung nooks and crannies. The **Breakfast Room** alone contains 150 mirrors, but never for their decorative value alone. Form without content was anathema to this precise man, who placed compass points at strategic locations to remind one of the direction of the sun.

For the sun played an integral part in Soane's interior alterations; most rooms have a skylight which, during his lifetime, contained yellow glass. The architect urged all the visiting 'amateurs and students' to arrive on a sunny day, when his antiquities would be surrounded by a mellow amber glow. Be sure to climb upstairs to the **North Drawing Room** for a view of the courtyard below — a shimmering world of glass octagons, tunnels and cuppolas.

So remarkable is this house that it tends to detract from the fine collection of paintings which hang on the walls themselves. Of particular note are two famous series by **William Hogarth**. *The Rake's Progress* was painted in 1735 to depict eight phases in the career of Tom Rakewell, from wealthy young heir to ruined madman. *The Election* is a steely satire on government procedures.

The basement of the house contains the **crypt**, the **catacombs** and the **Monk's Parlour**. The latter is a bizarre gothic fantasy hung with medieval casts and seventeenth-century bric-a-brac. We are told this grotesque effect was an entirely intentional and accurate parody of the fashionable cult of antiquarianism much disliked by Soane.

The **Sepulchral Chamber** contains the museum's principal treasure, the sarcophagus from the Tomb Chamber of Seti I in the Valley of the Kings. This antiquity from 1300 BC was first offered to the British Museum, but when it was declined Soane placed a bid of £2000. So great was the architect's delight in his acquisition that he constructed a special chamber where it could be admired from three separate floors. Then he gave a party. Today, standing by the sarcophagus and gazing up towards the skylight, no fewer than 200 friezes, stone heads, busts and urns can be seen hanging on the walls. (M.E.Z.)

Admission free. Hours: Tues–Sat 1000–1700. Public lecture tour every Saturday at 1430. Access to collections of books and drawings, on application. **12 Lincoln's Inn Fields WC2. Tel: 01-405 2107. U: Holborn.**

Highgate Cemetery

In an English horror movie, *Tales from the Crypt*, five people lose the rest of their party and are ushered into a cavernous vault by a figure who reveals what the future holds for them. One of them, Arthur Grimsdyke, played by Peter Cushing, later returns from his grave to extract revenge from the neighbour who drove him to suicide. In another, *Twins of Evil*, the Countess Mircella, vampire ancestress of Count Karnstein, whom he has accidentally brought back to life, rises from her sarcophagus and floats towards the terrified soon-to-be transformed vampire.

The set for these and many other graveyard horror scenes, with swirling mists, dense foliage and scattered tombs? Not an MGM back lot, but **Highgate Cemetery**, just north of London's tourist centre, where many of nineteenth-century London's wealthiest, brightest or most eccentric residents found their final resting places among the elaborate tombs, catacombs and memorials with which the Victorians celebrated — rather than shunned — death.

Open daily for tours by the **Friends of Highgate Cemetery**, a group of volunteers who rescued it from vandalism, Satanists and rapid natural decay, the cemetery can be appreciated both for its monuments of romantic Victorian funerary architecture and its most famous inhabitants: **Karl Marx, George Eliot, Michael Faraday**, the **Rosetti** family, **Charles Crufts** (of dog show fame), **Sir Raph Richardson** and many others. The guides are full of anecdotes and legends about Highgate's 160,000 buried inhabitants, and helpfully explain the symbolism behind the use of broken pillars, urns and empty chairs. They point out the architecturally-interesting tombs, such as one with a grand piano and another with a hot air balloon, and share the stories of the appearance of a dog on boxer Thomas Sayer's tomb, a prone lion on George Wombell's tomb and the golden mosaic on the tomb of newspaper tycoon Julius Baer.

The western side is in a wild, overgrown state — a condition much appreciated by the makers of horror films and visitors who share their romantic fascination with graveyards, or appreciate the ends as well as the beginnings of some of England's most distinguished citizens.

Burials still take place in the eastern cemetery — a flatter, more ordered site where Marx lies. The actor Ralph Richardson was among the most recent internees.

The cemetery can be reached from **Archway** underground station, but it is not very convenient. Sunday afternoon is the best time to go. Some of the most interesting parts of the cemetery are accessible only to special tours. Call for Highgate tour times: Tel: 01-340 1834. (L.M.V.)

Two other London cemeteries contain the graves of many famous people and make an interesting visit: **West Norwood Memorial Park, BR: West Norwood**; and **Kensal Green Cemetery, Kensal Green U or BR**.

Linley Sambourne House

Where do you go to see a perfect example of a London Victorian home? Linley Sambourne House was built in 1875 on the Phillimore Estate in Stafford Street, a turning off Kensington High Street. In that same year, Mary Anne Herepeth married Edward Linley Sambourne (great great grandfather of today's Viscount Linley), and her father purchased the house for the young couple.

Edward was an illustrator of *Punch* magazine, and many of his cartoons can be seen in the house, notably on the staircase. His salary, by 1883, was about £100 a month — sufficient in those days to furnish comfortably, employ three servants and entertain well.

In this connection, no doubt, the capacious wine-cellar under the street was extremely useful and much appreciated by Edward and his guests. The kitchen at that time was also in the basement, and orders for food and service went via bell-pulls and speaking tubes. However, the kitchen and one of the bathrooms have been modernized. This was necessary since Lady Rosse, Edward's granddaughter, and her husband lived in the house for 22 years until 1980.

But everything else is practically untouched. A ground-floor lavatory with marble floor is interesting; so, too, is the coffin-shaped bath in the first-floor bathroom. And the skilfull photographs, taken by Edward, which adorn the walls here are worth a closer look.

The first-floor drawing room and the reception rooms downstairs may seem somewhat dark and claustrophobic to modern tastes, but the Victorians set great store by their privacy. And the stained-glass windows seen here were very popular in many houses of this era, as was the beautiful but sombre wallpaper designed by William Morris, the eminent craftsman and poet.

Gilt decoration was also much approved of, and appears here on frieze, ceiling and panels in the sideboard. Plush and leather are much in evidence, as, of course, is brass. However, I understand that nowadays this is polished by dedicated volunteers rather than a little housemaid whose time-consuming task it would formerly have been. Perhaps this also applies to the dusting, since there are numerous knick-knacks, plates, vases and birds and flowers beneath domed covers — all beloved by the Victorians.

Needless to say, the furniture is large and the rooms crowded in accordance with the fashion of the day. That generation bought for posterity, and posterity is now benefiting. For time has stood still in this house, preserving for us a perfect piece of

history. This is more than just a museum, since people lived their lives here, and the whole house therefore feels like a home. (A.G.)
   Admission £1.50. Hours: Wed 1000–1600; Sun 1400–1700. March–October. **Stafford Street W8. U: High Street Kensington**. Further information from: The Secretary, The Victorian Society, 1 Priory Gardens, London W4. Tel. 01-994 1019.

18 Folgate Street

Dennis Severs is an intruder in his own house. Yet it seems he was predestined to live in the house that was built in 1724 on Folgate Street in the Spitalfields area of East London. The five-storey, 10-room house stood empty from the very day Severs was born (the day the last resident died) until the day he bought the property from the City of London for £20,000 in 1979.
   Severs, a native of Escondido, California, who moved to England 19 years ago, invites you to intrude on the house that he 'shares' with four generations of the Jervis family, Huguenot silk-weavers who lived in the house until 1919.
   They still seem to be at home. Their pictures hang on the walls. Their dirty dishes are left on the dining room table. The odour of stale smoke fills the smoking room. Children's playthings lie here and there on the floors that have been swept with lavender and damp tea leaves.
   But, as Severs' guest participating in a theatrical experience of the house, you will never see the Jervises. You will hear them moving about sometimes, arguing with a neighbour. But when you approach them, they've always just left the room. You will be caught up in the atmosphere created by the Jervis family's lifestyles from the eighteenth to the twentieth centuries, while wondering what lies around the next corner.
   You'll see the house by the light of 120 candles. You'll feel the warmth of the fires, peer through the smoke, smell the wig powder, and perhaps find yourself covered in goosebumps when the unattended door across the room suddenly, mysteriously, closes with a click of the latch. For three hours you will live in a different space and time.
   Severs doesn't allow the twentieth century to intrude on the atmosphere. Although he employs tape recordings of sounds of other days — horses' hooves and callers in the street — you'll never see the telephone, television or refrigerator which are carefully concealed so as not to interfere with the spirit of the house. Likewise, he doesn't allow his guests to interrupt the flow of the evening's theatricals, and he'll warn you not to lag behind.
   Severs has systematically furnished the house with bits and pieces that nobody else wanted — rejected things, chipped and worn, that he found at street markets. The host, however, does not dress for the eighteenth century, since 'we're not supposed to be in the house. We're intruders. We actually get locked in the room during the tour.'
   The tour is not recommended for children under 12, though Severs offers a one-hour **Special Christmas Event**, which he describes as an 'adventure with atmosphere — a sort of Christmas Dream'.
   To arrange a tour, ring Dennis Severs on **01-247 4013** between 1000 and 1230. The 3-hour experience costs £20 per person. The Christmas 'event' is £10. The time of the tour varies with the season, but always begins after dark.
   Liverpool Street is the nearest underground station. From there it is best to take a taxi, as it is important to be neither early nor late for the event. Once on Folgate Street, you'll recognize the house, at number 18, by the old gas lamp and the straw strewn on the doorstep. (L.K.)

Pollock's Toy Museum

This very special surprise tucked away in central London is a two-in-one adventure. The tradition of the toy theatre is still being kept alive through the shop: its history is charming and colourful and you'll be able to get a descriptive booklet that explains everything when you come. Mr Pollock, who devoted his life to making such theatres — a long piece of English history — died in 1937, but his museum is now housed in two tiny little homes joined together with narrow winding staircases (perfect for 7–12 year olds and adults). There are *generations* of toys, ancient dolls and teddies, magic lanterns, and playthings from Ecuador to Quaker Pennsylvania to Iceland, old and older. To detail them all here would require a whole section on its own; suffice it to say that on the right-hand side of the shop a truly enchanting experience awaits you and your children. Not just recommended — mandatory!

On your left is Pollock's **Toy Store**, a tiny wooden place with lovely old display cases and wooden floor. You're in another era here. In a divided box you'll find small wooden tops (35p); Chinese yarn dolls ((50p); 1-inch high perfectly-formed pewter soldiers (60p); flip books; cards; matchbox music boxes (£2.95); tiny wooden figures; *teeny* Paddington bears; minute face-paint crayon sets; an 8-piece brass tea-set that fits inside a large postage stamp (£1.50); speckled marbles; *wonderful* kaleidoscopes (I bought six for gifts); whistles, fans and whizzers made of tin that sparkle in the dark when you whizz them; replicas of 1890s paper dolls, and tin toys for the collector. You don't have to be one, though, to buy a pre-1914 Dutch wooden-jointed doll for £17.50 (if there are any left). Oh, and there are old-fashioned transfers and glow-toys and *wooden* yo-yo's and rubber mice and furry hand-puppets and wood monkey puzzles and wood puppets (gasp) and jack-in-the-boxes and pull-toys (wood) and glass balls with snow and more.

And if you're anything like the other adults (never mind the children) wandering about in a happy daze exclaiming 'I had this when *I* was little!' and 'They *still* make *these*?' . . . you may not even have to bring your kids at all . . . (J.E.)

Admission 80p adults, 40p children. Hours: Mon–Fri 1000–1700. **1 Scala Street W1. Tel: 01-636 3452. U: Goodge Street**.

Toy-history lovers may also enjoy the **London Toy & Model Museum, 23 Craven Hill W2, Tel: 01-262 7905**, which is especially good for trains. **U: Queensway or Paddington**.

Bethnal Green Museum of Childhood

Only 12 minutes by underground from busy Oxford Circus lies a delightful and little-known world — a world of dolls, of miniature manor houses, of tall wooden soldiers and things that go bump in the night. This is the **Museum of Childhood**, the 'baby' branch of the **Victoria & Albert**, whose prestigious collection of antique toys and games is amongst the biggest to be found anywhere. Under a great soaring roof is everything to interest children of any age, displayed at a level even a wriggly six-year-old would find comfortable. Cases are unbreakable.

The **Doll Gallery**, designed to illustrate the development of the doll from the mid-eighteenth century to the present day, is basically still in order. Its cases include **Sophie**, carved from a single block of wood and crowned with human hair; stern-faced china dolls, popular in Germany, to the teenage fashion dolls on every girl's Christmas list today. According to the excellent catalogue, in order to fully appreciate the evolution of the doll, it is important to view the social and industrial background of a particular period. For instance, in the eighteenth and nineteenth centuries, children were regarded as little more than miniature adults, and many dolls were purely decorative, designed to live under a glass dome — pristine, secure and very grown-up. The Victorians ushered in a new era with a new approach to play. Although strict and religious with their children, they also saw the need for juvenile recreation, and the toy industry boomed. Dolls changed from being little adults to models of the children and infants who played with them. The baby doll was born.

Little boys, on the other hand, opted for miniature soldiers, the earliest toys made of metal. The museum's collection of lead toys includes not only regiments of these stiffly marching figures, but also Dinky toys and twentieth-century spacemen.

Equally impressive is the gallery of teddy bears and stuffed animals; the Edwardian owners of 'Pumpie', the stuffed elephant, were so enthralled with their plump friend that they had him immortalized in photographs and sketches.

The dolls' houses present complete pictures of domestic life from as long ago as the seventeenth century. The 1673 Nuremburg house has a fantastically well-equipped kitchen, rows of gleaming pots meticulously reproduced.

The children's fashion collection echoes the development of the fashion in dolls — from the stiff bodices on the dresses of eighteenth-century 'little women' (to teach the rudiments of wearing boned corsets) right through to the easy-care romper suits modern mothers favour for convenience.

The **Museum of Childhood** relives and chronicles the wonders of being young as no other museum in London can. Should you wish to re-enact some of the pleasures at home, the shop, under a striped umbrella roof, stocks postcards, paper dolls, mock Edwardian toy theatres and traditional European children's games. (M.E.Z.)

Admission free. Hours: Mon–Thurs, Sat 1000–1800; Sun 1430–1800. Closed Friday. **Tel: 01-980 2415. U: Bethnal Green** (the museum is close to the tube station).

Specialist or curiosity museums

London has a growing number of small specialist museums devoted to a particular topic. Some are tourist traps. Those we've listed below are genuine museums of great value to those with a professional or hobby interest in (or to anyone whose curiosity is stirred by) their subject matter.

The Guards' Museum

Tells the story of the five regiments of the Queen's Foot Guards in peace and war over 350 years.

Admission £2. Hours: daily 1100–1700. **Wellington Barracks, Birdcage Walk. SW1 U: Victoria**.

Freud Museum

'Where's the couch?' is often the visitor's first question. They find it, covered with oriental rugs and cushions, in Sigmund Freud's study, which he used as a consulting room. There it is: the actual couch that's become the international symbol of psychoanalysis.

Everything is as Freud left it when he died in September 1939 aged 82. His wife, Martha, and their youngest daughter, Anna, made sure nothing was ever moved. And the layout of the furniture, books and Freud's beloved antiquities is as they were in Vienna, where he lived for 47 years.

Hitler's Storm Troopers goose-stepped into Vienna in March 1938. That same month Anna Freud was taken away for interrogation. Freud needed no more threats. He wrote to his son Ernst in London: 'Two prospects keep me going in these grim times: to rejoin you all . . . and to die in freedom'. Anna was returned unharmed. Two months later the family fled to London.

The US Government ensured that when the huge ransom demanded by the Nazis had been paid, Freud got immediate safe custody on the Orient Express. Three sisters left behind perished in Auschwitz.

But, though shocked, cancer-ridden and 81 years of age, Freud did not flee to England to be a bedridden invalid. At 20 Maresfield Gardens he saw three or four patients a day. In the evenings he finished writing *Moses and Monotheism* and started *An Outline of Psychoanalysis*. Knowing he could not have much longer to live, he often wrote in his study until 1 am.

£10 per annum will make you a Friend of Freud. This lets you off the admission charge and entitles you to 10 per cent discount in the shop, and a quarterly newsletter. (J.C.)

Admission £2. Hours: Wed–Sun 1200–1700. **20 Maresfield Gardens, Hampstead. Tel: 01-435 2002. U: Finchley Road** then five minute walk, or take bus **13, 82 or 113**.

Imperial War Museum

The name may be anachronistic, but many of the display methods are more up-to-date than other London museums. Push-buttons, videos and displays of uniforms, guns, war objects and even a Spitfire aircraft illustrate British and Commonwealth involvement in twentieth-century wars: principally the two world wars. Set in a Regency building on the original site of the 'Bedlam' mental hospital for the insane.
Admission free. Hours: Mon–Sat 1000–1730; Sun 1400–1730. **Lambeth Road SE1. Tel. 01-735 8922. U: Lambeth North.**

London Transport Museum

This museum, housed in what was the old Covent Garden flower market is fun for kids and those who are really interested in early red double-deckers and underground trains, trams and hackney carriages. You can walk through or climb up on many of the old vehicles on display, or you can push buttons and experience old black and white documentaries and London transport films on video. An old newsreel has a George Formby-like voice singing about a couple who would 'sit on the tram and spoon all the way'. If you don't want to pay the admission charge, at least visit the museum shop and have a gaze at the beautiful pre-war Art Deco reproduction underground posters. This is also where you can buy the famous London Underground T-shirt.
Admission £2.40. Hours: Mon–Sun 1000–1800. **Tel: 01-379 6344. U: Covent Garden.**

The Museum of Mankind

A little gem of a museum, improbably located in Mayfair's Burlington Gardens, near the opulent arcade of the same name. Actually, this is the home of the ethnographic collection of the British Museum, but it is unlike its parent in most respects. The museum's permanent collections of artefacts of tribal and village life from around the world is small, beautifully displayed, accessible and non-exhausting. The real star is always a major long-running exhibition (recent examples: **Arctic Hunters** (Eskimos) and **Ashanti** (Ghana)). Not just the items on display but the exhibit design itself is often stunningly creative.
Admission free. Hours: Mon–Sat 1000–1700; Sun 1400–1800. **6 Burlington Gardens W1. Tel 01-437 2224. U: Piccadilly.**

Wimbledon Lawn Tennis Museum

The only one of its kind in the world, and exhibits, which have taken years to build up, represent several collections and many gifts. The **Kenneth Rich Library** is filled with photographs, films, documents, postcards and autographs. There's a comfortable **Film Theatre** where films of great matches are shown, as well as a splendid video which not only traces the history of lawn tennis since the 1870's but also illustrates the kind of tennis played before the modern version.

The now-enlarged museum includes fashion, trophies, replicas and memorabilia representing the history of lawn tennis, invented in 1874. Other sections include tennis equipment through the ages, with a remarkably-interesting reconstruction of a racket maker's workshop. There are lifesize figures of lawn tennis 'greats', plus the opportunity to view the famous **Centre Court** from the museum, complete with a sound commentary.

From time to time, the museum features special or unusual small exhibitions in addition to the regular set pieces, and the shop offers a wide range of attractive souvenirs. (D.A.)
Admission £1.50 Hours: Tues–Sat 1100–1700; Sun 1400–1700. Admission during the championships is restricted to those attending the tournament. **Church Road, Wimbledon SW19. Tel: 01-946 6131. U: Southfields.**

National Maritime Museum and Royal Observatory, Greenwich
Full of navigational and ship instruments, ship models, drawings and plans. The history of astronomy is shown, as is a collection of boats. There's no reason to *miss* the museum during the extremely enjoyable day trip to Greenwich. Maritime afficionados may be the only ones to linger over some of the technically-sophisticated navigational aids and equipment, but there are also paintings by artists like **Van Dyke** and **Romney** and historical curiosities like the uniform that Nelson died in. And the view from the Wren-designed **Observatory** is magnificent.
Admission £2.20. Hours: Mon–Sat 1000–1800; Sun 1400–1730 (Easter–Oct). **Romney Road, London SE10. Tel: 01-858 4422. BR: Greenwich.**

Geffrye Museum
A must for anyone interested in interiors and lifestyles of the past 400 years. Housed in several restored eighteenth-century almshouses, somewhat out of the way in the East End. Period rooms are arranged chronologically on permanent exhibit to show the development of furniture and furnishings in English middle-class homes. Several special exhibits are shown each year.
Admission free. Hours: Tues–Sat 1000–1700; Sun 1400–1700. **Kingsland Road, Shoreditch. Tel: 01-739 8368. U: Liverpool Street** or **Old Street.**

National Army Museum
This museum can be visited along with a trip to Wren's **Royal Hospital** next door. History of the British Army from 1485 to the present.
Admission free. Hours: Mon–Sat 1000–1800; Sun 1400–1800. **Hospital Road SW3. Tel: 01-730 0717. U: Sloane Square.**

Public Record Office
The original **Domesday Book** and other famous documents on display.
Admission free. Hours: Mon–Fri 1000–1700. **Chancery Lane WC2. Tel. 01-876 3444. U: Chancery Lane.**

The Jewish Museum
This museum contains artefacts and items from English Jewish history.
Admission free. Hours: Tues–Fri, Sun 1000–1600. **Tavistock Square WC1. Tel. 01-388 4525.**

Wembley Stadium
For those who don't know, this is London's major sports venue, where the annual final of English soccer, the F.A. Cup, is played. The guided tour of exhibits, the locker rooms, player's tunnel, Royal Box and other parts of the stadium is extremely popular and includes an audio-visual show. For sports fans only.
Admission £2.00. Hours: daily (except Thursdays, public holidays, and the days before, during and after an event), call for times. **Tel. 01-903 4864. U: Wembley Park.**

National Postal Museum
London's chief post office is considered to have one of the best collections of stamps (British and foreign) in the world.
Admission free. Hours: Mon–Thur 1000–1630; Fri 0930–1130. **King Edward Street EC1. Tel. 01-432 3851. U: St Paul's.**

Shakespeare Globe Museum
Interesting, more than anything else, for its location beside the site of the original Globe Theatre, where a modern replica is being rebuilt under the direction of American actor Sam Wanamaker.
Admission £1.50. Hours: Tues–Sat 1000–1700; Sun 1400–1800. **Bear Gardens. Tel. 01-928 6342. BR: London Bridge.**

Apsley House: The Wellington Museum
The Duke's opulent home, conveniently located at Number 1 London (Hyde Park Corner). Uniforms, trophies, awards and fine paintings.
    Admission £2.00. Hours: Tues–Thurs, Sat 1100–1700; Sun 1430–1800. **Tel. 01-499 5676. U: Hyde Park Corner.**

The Royal Air Force Museum
Exhibits and aircraft on display at **Hendon Aerodrome** illustrate aviation history. An alternative is to be found at **Duxford**, but this requires a day-trip.
    Admission £3.00. Hours: Mon–Sat 1000–1800; Sun 1400–1800. **Grahame Park Way. Tel. 01-205 2266. U: Colindale.**

The Theatre Museum
A branch of the **Victoria and Albert**, this museum nonetheless has a separate Covent Garden address and admission charge. 'Theatre' is broadly defined to include music hall, variety and show business of all kinds. Some think the admission charge high. Innovative exhibitions — like one on rock 'n' roll in which visitors are invited to play their favourite records on an old Wurlitzer juke box — are fun.
    Admission £2.25. Hours: Tues–Sun 1100–1900. **Wellington Street WC2. Tel. 01-836 7891. U: Covent Garden.**

Taxi Museum
Out-of-the-way museum worth visiting only if you're really taken with London taxis or you happen to be in this somewhat unsalubrious neighbourhood. One large room, very atmospheric, with 14 vintage taxis illustrating their development in London. At the back of the **London Cab Company.**
    Admission free. Hours: Mon–Fri 0900–1700; Sat 0900–1300. **1 Brixton Road SW9. Tel. 01-735 7777. U: Oval.**

The Museum of the Moving Image
A brand new museum opened beside the South Bank's mammoth theatre, film and concert halls in late 1988. The Museum of the Moving Image traces the history of film and television with over 50 exhibit areas — many offering 'hands on' (visitor participation) displays. It's modern, fun and open late so you can combine with a show.
    Admission £3.25. Hours: Tues–Sat 1000–2000; Sun and Bank Holidays 1000–1800. **South Bank Arts Centre, Waterloo, London SE1. Tel. 01-928 3232. U. Waterloo.**

Palaces

One recent survey of visitors showed that many expected to be able to walk around the great royal palaces on their first trip to England. In London, they would have been a little disappointed. The three standing royal palaces are still residences, and not open to the public, with the outstanding exceptions of the **State Apartments** at **Kensington Palace**, the **Queen's Gallery** at the side of **Buckingham Palace**, and Sunday worship at the **Queen's Chapel, St James's Palace**.
    Windsor and **Hampton Court** are included under *Day and half-day trips*, as these are further out.

Buckingham Palace and the Changing of the Guard
Gazing through the bars of the front fence, you can't see much of Buckingham Palace apart from its square, flat and unexciting Regency front. However, you can get into the **Queen's Gallery** at one side and see those of Her Majesty's pictures that happen to be on display. Also, the royal carriages in the **Royal Mews** are exhibited to the public. Did you know you can register as a visitor at the sentry box to let her know

you've come to see her? None of these activities will shed much light on the royal mystique, but they're the closest you can come to the palace.

Buckingham Palace has been the principal London residence of British monarchs only since Victoria moved her family there in the mid-nineteenth century. To appreciate the Palace best, walk or ride a taxi under Trafalgar Square's **Admiralty Arch** and down **The Mall**, a long, tree-lined grand avenue with pretty **St James's Park** on one side and the elegant **Carlton Terrace** on the other, down to **Queen Victoria's statue** in front of the Palace — enough to give anyone something of the grand, majestic feel of being queen. (For more information on the **Mews** and the **Queen's Gallery**, see the section on *Museums*).

The Changing of the Guard is a ceremony most first-timers want to see. During the summer months you may not be able to see very much as huge tour buses disgorge vast numbers of tourists intent on the same thing. Don't expect grand pageantry. The changing of the **Queen's Guard** lasts about 30 minutes, from 1130–1200 daily, April to September, and every other day from October to March, and is interesting for those who haven't seen it before. If you want a good view, go during the winter, or at least half an hour or more early during the summer. There is another guard-changing ceremony at the **Horse Guards, Whitehall** — The **Queen's Life Guard** — at 1100 daily.

Buckingham Palace: U: Green Park or Victoria. Whitehall: U: Charing Cross.

Kensington Palace

A walk through the **State Apartments** at **Kensington Palace** provides the only London opportunity to enter a royal residence. Strangely, this major attraction is missed by many tourists, perhaps because the entrance is hidden away at the far end of **Kensington Gardens**. Today, the Prince and Princess of Wales live in a part inaccessible to the public where Princess Margaret lived until recently.

The original Jacobean building was acquired by William of Orange and Mary, who in 1689 hired Christopher Wren to undertake extensive alterations. Queen Anne made further changes. George II was the last reigning monarch to live there, until his death in 1760, but Queen Victoria stayed here until she ascended the throne in 1837. Her bedroom is open to the public and the nursery still contains her doll's house and toys.

Queen Victoria's Bedroom, Queen Mary's Bedroom, the **Grand Staircase** and the many fine paintings by Old Masters are the main attractions. There are separate admission charges for the **State Apartments** and the **Court Dress Gallery** (costume exhibit), or you can save money with a combined ticket. Stroll round the gardens afterwards.

Admission £2.60. Hours: Mon–Sat 0900–1700; Sun 1300–1700. Tel. 01-937 9561. **U: Queensway or High Street Kensington.**

St James's Palace

The public is not admitted to **St James's Palace**, site of the 'Court of St James' but no longer home to reigning monarchs of the United Kingdom. Still, you might want to stroll past the façade on St James's Street, or through the courtyard if you feel curious about where the Queen Mother (at Clarence House) and the Duke of Kent live. The Palladian **Queen's Chapel** is open for services of worship on Sundays from Easter to the beginning of August. The whole complex has undergone immense changes since Henry VIII, Bloody Mary and Elizabeth I lived there.

U: Piccadilly Circus.

Lambeth Palace and Fulham Palace

No connection with royalty, but with the Church of England. See *Churches and ecclesiastical buildings*.

Great country houses and town houses

You don't have to make a long out-of-town day-trip to see examples of the famous English country house. In fact, you don't even have to leave London. The area around Richmond is, well, especially rich in the genre. Of course, an even wider and more interesting range of choice lies within easy reach of the city (see *half-day and day trips*). Access to several of these London houses requires a little effort — a walk from the nearest tube, or a taxi (better a minicab) ride; but this extra effort puts these attractions out of the reach of the tourist hordes, and makes them all the more rewarding.

Kenwood

The name is now more closely associated with the famous summer Saturday evening concerts, which take place in the idyllic atmosphere of its former grounds, now part of the immense **Hampstead Heath Park** (see *Activities*). You might want to go early on a Saturday and make a day of it, wandering around the elegant white mansion remodelled in 1764 by Robert Adam. The front portico is pure classical Greek, and the library has been described as 'perhaps Adam's most inspired room'.

In this aristocratic setting visitors can enjoy at least a dozen paintings universally renowned as masterpieces. Two favourites are *Lady Howe* by **Gainsborough** and *Guitar Player* by **Vermeer**. You may prefer the *Self Portrait* of **Rembrandt**, or a **Turner, Hals, Reynolds, Van Dyck** or **Cuyp**.

Most of the treasures were collected by Lord Iveagh, the last person to live at Kenwood House in the 1920s. Inhabitants before him include a generous sprinkling of dukes and earls. One of the most famous was the great Lord Mansfield, who became Lord Chief Justice in 1756. Americans will have heard of one of his judgements — when he championed a negro slave who claimed his freedom when brought to England. (J.C.)

Hours: Mon–Sun 1000–1700. Tel. 01-348 1286. **U: Golders Green** then bus **210** to the top of **Kenwood House Drive**.

Burgh House

An English town house built in 1703 during the reign of Queen Anne. You can take tea there and visit the library to see a living artist's latest watercolours or oils; or you can sit in the panelled music room and listen to madrigals or Debussy played on the grand pianoforte? You can do it all at **Burgh House**, only 3 miles from the heart of London, off the usual tourist circuit. A strong conservationist movement has preserved most of Hampstead's eighteenth-century charm, and **Burgh House** (pronounced 'Berg') is part of it all.

A ticket for an afternoon concert costs only £3. Music is classical, interspersed with occasional international jazz musicians in person.

Home-made, traditionally English and wholefood lunches and teas in the **Buttery** are served by women in mob caps and aprons. It's also one of those places in London where a woman can go alone to eat and not feel self-conscious or threatened. The Buttery has an almost family atmosphere.

Burgh House has been taken to the heart of the local intelligentsia,and is run mainly by volunteers. It's only five minutes walk from Hampstead tube station. (J.C.)

Admission free to house, art exhibition, museum and bookshops. Hours: Wed–Sun 1200–1700 (Buttery 1200–1730 — advisable to reserve for lunch: 01-431 2516). **New End Square, Hampstead. Tel. 01-431 0144. U: Hampstead.**

Chiswick House

If you're seen **Kenwood** (see above) and you want to visit another Georgian era country house (albeit a small one) without leaving London, this is probably the most accessible, though it does involve a tube (Hammersmith) and a bus (290). Set in its own green expanse in the middle of a residential area, **Chiswick House** is a lovely Palladian villa designed by William Kent and built by Lord Burlington in 1725, after a trip to Italy.

If you've ever wondered what 'Palladian' means, this house is probably the clearest textbook example. The interior walls are adorned with classical statues and decorations. Then, as now, it was intentionally sparsely furnished for effect. It's hard to imagine anyone wanting to *live* there, but it is beautiful. This romantic classicism was heavily ridiculed by Burlington's contemporaries, like Pope, and Hogarth, who was a neighbour. Go and see *his* humble dwelling afterwards for the contrast, then maybe take a walk along the Thames back to a nearby tube, stopping at a pub *en route*.

Admission £2.00. Hours: Daily 1030–1800. **Burlington Lane W9. Tel. 01-994 3299. U: Hammersmith**, then bus **290**.

Osterley Park House
This Robert Adam house now owned by the National Trust is further out, set in an even larger green park surrounded by West London's dull suburban sprawl. Take the Piccadilly Line to Heathrow, but get off at **Osterley** and walk for about 20 minutes. An enormous majestic palace beside a pond, originally a Tudor mansion built by Sir Thomas Gresham, **Osterley Park House** was almost totally transformed into the classic mode by Robert Adam in 1767–81. Inside the entrance, high ceilings with blue and white plasterwork introduce you to a series of beautiful, gracious rooms. Wander the enormous grounds afterwards.

Admission £2.00. Hours: Tues–Sun 1100–1700 all year except usual holidays. **Osterley Park. Tel. 01-560 3918. U: Osterley.**

Ham House
A trip to see this fine 1610 Jacobean mansion is easily combined with a visit to nearby **Richmond**, the charming village of **Petersham** and local riverside pubs. **Ham House** has been called the 'sleeping beauty among country houses' on account of its dreamlike riverside and parkland setting. A grand staircase, sumptuous plasterwork, painted ceilings, original furnishings and Old Master paintings grace the fine interiors. Rare formal seventeenth-century garden.

Admission £2.00. Hours: Tues–Sun 1100–1700 all year except usual holidays. **Ham Street, Richmond. Tel. 01-940 1950. U: Richmond** then bus **65** or **71**.

Syon House
This family seat of the dukes of Northumberland has retained its original Tudor façade. Otherwise, like **Osterley Park** (see above), it was totally transformed into a classical palace by Robert Adam in the late eighteenth century. Sumptuous interiors, but visitors really come to see the **Capability Brown** landscaping, the **Gardening Centre** and the **Butterfly House**. Gardening fanatics shouldn't miss the 55-acre grounds with the excellent rose and water-lily collections. **Syon House** is near **Kew Gardens**, and the two could be combined, but unfortunately they are on opposite sides of the Thames, with no easy direct link.

Admission £1.75. Hours: House 1000–1600, except Fri and Sat (Mar–Sept); Park open all year (summer) 1000–1800: (winter) 1300–dusk. **Brentford. Tel. 01-560 0881 U: Gunnersbury** then bus **237** or **267**.

18 Folgate Street
See *Favourite small museums*.

Marble Hill House
Another Palladian mansion, designed for the mistress of George II in 1724–29, containing early Georgian furniture and paintings. More restrained than **Chiswick**

House. Open-air exhibitions during nice weather, with open-air theatre. Delightful riverside nearby, and pubs. **Orleans House**, built in 1720, is nearby — now a municipal art gallery.

Admission free. Hours: Sat–Thurs 1000–1600 (open all year). **Richmond Road, Twickenham. Tel. 01-892 5115. U: Richmond** then walk across the bridge, or any bus except 71 or 65.

Famous people's houses

Apsley House (Duke of Wellington)
See *Museums*.

Carlyle's House
A visit here is really an excuse to see this charming area of Chelsea not far from the Thames, especially the fashionable **Cheyne Walk**. The row of Georgian houses in which it is set has had many famous residents, including George Eliot (at Number 4) and J. M. Turner (Number 119).

The Victorian sage Carlyle lived here at Number 24 from 1834 till his death in 1881. This National Trust house is supposed to be as he left it, with his hat still on the peg. Good pubs nearby (see *Pubs*).

Admission £1.60. Hours: Tues–Sun 1100–1630 (April–October). **24 Cheyne Row SW3. Tel. 01-352 7087. U: Sloane Square**.

Hogarth's House
Again an excuse to see an out-of-the-way neighbourhood in a non-tourist area. London has grown up all around his country retreat. Extensively restored, with no original art and little furniture, it is worth visiting only for fans of this eighteenth-century painter. Combine with **Chiswick House** or take a walk along the Thames afterwards and stop for a drink at one of the riverside pubs along the mall.

Admission free. Hours: Wed–Mon 1100–1800; Sun 1400–1800. **Hogarth Lane W4. Tel. 01-994 6757. U: Turnham Green** then 8 minute walk.

Charles Dickens' House
Dickens only lived here for two years, but this is where he wrote *Oliver Twist*, and there are numerous Dickens relics and memorabilia.

Admission £1.50. Hours: Mon–Sat 1000–1630. **48 Doughty Street WC1. Tel. 01-405 2127. U: Russell Square**.

Samuel Johnson's House
The famed writer compiled his dictionary between 1749 and 1759 in this four-storey Queen Anne house, approached from the same alley off Fleet Street as the **Cheshire Cheese**. Atmospheric, with prints and mementos.

Admission £1.30. Hours: Tues–Sun 1100–1730. **17 Gough Square EC4. Tel. 01-353 3745. U: Blackfriars**.

John Keats' House and Museum
Keats lived in a handsome Regency house in what was then the charming spa resort of Hampstead. Still charming today, and a chance for a look round.

Admission £1.30. Hours: Mon–Sat 1000–1300; 1400–1600; Sun 1400–1700. **Wentworth Place, Keats Grove NW3. U: Hampstead**.

Michael Faraday's Laboratory
The place where the great scientist made most of his important discoveries, restored to its original 1845 look.

Admission 40p. Hours: Tues and Thurs 1300–1600. **21 Albemarle Street W1. Tel. 01-409 2992. U: Green Park**.

Wesley's House and Wesley's Chapel (Museum of Methodism)
If you are a Methodist, this is a must. If not, it will still give you an insight into the
social origins of non-conformism. See **Activities: Religious services.**
    Admission £1.20. Hours: Mon–Sat 1000–1600. **47 City Road EC1. U: Old Street.**

William Morris Gallery
Morris lived here during his childhood. Now run by the **William Morris Society**, the
collections include the famous textiles, furniture and wallpapers of the great
designer, the Pre-Raphaelites and contemporaries.
    Admission free. Hours: Tues–Sat 1000–1300; 1400–1700. **Water House, Lloyd
Park, Forest Road, E17. Tel. 01-527 5544. U: Walthamstow Central.**

Parks and gardens

London is fortunate to have several large green open spaces left as relics of the days
when they served as Henry VIII's hunting and leisure grounds. Though central
London has many pleasant squares, these are often private in residential areas.
Kensington and Chelsea are particularly bad for squares that should be public but
require a key to enter.

Parks
Our favourite parks are mostly the less common, smaller ones. This is not to
disparage larger parks, it's just that the big ones are conglomerations of small bits,
whilst the smaller ones have their own special personalities.

Holland Park
This relatively small (55 acres) park is our favourite. Part of it is wild and brushy; it
stretches in an unlikely sliver between **High Street Kensington** and **Holland Park
Road** and contains several fenced-off pathways, where you and the kids can look at
geese, chickens, rabbits, peacocks and an ostrich in comfort.
    These were formerly the grounds of **Holland House**, once a country house,
bombed in World War II, and now a youth hostel. There is also a playing field, an
open-air theatre (Tel. 01-633 1707), a rose garden and a café — a pleasant place for tea
or an ice cream. Concerts are sometimes held in the summer.
    Two expensive restaurants, the **Belvedere** (English) (Abbotsbury Road W8. Tel.
01-602 1238) and the **Al-Basha** (Lebanese) overlook parts of the green expanse. **U:
High Street Kensington** or **Holland Park.**

St James's Park
The oldest and possibly the prettiest of London's parks, it would be even lovelier for
its flowers, ponds and bridges if the location were not so central: between the
Whitehall government buildings and Buckingham Palace. On the rare sunny summer
day this ensures that it is filled with office-lunchers, tourists and passers-by — many
of whom sunbathe their bareable parts to a state of ripe pinkness. Still, bands often
play in the bandstand, and in the shade you can still escape some of the London
tourist and business hurly-burly. **U: St James's Park, Westminster** or **Charing Cross.**

Green Park
The former duelling ground doesn't have much of a personality. Mainly a broad
expanse of green lawn between Piccadilly and Buckingham Palace, with tree-lined
borders, it is best known for the very amateurish artists who hang up their wares for
sale on the railings on Sundays (and along Hyde Park's Bayswater Road railings).
Still, it can be a good retreat to take your lunch or snack and sit and eat *al fresco*. **U:
Green Park.**

Hyde Park and Kensington Gardens
A former royal hunting reserve, this 400-acre park is so improbably huge that it's best appreciated in parts rather than in its pretty but rather non-descript whole. At the north-east corner is the famous **Speakers' Corner**. On Sunday afternoons crowds drift and congregate around the speakers exercising their right to free speech. Some are charming, some are brash, some are provocative, some are nutcases and not a few are just plain boring. Near the southern boundary and **Hyde Park Corner** lies **Rotten Row** — where you can see fully kitted-out horseriders exercising their hunters and jumpers. In the centre is a long kidney-shaped lake called the **Serpentine**: feed the ducks, rent a paddle boat, enjoy a café meal or simply sit in a deckchair and watch the cosmopolitan promenade.

Kensington Gardens adjoins **Hyde Park** on the western side, and many people consider it to be the same park. At the extreme west end is **Kensington Palace**, home of Prince Charles, and you can sometimes see helicopters coming and going. In springtime there are some beautiful floral displays, particularly around the boundary areas. In the centre is the huge **Round Pond**, where kids and grown-ups sail toy boats, a huge promenade where all the world seems to be walking to and fro, and many wooded paths lined with ancient oaks. On Sundays, amateur artists and craftsmen sell their works from the railings along the Bayswater Road, all the way from Kensington Palace to Marble Arch. **U: Marble Arch, Hyde Park Corner, Lancaster Gate, Queensway**.

Regent's Park
Another former hunting reserve, 472-acre **Regent's Park** is almost a world in itself — with a zoo, a rose garden, a college, a bandstand, and open-air Shakespeare and concerts in the summer. In the spring, the floral displays along the canals are wonderful. **Queen Mary's Rose Garden** has a magnificent display of summer roses on 40,000 bushes and climbers. Summer Sundays bring out many picnicking London families. Broad expanses for kite-flying or frisbee games. **U: Baker Street** or **Regent's Park**.

Hampstead Heath
Much of the Heath is a vast area of wilderness surrounded by grown-up London. Walk along secluded forest trails — it is quite possible to get lost, at least for a while — or fly a kite on the open stretches of **Parliament Hill**; you'll also see some fantastic views of London. **Kenwood**, with its open-air concerts and art gallery, is an eighteenth-century mansion within the park. In the summer there are carnivals, funfairs and bands. Also some unusual facilities: separate single-sex outdoor nude bathing in secluded areas. **U: Hampstead**.

Battersea Park
Covers 200 acres along the edge of the Thames. Little known but pleasant, with a boating lake and a Chinese pagoda. Scene of the annual Easter Parade. **BR: Battersea**.

Dulwich Park
A visit to see the famous azaleas, rhododendrons and rock gardens of this charming park can be combined with a half-day visit to **Dulwich Picture Gallery** (see *Museums: Smaller collections*) and **Dulwich Village**. **BR: West Dulwich**.

Richmond Park
We are drawn back again and again to this 2500-acre park sprawling across 2½ miles in both directions. There is always something new to discover, whether the changing of the seasons in the spectacular rhododendron- and azalea-filled **Isabella Plantation**, or the many views over the Thames Valley into central London. But it is

really the deer which have totally captivated us. For unless you are lucky enough to be a game warden or live in a forest, where else can you stand eye to eye with a huge buck or observe a herd of fallow deer playing with their young from 20 yards? There are currently 250 red deer and 250 dappled fallow deer, descended from the original inhabitants which Charles I enclosed.

There are maps all round the park to direct you, but to get a description and picture map of the park or highlights of the surrounding area, go towards **Pembroke Lodge** near **Richmond Gate**, where a mobile tourist information van is stocked with maps and information. You can stop for a cup of tea and a snack at the lodge, and visit the mound in the 13-acre gardens where Henry VIII is supposed to have received the news of Anne Boleyn's execution. The views from here and behind the lodge are excellent — provided it's a clear day. Don't miss the **Isabella Plantation** (see *Notable gardens* below). **U: Richmond.** (L.M.V.)

Notable Gardens

Kew Gardens (see *London's Britain* chapter)

Cannizaro House
Just take a look behind **Cannizaro House** in Wimbledon. Here, unbeknownst to many a Wimbledonian, lies one of the finest collections of rhododendrons and azaleas in the whole of the south of England. Follow the narrow walkway to the right of the house, between the elaborate displays of Victorian-style bedding plants, and you will emerge to a charmingly rural view across a rolling lawn towards distant hills and the spire of Richmond Church. **U: Wimbledon.**

Chelsea Physic Garden
Perhaps you prefer a hideaway closer to the city centre? Visit the **Chelsea Physic Garden** on Swan Walk. It is open only on Wednesday and Sunday afternoons between mid-April and late October (and there is an admission charge), but here, just one mile from Victoria Station, lies England's second-oldest botanic garden.

Founded by the Worshipful Society of Apothecaries in 1673, it is nearly 100 years older than the Botanic Gardens at Kew. Crammed into a mere 4 acres are over 7000 species of plants, including several of London's most notable trees and Britain's largest specimen of the olive. **U: Sloane Square.**

Tradescant Garden and Museum of Garden History
Across the river is an even smaller hidden garden, but one worth visiting for its historical associations: the **Tradescant Garden**, behind the newly-founded **Museum of Garden History** on Lambeth Palace Road. The museum and garden were both inspired by the fact that the two famed seventeenth-century plant collectors and royal gardeners, John Tradescant (father and son) were buried here. Open Monday to Friday, 1100–1500, and Sunday 1030–1700. Closed in winter. **U: Lambeth North.**

The Isabella Plantation
South-West London's equivalent of The Hill Garden, set in **Richmond Park**. Again, one could roam the huge park for a day and never even notice this woodland garden, enclosed within a fence and hidden from view by a belt of leafy trees. Best to go in late April and early May, but worth a visit at any time of the year. The **Isabella Plantation's** pride is its collection of azaleas and rhododendrons, but the trees are remarkable for their variety too: you will find the pocket handkerchief tree, the strawberry tree, the tulip tree, the dawn redwood and the roble beech, to name but a few. **U: Richmond.**

Syon House
Landscaping by Capability Brown and home of a big **Garden Centre**. (See *Houses*)
(A.C.)

Walks

The best way to see any city is on foot, but it would take an eternity to walk around the
sprawl of even just central London. Of course, numerous very informative walking
tours are available, but there are immense pleasures to be had from just wandering
about on your own. Just to scratch the surface, here are a few suggestions that will
take you through especially atmospheric areas.

Riverside walks
See our suggestions above, under *Major sights: The River Thames*

The royal parks
Begin at the **Admiralty Arch** off **Trafalgar Square**. After a look down **The Mall**, have a
wander along **St James's Park's** pondside paths, feed the ducks, admire the flowers.
The Stuart kings kept a menagerie of elephants, alligators and crocodiles here. Much
more peaceful now, except at 4pm in the summer, when a mass duck feeding takes
place. Walk on up to the gates of **Buckingham Palace**, take a peep through the bars,
then move across the road to **Green Park**. Picture it in your mind's eye as a duelling
ground, which is what it was before Charles II moved them away to make room for ice
houses 'to cool drinks in the continental fashion'.

Up at **Hyde Park Corner** you might want to stop and see **Apsley House**, the former
home of the Duke of Wellington, who rejoiced in the address of No 1, London. If you
can dodge the cars, make your way to **Rotten Row** in **Hyde Park**. The name is thought
to be a corruption of *Route de Roi* — way of the king. Today you can watch elegantly-
dressed riders exercising their serious horses on the dirt track.

A little ways from here is the long pond, the **Serpentine**, with its rowers, paddle-
boaters and toy-boat sailors. Follow its length (perhaps stopping at the café), cross
the busy road, and you're in **Kensington Gardens**. You might like to visit the
Serpentine Gallery. Guidebooks say there is a clear difference between the two
parks. You do see more children, monuments, sculptures and pets in Kensington
Gardens. There is even a pet cemetery now open.

Now you have a choice: swing south past the **Albert Memorial** and the carefully-
tended flowerbeds and on towards **High Street Kensington** tube station, or north
past the **Sunken Garden** towards **Queensway** tube station.

Taken at a leisurely pace and allowing for stops, this walk takes you across the
heart of London's interconnecting green parkland in about four and a half hours.
Thank Henry VIII for preserving the hunting grounds that are today's royal parks.

Bloomsbury
Bloomsbury is full of literary associations and today blue plaques mark the places
where many of the famous lived. No prescribed walk can do full justice to the area,
but especially recommended are **Bloomsbury Square** (Gertrude Stein), **Russell
Square** and **Bedford Square** (Bertrand Russell, Thomas Grey, Thomas Wolfe, R. W.
Emerson). **Gordon Square** was home to many of the Bloomsbury Group: J. M.
Keynes, Duncan Grant, Lytton Strachey and his brother James. Virginia Woolf and
her husband lived in nearby **Tavistock Square**. Stroll through these and adjoining
streets and keep your eyes peeled for the blue plaques. Some parts of the area have
hardly changed in 60 years.

The Grand Union Canal Walk
For most of its length the **Grand Union Canal** has a fine footpath on at least one bank.

The most pleasant section parallels the excellent **Canal Boat Trip** (see below) between **Camden Lock** and **Little Venice**. There is only a short stretch (between **Lisson Grove** and **Edgware Road**) where it is necessary to leave the canal bank. On the way, you skirt the edge of **Regent's Park** and the **London Zoo**, and pass many pleasure-boaters, backs of Regency houses, greenery and birds, fish and Londoners out to spot them. The canal bank is a cool place on a hot day, and there are pubs and refreshments at either end. **Camden Lock** area has an extensive market area. U: **Warwick Road** (Little Venice) or **Camden Town** (Camden Lock).

Riverside Chelsea
Take a tube to **Sloane Square** then walk south on **Lower Sloane Street** to Wren's **Royal Hospital**. You might want to visit the magnificent rooms open to the public, have a chat with a uniformed **Chelsea Pensioner** or stroll around the nearby gardens. Continue down **Royal Hospital Road** or weave around the little streets and mews north of it to **Cheyne Walk**. Around this area are a number of fascinating Georgian houses, including **Carlyle's House** — a museum which you can visit. Unfortunately, busy traffic on the riverside road somewhat mars the English setting. You can then head up **Oakley Street** to **King's Road** for the shopping, or cross the **Albert Bridge** to enjoy the view of Chelsea from **Battersea Park**.

Fleet Street
Begin or end at the **Punch Tavern**, a comfortable old-fashioned pub, with framed cartoons from the magazine. Have a look at Wren's **St Bride's Church**. In the crypt are Roman remains and a framed newspaper article telling of the church's destruction in the blitz in December 1940. West of the church, along **Salisbury Court**, is a plaque marking the site of the home of **Samuel Pepys**. Pass the black glass **Daily Express** building, where passers-by could once see the paper being printed through the windows. Just to the west is **Wine Press Alley** and London's most famous pub, **Ye Olde Cheshire Cheese**, haunt of Voltaire, Goldsmith, Pope and Dickens, to name but a few. Still atmospheric, but now inevitably touristy. Up the alley, at **17 Gough Square**, you can visit the house where **Samuel Johnson** compiled his famous dictionary.

Take a detour to visit the peaceful environs of the **Middle Temple Church** in one of the **Inns of Court**, off the south side of the street, then continue west past the classy **Wig and Pen Club** (lawyers and journalists — members only). Have a look at the **Cock Tavern**, a haunt of Samuel Pepys, with a famous sign said to have been carved by Grinling Gibbons. Browse among the tea varieties offered in **Twinings**. Like a number of buildings along the street, this is a modern replacement of a building destroyed by bombs. In spite of this, the whole area remains one of London's most atmospheric. Although newspapers are no longer printed here, monuments such as **Temple Bar** remain to remind us of the past.

London by gaslight
Does Dickensian London still survive? Indeed it does. Although the city no longer has 'pea-soupers' or hansom cabs, there are a number of gaslamps still in use, and historic areas where the soft mellow light of the gaslamps casts its quiet spell. One of the most famous of these is **The Temple**, home of London's legal profession. Over 100 lamps are still tended daily by London's only lamplighter. At the height of summer he lights the lamps at 2200 and extinguishes them less than six hours later.

The Temple can be reached from **Fleet Street** via seventeenth-century gateways and narrow cobbled alleys, and consists of the **Inner** and **Middle Temples**, two of the great **Inns of Court**. Many of the buildings here date from earlier centuries. In those days there was no roar of traffic from Fleet Street, as there is today, but the area was full of chop houses and coffee houses from which literary figures like **Samuel Johnson** and **Boswell** would observe the world.

Many of the entrances into the **Temple** from **Fleet Street** are easy to miss, so discreetly hidden are they from the casual passer-by. Some are small and narrow, often nothing more than a slit between buildings. The entrance at **No 17**, squeezed between a print shop and a book shop, has an arched wooden doorway above which is a projecting upper storey built in 1610. On the first floor is a chamber known as **Prince Henry's Room**, after the elder brother of **Charles I**. Walk under the Prince's room and you enter the precincts of the **Inner Temple**. The area is a peaceful warren of courts and alleyways, and must be explored at leisure and on foot. To walk here in the dusk is to step out of the twentieth century and back into an earlier time.

It is at this hour of the day that the lamplighter does his rounds. Riding his bike and carrying his long pole under his arm, he stops in the quiet nooks and crannies and lights up the beautiful lamps, the soft glow illuminating their elegantly-ornate design.

You will find it more rewarding to wander at your inclination rather than follow a prescribed route through the alleys and courtyards. The area is spread over less than a mile and each corner you turn leads you back into the past.

Walk through the cloisters to the graceful row of houses in **Kings Bench Walk**. Look for a beautifully-carved stone archway with elegant apartment above — this is the **Temple Gate**, the entrance to which is on the **Victoria Embankment** with its gardens.

Lawyers and journalists congregate in the taverns and restaurants which abound in and around this area. **The Devereaux**, in Devereaux Court within the precincts of the **Temple**, is a comfortable old pub which also offers accommodation. Three other pubs in the immediate vicinity are also worth a visit: **The Clachan** in **Mitre Court**, **The Edgar Wallace** and **The George**. Another well-known drinking establishment is the **Cock Tavern**, situated between Chancery Lane and Fetter Lane, nearly opposite the church of St Dunstan-in-the-West. Also worth trying are **The Wellington** and **El Vino**. (C.R.S.)

NB The Gas Board refuses to give exact times and itineraries for the lamplighter's rounds. Just go and look around at dusk. If you find him — it's an added bonus!

Activities and activity sights

Like the walks in the last section, and the river trips (see *Major sights*), some sights are 'activity'-oriented — places that are more significant for your participation than for what they are. We also include under this category a number of suggested activity ideas that might increase your enjoyment of your trip to London. Check the appropriate sections of this book for more information.

Arcades
London's Regency and Victorian shopping arcades are great places to browse and enjoy the old-fashioned atmosphere. **Burlington Arcade** in Piccadilly is, of course, the most famous, with its out-of-sight prices and old-fashioned 'Beadle' police. Between Jermyn Street and Piccadilly, on the opposite side, is the **Piccadilly Arcade**. The **Royal Arcade** starts at 28 Bond Street W1 and the **Royal Opera Arcade** is behind New Zealand House off St James's Street SW1. All are worth a visit.

Art auctions
Anyone can attend most of the famous auctions at **Sotheby's**, **Christie's**, **Phillips** and particularly **Bonhams**. A fascinating experience, but don't scratch your nose.

Barber shops and hairdressers
London has at least two famous old-fashioned gentlemen's barbers. Having your hair cut there is a fascinating experience. Ladies can choose from fashionable salons.

A public bath and private spa
One of the few Victorian institutions to survive in modern day Britain is the 'public baths'; these still exist in many British cities, sometimes only in the form of a swimming pool and individual baths or showers. Originally, these were intended to fulfil a social need for public hygiene, but many, such as London's **Porchester Baths**, became much grander institutions, with Turkish and Russian baths, plunge pools, exercise facilities and snack bars. Today, expensive private clubs like **The Sanctuary** seem to have assumed much of the functions of the traditional baths, but it is still possible to sample both. As one friend said, these baths provide a kind of relaxation that is the 'best possible antidote for jet lag'.

We recently visited both the above. Let's begin with **The Sanctuary**, which describes itself as a women's private club, though most of its 'members' are of the one-day kind who pay a fee of £28.50, or an evening membership fee (after 1700) of £19.50. But you can join for a month (£225), six months (£550) or a year (£900). To get the full benefit of a day fee, you should plan on spending an entire day there. Lately it's become the fashion for London women to take a friend for a birthday treat.

The Sanctuary is primarily a place for relaxation, though it is connected (but not at the moment) with an exercise room and dance studio next door. The fee allows use of the pool, jacuzzi, sauna, and a sunbed token for 30 minutes, and free body lotion, conditioners, shampoo and tissues. Beauty treatments are an expensive extra.

A walkway stretches across an indoor pool filled with huge colourful carp and surrounded by tropical plants. Brightly plumaged and caged tropical birds eye you across the water and the screeching of the tethered macaws fill the air. Overlooking the pond is a health food snack bar with good salads, carrot cake, juice and very good coffee.

Down below is a bath-water temperature swimming pool beneath towering Moorish arches (but some complain that it can be crowded at certain times). You can swing above it, sitting on a trapeze. In a side area is a jacuzzi with turbulent but silky herbal waters. Nearby you can get beauty treatments such as mud treatment or 'seaweed envelopment' (both £24).

The Sanctuary is definitely worth a visit for the experience, but our own feeling was that the club too faithfully reflects its Covent Garden location. Some staff were a bit snooty. Also, the Sanctuary is not unlike health clubs elsewhere.

Of the more local interest to the foreign visitor to Britain are the **Porchester Baths**. Unlike The Sanctuary, the **Porchester Baths** alternate between men-only and women-only days. The baths are out of another century. Located in a Gothic-revival building just off Queensway in W2, its interiors also seem out of a more gracious age. Also unlike The Sanctuary, the carpeted changing rooms are individual cubicles with beds divided from one another by maroon-plush curtains. You are given a towel and a length of gingham cloth.

There is a door to an always-mixed swimming pool, but within the baths area you may walk around as you please. We were amazed at the number of foreign women walking around naked but loaded down with jewellery.

The bath facilities include steam rooms, dry heat rooms, showers, plunge pools and a snack bar (not so upmarket as the one in The Sanctuary). We found the massages to be very relaxing and extremely skilful. The **Porchester Baths** do not have the extensive and exotic beauty treatments offered by The Sanctuary, but the staff are much friendlier and more down-to-earth. It is also cheaper, unless you plan to spend a whole day (£7 for three hours; massages £5 for half an hour).

Which did we like best? **The Sanctuary** offers a modern, luxurious, exotic but somewhat toffee-nosed experience. The **Porchester Baths**, with their ageing but well-kept cubicles, grand staircases and mirrors, offer a nostalgic and friendly excursion into the past. Both are spotlessly clean. Try both, if you have the time. If you can only go to one (or you are a man), we recommend the **Porchester Baths**. (L.S.)

The Sanctuary: 11 Floral Street WC2. Tel. 01-240 9635. Hours: Mon–Fri 1000–2200; Sat 1000–1800; Sun 1200–2000. **U: Covent Garden.**

Porchester Baths: Queensway W2. Tel. 01-229 9950. Mon, Wed, Sat — men only; Tues, Thurs, Fri — women only. Hours: Mon–Fri 0900–2200 (last ticket 2000); Sat 0900–2100 (last ticket 1900). **U: Bayswater, Queensway** or **Royal Oak.**

Visit a betting shop
London's betting shops are mainly geared to the race tracks, though a number are willing to quote odds on many sporting events, or even American elections or royal births. Even if you don't want to place a bet, go inside and view the human drama on a race day as anxious punters watch the TV and video display units. To find a betting shop, look for the sign **Turf accountants**, or one of a number of chain names, like **William Hill, Mecca,** or **Coral.**

A blimp's-eyeview of London
Every year the question arises whether Airship Industries will be allowed to fly passengers over London during the April–September season. If seats are available, it's an astounding, if expensive (£150) view. To find out phone 01-995 7811 (public relations).

Brass rubbing
A hobby that's easy to take up, and the results are great gifts to take home. Your first stop should be the **National Centre**, now at **St Martin-in-the-Fields** church in Trafalgar Square.

Canal boat trips
We highly recommend the boat trips between **Camden Lock** and London's charming **Little Venice** on the **Grand Union Canal**. The season lasts from Easter to October. Two companies run similar excursions, but we prefer **Jason's Trip** (60 Bloomfield Road W9. Tel. 01-286 3428). (Ring **Camden Lock Cruises** on 01-485 4433 for information on the other one.) Options include dinner cruises, lunch on board or a stop at **London Zoo**, which you pass *en route*. Other sights include the **Maida Hill Tunnel**, the **Mosque, Regent's Park** and the canalside Regency houses. You might want to take the boat one way and enjoy a walk along the canal path the other way.

The trip is best enjoyed if you take the morning or lunch run from **Little Venice** to **Camden Lock (Jason's Trip)** to enjoy the market, but you can do it either way. Takes about 1½ hours. Reserve your seat. **U: Warwick Avenue** (for Little Venice); **Camden Town** (for Camden Lock).

Weekend car hire
Like to see famous houses or other country attractions just outside London, but don't have a car? Many firms offer weekend hire from Friday to Monday at a bargain inclusive rate. Check with your hotel or look in the Yellow Pages.

Visit a cemetery
Highgate, Kensal Green and **Norwood** are places where you can see some grandiose Victorian monuments and quaint tombstones.

Children
Visit the **Zoo** (see below), **Pollock's Toy Museum**, the **London Toy and Model Museum**, and **Hamley's** toy shop. The **Space Adventure**, at 92 Tooley Street, next to the **London Dungeon**, provides a simulated space trip. **U: London Bridge.**

The **Unicorn Theatre** stages plays and shows of all kinds for children from September to June (info on 01-836 3334).

Kids also enjoy a **canal trip** or a **boat trip** on the Thames. During the summer you may find a **carnival** somewhere along the northern side of **Hampstead Heath** or in some of the other parks. **Smolensky's Balloon** restaurant has babysitting for diners' children on Saturdays. Kids also like the hamburgers at the **Texas Lone Star Cafe** (U: Gloucester Road). The closest thing to Disneyland in this part of the world is **Thorpe Park**, which involves a train from Waterloo to Staines, then a taxi; rides and British history-themed attractions (£6 adults, £5 children; open April–September 1000–1800).

Chinatown
Like most big cities, London has a small Chinatown, along Gerrard, Lisle and adjacent streets in Soho. Despite recent corny touches (classical gates and Chinese phone-boxes), London's Chinatown still hosts a real Chinese community with fascinating oriental supermarkets, bakeries, restaurants, and shops selling Chinese-character typewriters and Encyclopaedia Britannicas. And see *Dim sum* (below). U: **Piccadilly Circus**.

Cricket
London has two famous venues: the **Oval** in Kennington, and **Lords** in St Johns Wood. The game is almost incomprehensible to non Commonwealth foreigners. Go with someone who can explain it, or just buy a cheap ground ticket and take in some of the atmosphere. **Lords** also has a small museum and a shop where you might buy an unusual gift.

Dim sum
At **Cheng Cheung Ku** and **New World** and several other Chinese restaurants, you can watch a Sunday spectacle of big Chinese families enjoying a feast of trolley-borne delights — while you sample them youself, of course.

The Docklands Railway — Greenwich — River Circuit
Take the **Docklands Railway** to **Island Gardens**. The trip takes 13 minutes and provides a new perspective on the city. You can return the same way, or, better still, cross under the Thames through a 1906 pedestrian tunnel to **Greenwich** and return by river boat. Actually it's best to do this in reverse, because the last boat from Greenwich is usually no later than 1600, but trains return from Island Gardens well into the evening.

Evening Classes and Adult Education Courses
Every year ILEA (the Inner London Education Authority) has run a series of short evening courses in a vast number of fields. The emphasis in most cases is on fun rather than hard academic work. for those who are staying in London for a short period, these are great places to meet people. An annual directory, *Floodlight*, details courses and meeting times, but the future of ILEA, and therefore these courses, is now in doubt. You might want to ring 01-633 5000 for information.

Exotic dining
Where else in the world is a city where you can sample all these exotic cuisines — Burmese, Polish, Ethiopian, Korean, Caribbean, Mexican, Brazilian? And the list is by no means exhaustive (see *Going out to eat* for more details).

Factory shops
London has a few of these bargain outlets (the **Reject China Shop** is a distributor). **Stoke-on-Trent** is an easy day trip if you're after china. A day trip to **Bradford** would be very rushed, but the whole area is full of woolshop bargains. Gillian Cutress, 34 Park Hill SW4 Tel. 01-622 3722 publishes a series of inexpensive **Factory Shop Guides**.

Films: vintage and repertory
London offers a number of opportunities to see your favourite old and repertory films, as well as the latest releases, at the **National Film Theatre** and several repertory cinemas. Check the detailed listings in *Time Out* or *City Limits*.

Good fish and chips
What many foreign visitors are looking for. Go to **Geale's** or **Seashell**.

France for a day
You can visit the Channel ports of France (Calais, Boulogne) on a day trip for good eating and shopping. Less exhausting if you spend the night, however! See *Day trips*.

Fringe theatre in suburban London
Richmond, Greenwich and Guildford all have high-class repertory and experimental theatre — a good excuse for a half-day out of central London.

Garden centres
If you're a keen gardener you may enjoy a visit to one of London's many garden centres (nurseries). One of the largest is, of course, the **Gardening Centre** at **Syon House**, with its huge choice of plants, seeds and tools. If you are in the area, the **Petersham Garden Centre** (143 Petersham Road, Surrey, Tel. 01-940 5230) is a charmer. Closer in is the **Clifton Nurseries** (5a Clifton Villas, Warwick Avenue W9, Tel. 01-286 9888) in London's Little Venice.

Ghost tour
A company called **Tragical History Tours** specializes in horror, mystery and murder tours. Their nightly Monday-Friday *Bus Trip to Murder* bus tour leaves **Temple** underground station at 1915 (call 01-857 1545 to check for seat availability) and visit the haunts of **Jack the Ripper** and several other murderers and ghosts. They also run day trips to Pluckley — reputedly the most haunted village in England.

Indian food
Although Indian restaurants are spreading all over the globe, London still has the best, and Indian restaurants are now to be found on every major street in some areas. **Sunday buffets** provide an opportunity to sample several specialities at an inexpensive set price. See *Restaurants*.

Kenwood
On summer Saturday evenings concerts are held in the idyllic pondside lawn setting of **Kenwood**, an eighteenth-century mansion in Hampstead Heath. Take a picnic lunch. On some evenings there are fireworks after the concert.

Lectures at public museums and galleries
The **British Museum**, the **National Gallery** and other institutions often give inexpensive or free lectures — particularly on subjects related to current exhibitions. Ring for details or check magazines like *Time Out* or *City Limits*. Again, a good place to meet people.

Lloyd's Public Gallery and the Stock Exchange
Lloyd's has a public gallery and a coffee nouse. The **Stock Exchange** is a less interesting exhibit now that most trading is computerized.

Markets
Don't forget London's street markets — a great opportunity to people-watch both Londoners and tourists. And in fact you are more likely to get satisfaction out of that than out of your bargain hunt . . .

Minibreaks
Especially during the non-summer months, many of Britain's hotels and hotel chains offer 'minibreaks' or short breaks. For an inclusive bargain price you usually get two or more nights' accommodation, breakfast, dinner and maybe some other extras. Some of our subscribers, sated with London, have booked these breaks (most often available over weekends) to spend a couple of days in Lincoln or York or Harrogate without the pressures of day tripping or organizing a full-scale trip. Reduced prices for transportation are sometimes included. Check with the **British Travel Centre** at 12 Regent Street (Tel. 01-730 3400) or a local travel agent. The BTA's booklet *Let's Go* provides a listing of hotels offering bargain breaks.

Murder weekends
Hotels in Brighton and other seaside resorts offer all inclusive **Murder weekends** where guests try to find out 'whodunnit'. The most well-known are run by **Quality Hotels**, 72 King Street, Southport PR8 1LG, Tel. (051) 924 1124.

The Royal School of Needlework
The school holds short classes that several of our subscribers have enjoyed. 5 King Street, WC2, Tel. 01-240 3186.

Opera in English
If you've always avoided opera because you don't speak foreign languages, try the **English National Opera** at **The Coliseum** on St Martin's Lane WC2. All productions are sung in English. Standards are high, and prices are much cheaper than at the nearby **Royal Opera House** in Covent Garden.

Parks
Especially in summer, London's parks are full of happenings and events. Bandstands provide music and there is open-air theatre in **Regent's Park** (the *Open Air Shakespeare*— see *Entertainment*) and **Holland Park**. **Battersea Park** is the venue of an annual Easter Parade.

Parliament — The Public Galleries
Worth it, but you must queue.

Picnics
Go to **Marks and Spencer** and get some excellent prepared foods, or to one of the more expensive gourmet food shops and delis. Head for one of London's parks. **Richmond Park** (for deer watching) and **Kew Gardens** (botanic curiosities) are particularly recommended.

Pub crawling
Now that hours have been lengthened you can spend an evening or an afternoon visiting several pubs and drinking in the atmosphere. Pick several in geographic proximity or within easy reach of public transport (but be prepared not to fulfil *all* your ambitions). We particularly recommend the pubs along the **Hammersmith-Chiswick** mall beside the Thames in West London. **U: Hammersmith**.

Pub theatre
London has a number of fringe theatres operating in rooms above pubs. Have a drink with the actors before or after, and enjoy some good productions.

Pub jazz and folk
A number of London pubs have live music — makes for a cheap atmospheric evening out.

Races

Kempton Park, Sandown and **Epsom** race courses are reachable by short train trips from London. Racing is held on many weekends throughout the year. Admission prices are low and bets are up to you.

Radio and TV

Foreign visitors should not turn up their noses at the idea of 'tuning in' to British radio and TV during their visit. After all, the broadcast media are a vital part of any modern culture.

In Britain's case, there is a worldwide reputation for quality television that visitors may want to test for themselves. Some will be amazed at the amount of junk — boring sitcoms, game shows and soap operas — but alongside these programmes on Britain's four channels (two state-owned — BBC — and two commercial) is a wealth of excellent drama, films and documentaries. Even many of the commercials are clever, and tend to come in airtime blocks with fewer programme interruptions than in some countries. There's nothing wrong with staying in to watch TV. At the least, it must be more educational than going to the movies to view an international blockbuster that you can just as well see at home.

Radio, similarly, is both state- and privately-owned. There is now a proliferation of commercial stations that will sound very familiar to many visitors. The national BBC has four channels. Radio 1 is a pop station, but (is this a contradiction in terms?) *sans* commercials. Radio 2 is easy listening, Frank Sinatra-type music. Radio 3 is classical. Radio 4 is an unexpected delight — carrying news, current affairs, consumer interest and, above all, high-quality drama.

Americans in particular may enjoy tuning into Radio 4 because there is nothing quite like it in the States. Older people will be reminded of the golden days of radio, before pop music took over the airwaves. Younger people will learn to appreciate the unique quality of radio drama: you listen while your imagination conjures up the imagery. But there's more. *Yesterday in Parliament* features recorded slices of the proceedings — complete with the hisses and boos and attempted interruptions. Will the new TV coverage put the politicians in a better light? *Medicine Now* and *Science Now* make the latest discoveries in these fields understandable and entertaining. But many of the programmes are just for fun. On *Desert Island Discs*, a celebrity is asked to pick the eight records he/she would take with them to a desert island. The host interviews the guest and plays the records at intervals.

Religious services

There is hardly a tourist in London who doesn't stand in awe in the magnificence of St Paul's Cathedral or marvel at the age-old beauty of Westminster Abbey. Yet when it comes to finding a place for personal worship, London's visitors aren't sure which way to go. The places of worship suggested below each have a special emphasis or bit of historicity that might make it easier for worshippers to choose. Phone to check times of worship.

Baptist

Bloomsbury Baptist Church was the first nonconformist chapel to stand prominently on a main London thoroughfare, and was built by Sir Morton Peto, who also built Nelson's Column and the Houses of Parliament. The modern sanctuary is housed in the shell of the old building, and the basement was transformed in 1967 to a Friendship Centre where people could meet for meals and coffee. **235 Shaftesbury Avenue** (northern end), **Tel. 01-836 6843. U: Tottenham Court Road. Sunday services: 1100 and 1830**. Coffee, lunch and afternoon tea available in the Friendship Centre downstairs.

Church of England
All Hallows by the Tower has a history that goes back to Roman times, and has more links with America than any other church in London. William Penn was baptized here; John Quincy Adams was married at the All Hallows altar, and today the church is linked with several parishes in the United States, providing a connecting ministry between the two countries. Don't be surprised to see cats and dogs attending service with their owners. **Byward Street EC3, Tel: 01-481 2928. U: Tower Hill. Sunday services: 1100 first Sunday of the month, otherwise 1000. Also Matins.** Coffee, tea and sherry (!) after the service.

St Marylebone Parish Church is noted for its excellent music. Its Choral Eucharist is set to the music of Beethoven, Haydn, Mozart, Schubert, Stravinsky and other classical and modern composers. The crypt has been developed as a Centre for Christian Healing and Counselling. Historically, the names of Charles Wesley, Nelson, Charles Dickens, Robert Browning and Elizabeth Barrett are connected with this church. **Marylebone Road, Tel. 01-935 7315. U: Baker Street. Sunday services: 0800 Holy Communion; 1100 Choral Eucharist; 1830 Evensong (except first Sunday: Ministry of Healing)**

Church of Scotland (Presbyterian)
The **Crown Court Church** originally served the Scottish Commissioners in Scotland Yard, Whitehall. The church serves the Scottish community from all parts of London and the home counties. **Russell Street WC2, Tel. 01-836 5643. U: Covent Garden. Sunday services: 1115 and 1830.** Tea and coffee after the services; modest lunch after morning service.

Jewish
The **St John's Wood Synagogue** is a liberal Jewish congregation that welcomes American visitors. Tickets are required for high holy day services. Information about services here and at other liberal and progressive synagogues is available from the **Union of Liberal and Progressive Synagogues at 109 Whitfield Street W1, Tel. 01-580 1663.**

Methodist
Wesley's Chapel was opened in 1778 and reopened after restoration in 1978. In addition to worshipping in the church built by the founder of Methodism, visitors may participate in a 'walk-about' with the church historian following the service and lunch. This enables them to walk through Wesley's house, sit in the small foundry chapel that houses hymn-writer Charles Wesley's organ, and browse in the recently-opened Museum of Methodism housed in the crypt. **49 City Road, Tel. 01-253 2262. U: Old Street or Moorgate. Sunday services: 1100.** Eucharist followed by coffee in the Radnor Hall, Lunch Programme and Wesley Walkabout.

Society of Friends (Quaker)
Friends House is the headquarters of the Religious Society of Friends in Great Britain. Its library houses a large collection of Quaker literature and many seventeenth-century manuscripts, including the journal of George Fox. **Euston Road, Tel. 01-387 3601. U: Euston. Sunday meeting: 1100.**

Roman Catholic
Westminster Cathedral is the Mother Church of the Diocese of Westminster and stands on a piece of land once used by the Benedictine monks who built Westminster Abbey. After the monks were evicted during the Reformation, the site was used variously as a maze, a pleasure ground, a ring for bull-baiting, and a prison. **Victoria Street. Tel. 01-834 7452. U: Victoria. Sunday Masses: 0700, 0800, 0900, 1030 (Solemn High Mass, 1200, 1730 and 1900.**

United Reformed Church
The City Temple is the main central London church of the United Reformed Church. It has a reputation for good preaching and lively worship, with the evening service being informal and participatory, often with a group of musicians or an occasional drama. It is one of the oldest free churches in London, dating from the 1570s. **Holborn Viaduct (near Holborn Circus), Tel. 01-583 5532. U: St Paul's. Sunday services: 1100 and 1830**. Coffee and tea; lunch available first Sunday of the month.

Non-Demoninational
The American Church in London welcomes visitors to a warm, charismatic service that is less liturgical than most English counterparts. **79 Tottenham Court Road W1, Tel. 01-580 2791. Sunday service: 1100**. Tea and coffee; child minding. (L.K.)

Rugby
Twickenham is the site of many important rugby matches. Often it's hard to get a ticket, but you can take in the atmosphere by hanging out with the crowds in the nearby pubs of Twickenham and Richmond.

The sales
London's stores hold major sales in January and mid-June to August. You might like to arrange your visit to take advantage of the bargains on offer.

London's seaside
The seaside resorts of **Brighton, Eastbourne, Hastings, Margate** and **Southend** are no more than an hour and a half by train from London. However, the water's cold, the breeze is cool and the beaches are more often pebbles than sand. The emphasis is on sunbathing, paddling, eating fish and chips, and enjoying the tatty old-fashioned seaside atmosphere. A good escape from dirty humid London on a summer day.

Speakers' Corner and Artists' Sales
Sunday afternoon at **Speakers' Corner** is described elsewhere. After you've had your fill, stroll along the Bayswater Road and look at the amateur arts and crafts hung for sale on the railings.

Stay with Shakespeare
The **Royal Shakespeare Theatre** in Stratford has good-value deals inclusive of meals, accommodation, tickets and sometimes transportation from London.

Sunday lunch
Have a traditional Sunday lunch, brunch, Indian buffet or dim sum, then have a lazy afternoon in one of the parks.

Take tea
Go to one of the famous major venues like the **Ritz** or **Brown's Hotel** or one of the cheaper, less formal places.

Theatre tours
A company called **Stage by Stage** organizes tours to seven different London theatres to learn about their histories and what happens backstage. Among the most interesting is the tour to the **Old Vic**.

Time travelling
18 Folgate Street (Georgian) and **Linley Sambourne House** (Victorian) are two attractions which aim to preserve houses exactly as they were in earlier times. Similarly-preserved are the **Cabinet War Rooms**.

Trial by jury
Attend a trial or court proceeding — best at the Central Criminal Courts, the **Old Bailey**.

Drive an underground train
One of the exhibits at the **London Transport Museum** simulates this activity.

Viewpoints
Four good views: The **Monument** has a lot of steps to climb; **Tower Bridge**, next to the Tower, is a great riverside vantage point, and has a lift (elevator); **Westminster Cathedral** also carries you to the top of the tower; **Queen's Tower** at Imperial College is open during the summer.

London Zoo
Zoos are a necessary evil. The London one in **Regents Park** has at least been cleaning up its act and getting rid of the old iron-bar cages, and it is considered one of the world's best. Hours: daily 0900–1800 summer and 1000–1800 winter. Tel. 01-722 3333. Also famous for its **Adopt an Animal** programme. You pay the annual cost or part of the cost of maintaining individual animals, ranging from an elephant (£5000) to small mammals (£30). In return, you get a photo, your name on a plaque, and a discount ticket.

Tourist attractions

Beware of the 'tourist attractions' — what we define as artificially-created tourist draws, mostly without historical associations. Most of them describe themselves as 'museums'. This has become big business in Britain — on average, a new one opens every two weeks — and most are privately-owned and run. Many charge high prices. A lot of them serve a useful child-oriented entertainment purpose in quiet holiday areas, where families look for things to do on rainy days. But not in London — a world city full of history, entertainment and real attractions. Here, they may add up to a big admission bill without much in return. If the kids are desperate (and old enough), one solution might be for parents to let the kids go inside while they have a beer or coffee outside.
  The tourist attractions listed below are included because they are London's most famous and popular. With these, as with less well-known attractions, consider whether you really want to go in for the price charged.

Madame Tussaud's
Probably the world's oldest tourist attraction. We are going to upset a lot of people by saying that this is London's most overrated and overpriced sight. In the summer, lines are long and the museum is chaotic with wild kids. If you must go, better to wait until about 1530 or 1600.
  Nevertheless, this is still the world's most famous wax museum, attracting two million visitors a year. New figures and exhibits are constantly appearing. Kids enjoy it more than adults because, although the wax figures are undoubtedly of the highest quality, you really do have to suspend your critical faculties or else be taken by surprise (the museum is fond of this practical joke — particularly with Beatle-lookalikes) to be very impressed. Admission is a steep £4.30 adult and £2.80 children. Better value is the Royal Ticket (£5.60 and £3.40) which also admits you to the only average **Planetarium** next door. **Madame Tussaud's** is very close to **Regent's Park**, and might be combined with a canal trip or a visit to the **Zoo**.
  Marylebone Road NW1, Tel. 01-935 6881. Hours: Mon–Sat 1000–1730; Sun 0930–1730. U: Baker Street.

London Dungeon
The wax figures in this massive series of exhibits of the more macabre and murderous aspects of British history (witchcraft, cannibalism, head-chopping, torture and assorted mayhem) are not even as convincing as those in **Madame Tussaud's**. The place does manage a gloomy, grim, candlelit atmosphere, occasionally punctuated by weird noises and screams. Not for very young children or adults, but pre-teens and teens (9–14) may find it either exciting or funny. Expensive family admission total for what it is (£3.50 adults, £2 under-15s).
   28/34 Tooley Street SE1. Tel. 01-403 0606 Hours: Apr–Sep 1000–1745; Oct–Mar 1000–1630. U: London Bridge.

Guinness World of Records
Overpriced (£3.50) tourist attraction in the new **Trocadero** building. Should be in a holiday town, not an exciting world city where there is already lots to do. Good and innovative displays, but again strictly for the kids.
   Coventry Street W1. Tel. 01-438 7331. Hours: daily 1000–2200. U: Piccadilly Circus.

The London Experience
An audio-visual experience, also in the **Trocadero**, showing glorious film views of London. Some tourists prefer it to the real thing . . .
   Coventry Street W1. Tel. 01-439 4938. Hours: daily 1020–2220. U: Piccadilly Circus.

The Light Fantastic Gallery of Holography
Inexpensive and OK if you're into holographs, but you can see very similar exhibitions in most major world cities, and not a few American shopping malls.
   48, The Market, Covent Garden WC2. Tel. 01-836 6423. Hours: 1000–1800 Mon–Fri. U: Covent Garden.

Royal Britain
A new (1988) audio-visual tourist draw, which aims to take visitors through '1000 years of royal history'. For royalty-watchers only. Admission £5 adults, £3 children.
   Aldersgate EC2. Tel. 01-588 0588. Hours: daily 0900–1730. U: Barbican.

12   *London's Britain*

Going out of London for a day or more

Most overseas visitors want to see at least a bit of Britain beyond the reach of the easy-to-use London Underground and bus networks. Some want to choose the easy option of the many organized bus tours or British Rail's own day trips. Tours often include lunch and cut aggravation and local hidden costs of independent travel like local transfers and tips. The disadvantage is that you must travel around with the group, schedules may be hectic in order to cram everything in, and time to wander, see and discover the things you enjoy most may be severely circumscribed.

Travelling independently in Britain is almost as easy. You might not see as many sights, but you'll probably enjoy and remember more. The short distances of these islands are served by a vast internal network of rail, bus and air routes. Most cities and larger towns have extensive public transportation systems and local taxi and car hire facilities. Tourism is big business in Britain, and efficient local tourist offices (often near the railway station) can help you find and book hotels, B&Bs and local attractions on the spot.

Our recommendation to most day trippers or travellers with limited time is to **go by rail**: it is usually quicker and there are a variety of fare bargains from which to choose. Buses are subject to traffic and weather problems, though there are places that don't have a convenient train station, and bus fares are cheaper than the train.

Deregulation has cut the cost of air travel to Ireland and the far corners of the kingdom, but it's still not competitive on shorter routes, nor is it likely to be attractive to scenery-minded tourists.

Although many visitors are frightened by the idea of driving on the left, for those with more time, car hire, though not recommended for central London, is really the best way to see the countryside and make your own discoveries of off-the-beaten-track pubs, hotels and attractions.

Some tips

- Rail is generally the most comfortable and efficient transport for self-guided day-tripping. Trains run on their own road, so traffic is not a problem and schedules are more easily kept.

- If your time is limited, you might be better off with a direct bus or coach tour to these destinations: most individual country homes and castles, **Stonehenge** and other places that require a connecting local train, bus or taxi. If you're short of time, the hassle may not be worth the feeling of independent accomplishment. **Green Line** coaches run direct services and tours to many of these attractions during the April to September period (Tel. 01-668 7261). A useful minibus company called **Trust Tours** provides transport to country houses and other hard-to-reach places near London. Tel. (0732) 451 731.

- The extreme limits of day tripping are probably destinations that are 2 to 2½ hours away, but you must consider two things. (1) How much is there to see? For example, York (2 hrs 15 min) is now being promoted as a day trip — but there's no way that a single day's visit can do justice to that city's many attractions. (2) Travel is tiring: how fit are you to benefit from a quick visit? With a few notable exceptions, you should probably limit your day-tripping to the boundaries of British Rail's **South East** region.

- Dedicated day trippers plan in advance and know exactly what they want to see. Alternatively, you might want to commit yourself just to wander, enjoy the day and not worry whether you see the major sights.

- Unless you've made extensive plans, a first stop at the local tourist information centre for an inexpensive map and local information brochure is a good bet.

- For those who do not want to travel far away, Greater London and its fringes offer plenty of green spaces, stately homes and changes of scene and pace.

- If you plan to visit many stately homes administered by either the **National Trust** or **English Heritage** (includes the Tower of London), you can save money by joining either of these organizations at the first of their properties you visit.

British Rail

British Rail (BR) and rail travel have been almost synonymous in Britain since 1948 when the entire network was nationalized. Today, the only exceptions are local steam excursion lines and city transit systems. All major cities and most good-sized towns are served, though the backbone of the system is the skeletal **Intercity** set of routes that run south-north, mostly linking provincial cities and London's uncentral hub in south-east England. East-west connections between provincial cities, local trains and suburban services rarely match the quality and standards of service of Intercity trains. Some London commuter trains are disgracefully overcrowded during morning (inward) and evening (outward) rush hours.

BR is now trying to improve non-Intercity trains by creating regional companies to run local services and encourage travel. For example, British Rail's subsidiary for south-east England is called Network SouthEast; for Scotland, ScotRail. New local Sprinter trains and up-to-date surburban trains are being introduced. Nevertheless, these efforts have a long way to go, and you'll still notice a difference between Intercity trains and many provincial and local services.

Even on Intercity routes, many of us feel that British Rail still needs a significant improvement in quality. Strikes and labour disputes are now less common than on Network SouthEast and local services, but disruptions still occur. Poor management and union work practice dermarcations still lead to occasional inefficiencies and poor service. Catering has been vastly improved but buffet cars too often run out of food. We've been on too many trains where the only food on offer has been overpriced coffee, beer, bacon sandwiches and odd items, not the full range advertised.

Tip We've learned our lesson and now buy our sandwiches beforehand. BR's own station buffets have vastly improved the quality and range of sandwiches and other take-away items on sale. The larger stations now have stands selling hamburgers, cookies, croissants, and even take-away breakfasts.

On several trains we've experienced, advertised restaurant cars have not opened. Anyway, BR's policy is to phase these out in favour of a new programme called Cuisine 2000, in which only First Class passengers will enjoy a hot meal service at their seats, served from a trolley. Standard Class (the new name for Second Class) passengers will be restricted to buying snacks and warmed-up meals from the buffet cars (except some may be allowed to come up to the First Class to eat breakfast if there's space). BR seems determined to preserve the old British class system . . .

. . . and to kill off romance. Before BR began to do away with restaurant cars, they discontinued the old-fashioned panelled seating compartments. In that particular case, we accept the argument of many women that such trains were unsafe. And it's obvious that new, open railway cars make more economic sense. But in designing these, did they really think that most people really want to share an immovable table with three strangers? When you have to squeeze in and out and ask someone else to move out of their seat when you want to go to the toilet or the buffet or simply to stretch your legs, one of the main advantages trains have over buses is diminished. The design of these trains, and BR's lack of cleaning personnel, can give some trains a cluttered, trashy look after only a couple of hours out.

Don't expect the Orient Express. These days there won't be a dining car on a sleeper train, and bar cars are rare. Sleeper trains are just that, but the Pullman ones are especially nice and you might try them just for the experience of sleeping on a train.

But don't get us wrong — BR has improved and is improving, but it aspires to the modern philosophy that train travel should be a standardized, fast, efficient form of transportation between points. For taking day trips or getting about the country, there is no substitute for British Rail, because it runs on its own road, free from traffic jams and mostly free from weather problems. And some of the country's most gorgeous scenery can be seen from train windows.

British Rail information
BR has a whole host of information numbers, including 24-hour dial and listen recordings (see the Telephone Directory **White Pages** or call **Directory Enquiries** — (dial 192). Here are the General and Reservation Enquiries numbers for trains to:

Southern England and the south-east, south London, Essex/East Anglia	928 5100
West Country, South Wales, West Midlands	262 6767
East Midlands, North Wales, North-west England, Scotland via west coast (Glasgow)	387 7070
North-east England, north London, Scotland via east coast (Edinburgh)	278 2477

Alternatively, you can get information about any route from any railway station information counter, though the most informed personnel are usually in the bigger stations.

Tip If you are departing London by train, it's a good idea to be sure *which London station* you are leaving from. There are fourteen stations, but only about seven of these are major termini! In general, **Paddington** handles trains to Bath, Oxford and the West Country; **Euston** to Manchester, Liverpool, the north-west, Glasgow and all Scottish sleeper services; **King's Cross** to Edinburgh, York and north-east England, **Liverpool Street** to Cambridge, Colchester and much of East Anglia; **Charing Cross** to Canterbury and Dover; **Waterloo** to Portsmouth and Salisbury; and **Victoria** trains to Brighton, Chichester, Gatwick and the Continent. *But double-check.*

Tickets
Tickets can be bought from BR stations or authorized travel agents in Britain and abroad. There is a small charge for reservations (cheaper here than overseas) for both first and standard class seats, but these are particularly worthwhile on weekends and during July and August and the periods around national holidays.

First class tickets
Exorbitantly expensive. Most of the passengers seem to be businessmen on expense accounts, well-heeled elderly people paying for extra quiet, and First Class Britrail Pass holders. The special **Intercity Day Trips**, which may include meals and seating in the old wood-panelled carriages, are the best first class day trip deals.

Standard class ordinary single or return tickets
These are also relatively expensive if you must pay the full price. Few Britons do so, and visitors shouldn't either. Investigate cheap day returns, saver returns, passes and other discounts outlined below.

Travelcards
(See *Getting around* section.) Useful if your final destination is within the Greater London zones of the card's validity, though limits are roughly similar to those of the Underground system.

Cheap day returns
Available from London to most cities and towns within a day's journey from London, and probably your cheapest ticket for these trips (especially with a **Network Card** — see below). There are additional restrictions to some destinations — no travel before 0930, on Fridays or on some peak days — but commonly you need only travel out and return on the same day.

Saver returns
These discounted tickets allow you to travel out and return any time within a month. Useful for a discount on longer distance travel or spending the night. Savers are not valid on Fridays, though a higher-priced **Peak Saver** is available on most routes. **Network Savers**, sold for stations in south-east England, will not allow you to travel before 0930 Monday–Friday.

All-line rail rovers
Standard class tickets good for one or two weeks, which allow unlimited travel anywhere in Britain. Second class fare is £135 for one week and £215 for two weeks. If you can't get a Britrail Pass and want to do a lot of travelling in a short time, this is the next best thing.

Local rovers
Standard class tickets good for one or two weeks which allow unlimited travel within one of 19 specific areas for as little as £18. Of special interest is the **Freedom of Scotland**, which allows unlimited travel throughout Scotland for only £42 for seven days.

Circular saver
Another bargain often missed by the tourist. If you plan to take a trip round Britain, say starting and ending in London, but travelling up to Scotland, across to Wales, and stopping in chosen locations on the return route, you simply add up all your single fares and divide them by half, giving you a round trip to all these places for the price of a one-way ticket. This is done through a British Rail Office. If, for example, you combine this with a **Family Rail Card**, the savings may allow you to travel at about a quarter of the regular price.

Nightriders
Cheap return fares of only £19 or £25 for first class travel from London to Edinburgh, Glasgow or Aberdeen. The catch is that you must travel on certain late night trains.

Upgraded tickets
Standard class tickets upgraded to first class are sometimes available at short notice. Look for a small notice on the train window. The fee is sometimes as little as £2, payable on board.

Britrail passes — are they worth it?
Many eligible overseas visitors will ask this question, even though many travel agents will automatically insist on it. **Britrail passes** come in several types: the **Gold Pass** allows unlimited first class travel and has a variant type, the **Senior Citizen Pass** for those aged 60 or over, who get a 15 per cent discount. The **Silver Pass** allows unlimited standard (second class) travel and has a variant type **Youth Pass** with a 15 per cent discount for those aged between 16 and 25. Cheaper **Child Pass** versions of the Gold and Silver Passes are available. Passes are valid for 8, 15, 22 or 30 day periods, which begin the first time you use them. Two new Gold and Silver variants, the **'8 out of 15'** and the **'4 out of 8'** allow the purchaser to travel for as many days out of the total validity period. All Britrail passes must be bought before you leave for Britain, so you have to make your decision early.

There are three factors to consider:

1. The amount of travelling you plan to do.

2. The current exchange rate — has the value of the dollar (or other foreign currency) gone up or down since the price of the pass was set?

3. Whether the simple convenience of the pass outweighs other factors.

Note: Since most passes are sold to Americans for US dollars, we have used that currency as an example. Examples are based on presstime prices and a rate of US$1.86. Check current rates.

First Class Gold Pass
With the decline of the dollar, first class passes are now good value — if you are going to travel long distances in a short time period and/or you would have travelled first class even if the pass had not been available. Ordinary first class fares are so horrendously expensive that few Britons, other than businessmen, ever pay them. For example, a London-Edinburgh first class return ticket is the equivalent of US$250, whilst an eight-day Gold Britrail is the same price. A '4 out of 8' would be only $210. And BR is in the process of switching over to Cuisine 2000 (see above). Although they

are behind schedule, this will eventually mean that dining privileges will effectively be restricted to first class passengers. First class is more comfortable, less crowded and less plagued by screaming tots. A chief drawback is that most of your classmates are either pin-striped businessmen or fellow foreign visitors.

Standard Class Silver Pass
If you're going to make *more* rail journeys than just one long-distance return trip (say to Edinburgh, for example), a couple of medium length trips, or a few short trips around London (say Brighton, Oxford and Bath), then you'll probably save by buying a Silver Pass. These passes are particularly valuable for a series of single or interrupted journeys. But don't be too taken in by the *Go Britrail* brochure's table of regular individual dollar-equivalent fares. Few of us ever pay these prices. Instead, most non-businessmen (and not a few businessmen) buy the far cheaper 'saver fares' that are available to everybody, whether resident or not, or use the discount cards available to senior citizens, students and families.

For example, if I go to Edinburgh by train, I travel on a saver for £52 return (approximately $96) — not the full fare of $172 dollars quoted. A standard class Britrail Pass holder would have paid $179 for an eight day pass or $149 for a '4 out of 8' and he/she would have needed to make a similar trip, in addition to this one, or several trips, to get full value from the pass. The only current restriction on saver tickets to Scotland is that the ticket costs £10 more if you plan to travel on a Friday. Some saver tickets to other destinations may restrict departures between 0700 and 0900 or 1700 and 1900, but all allow you to return at any time within a month. Some other recent examples of saver fares: Bath £19 ($35); Inverness £63 ($118); Cambridge £12.50 ($23); Penzance £41 ($76). But 'saver' prices are both seasonal and constantly rising.

Travel Pak
If you're just coming over for a week and want to spend half that time in London, then you might want to consider the new **Capital Travel Pak** for $129 (7 days) or $99 (4 days) the Pak includes unlimited tube and bus travel in Greater London and all British Rail's Network South East network (see below). Alternatively you might just buy one day Travelcards (approximately $4) and a Network Card (approximately $18 — see below) and get discounts on the trips you choose.

The real advantage of either the Britrail Pass or the Travel Pak is *flexibility* — hop on any train, any time within the period. You aren't tied to fixed routes and schedules. But you may want to have a look at some of the other discount deals on offer.

Other discount passes
These passes can be bought in Britain and used for big discounts on British Rail tickets, provided you can meet their requirements. You just obtain a form from a railway station, fill in the details with any local address, and pay a small fee. Some passes require proof of age. And their benefits are subject to change.

A. Network Cards
Network SouthEast is a huge area centring on London and stretching from Salisbury, Weymouth and Oxford in the west, and Northampton, Cambridge and Ely in the north, to the eastern and south-eastern coasts, including places like Winchester, Portsmouth, Arundel, the Isle of Wight, Brighton, Canterbury, Rye and Dover. In effect, it covers most of the nearby day-trip areas. A Network Card costs £10 for 12 months or only £5 if you're over 60 or the holder of a **Young Person's Railcard** (see below). The cardholder plus up to three other adults can travel for one third off most tickets, including savers, plus up to four children can accompany at only £1 each any time after 1000 Monday–Friday and all day Saturdays, Sundays and holidays.

B. Family Rail Cards

If you are travelling with children, your best long-distance travel investment is the **Family Rail Card**. This costs £15 a year (or any fraction thereof). For an entire family (anywhere from one adult and one child to four adults and four children) it offers adults a third to a half off second class travel, while children pay only £1 per journey, no matter how far they are travelling. The catch is that these cards can only be used if there is at least one child under 16 travelling with you and one adult (named on the card) in the party.

If you can avail yourself of a Family Rail Card, this entitles you to an additional half off on Cheap Day Returns, and an additional third off on saver tickets, thus making your saving really phenomenal.

C. Senior Citizen Railcard

Special rates are given to senior citizens — all outlined in specific brochures available from most British Rail stations. For example, senior citizens who can show a UK address of any kind can obtain a Senior Citizen Railcard for £15, and save half on cheap day returns, one third on saver tickets, and one third to a half on standard tickets, plus numerous other benefits.

D. Young Person's Railcard

People aged between 16 and 24, or who are full-time students attending an educational establishment in the UK, can obtain this card (£15), which entitles them to benefits similar to the Senior Citizens Railcard.

Bus services

If you prefer the bus, you also have the benefit that it is probably cheaper. The deregulation and privatization of the passenger coach (bus) services in Britain have led to reduced fares and fierce competition between rival companies. The most comprehensive selection of tickets and deals is under the **National Express** banner, but on routes such as London-Oxford, several London firms battle with hourly departures and single fares as low as £2.50 (many daily departures from **Victoria Coach Station** and **Marble Arch**).

On long-distance routes you can have the option of taking a luxury bus complete with stewardesses, food and drink services, videos and other amusements; or you may prefer a no-frills cut-rate service.

Tickets, information and departures

The **Victoria Coach Station Travel Centre**, Buckingham Palace Road, open 0730–2230, many **Tourist Information Centres**, and affiliated travel agents sell coach tickets. For telephone information, you now have to phone the individual companies. **National Express** offers the most services and takes credit cards. Tel. 01-730 0202.

Most long-distance departures from London leave from **Victoria Coach Station**, about 200 yards down Buckingham Palace Road from Victoria Station. It's a fairly grotty, old-fashioned, functional place, but it is safe and there's a taxi rank outside should you arrive early in the morning. **Green Line** and some other coaches depart or pick up passengers from other London points. For those with heavy bags, **Shuttle Bus** (40p) connects the coach station with Victoria railway station.

If you're travelling on **National Express'** nationwide network of routes, the quickest and most comfortable are those designated **Rapide**. Overnight services available on many routes allow passengers to save by sleeping *en route*.

Discounts

Like British Rail, coach companies offer a variety of special deals and discount fares. Among those offered by National Express are: day return, midweek return, period return, and child and senior discounts (one third off).

Other passes and deals

Britexpress Card
This card is available to overseas visitors only, but it can be bought from the Victoria Coach Station or the Coach Travel Centre for £8, and gives up to 30 days discounted travel (one third off standard fares) and reductions on **Great Days Out** (see below) and **Minibreaks** (see below).

Great Days Out
Special day fares to Bath, Brighton, Bristol, Cambridge, Canterbury, Norwich, Portsmouth, Salisbury, Stratford, Winchester and Warwick that allow you complete freedom once you get there, and often a choice of return times. Average National Express fare £6–£8.

Minibreaks
This National Express package includes travel, transfers and hotels for 2–3 nights in Chester, Edinburgh, Stratford, Windermere or York at reduced prices.

Ordinary red London buses
These go to many outer London points. You could buy a **Travelcard** or a **Capitalcard** (see above) and transfer to a local bus at a tube or railway station.

Green Line buses
These travel to many suburban and south-eastern towns and attractions, with departures from several places in London. Tel 01-668 7261.

Air travel

Domestic air travel has undergone a boom in Britain in recent years, with a growing number of airlines and routes. Deregulation has led to lower prices within Britain and there are hopes that the EEC will further deregulate inter-Europe travel, making London even more of a world travel centre. Within these islands, air travel is most useful and valuable to Ireland, Scotland, the Channel Islands, and more distant parts of the kingdom.

Many bargain fares are available if bought in the UK. For the foreign visitor, the biggest problem is that many of the ultra-cheap fares have advance purchase requirements. Fares are least expensive if you book early, but now there are also many tickets with non-refundable, standby and other restrictions which can be almost as cheap. It pays to shop around by phoning several airlines. We've found that an unfortunate number of travel agents will automatically book the walk-in customer on British Airways at standard rates.

Many visitors want to save time by flying from London to Scotland. Some automatically choose British Airways' hourly **shuttle** to Edinburgh and Glasgow. You are guaranteed a seat, but the shuttle isn't particularly cheap if you pay one of the unrestricted fares. Phone British Airways (897 4000) in advance, or, better yet, call competitor **British Midland** (589 5599), whose 'we try harder' approach has made it our favourite go-ahead domestic airline.

Special fares are also on offer from London to distant out-of-the-way parts of Scotland like Shetland, Orkney and the Outer Hebrides. Another competitive route is London-Dublin, where the small but quality Irish carrier **Ryanair** (Tel. 01-435 7101) has sparked off a fares war, and the airline's low fares are now frequently matched by AerLingus, British Airways and Virgin. A host of carriers fly to the Channel Islands of Jersey and Guernsey (about one hour away) at rates as low as £29 for a single journey.

Car hire

Visitors to the UK are confronted with a bewildering variety of car rental ads and offers. Because these change often, sometimes abruptly, it's difficult to say anything current and accurate about the different deals that may be available by the time you read this guide. But over the past four years of publication we've found several generalizations to be useful.

- Our favourite big nationwide company is **Town and Country** (834 8415). They have consistently offered good-value deals and friendly service.

- **Budget** (935 3518) is our second choice for value deals. Other useful companies are **Swan** (828 9291) and **Central** (727 7812). **Team Cars** (327 King Street W6, Tel. 748 8465) is a good-value small company praised by several subscribers.

- *Off-season* (October–April) rates are more competitive.

- Visitors to London who want only 2–3 days in the nearby countryside should investigate *inclusive reduced rates for weekend hire* available from many firms. These can be particularly valuable over long weekends (when Monday or Friday is a national holiday).

- Some firms have several locations in London and will offer a better rate if you agree to pick up the car from a particular location (often, this is one of the airports).

- Big discounts are often available by booking with one of the major international companies before you leave home.

- **Inclusive fly-drive** deals from the airlines are generally good value, though you should check that they include insurance and all applicable charges.

- Local minibreak or shortbreak packages often include attractive car hire rates.

- **Godfrey Davis Europcar** (950 5050) has long been affiliated with British Rail with offices and pick-up facilities in the major railway stations nationwide. Their **rail-drive** promotions (info from BTA offices abroad) have varied in relative value depending on exchange rates. But some of these deals have offered the outstanding convenience of enabling travellers to pick up a car at one railway station and drop it at another. On 1 April 1989, **Hertz** becomes the British Rail affiliate. Check with them to see which value deals are still available.

- Drivers over 65 may need either to book with one of the larger companies before they leave home or to make enquiries about age requirements with other companies. Some small firms have insurance problems with older drivers.

- Small and local car hire firms often have bargain rates, widely advertized in overseas tourist literature and in **In Britain** magazine. As with the larger companies, low rates may only be the bait, and 'extras' can bring your bill up considerably.

  It is also necessary to pay close attention to small print in insurance matters — some contracts specifically exclude tyres, caps or wheels, or exclude a high waiver or 'excess' amount. You might want to pay the supplement to make sure you're fully covered. Local firms also may lack nationwide drop-off, emergency breakdown and car replacement service. These are not problems for those who confine their travels to southern England, but if you break down in the Scottish Highlands or Ireland, you might have real problems. Ask about these concerns.

- Most rental cars are manual (standard) gear. Automatics are available, usually in the mid-to-higher range of cars, but it's a good idea to book these in advance. One agency with many automatics is **International Car Rental** (40 Kensington Park Road, London W11, Tel. 727 1467).

- As a rough guide, a small economy car can be rented for £90–£130 a week inclusive; a mid-sized car will cost £140–£160 or more. Petrol is currently about £1.80 per imperial gallon.

Driving hints for overseas visitors
Driving is the best way to see many parts of Britain. With a car, your choice of things to see is virtually unlimited. While the basic idea of driving on the left is not that difficult, there are some things that require extra consideration or concentration.

A good map is an absolute must; a ratio of three miles to an inch is preferable. If your driving will take you through several areas of the country, you will find a road atlas useful: **Collins** or the **National Ordnance Survey** road atlases are easily obtainable, up-to-date and relatively cheap.

Driving on the left takes only a day or so to master. Take along a companion who'll let you know if you stray into the wrong lane. This happens most often when making a left turn. Have him/her poised to shout 'left!' whenever you begin to turn into the right lane.

On longer trips an attentive and cheerful **navigator** is needed to watch the map and the road signs. Following the road signs to your destination is not easy. Just knowing the road number is usually not sufficient; the signs will show the names of towns you are headed towards, and so your navigator will need to have an eye on the map to know which towns are on your route and in your direction. When a parenthesis surrounds a road number it means that you are not on that road yet, but heading towards it. Yes, it takes some attention; and you and your navigator will have to be prepared to laugh it off when you take a wrong turn — after all, you're on vacation ('on holiday', that is)!

The **centre line** on two-lane roads is not well observed in Britain. If a driver coming towards you needs to pass a parked car or a bicycle, etc. on his side, watch for him to veer over the centre line if he thinks that you have room to move over. This is so universal that you should expect it from any car coming toward you.

British **roundabouts** are so practical that you'll miss them when you go home. Your side of the road usually widens just before you enter the roundabout. If you are turning left, get in the left lane, signal left, and yield to cars coming at you from the right before proceeding on around. If you are going straight, get in the left lane or the right lane, yield to cars coming at you from the right, and signal left when passing the exit before the one you are taking. If you are turning right, get in the right lane and signal right, yield to cars coming at you from the right, drive towards the inside of the roundabout and stay on the inside until you are nearing your turn; switch your signal to the left when passing the exit before the one you are taking, and as you pull out into the left lane to take this exit.

Motorway driving is somewhat different than elsewhere. The 70mph speed limit, much exceeded, makes for a fast pace. In the major three-lane carriageways, the far right lane is used strictly for passing ('overtaking'). Cars will pass you and cut in front of you much more quickly than you are used to, and will (illegally) pass you on the left if they think you are going too slow. The big trucks are usually good about staying in the two left lanes. Again, it's the fast pace that takes the concentration.

The speed limit is 60mph, except on motorways and other dual-carriageways, but you won't be driving anywhere near this speed most of the time. Signs posting 30mph limits often come up quickly and should be strictly obeyed. Watch for **zebra crossings**, in towns of any size, where pedestrians have right of way.

You and your front-seat passenger must both wear **seat belts**; it's the law — and well observed in Britain. Use of rear seat belts, particularly for children, is advised, but is not yet the law.

Parking can be a problem in towns and cities. Double yellow lines mean no

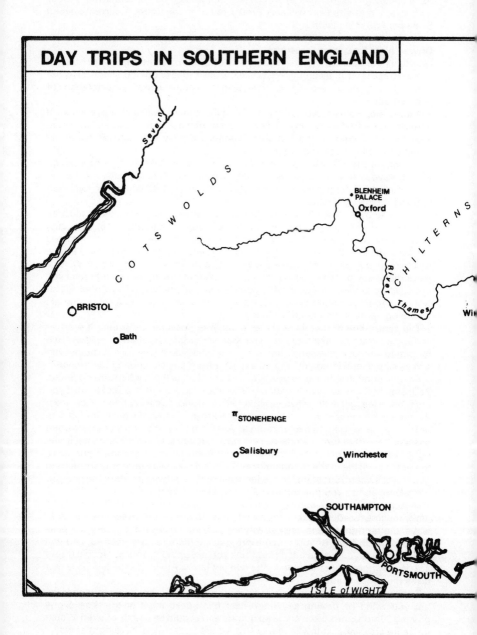

DAY TRIPS IN SOUTHERN ENGLAND

COTSWOLDS

CHILTERNS

Severn

River Thames

BLENHEIM PALACE

Oxford

○ BRISTOL

● Bath

π STONEHENGE

○ Salisbury

● Winchester

○ SOUTHAMPTON

PORTSMOUTH

ISLE of WIGHT

Cambridge

Bedford

BURN
EY

Colchester

Hatfield (House)

St Albans

rsham

Highgate   Kenwood
Hampstead
Osterley   **LONDON**
Park House
HEATHROW   Syon Hse
            Chiswick
Marble   Hse   Greenwich
Hill Hse   Kew
            Richmond   Dulwich
            RICHMOND
mpton Court PARK
            Ham House Carshalton
                                    Rochester
Quebec House   Chartwell

Southend

Broadstairs

ildford   Sevenoaks   LEEDS   Canterbury
                        (Knole House) CASTLE
GATWICK   Tonbridge
                        (Penshurst Place)
                         Ightham Mote
                        Tunbridge   Dover
                        Wells

Arundel   Lewes   Burwash
                       (Kipling's
         Brighton   house)   Hastings
              Eastbourne

Miles 0   10   20
Km 0   10   20   30

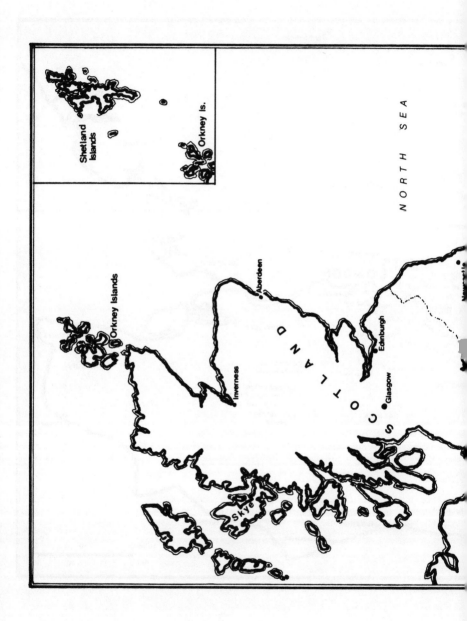

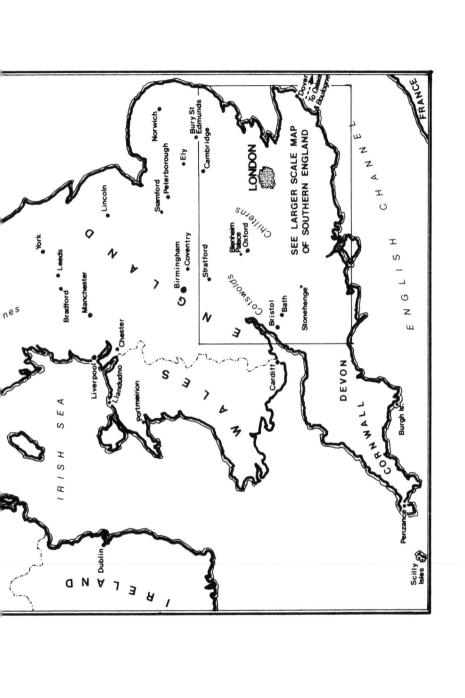

parking at any time. Single lines denote a restricted area: look for small signs that give permitted hours. Look for signs with a white 'P' on a blue background to find parking lots. Keep some parking meter change, and keep your humour if the search for parking takes some time — the rewards will be well worth it. (R.H.)

Recommended day and overnight trips

London is at the hub of a vast network of railways and highways. With faster (especially Intercity) trains, and the building of the M25 orbital motorway, ever-larger areas of south, eastern and western England have come within the range of the casual day tripper who sets out from London in the morning, sees the sights, and returns to his London hotel at a decent hour for bedtime. Formerly, day trips were confined to the famous destinations — Oxford, Cambridge, Bath, Brighton and Stratford. Now London's backyard is limited only by the visitor's capacity for endurance. Some even go to France for the day.

One determinant is the weather; if rain is forecast, you might want to pick another day. Nothing can be quite as grim as, say, traipsing from one Oxford college to another in pouring rain and soggy clothes. Wait till a clear day and spend the wet one in the British Museum or at a West End matinee.

What then is the realistic range of the day trip? Partly, it depends on how much you want to see and how much a destination offers. Much simply depends on the individual. For some people, just leaving London is a tiring hassle. Another consideration for those who don't have rail passes is that some 'saver' tickets require the holder to begin his journey after 0900 or 0930, wasting part of the day.

Destinations that have a major place of interest and few other attractions make the best day trips. My own ideal of a day trip is to arrive, spend 2–3 hours sightseeing, have an atmospheric pub or restaurant lunch, then spend a lazy afternoon browsing in antique shops or walking in a park, finishing with a cup of tea and back to London. Unfortunately, limited time and train schedules mean that such leisurely trips are not always possible. And the more you learn about most places, the more (probably) you want to see. You wish you'd spent the night.

Consider carefully whether you wouldn't be better off spending the night at your destination. You'll be less rushed, see more, and enjoy it better. Obviously, the further away you're going, the more this makes sense. Local tourist offices can find you a bed and breakfast, or you can book ahead through the BABA system.

Although several day trips are on the heavily-beaten tourist path, all foreign visitors should try to get out of London for at least a day. If nothing else, it provides a breather and a new perspective on this 'green and pleasant land'.

Selections
Our selections below are designed to help you discover possible half-day, day and overnight trips around London. There isn't space to describe all the attractions, restaurants, hotels and historical background of each destination. More detailed information is readily available at the local tourist offices, either free or at very inexpensive prices. Our own aim is to provide enough information to point you in the right direction — for you.

Favourite half and day trips within Greater London
London's sprawl is so enormous that it is senseless to try to include separate visits to farflung parts of the city in a single day. Parts of the metropolitan area are well-suited to day or half-day trips that allow you to soak up the atmosphere of a London far-removed from burger bars and tourist hustle. Eat in a neighbourhood pub, try local shops and see how pleasantly ordinary life is away from the bright lights. Particularly in the humid, noisy London summers, a slower pace makes a welcome change. Here are our recommendations.

Amersham

Amersham is at the end of a spur of the Metropolitan Underground Line, and as such is part of the area of suburban sprawl known as 'metro-land'. Nevertheless, the history of the town dates back to the *Domesday Book*, when it was called Elmodesham, and many historic Georgian and Tudor buildings remain. Obtain the useful tourist pamphlet (20p) from The Bookshop, 3a Sycamore Road, or Amersham stationery shops, and take the hour's walk that gives views of the town, crosses the **River Misbourne** and takes you across **Barn Meadow**. Good pubs, shops and market (Tuesdays, Fridays, and Saturday bric-a-brac) for those who want to avoid day-tripping tourist mobs. If you can't get out of London to see traditional English country towns, this is one of the next best things.

To get there
U: **Amersham** (Metropolitan Line) or BR from Baker Street or Marylebone (30 minutes).

Carshalton

Despite the sprawl of outer London all around, this little waterline Surrey village remains picturesque. Local conservation groups have been determined to preserve it, and, again, if you can't get out to the country, a few hours in Carshalton may provide you with an image of a gentle, more rural, England. The tranquillity of the ponds with swans and wildfowl, the timbered and clapboard cottages of the rich and not so rich, and the geniality of the locals in their ancient taverns, all seem to fit this picture.

Seen on a misty day, with the sun trying to break through, **Carshalton Ponds** have a delicate Japanese-print quality about them. They have been known to dry up a little at times, but seldom to freeze. **All Saints Church** (*c.* twelfth century) stands opposite the ponds, occupying the same central position it has enjoyed for centuries. Weather-boarded Georgian pubs and timber Georgian houses (unusual for Britain) complete the scene. (A.P.)

To get there
BR from Victoria (40 minutes).

Chiswick-Hammersmith riverfront

Please see *River walks* in the *Sights* chapter.

To get there
U: **Hammersmith** or **Ravenscourt Park**.

Dulwich

One of London's most unjustly ignored museums is the **Dulwich Picture Gallery** — largely because it is down in south London and therefore in *terra incognita* for most tourists. Otherwise, it's hard to understand why. The Gallery, designed by Sir John Soane, has been beautifully restored after 1944 bomb damage, and houses a collection that includes works by **Rembrandt, Reynolds, Cuyp, Van Dyck, Rubens, Poussin, Murillo** and **Gainsborough**. Afterwards, wander through **Dulwich Park** — famous for its rhododendrons, azaleas and rock gardens. Then have tea, a drink or a meal in **Dulwich Village** — the main street that still contains a number of handsome Georgian structures. **Dulwich College** is a famous public school with some interesting buildings. Dickens afficionados will remember Dulwich as Mr Pickwick's retirement home. More recently, this bucolic suburb attracted attention when Mrs Thatcher bought her retirement home here. Speculators wondered whether it would ever be used . . .

To get there
BR from **Victoria** to **West Dulwich** (12 minutes).

Greenwich

Greenwich is an old seafaring Thameside village which is, today, a London borough fast filling up with well-heeled commuters. They like the nautical character of the old central part of town, and tourists increasingly appreciate its charms too. Along the riverfront are the famous brig *Cutty Sark*, Sir Francis Chichester's *Gypsy Moth IV*, and several interesting exhibits. The Georgian town centre has a number of antique, print, model and nautical theme shops (try **Nelson Road** or **Nelson Street**, or **King William Walk**). Just off King William Walk is a tiny byway called **Greenwich Market Square**, with its mix of clothes, jewellery and curiosities. On Saturday mornings there is a small antique market.

But Greenwich is famous all over the world as the home of the **Prime Meridian** and **Greenwich Mean Time** (GMT). At the **Royal Observatory** you can stand on the Prime Meridian line and also see an interesting exhibit of clocks and nautical instruments. Wren's magnificient **Royal Naval College**, below, has other maritime exhibits. The broad expanses of **Greenwich Park** on the observatory hill afford stunning views of London and the Thames. A more modern attraction is the **Thames Barrier** flood control system, which is best viewed on a tour from Greenwich pier.

To get there
BR from **Charing Cross** (14 minutes); or **Docklands Light Railway** from **Tower Gateway** (13 minutes), then foot tunnel (free). The real treat is a boat trip to/from **Westminster Pier** or **Charing Cross Pier** on the river (45 minutes).

Tourist info
Cutty Sark Gardens, Tel. 01-858 6376. Open 1100–1730 daily June-August, 1100–1600 daily April, May, September, October.

Hampstead and Highgate

These two charming suburban 'villages' can be reached from central London in a few minutes for the price of a tube pass or ticket, but there's enough here to occupy and enchant the visitor for a day or more: beautiful wild open spaces, historic architecture and neighbourhoods with literary associations, good cafés, pubs and restaurants. Today, both are an upmarket part of London's sprawl. Hampstead, in particular, has an image as the home of the intellectual, left-leaning well-to-do, hence the familiar sneer: 'Hampstead Socialist'.

Hampstead and Highgate have long histories as country retreats for the rich and famous. Until the nineteenth century, both were separated from London by country and hunting estates. We can think of only two drawbacks to visiting: (1) traffic on the high streets can be very noisy and congested, and (2) casual strollers will find both neighbourhoods to be quite hilly.

Hampstead
Early popularity as a retreat was due to the presence of a spring, and between 1700 and 1800 a spa grew up. **Burgh House**, a pleasant eighteenth-century townhouse, is one of the relics of this era. The house, its **Buttery Restaurant** and the atmospheric nearby narrow streets, like **Flask Walk**, can be visited today (see *Sights: Houses*). Not far away is **Keats Grove**, where you can see the home of the famous poet John Keats, now a museum (see *Sights: Famous people's houses*). Also within these nearby streets are **Fenton House**, built in 1693 as a prosperous merchant's house and now a museum of keyboard instruments, and **Admiral's House**, built in the eighteenth century with a roof like a ship's deck.

The nearby **High Street** and adjoining streets have good shopping facilities and pleasant tea, coffee and bookshops. Particularly recommended pubs include **The Flask** (14 Flask Walk), and the **Horse & Groom** and the **Nag's Head** on Heath Street. Further up the hill are more historic pubs like the **Bull and Bush**, famed in the song *Down at the Old Bull and Bush*, and **Jack Straw's Castle** and **Spaniard's Inn**, two big atmospheric pubs that were once haunts of notorious highwaymen like Dick Turpin. Good walking tours from **Footloose** Tel. 01-435 0259.

Don't miss the massive **Heath** — a huge park with ponds, woods and open spaces for flying kites — or the magnificient views of London from **Parliament Hill** in the south (on a clear day). In the north is **Kenwood**, an eighteenth-century Adam mansion with an excellent art collection and the famous summer outdoor concerts. On the opposite side of the park is **Highgate Village**.

Highgate Village
Not quite as affluent as Hampstead, Highgate is just as rich, if not more so, in historical associations. Highgate grew up around a medieval toll gate called the Hedge Gate on the main road to London. The narrow streets still hold a number of Georgian buildings and charming 'locals'. Like Hampstead, Highgate has a pub called **The Flask** — this one is a coaching inn dating back to 1663. Also enjoyable is the **Prince of Wales** at 53 High Street. And, on this street are a number of galleries, antique shops and good tea and coffee at the **Highgate Tea Rooms and Coffee Company**. Fronting onto the High Street is **Waterflow Park** with ponds, an aviary and summer band concerts. Walk down **Swain's Lane** to the famous **Highgate Cemetery**, where Karl Marx and several Victorian luminaries are buried (see *Sights: Favourite museums*).

To get there
Hampstead: U: Hampstead. Highgate: U: Archway or **Highgate.**

Kew Gardens
Anyone who loves plants and gardening can easily spend the whole day at this Royal Botanic Gardens, famed all over the world for research as well as for the thousands of varieties of trees and smaller plants in the well landscaped 300-acre grounds. More delicate tropical and desert plants are housed in elegant walk-through glasshouses with controlled temperatures. Unfortunately, the terrible gale of October 1987 laid waste many beautiful trees at Kew, and it will be hundreds of years before it is restored to its former glory. **Kew Palace**, a former royal Georgian residence, is within the gardens and is now a museum, open during the summer months. Other highlights include a **pagoda**, erected during a craze for all things Chinese in 1761, and the half-timbered **Queen Charlotte's Cottage**, built in 1772 for the wife of George III. Kew is a fabulous place for a picnic beside the Thames.

If you're a gardener and you still can't get enough, **Syon Park** and its big **gardening centre** are just across the river. Unfortunately, there is no longer a pedestrian ferry, and so you have to walk the long, long way round via Kew or Twickenham bridges; or you can visit nearby **Richmond**.

To get there
U: Kew Gardens (District Line). Open 1000 to sunset daily.

Richmond
The address is Richmond, Surrey, and much of the town doesn't seem like a London borough but rather an affluent country suburb, with pleasant riverside walks and quaint pubs, art galleries, antiques, boat-hire, little restaurants and old-fashioned tea shops. Nevertheless, Richmond is part of London (telephone

numbers begin with 01 and, more importantly, you can get there on the Underground — it's the last stop on a spur of the District Line). The next to last stop is **Kew Gardens**, and many people try to combine the two, but if you have any love for plants, you may find that it's too much for one day.

Like Hampstead, Richmond has a number of fine houses with literary and historic associations. The two most spectacular are **Ham House** (65 or 71 bus from Richmond) and **Marble Hill House**, a former country house filled with fine antiques and surrounded by gardens. Take in the View from Richmond Hill — inspiration of several pastoral masterpieces — or get closer to nature in **Richmond Park**, the giant 2500-acre walled-in park heavily populated with wild deer who roam at will. Richmond also has two well-regarded theatres where plays are often given trial runs: the **Orange Tree** and the **Theatre on the Green**.

A final note: don't be too put off by the noisy busy High Street in front of the station; if you head down toward the river, it's a different world.

To get there
U: Richmond (District Line) or BR from **Waterloo** (20 minutes).

Tourist info
Central Library, Tel. 01-940 9125. Open Mon–Sat all year except Christmas and New Year.

Some atmospheric towns in easy reach of London
These towns are nothing extraordinary, but they do provide a glimpse into a relaxed, more ordinary England, and a direct-access escape from noisy London and the heavily-beaten tourist path.

Bedford
John Bunyan Museum; pleasant buildings and riverwalks. *Getting there*: St Pancras Station (56 minutes).

Broadstairs
Dickens' Bleak House and Museum; traditional seaside town. *Getting there*: Victoria (50 minutes).

Colchester
Castle and Roman remains; museums; old Dutch Quarter; Gainsborough and Constable country. *Getting there*: Liverpool Street (52 minutes).

Guildford
Cobbled high street; pretty riverside castle ruin and St Mary's Saxon church; famous theatre. *Getting there*: Waterloo (35 minutes).

Lewes
Beautiful town retaining some medieval character. Good views from castle ruins over surrounding countryside. Barbican Museum; Anne of Cleves' house; needle-makers restored factory housing craft shops; antique shops. *Getting there*: Victoria (60 minutes).

Tunbridge Wells
Pleasant commuter town. The Pantiles is a Georgian shopping mall left over from spa days. *Getting there*: Charing Cross (55 minutes).

Castles within a day
Most visitors from outside Europe want to see a castle. A surprising number are

unaware that they saw a particularly fine example of one when they visited the **Tower of London**. Castles dot the countryside around London, but most of these are now somewhat pitiful ruins, worn down by centuries of war and stone pilfering. If you want to see the storybook ideal, it's best to go to Wales. Nearer London, the most physically impressive is **Windsor**. The most romantic is probably moated **Leeds Castle** near Maidstone.

Windsor

Windsor Castle lies out of the Western periphery of London commuter-town sprawl. Travellers on the motorway from Bristol can often see the outline of its great stone towers from miles away as a sign that they are nearing London. Legends say you could once see the castle's outline from Notting Hill and other London high spots. Smog and high-rise buildings now make this impossible to verify. The castle, surrounding town and neighbouring **Eton**, across a Thames bridge, still seems worlds away from busy central London, especially in the tourist off-season.

The huge grey stone castle is just as impressive close-up, though the number of windows that have been cut in the walls and battlements over the centuries give it the look of what it is today: a lived-in castle, 'the oldest inhabited castle in the world', rather than the medieval stronghold envisaged by its founder, William the Conqueror. Most of the later Norman and Plantagenet kings lived here part of the time and made additions and improvements. Later monarchs were fond of the place, especially the Georgians and Queen Victoria, who renovated and redecorated the interiors.

These interiors, the **State Apartments**, are a royal treasure house that should not be missed if you're lucky enough to visit when the royals are not in residence (no set period, but March–April (around Easter) and the period around the Ascot races in June are likely times for royal visits). A trip through the **State Apartments** allows a bigger peek at something mostly forbidden to tourists at Buckingham Palace: the monarchy's vast wealth of pictures (including a Van Dyck, a Rubens and numerous Old Masters) and fine furnishings. There is a separate admission charge for the Old Master drawing collection.

Even if the **State Apartments** are closed, **Queen Mary's Dollhouse** should not be missed by curiosity-lovers. It's a fully-working tiny model of a palace, with electricity, running water and miniatures of all kinds. There's again a separate charge for this, and for **St George's Chapel**, a beautiful church dating back to medieval times. If all these charges are too much for you, then have a free walk around the battlements (as far as is permitted) and enjoy the majestic views. Also free is the impressive 1100 **Changing of the Guard**.

The cobbled streets surrounding the entrance to the Castle are pretty with Georgian and Victorian buildings, but, I'm sorry to say, full of tourist traps. Even a McDonald's and a Pizza Hut face the castle — which you may in fact find useful, if not exactly atmospheric.

I much prefer to walk down the **High Street**, then follow the curve of **Thames Street** to **Eton's** riverside, where the hustle is toned down and you seem to be again in a more tranquil England. Have lunch at the elegant **House on the Bridge** or the cheaper **Buttery** — both have magnificent views of the river and the massive, dominating Castle. If these are too crowded, walk down the **Eton High Street** and enjoy the pleasant tea shoppes and pubs. The famous **Eton College** is a fair walk further down the street, but Anglophiles will find the otherworldly-atmosphere of the grounds and buildings, some of which date back to the fifteenth century, to be worth every step. Guided tours are available from April to October at 1415 and 1515, but a few of the buildings and a museum are open all year round.

Before you board your train to go back to London, you might want to take a boat trip (available from the **Promenade** and lasting about 35 minutes), or to explore the 4800-acre **Great Park**. And there's the **Royalty and Empire** exhibition in the Central Station. I can't personally recommend it, but if you liked Madame Tussaud's you may be prepared to pay nearly £3 each to view a scene of a lifesize wax Queen Victoria boarding a train, and another of her taking a carriage with the guards on review and martial music in the background. There's also an audio-visual presentation, and, of course, a shop. Inclusive return rail and exhibition tickets are available from BR.

To get there
BR from **Waterloo** (47 minutes) or from **Paddington** (change at Slough — 35 minutes). Many tour companies run inclusive bus tours, and some combine with **Hampton Court**.

Arundel Castle
Seat of the Dukes of Norfolk for 700 years, the soaring, majestic castle has been extensively renovated and restored. Only a few parts date back to Norman times, but the restoration is superb. The present home is mostly Victorian Gothic, with much earlier art and furnishings. Both the castle and the tiny streets of the town have a charm which attracts many tourists. Don't miss the highly-peculiar **Potter's Museum of Curiosity**. A 'curiosity' is hard to define, but includes such things as a stuffed guinea pigs' cricket match and other Victorian notions. Another, similar experience is to be had at the **Toy and Military Museum**, also on the **High Street**.
   All these attractions are open only from April to October (the castle is closed on Saturdays) but the town itself is charming, with many old buildings and small shops, several atmospheric pubs and tea shops.

To get there
BR hourly from **Victoria** 1 hr 15 minutes) or combine with a trip to **Brighton**. Castle open June–Aug Sun–Fri 1200–1700; April–May, Sept–Oct 1300–1700; Nov–Mar closed.

Leeds Castle
This commercially-owned and run castle promotes itself as the 'loviest castle in the world'. The setting is indeed charming: on two islands in a moat-lake, with surrounding parklands and gardens. It is a great place for a picnic — and picnicking is encouraged.
   Leeds Castle dates back to Anglo-Saxon times, and was used as a fortress until Henry VIII extensively renovated it as a lavish palace.
   We rate this a pleasant excursion rather than a place to learn much about castles.

To get there
The **Orient Express** occasionally runs a relatively expensive day trip: the real star is, of course, the train. During the summer, BR sells a much more sensibly-priced combined ticket for a day excursion from **Victoria**. (Not near Leeds, as you might think, but only about an hour away from London, near **Maidstone**.) Open June 1–Sept 30 1200–1700; Nov–Mar weekends only.

Dover Castle
The castle is probably not the usual reason for a trip to Dover, a ferryport for France, though it is worth a visit both for the impression of powerful strength conveyed by the thick walls and the impressive views over the Channel commanded by this ancient bastion. Earliest parts date back to Henry II in 1180, and later rulers added walls, battlements and gatehouses.

Most visitors will want to see the famous **white cliffs**; the best are west of town and known as **Shakespeare Cliff**. A better impression is gained by taking a local boat trip or a round trip to the French ports of **Calais** or **Boulogne** (about an hour away) and then returning to English soil. In the winter bargain season, a round trip can cost as little as £6.50 (See *France for the Day*).

Dover was heavily bombed and rocketed during the war, and is not particularly charming, though it does have a few other interesting sights, including *Pharos*, a (mostly) Roman lighthouse, other Roman ruins and a Norman church.

To get there
Quickest trains at 55 minutes past the hour from **Charing Cross** (1 hour and 26 minutes).

Other nearby castles
The following castles may also be worth a visit. Most haven't been given more extensive treatment because of their isolation, away from public transport, or because they date from after the medieval period, or because (like most castles today) they are nothing much but ruins.
Deal Castle and **Walmer Castle** are coastal fortifications in the Channel port of Deal, built by Henry VIII (BR from **Charing Cross**). **Rochester Castle** is a fine example of a Norman keep (see *Day Trips: Rochester*). **Hever Castle** is a commercialized historic fortified manor house, best reached by car or tour. **Pevensey Castle** is an ancient ruin, 4 miles from Eastbourne; some of the walls are Roman. **Bodiam**, 10 miles north of Hastings, is considered by many to be the 'finest ruined castle in England'. **Lewes Castle** has very few remains but is worth a visit if you happen to be in Lewes. On the other hand, **Warwick Castle** is outstanding, and should be combined with **Stratford** or **Coventry** (see entries).

Country houses and stately homes
The stately home fits somewhere in every foreign visitor's image of England. London has grown so much in the last 200 years that it has absorbed several into its urban sprawl — **Ham House** and **Marble Hill House** are the two most prominent Richmond examples. If you can't get out of London, either of these places will give you some idea of the English country house without extensive travel, time or trouble.

Many more delightful homes and gardens are within easy reach of London. Unfortunately, it is in the nature of their being — as country homes — that most are not readily accessible by public transport. Usually, you have to have a car, take a tour, or make train-bus connections and taxi connections (if available). More information is available from the **National Trust, Tel. 01-222 9251** or **English Heritage, Tel. 01-211 7589**.

Country homes within Greater London (see *Houses*)
Chiswick Park
Ham House
Kenwood
Marble Hill House
Osterley
Syon House

Blenheim
Fabulous, opulent **Blenheim Palace** is perhaps a textbook example of what can happen when even a fine architect (Sir John Vanbrugh, in this case) is given an unlimited purse and the opportunity to run wild. This vast, rambling, early eighteenth-century palace and grounds of Versailles dimensions were a gift from

Queen Anne to John Churchill, Duke of Marlborough, to thank him for his victory over Louis XIV at Blenheim, an obscure German village. And as if the hundreds of rooms, the scale and the lavish decor weren't already too much, the house also has a vast collection of tapestries, old paintings and antiques. I should also add that Winston Churchill, a descendant, was born here, and one bedroom is an exhibit of Churchilliana.

Landscaping of the extensive grounds is by Capability Brown, on an equally huge but more pleasing scale. The park is open 0900–1700 daily most of the year. The palace is only open mid-March to mid-October, 1100–1800. You must go on a brief house tour to see the interiors.

Woodstock is a charming nearby village for stays or refreshment. Tel. (0993) 811325.

To get there
Eight miles north of Oxford. At least two buses a day from Oxford's Cornmarket Street. Oxford, of course, can be reached by train or bus from London.

Chartwell
Churchill's country home is best seen as part of a tour or trip around the area, which includes other attractions. Otherwise, it is not likely to be of much interest except to Churchillians. The house is architecturally undistinguished Victorian, but it does have a beautiful view and is attractively furnished with Churchill's own paintings and memorabilia.

To get there
Difficult without a car or on a tour. Near Westerham. Tel. (0732) 866368. Open Mar–Nov Tues, Wed, Thur 1200–1700; Sat, Sun, Bank Holidays 1100–1700.

Hampton Court
Cardinal Wolsey's famous 1514 palace, coveted and seized by Henry VIII, and now a symbol of Henry's reign. Indeed, he loved the place and made a number of additions and renovations, but much of what we see today is actually the later classical work of Sir Christopher Wren for William and Mary.

Hampton Court's buildings are vast and rambling. The **State Apartments**, the main part open to visitors, are treasure-houses of tapestries, woodwork panelling and fine Delft porcelain. A fabulous hammer-beam ceiling adorns the **Great Hall** and Old Masters hang on the walls. But perhaps the most famous feature is the outdoor shrubbery **Maze**.

Next to the palace is a lovely huge walled-in park beside the Thames. A popular misconception is that **Hampton Court** is out in the country. Actually, the palace and the adjacent green parkland are surrounded by miles of built-up London suburbia. Still, there are some lovely Thameside walks as a bonus to your visit.

To get there
BR from **Waterloo** twice an hour (32 minutes). Open April–Sept, Mon–Sat 0930–1800 and Sun 1100–1800; Oct–Mar 0930–1700 and Sun 1400–1700.

Hatfield House
A superb, easy-to-reach Jacobean house with a magnificent carved **Great Hall**, oak staircase and **Long Gallery**, built by Robert Cecil in the reign of James I. Rich in furnishings and paintings, the house has the famous Hilliard painting of Elizabeth I and the Oudry portrait of Mary Queen of Scots. In the same grounds are the remains of the old **Hatfield Palace** where Elizabeth I learned of her accession to the ʌnrone. Now it's a restaurant hosting evening Tudor banquets.

The town and church are also well worth a stroll. Try the **Eight Bells** on Park Street for lunch. Dickens fans will remember it.

To get there
Near **Hatfield Station**. BR from **King's Cross** (only 23 minutes) Open Mar 25–Oct, Tues–Sat 1200–1700; Sun 1400–1730.

Ightham Mote
(Pronounced 'item') My special favourite National Trust country manor house in England. The fifteenth-century half timbers, stone and brick, and the green moat with the sound of water flowing in and out — as it has for centuries — give the place a special atmosphere. There's a strong touch of the Gothic too: one renovation uncovered a seated female skeleton . . .

The secret of the Mote's charm, so a guide told me, is: so much in so small a place. Hidden away in a green valley, but worth going out of your way to see with a car or on a tour.

To get there
Near **Sevenoaks**, Kent. BR from **Charing Cross** (40 minutes). Taxis can be arranged from the station. Open April–Oct daily, except Tues and Sat, 1100–1700. Tel. (0732) 810378.

Kipling's House (Bateman's)
Like Churchill's house, this is mainly a treat for admirers, but the house dates back to Jacobean times and is interesting for that reason. Maintained as a Kipling museum, it is much in the condition he left it at his death in 1926.

To get there
Near Burwash, Kent. Again, you need a car. Open April–end Oct daily, except Thurs and Fri, 1100–1800. Tel. (0435) 882302.

Knole
Like Hampton Court, **Knole** was originally built by a leading churchman and then coveted and taken over by none other than Henry VIII. Here, too, he added to and renovated the existing structure. Later, the house passed into the ownership of the Earl of Dorset's family, the Sackvilles, who totally transformed it during the sixteenth century. Exquisite panelling and plasterwork, tapestries, rugs, Elizabethan furniture and five long galleries. Worth seeing for massiveness alone — the house covers several acres.

To get there
BR from **Charing Cross** to **Sevenoaks**. Open April–Sep, Wed–Sat and Monday holidays 1100–1700; Sun 1400–1700. Tel. (0732) 450608.

Penshurst
An outstanding country house that shouldn't be missed if you are in the area for any reason, **Penshurst** has a fascinating history and architectural background. The **Great Hall** dates back to the fourteenth century. Other parts were added during the next 300 years. This is the family seat of the Sidneys, who included Sir Philip Sidney, the famous Elizabethan poet and courtier. Splendid gardens as well as interiors.

To get there
BR from **Charing Cross** to **Tonbridge**, then taxi (3½ miles). Open April–early Oct daily, except Mon, 1300–1730. Tel. (0892) 870307.

Quebec House

Canadians may take a special interest in this eighteenth-century house near Westerham. The square red brick structure is full of memorabilia of the famed General James Wolfe, killed in the course of victory at the battle of Quebec.

To get there

Near Westerham. BR from **Charing Cross** to **Sevenoaks**, then taxi. Open April–end Oct daily, except Thurs and Sat, 1400–1800. Tel. (0959) 62206.

Woburn Abbey

Not an abbey, but built on the site of one, this is one of Britain's most-famous (and most-publicized) stately homes. The eighteenth-century house is the seat of the Dukes of Bedford and the current family are much in the news for their commercial efforts to pay the huge costs of keeping up their giant estate, which includes a priceless collection of furnishings, porcelain and paintings by Holbein, Rembrandt, Gainsborough, Reynolds and many other Old Masters. Money-making activities now include a **Safari Park** with a gondola ride over it and a respected French restaurant. These efforts pay off: over a million visitors a year now visit the house and grounds.

To get there

Notoriously hard to reach by public transport. Best to go by car or take one of the many organized tours. Open April 1–Oct 27 Mon–Sat 1100–1745 and Sun 1100–1815; Oct 28–Mar 31 Sat and Sun only, 1100–1645. Tel. (0525) 25666.

Other day trips: popular and little-known

The five most famous and popular day trips — **Bath, Brighton, Cambridge, Oxford** and **Stratford** — have a steady path beaten to them by millions of tourists each year. Amazingly, only little Stratford seems too obviously impacted by the rush. All still have something genuinely worthwhile to offer. Further possibilities are endless, however, and we include more recommendations.

Bath

Sooner or later, most travellers find their way to Bath, a city with endearing and unusual qualities. Cream stone Georgian houses tumble down the surrounding hillsides into a city centre that has achieved an amazing mix of sophisticated shopping facilities and historic charm — a skyline of chimney pots and hills, vistas of cobbled mews and eighteenth-century street lamps.

In the first century AD the Romans built their version of the city, Aquae Sulis, around the hot springs that bubble up in a sheltered crook of the River Avon. A thousand years after the empire had collapsed, and much of the city with it, Georgian architects began to rebuild on a crumbling spa town and its ancient reputation. Somehow, the urban renewal planners were kept away and it has become one of the nation's treasured centres of Georgian charm.

Your first stop should be the **Tourist Information Centre** in the Abbey Church Yard behind the enormous **abbey** that dominates this part of the city. Here you will be spoilt for choice with ways of seeing what Bath has to offer. There are coach tours, walking tours and open top double-decker bus tours. Or you could spend 20p on the excellent mini-guide map and wander off on your own. The basic coach tour costs about £3 and lasts about two hours, including out to the surrounding hills.

The **abbey** is a majestic old building, closely flanked by Roman and Georgian neighbours. Inside you get an overwhelming sense of awe and space. This is a magnificent example of Late Gothic architecture, with high imposing arches and an impressive stone fan-vaulted ceiling. From here, cross the Abbey Church Yard to the **Pump Room**. This enormous stately hall with chandeliers dates from 1796. Even if you don't want a glass of hot spa water, a meal or afternoon tea, just wander through it and listen to the chamber music as the steam rises from the old Roman Baths below and drifts across the window.

The **Roman Baths Museum** (attached to the Pump Room) is very absorbing. The Roman ruins are some of the best in Britain, and you can easily spend a couple of hours here. It's easy to forget you are surrounded by a modern city centre.

The **Theatre Royal** is a short walk away (all walks to anywhere in Bath are short, but most are full of interesting distractions: captivating little alleyways, fascinating shop windows and hot Bath buns!). Built in 1805, the theatre previews many West End shows before they reach London. Tours of the theatre take place at midday on most Wednesdays and Saturdays, lasting about 45 minutes and costing only 50p. Underneath the theatre in the old stone vaults is a **Brasserie and Bar**, well worth a visit. If you have dinner after a show, you are likely to recognize a few famous faces from the stage, as the actors often eat there too. Main courses average about £7 and snacks about £2. All the food is homemade and the bar stays open. This is an intimate little underground eatery with lots of character, open Mon–Sat 1000 till very late.

Pulteney Bridge crosses the River Avon in three wide arches. On the bridge itself are the kind of shops you could browse around for hours, but then you can easily lose all sense of time in Bath, so it really doesn't matter. When you are ready, take the steps leading down to **Riverside Walk**. Here the water is peaceful as it emerges from under the arches, but the air is filled with the thunder of the weir ahead. The short amble down to the next bridge is a photographer's paradise, with some of the best views of the Abbey, bridge, weir and outskirts of Bath.

Bath is essentially a city for walkers. Much is lost in a fleeting glance through a coach window, and it costs nothing to admire architecture like the great sweeping arc of Georgian terraces in the **Royal Crescent** (No. 1 has been furnished as it would have been in the eighteenth century, and is open to visitors). The crescent and the nearby **circus** are as elegant as any Regency squares you have seen in London or elsewhere.

In the High Street stands the **guildhall**. A look at the pale green and gold Banqueting Room is worth a few minutes of your itinerary. Highly-decorative ceilings support the weight of three spectacular chandeliers.

Every Bath guidebook will list an abundance of little museums. All are worth a visit, but few are free, so you lose nothing in being selective. The **Museum of Costume** is included in your £2.50 ticket to the Roman Baths; an interesting collection displays the history of fashion. The **American Museum** is housed in an 1820 manor and portrays the history and culture of North America. The **Bath Industrial Heritage Centre** is a reconstruction of provincial working life at the turn of the century; and then there is still the **Museum of Bookbinding**, **Bath Postal Museum**, the **National Centre of Bookbinding**, the **National Centre of Photography**, and the **Victoria Art Gallery**, amongst others.

If you decide to cancel anything from your list, let it not be **Sally Lunn's Kitchen Museum and Teahouse**. This fifteenth-century timber-framed building is the oldest in Bath, but it was 1680 before the young French Huguenot refugee made it famous as a bakery. Sally Lunn brought a traditional French recipe with her and produced the bun now named after her.

One final drool is the **Fudge Kitchen**. You can pop in to see the fudge-maker at work (usually between 1000 and 1500), mixing rich and mouthwatering ingredients in a large copper kettle and producing a long loaf of fudge on a marble table. (A.B.)

To get there
BR from **Paddington** (1 hour 20 minutes).

Brighton
One of the most popular bathing resorts in Victorian times, Brighton still attracts thousands of visitors every year. It is unlike many seaside resorts in England in that it is both a resort and a thriving town in its own right, bustling with locals, students, artists and London commuters.

Tip
Some foreign tourists now prefer to stay in Brighton and commute to London on their BritRail passes (check with the **Tourist Information Centre, 54 Old Steine**). Accommodation is certainly cheaper and often better value for money. The last late train from London is at 2359. You might see one of Brighton's actor residents, like Sir Lawrence Olivier, on their way home from work.

If you wander about in the area called **The Lanes**, in central Brighton just behind the Stein, you will find every sort of cuisine on offer, as well as a number of curio and antique shops. **English's Osyter Bar** is probably the best fish restaurant in town. Or try a Russian restaurant called **Blinnies**, or **The Black Chapatti** for good vegetarian Indian food. **Al Forno** and **Al Duomo** are the twin Italian pasta and pizza places. For an American burger plus try **Browns** in Dukes Lane.

Well-fed by this time, you will want to walk it off. A stroll along the seafront between the piers can be pleasant. You can also walk up and down the **East Pier**, on which there is a traditional seaside funfair, with ghost trains, slot machines and fortune-tellers. The shorter **West Pier** is being restored.

If you extend your walk eastwards, you will be heading for the **Marina**. There is a train between the pier and the Marina in case you begin to tire. The Marina is huge and from under the cliff walk you can survey the expensive yachts berthed there and watch them sailing in and out. For a small cost you can go into the Marina, where the annual boat show is held, and see the crafts at close range.

The undercliff path carries on as far as **Rottingdean**, which is a very pleasant place to stop for a pub lunch or tea and cakes. From there, the very energetic might walk home; others can catch the bus back to Brighton.

During the day there is the obvious attraction of sitting on the beach in the sun, or swimming. For the sporty it is possible to hire a windsurfer, or do some water skiing. When you tire of the beach you could wander west along the front and play tennis or go east for a round of crazy golf; or visit the **Aquarium** or the **Dolphinarium**. Let's not forget the **Royal Pavilion**, which is a must. This famous Regency-era Arabian Nights fantasy palace has to be seen to be believed. Have a walk through.

A short journey by car or bus (pick-up point is the **Old Steine Bus Station**), will take you out to the **Devil's Dyke**, where you can look over the Weald of Kent to the North Downs on a clear day. From here the intrepid leap into the air on hang-gliders.

Another five-star viewing point is **Ditchling Beacon**. You can walk from here on the top of the Downs along part of the **South Downs Way**, which will eventually bring you to **Newhaven**. Beyond Newhaven at Seaford is the **Seven Sisters Country Park**. The **Living World Exhibition** at the information centre on the A259 will show you what to look for as you walk through the beautiful park, which runs down to Cuckmere Haven and the sea. (S.M.)

To get there
BR from **Victoria** (1 hour).

Bury St. Edmunds
This historic little East Anglian town is better as a day trip from Cambridge (45 minutes), but you can make a day trip from London with properly-timed train schedules (about 2 hours).

If you want a slice of relatively untouristed rural market-town England, this is it. Laid out according to a Roman plan, the centre streets are lined with historic buildings. These are mainly Victorian or Georgian (see especially the **Athenaeum**, where Dickens used to give dramatic readings), but there are several more ancient structures — a ruined **abbey** (founded 1021) and a **guildhall** dating back to the 1200s. On Wednesdays and Saturdays there is a colourful market in the square. Bury promotes its famous Wednesday cattle market as a tourist attraction. Some also want to see the **Parkington Collection of Clocks and Watches**.

If you have a car, **Lavenham** and **Long Melford** are two nearby half-timbered villages that are almost too good to be true. Journey time is perhaps a little long, but Bury does provide a pleasant day's wander, especially on a market day. It's about the right size.

To get there
BR from **Liverpool Street**; change at Ipswich (about 2 hours).

Cambridge

If we don't do Cambridge justice in terms of space, perhaps we can make up for it with the following sentence. If you have to choose between visiting Oxford and visiting Cambridge, you should pick Cambridge. Why? Cambridge is prettier, smaller, more self-contained and will give you a better understanding of the medieval mystique that influences both their views on the world and British society's continued deference to them as the country's top-ranking universities. Oxford is partly industrial and partly mauled by urban renewal, and the main roads always seem busy. Cambridge has become a popular locale for high-tech 'soft' industries.

Cambridge is the younger of the two, founded in the early thirteenth century by a group of disgruntled Oxford University students. Like Oxford, Cambridge is organized on the college system. Cambridge has 31, each with its own group of buildings, gardens and traditions. **Peterhouse** is the oldest (1284); **Churchill** is the newest (1959).

We recommend that you take one of the standard two-hour tours, or pick the colleges you want to see. These are some of the favourites: **King's College** is worth seeing for its world-famous fifteenth-century chapel with fan-vaulted ceiling, spectacular perpendicular stained glass windows, carved wooden screens and the altarpiece by Rubens. Try to take in a choral performance here (1730 on many evenings). **Emmanuel** has a baroque chapel designed by Wren. **Trinity** is the largest college, with a sixteenth-century chapel, a huge courtyard and a Wren-designed library; **St John's**, like Venice, has a Bridge of Sighs, which joins its two parts across the River Cam.

Along the river are the famous 'backs' where several college grounds meet the river with views of spires and green spaces. If you have the time, hire a punt and pole your way along the lovely, languid stream. The flatness of Cambridge also make it an ideal place to hire a bike.

There are other things to do. The **Fitzwilliam Museum** is hidden away on Trumpington Street. Inside you will find works by Da Vinci, Michelangelo and Dürer, as well as many antiquities. The city also has several scattered specialized museums: **Zoology, Archaelogy and Ethnology, Folk**, and the **Scott Polar Institute**. Wander through the quiet of the **Botanic Gardens** or browse in **Heffer's**, one of Britain's better bookshops. Pubs are also a big Cambridge attraction; they are at their liveliest when the students are in residence.

If you don't know what else to do, just walk along the river and through those college areas where visitors are allowed. Even without a guidebook, the ancient buildings, open spaces and dreamy atmosphere make for a pleasant day out without trying too hard. But do avoid the period from mid-May to end of June when exams are in progress.

To get there
BR from **Liverpool Street** (1 hour).

Canterbury

It is still possible to join a 'pilgrimage' to the shrine of Thomas à Becket in **Canterbury Cathedral** (details available from the Church of England). For the ordinary tourist, **Canterbury** is 80 minutes from London, and makes an ideal day trip. Those who've just come from France will be struck by the lighter atmosphere of one of England's most important and historic churches. It is not the biggest, or the most beautiful, but the place has its own unique medieval ambience, belied by the vast clutter of shrines, tombs and monuments. Have a long wander, read as many inscriptions as interest you, and lastly climb the north-east tower for a panoramic view. For perspectives of the Cathedral from the town, look down **Mercury Lane** or from the grounds of **King's School**.

The town itself often disappoints tourists and pilgrims alike. Canterbury's proximity to the Channel means that it was badly ravaged by German bombs, and later urban planners did further damage with their shopping malls. But enough bits and pieces of medieval Canterbury survive in the **West Gate** (the only remaining city gate), parts of the walls, the street plans and a few buildings to lend charm.

A new attraction, the **Pilgrim's Way**, provides a Disney-type experience of Canterbury's history.

To get there
BR from **Victoria** (1 hour 20 minutes).

Chichester

A charming town of mostly red-brick Georgian architecture on an ancient Roman grid pattern. That summarizes the place, except for the **cathedral**, which is worth seeing not so much for the usual Normal features but for the unusual modern art that livens them up, including a stained glass window by Marc Chagall. The town, especially the city-within-a-city called **Pallant**, offers pleasurable easy-to-navigate strolling and brass rubbing. Unless you go during the **May Festival**, though, you may find it rather dull and unexciting.

To make this a worthwhile day trip, you might also want to see the old harbour and Roman remains at nearby **Fishbourne**, about 2 miles away. The Fishbourne **Roman Palace** is an excavated villa, the largest Roman building yet found in Britain. Perhaps you've seen a picture of the famous floor mosaic of a boy riding a dolphin?

Chichester really suits car tourists better than rail day trippers, because they have access to the real charm of the area: little villages and vantage points on the beautiful sailing 'harbour' — a series of channels ideal for boating. A chance to sail or take a short boat excursion (available in summer) should not be missed.

To get there
BR from **Victoria** (60 minutes).

Coventry

Many visitors want to go and see the famous **cathedral** blitz ruins and the new, modern one rising Phoenix-like beside them. Some also know that this was the legendary home of Lady Godiva — but alas, there's nothing more to that than a statue in a park. The bombed-out ruins of the earlier **Cathedral of St Michael** cannot fail to impress, with its altar of broken rubble and burnt cross. The new one is very modern, with once-controversial pieces of art, including the Epstein statue of St Michael, and the huge Graham Sutherland tapestry behind the altar.

Coventry has a **Transport Museum** and a lively theatre, but otherwise there's little to see, and so it's best combined with nearby attractions like **Warwick Castle** — a fine well-preserved medieval castle with magnificent battlements, a Capability Brown park and a gruesome dungeon. Check to see whether the hourly bus is still running — it takes about 20 minutes; Warwick is also accessible by bus from Stratford.

To get there
BR from **Euston** (1 hour 10 minutes).

Duxford Aviation Museum
Just south of Cambridge is a place with a particular appeal for many Americans — **Duxford Airfield**. Now part of the **Imperial War Museum**, this was the home of hundreds of US Army personnel of the 78th Fighter Group, USAAF, whose HQ it was during the war. Duxford now displays the finest collection of military and civilian aircraft in Britain, together with the best line-up of American military aircraft in Europe. Many of the exhibits are airworthy, including the last B17 Flying Fortress in Europe, the 'Sally B'. Many military vehicles are also on display. A free transport system is laid on to help you see as much as possible.

To get there
An hour's drive from London, or 15 minutes by taxi from Cambridge railway station. A special bus runs at 1000 days from **Victoria Coach Station**, most returning at 1730, arriving back in London by 1930. Open all year except New Year, Good Friday, May Bank Holiday and Christmas. Mid-Mar–end October 1030–1730. Admission £2.50. Tel. (0223) 833 963.

Eastbourne
This is the quintessential faded elegant English seaside restort that has not seen really good days since the cheap package holiday to Spain became available to the mass British public. Lots of ageing pensioners, a slightly seedy pier with amusement arcade, and big, grand hotels that still hold tea dances in palm courts to attract nostalgic winter weekend Londoners. A few, more modern, attractions like the **Butterfly Centre** do not detract from the old-fashioned melancholic ambience that some people come to Britain to find.

To get there
BR from **Victoria** (1 hour 20 minutes).

Ely
Off the mass tourist track and thus a plus for daytrippers who want to experience an East Anglian market town without tourist hordes. However, it also has a famous **cathedral**, founded by St Etheldreda in AD 673. Most of the present building was rebuilt by the Normans, but the Saint's dramatic story is preserved in carvings on the ceiling. Even cathedrals have to make a living nowadays, and volunteers run a stained glass museum and sell brass rubbing materials.

Ely also has the **King's School**, **Cromwell's House** and several minor attractions. Down by the river are some interesting old buildings and eateries. For an upmarket meal, try the **Old Fire Engine House** in St Mary's Street. There isn't a lot to do in Ely — but it's a pleasant day out.

To get there
BR from **Liverpool Street** (1 hour 25 minutes).

France for the day
Incredible as it may seen, you can pop over to France for a day of shopping, eating and sightseeing, and be back in your London hotel at bedtime. Two channel ports, **Calais** and **Boulogne**, are especially accessible to the London daytripper. Contrary to popular belief, it is not yet possible to enjoy a 'day' (18-hour, in this case) trip to Paris unless you are very rich or fit — a Paris journey by boat train is a minimum of 5½ hours each way. When the new Channel Tunnel trains come into service in 1993, this journey time will be cut in half. Meanwhile, you can still enjoy a trip to the Channel ports.

Calais is thought by some to be better for shopping, but Boulogne is the better all-round choice. Unlike Calais, Boulogne wasn't bombed flat in the war; the city has well-preserved ramparts and medieval quarter, a cathedral and a castle. British shoppers come across the Channel on regular huge shopping expeditions to load up with wine, beer, food specialities, linen, kitchenware, china and, of course, French clothes. Their French counterparts go to Dover for the British versions of these things and — of course — Marks and Spencer.

As you would expect, Boulogne has scrumptious pastries available from patisseries, and little restaurants serve enormous multi-course seafood lunches, or abbreviated versions for £5–£10. Somehow the Camembert and bread-and-chocolate always taste better on French soil.

Weekends and Mondays are best avoided. During the mid-week, especially outside the summer months, the ferry companies offer some very cheap deals — as little as £6.50 return from Dover. (Rail pass holders take note.) Otherwise, you'll want to look into combined rail/ferry or rail/hovercraft tickets. The **Travel Centre** at **Victoria Station** can fill you in, but the hovercraft is only a few pounds dearer and shaves 45–60 minutes off the travel time, though bad weather conditions can cause sailings to be delayed, if not cancelled. And Americans — remember you'll need a French visa. At the time of writing, a return ticket from London costs from £18.50.

To get there
BR from **Victoria**, the hovercraft or ferry (2–3 hours).

More information
The Travel Centre, Victoria Station. Tel. 01-834 2345.

Hastings
We all know about the battle. Today's Hastings is a sleepy, atmospheric little seaside resort that lacks the ugly large-scale garishness of many English Channel resort towns. The promenade is kitschy, but there is little in the way of hard hustle. Have a fish and chips, play Space Invaders; maybe you'll hear 'I do like to be beside the seaside' on an antique barrel organ (or at least a recording of one). On a rare sunny day you might want to rent a deck chair and turn pink with the multitude on the pebbly beach.

Head down to the far end of the town for old Hastings, where you'll see rows of historic fishermen's huts used for drying their nets. Up above are a number of old half-framed houses with pretty mullioned windows. If you have kids, they'll love the funicular railway ride to **St Clement's Caves**, a former smugglers' haunt. Both you and the kids may enjoy the brand-new **Shipwreck Museum**, which conducts low-tide guided tours to the many shipwreck sites (closed October to March).

And of course there's that battle — the site of which is closer to **Battle** station than it is to Hastings itself. Like all battlefields, there is not a lot to see of the actual battle, but William the Conqueror had an abbey built here, supposedly on the very spot where Harold died. Little is left except for the gate and a series of monks' rooms. Take the **Battlefield Trail** and enjoy the views as well as the history.

To get there
BR from **Charing Cross** (1 hour 30 minutes).

Lincoln

The ancient city of Lincoln is at the northern limit of daytripping (about 2 hours away). Some might want to make an overnight stop and include **Stamford** or **Ely** in the trip. Nevertheless, a stop in Lincoln is very rewarding: it is perhaps England's most underrated provincial town, and relatively untouristy, which makes it a favourite for lovers of English towns. A stunning hilltop location in a generally flat area, three great distinctive bulky towers and a wealth of carvings and window detail give **Lincoln Cathedral** a unique personality. The strongly medieval atmosphere is true to its age — most of the building dates from before 1200. The cloisters and library were designed later by Sir Christopher Wren.

Little is left of **Lincoln Castle**, dating back to the Conqueror, apart from a few walls and the remains of a small twelfth-century keep. There are other scattered medieval buildings, half-timbered houses and narrow winding streets that give the city itself an ancient feel that has been lost in many similar-sized English towns. The **Jew's House** on Steeple Hill is a very rare surviving early merchant's urban house, and down Henry Street **High Bridge** is the last bridge in Britain still supporting medieval houses.

The special character of the city may be due to the fact that it was already an old town in the Middle Ages — it had been founded by the Romans as the city of Lindum, and there are some notable Roman remains, much of them only recently unearthed. You can actually still pass through the **New Port Arch**, the northern gate to the Roman city. The local museum is better than most, housed in a thirteenth-century friary and displaying many pre-Roman, and pre-historic, items and armour.

To get there
BR from **King's Cross**; change at Newark (2 hours).

Norwich

The unofficial capital of East Anglia, Norwich is another underrated tourist destination, with a restored stone block **castle**, a twelfth-century **cathedral** with Norman buttresses, many old churches and plenty of pleasant walks or bike rides. Along **Elm Hill** and **Tombland**, a maze of streets and alleyways recall the city's medieval origins. Norwich claims to have England's largest outdoor market (Monday--Saturday). Several museums and galleries and a chance to visit nearby country houses round out the list of attractions.

To get there
BR from **Liverpool Street** (2 hours).

Oxford

Like Cambridge, Oxford is about an hour away from London by train (or the new cut-rate bus service from Victoria Coach Station or Marble Arch will get you there for about half price). And, like Cambridge, it seems a world away; but Oxford is bigger, busier and more industrial. For that reason, we recommend, if you have to choose, you should pick Cambridge. Please don't take that too literally — the preference is slight!

Oxford, of course, was first 'Oxen Ford' — a place for teams to cross the rivers Thames and Cherwell — long before scholars from the University of Paris and local monks established Oxford University as the first centre of learning in England. **University College** was the first college in 1249, followed by **Balliol**

(1263) and **Merton** (1264). Over the next 700 years the other colleges were founded, and this system of division into colleges was later copied by Cambridge University. No other British university has anything quite like it.

The heritage of the last 750 years has begat a variety of architectural styles. Beware — much of the atmosphere of Matthew Arnold's 'sweet and dreaming towers' is really nineteenth-century academic gothic rather than the real thing; but nonetheless it is enchanting.

Daytrippers will need to pick which colleges to see. Walking tours are available at very reasonable prices; but, regardless of which colleges you pick, don't miss **Christ Church**. Considered the most majestic of all the university colleges, it was founded in 1525 by Cardinal Wolsey and refounded after the Reformation by Henry VIII. It is a study in superlatives: here you'll find the largest quadrangle, the biggest pre-Victorian hall, and its own art gallery containing an unparalleled collection of rare Italian prints. The college chapel serves as the city cathedral, having the double distinction of being the smallest cathedral and having the oldest spire in the kingdom. **Tom Tower**, the bell tower above the main gate, was designed by Sir Christopher Wren. It houses the bell 'Great Tom', which weighs over 6 tons and rings 101 times every night at 2105. Once this was the curfew warning that the gates were being closed — all who were late had to pay gate-money to get inside.

Other colleges are spread throughout the town. There is no 'campus', but most are within walking distance. Here are a few college highlights:

Magdalen (pronounced 'Maudlin') is compulsory for anyone in search of English tranquillity, with its monastic cloister, impressive main quadrangle, a private river walk and its own deer park. **Merton** has a notable chapel and lovely gardens. **Queen's** was redesigned by Wren and Hawksmoor. **Balliol's** buildings are mostly nineteenth-century, but it is worth a visit simply for the fame of its graduates, who include Matthew Arnold, G. M. Hopkins, Swinburne, Aldous Huxley, Grahame Greene, and a huge number of prime ministers and other politicians. Opposite the college is the spot where Ridley, Latimer and Cranmer were burned to death by Bloody Mary in 1555. **Keble** has interesting Victorian buildings. **Hertford** has a bridge modelled on Venice's Bridge of Sighs (or is it on the one at Cambridge. . . ?).

Oxford has many other worthwhile sights apart from the colleges. The centre of Oxford is called **Carfax** — from the Latin for 'four forks'. If your time is short, concentrate on this area. On a clear day, the fourteenth-century **Tower of St Martin** at the centre of Carfax is a 'must'. For 30p you may climb the twisting spiral staircase for a superb roof-top view of the city to help you get your bearings.

Shakespeare-lovers will not want to miss out on the colourful sixteenth-century murals found in No. 3 Cornmarket — the **Painted Room**, where Tudor wall-paintings were accidentally preserved through the years by a succession of Stuart, Georgian and Victorian occupants who applied oak panels and wallpaper over the murals. (Mon–Fri 1000–1200; 1400–1500.) Down The High on the left is **St Mary the Virgin** church, whose tower and spire are among the finest in England. The grey limestone tower, 188-feet tall, is open every day from 1000–1700.

To the north and west of Carfax you will find the **Ashmolean Museum**, named after Oxford's eccentric antiquarian, Edward Ashmole. Unlike most European museums, this one is not too large to explore in one afternoon, and comfortable seating is provided in each room for people with hot tired feet. The **Tradescant Room**, which is the remnant of Ashmole's earliest collection, is the most unusual room of all. Here you may examine the exhibits which were seen by the museum's first visitor in the late seventeenth century, such as a lock of King Edward II's hair, snipped from his skull 400 years after his death, or an unflattering pair of gloves made for Elizabeth I, who is reputed to have been so insulted by their large size that she left them in Oxford in disgust. The most famous exhibit in the **Tradescant Collection**, and perhaps the most important North American Indian relic to survive anywhere, is **Powhatan's Mantle**, associated with Pocahontas' father.

The world-renowned **Bodleian Library** is north and east of Carfax. Have a look at the current books on exhibit and at some of the splendid rooms. The **Sheldonian Theatre**, a fine assembly hall designed by Sir Christopher Wren, is a street away.

Boats for punting on the Thames may be hired from Mr Hubbock at Folly Bridge ((0865) 244 235). Bicycles can be rented at 14a Worcester Street ((0865) 726 643), but be warned — the streets can be very busy, as Oxford is also an industrial car-making (Austin Rover) town. One attraction I never miss is a browse in **Blackwell's**, the world-famous bookshop at 50 Broad Street.

Daytrippers looking for an atmospheric lunch should try **The Perch** or **The Trout**, on opposite banks of the Thames. **The Perch** is on Binsey Lane in West Oxford. Fresh fish, good grub and real ale are dispensed to students and dons alike. **The Trout** is genuinely Tudor, and serves excellent meat pies and sandwiches at lunchtime. Another inexpensive place to eat is the coffee shop of the **Randolph Hotel**, Oxford's fine old Victorian hotel, which, on some days, amazingly serves Mexican food . . . (M.A.)

To get there
BR from **Paddington** (60 minutes). City Link, Oxford Tube and other cut-rate bus companies run very competitive services from Victoria Coach Station that are almost as fast as, but cheaper than, the train.

Portsmouth, the Mary Rose *and the Isle of Wight*

Portsmouth has been an important naval base for centuries. Today much of the city is run down, but in a special dry dock you will find the breathtaking spectacle of the **Mary Rose**, Henry VIII's favourite Tudor warship. Visitors are able to view the hull as if it were a giant cutaway model, with the ship's structural detail exposed. Nearby, in a Georgian timber boathouse, an exhibition features displays of the historical treasures recovered from the ship — everyday items that she was carrying on that fateful July day in 1545 when she slipped into the murky depths of the Solent. An absorbing audiovisual presentation is also available.

Not far away you will find the ***HMS Victory***, Lord Nelson's famous flagship from the Battle of Trafalgar, plus the **Royal Navy Museum**. This depicts maritime history from Tudor times up to the Falklands campaign of 1982. *HMS Warrior*, Britain's first iron-clad battleship, launched in 1860, is also scheduled to be sited here. Admission £2.80. Open 1000–1730 daily.

Portsmouth is also the ferryport for the lovely **Isle of Wight**, with its beautiful countryside and subtropical gardens; but total journey time from London, including hydrofoil, is 2 hours 20 minutes, so you might make the Isle an overnight trip, or just enjoy a return ferry or hydrofoil (30 minutes) trip. (C.B.)

To get there
BR from **Waterloo** (90 minutes).

Rochester

For some reason, few tourists seem to be familiar with Rochester as a day trip. This is strange, because the city has the remains of a **castle** — the 'finest square keep in England' — dating from 1127–1135. And on the High Street is the Norman **Rochester Cathedral**, begun in 1082, with thirteenth-century choir-stalls. A few miles outside town is **Cobham church**, dating from the thirteenth century, with the largest collection of memorial brasses in England. But Rochester is probably best known as the home of Charles Dickens. **Eastgate House** is now a Dickens museum, open 7 days a week 1000–1230 and 1400–1730.

Most of us in-the-know foreign residents are familiar with the city as the home of the remarkable **Reeves of Rochester**, a china shop that has advantageous prices on some 800 patterns from famous and not-so-famous makes, as well as crystal and porcelain figures. Like the Reject China Shops, they are well- versed in the export trade. (**Reeves & Sons**, 142 High Street, Rochester, Kent ME1 1ER. Tel. (0634) 43339)

To get there
BR from **Victoria** (1 hour).

St Albans

London has very little left of the Roman period (and much of it is buried under concrete). Nearby **St Albans** and its (mostly) Norman cathedral are named after a Roman citizen who became the first Christian martyr in Britain. As Verulamium, it was one of the largest Roman towns in Britain. Today, St Albans has some of the country's most impressive Roman remains: a Roman theatre (the only one of its kind yet found in Britain); a superb, beautifully-preserved mosaic floor, and a substantial segment of Verulamium's city wall. A museum displays many smaller artefacts. The **cathedral** (1077), **clock tower** and central maze of narrow streets still give the modern city a pleasing medieval feel.

To get there
BR from **St Pancras** (20 minutes).

Stamford and Peterborough

Most visitors in search of day trips to the 'real' tranquil market-town England miss Stamford because they have to make a train connection in Peterborough to get there. But it is worth the effort. Ancient historical buildings abound, from the twelfth-century church of **St Martin's** to the Georgian and Victorian façades found throughout the town. Small pedestrian lanes hide shopping places of interest: second-hand books, antiques and curios, pubs and coffee shops. Stamford's most famous historical home is **Burghley House**, a fine Elizabethan house built on land given by Elizabeth I to Lord Cecil, one of her most trusted advisers. The house is open to the public and is still occupied by the descendants of the original owner. The deer park was landscaped by Capability Brown. Information is available from Stamford Walk on (0780) 65944.

There is plenty for those whose interests lie in history, art and photography, or who simply want to admire buildings from an earlier era, well maintained by its present inhabitants. Several pubs and old coaching inns serve good food. Make a stop in Peterborough while making your connection to see the magnificent **cathedral**. (E.K.)

To get there
BR from **King's Cross**, changing at Peterborough (1–2 hours).

Stonehenge, Salisbury and Old Sarum

Unless you're overwhelmed by the mystery of **Stonehenge** and want to spend a day at the stunningly bleak site, it's best to combine it with a day trip to nearby **Salisbury**, a pleasant cathedral town. Locals claim that only the spire of Cologne cathedral is taller than theirs. You can see the 404-foot tower for miles. Dating from 1220, its history is one of redevelopment to support this tower at all costs. The spire still doesn't seem really secure, but you can climb up to its base on a guided tour. The cathedral also boasts the oldest working clock in Britain (1386), one of the four surviving copies of the **Magna Carta**, in the **Chapter House**, and the largest cloisters in England.

Except on market days (Tuesday and Saturday), and during the summer festival, Salisbury is a quiet, picture-perfect Englishy cathedral town — pleasant for strolls, but it doesn't offer much if you're not a cathedral fan. Fortunately, there are several nearby attractions. Those who enjoyed the recent best-seller **Sarum** may like to see the original Norman motte built on the site of an Iron Age hill fort. In summer you can get a bus every half hour from Salisbury bus station. Or, you can visit the main attraction, Stonehenge, 10 miles away. Several buses leave from Salisbury railway station most days or, much more expensively, you can go by taxi. Need we say much about **Stonehenge**? This ancient circle of stone megaliths has stood on the desolate Salisbury Plain for at least 4000 years. Many theories have been advanced to explain their significance. Maybe one day someone will prove that the whole place is a massive hoax played on us by the ancients. I'd wager that even then the site would still be a major attraction. Despite today's hidden snack bar, car park and souvenir stall, most visitors are still impressed. Open daily 0930–1630.

To get there
BR from **Waterloo** (1 hour 30 minutes).

Stratford

Our advice: don't worry about not going. If you have even a mild interest in Shakespeare or his plays, you may want to visit **Stratford-upon-Avon**, possibly Britain's most over-visited and overrated tourist mecca. But if not, there is no reason to be ashamed (after all, the question of whether he or somebody else wrote some or all of his plays is still a hot controversial issue . . .). You might give Stratford a miss. Despite years of heavy promotion there is still no scheduled direct train service — you have to change at Coventry, Reading or Leamington Spa. But that in itself is not a good reason to miss Stratford. The real reason stems from the over-promotion to tourists who have no real interest in the Bard or his plays.

Stratford hotels are in a continual hectic state because many of their guests are 'one nighters' — people who come up on tour packages from London, take in the standard roll of sights and see the current production at the Royal Shakespeare Theatre (many don't appear to know which play they are going to see), before returning to London or moving on to the next stop on their itinerary the next morning. The pubs and restaurants are crowded out with daytrippers. To be fair, many are Londoners with a genuine interest in a play they've come up to see. The trouble is, little Stratford seems to be continually trying to fleece the 'instant Shakespeare seekers' as well. The town centre has little visible real life that is not concerned with catering to tourists.

Stratford has a sizable proportion of half-timbered houses, and the gardens along the River Avon are lovely. They provide the only reasons for visiting Stratford unconnected with the Bard.

If you are still with me, I'll now go into the major reasons why those who *are* interested in Shakespeare should visit Stratford. I suppose they should make one tour of the sights. It's easiest if you beat the coach parties by going before 1100 or after 1600. The **birthplace**, on half-timbered Henley Street, has an almost unending flow of filers-by through the corridors and twisting staircases. If you're not too rushed you can learn something about sixteenth-century life. Nearby **New Place**, in Chapel Street, is where he retired. **Harvard House**, on the High Street, is a less-hectic Tudor home, blessedly unrelated to Shakespeare. You can't see the inside of the still functioning **Grammar School**, where Shakespeare was educated, without special permission, but the **Build Chapel** next door is open. **Hall's Croft**, Old Town Road, was Shakespeare's daughter's home, and has a worthwhile pretty walled garden. Houses and landmarks of other relatives abound. Much ado about nothing is especially made about **Anne Hathaway's Cottage**, about a mile away, and **Mary Arden's House**, 4 miles away — perhaps worth it for the enjoyable walks to get there on well-maintained footpaths. The modern **Shakespeare Centre**, on Henley Street, has an exhibit of sixteenth-century books, and hosts an annual party festival. They will even charge you (20p) to see the poet's simple grave in **Holy Trinity Church**.

Perhaps I should at this point declare my interest. I enjoy Shakespeare's plays (when well-performed — few things are worse than bad Shakespeare) but am less than fascinated by his life story, and that of his wife, daughter and cousins twice-removed. With this in mind, I recommend a visit to the **Royal Shakespeare Theatre** in Stratford (the RSC at the Barbican in London is equally good, but there is something special about Shakespeare-in-Stratford). Plays by Shakespeare's contemporaries may be seen at the **Swan Theatre**, and modern plays at **The Other Place**.

If you can afford it, and have a car, I recommend that you stay a few miles away from all the hustle at one of Stratford's two excellent country house hotels, **Ettington Park** or **Billesley Manor**. Both have excellent food and pleasant quiet surroundings, where you can escape from traffic and Shakespeare T-shirts. If you can't, you might avail yourself of BR's **Shakespeare Connection** — day or 'period' return tickets on British Rail via Coventry that allow you to return to London after the play. Alternatively, the **Shakespeare Stop Over**, Tel. (0789) 295623, combines a play, a meal, and accommodation in a broad range of hotels ranging from guest houses to the aforementioned country house hotels, at a range of package bargain prices. If you're seeking your own accommodation, even in a B&B, in summer it's best to reserve in advance, especially for weekends.

And *take note*: Stratford's theatres are closed between January and April.

To get there
No direct connection — the easiest way is a combined ticket from **Euston Station** to **Coventry**, then bus to Stratford (2 hours).

Winchester
Once the capital of King Alfred's kingdom, and later an important medieval commercial centre, this is now a very quiet town: so quiet, most bus tours only stop for an hour at the **cathedral**. It is true that, apart from the cathedral (1093) and the nearby collection of buildings known as **Cathedral Close**, not much is left of its medieval past. There is a very good guided tour of the fourteenth- century buildings of **Winchester College**, and you can see the **Great Hall** — the remains of the castle — with a table reputed (falsely) to have been King Arthur's.

Should you visit Winchester? An amazing number of the 'seen one, seen them all' school still seem to like the **cathedral**. With the longest nave in England, a rib-vaulted ceiling, the remains of the Saxon kings in memorial chests, Jane Austen's tomb and an especially eerie crypt only open in summer (because it floods in winter), the **cathedral** seldom fails to enchant. Winchester seems to be at its best in autumn, when the leaves are turning. See the cathedral, then go on one of the town's pleasant walks — through the water meadows to the twelfth-century **Hospital of St Cross**, Britain's oldest functioning almshouse, or up to the magnificent view on **St Giles' Hill**.

To get there
BR from **Waterloo** (1 hour 10 minutes).

13   *After London*

London is really only a small part of that diverse nation and collection of islands known as the United Kingdom. Beyond the limits of day tripping are more fascinating places than we have room to describe here. Foreign visitors should take at least a few days out of the London area to discover the world of Cornwall, Yorkshire, Scotland or Wales. Our advice to first-time foreign visitors would be to limit yourself to one of these regions, besides London, unless you have a lot of time. Alternatively, whether first time or thirtieth, consider some of our suggestions.

Some suggestions for enjoying accommodation

Country Hotels
Try a few days or a weekend at a country hotel or a 'country house' hotel. Some are expensive and pamper their guests with extras and luxuries, but many more modest places offer antique furnishings, good food, relaxed surroundings and opportunities for walking, fishing, golf or just taking tea on the lawn. Here is our list of some of the best: **Sharrow Bay**, Ullswater (the Lake District); **Chewton Glen**, New Milton (the New Forest near London); **Bodysgallen**, Llandudno (North Wales); **Gravetye Manor**, East Grinstead (near London); **Maison Talbooth**, Dedham (East Anglia — beside the River Stour), and **Gidleigh Park**, Chagford (edge of Dartmoor). The *Good Hotel Guide*, published by the Consumers' Association (and in the US as *Europe's Wonderful*

Little Hotels and Inns) is an excellent guide. **Let's Go** is a useful BTA booklet listing many English hotels with value minibreaks.

Quality bed and breakfast

For a few pounds more than the norm you can stay in a better-quality distinctive bed and breakfast. Sometimes the houses are historic and hosts are titled. The following three agencies carefully screen their hosts.

Wolsey Lodges carefully screen both houses and hosts. Farms, country houses and village parsonages are some of the places on offer. A brochure giving detailed descriptions of accommodation, local attractions and facts about the host in each entry is available from BTA offices overseas or from **The Secretary, Wolsey Lodges, 17 Chapel Street, Bildeston, Suffolk 1P7 7EP**; Tel. (0449) 741297; Telex 987067 WOLSEY. Booking can be made direct to the above address (quote Amex or Visa number) or to the individual lodge owner with a £10 deposit.

The Best Bed and Breakfast in the World (**World Wide Bed and Breakfast Association**) and the *Prestige Bed and Breakfast* offered by **Bed and Breakfast (GB)** have already been mentioned in the *Getting a Place to Stay* chapter. They have members throughout the country.

Rent a country cottage

Many foreign visitors are surprised at how easy it is to rent a country cottage. Agencies are legion and most put out glossy brochures detailing their listed properties. Quality varies greatly and, like other forms of accommodation, you get what you pay for. But a family or a group can have a very economical holiday because charges are *per cottage* and generally it's cheap — £150–£400 per week, depending on the season. Many cottages are fully-modernized, with colour TV and central heating. Others aren't, so check the brochure descriptions. It also pays to research your desired locality — some areas have cheerful village pubs, beaches and pleasant walks that make for a great, cheap holiday. You'll probably want a rented car. If a motorway is nearby you'll be able to visit a wide area of attractions.

Private agencies

These are two of the bigger agencies. July, August and early September (school holiday times) are busy periods when you need to book early to have a choice.

English Country Cottages
Claypit Lane, Fakenham, Norfolk NR21 8AS; Tel. (0328) 4041.

Country Holidays
Spring Mell, Stonybank Road, Earby, Lancs. BB8 6RN Tel. (0282) 455 566.

Landmark Trust

This unusual organization preserves historic buildings and structures that might otherwise fall into ruin, by renting them out as unique and out-of-the-way places to stay. Disused railway stations, Martello towers, fortresses, island cottages, Georgian town houses and old country houses throughout the country make up the varied range available. Generally, standards of accommodation are high and properties are well maintained by caretakers who live nearby. The Trust is very popular and some of the more luxurious places need to be booked months in advance. All accommodation on **Lundy Island** is handled by the Trust and this too requires advance notice. Most places don't furnish sheets and towels. Total per night charges range from £30–£90; per week from £75–£435 — depending on the season.

The Landmark Trust
Shottesbrooke, Maidenhead, Berkshire; Tel. (062882) 5920. The catalogue costs £5. Americans should send $9 c/o **Mr and Mrs Philip J Myerly, 248 So. Prospect Street, Hagarstown, Maryland MD 21740.**

Distinctly Different
A consortium of 26 hotels and guesthouses located in buildings of historic interest in England and Wales. These include wind and water mills, railway carriages and stations, granaries and oast houses, chapels and schools. Prices are reasonable, ranging from £9–£25 per person per night. A brochure is available (overseas residents should enclose two reply coupons).

Distinctly Different
The Round House, Masons Lane, Bradford on Avon, Wiltshire BA15 1QN; Tel. (02216) 6842.

National Trust Cottages
The **National Trust** is the country's largest private landowner and conservation agency. Many houses and cottages are donated to the Trust, and, rather than putting them on display, the Trust rents them out to holidaymakers to help pay the bills. Prices range from £80–£300 per week, depending on season. Rates are per cottage, so a group can stay there very economically. Each property has been fully restored and modernized, most have colour TV, electricity, hot water and indoor plumbing. Because the Trust is a major coastal landowner, many cottages are on the sea or have a seaview in Devon, Cornwall and other scenic areas. Some have special arrangements for the disabled. Those in Scotland are administered by the separate **National Trust for Scotland**. Standards are high and some places are outstanding. Even the famous flat given to General Eisenhower in Culzean Castle on the West Coast is available.

For England:
Attn: Jackie Gurney, National Trust, 36 Queen Anne's Gate, London SW1; Tel. 01-222 9251 (specify region).

For Scotland:
National Trust, 5 Charlotte Square, Edinburgh EH2 4OU; Tel. (031) 226 5922.

Minibreaks
Like to get out of London for a few days in the country or smaller cities? Too few visitors seem to make use of 'minibreak' or short break value holidays, whilst many British people wouldn't go any other way. What is a 'minibreak'? Basically, it's a deal between you and the hotel. Usually, it involves agreeing to stay two nights, often on a weekend. Breakfast, dinner and other extras may be part of the package. Room rates are greatly reduced. On weekends and out of season, hotels hope to fill rooms, break even and maybe convince you to help support their bar.

Hotel chains like **Trusthouse Forte**, and consortiums like **Best Western** offer nationwide brochures showing 'mini' or 'short break' savings. Two of the best value agencies in the country are Gold Star Holidays' **Great English City Breaks** and **Superbreaks**. **Great English Breaks** allow visitors to stay in high-quality city centre business hotels throughout the country for as little as £16 per person per night on weekends and all week in July and August. **Superbreak** offers hotel discount minibreaks any night of the week for one night or more in hotels throughout the country. Enquire at the **British Travel Centre** or travel agents in London to find out whether minibreaks are available at a destination hotel or ask the hotel when you make the booking.

Trusthouse Forte
24 New Street, Aylesbury, Bucks HP20 2NW; Tel. 01-567 3444.

Best Western
(Minibreaks available only within UK.) Vinehouse, 143 London Road, Kingston on Thames; Tel. 01-541 0033.

Great English City Breaks
Gold Star Holidays, P O Box 12, York Y01 1YX; Tel. (0904) 38973.

Superbreaks
305 Gray's Inn Road, London NW1; Tel. 01-278 9646.

Staying on a farm
Farm stays in most areas throughout the country are easy to arrange. The quality of accommodation is usually higher than the average B&B, and there is often more of a chance to get a glimpse into local life. Some farms are even within commuting distance of London! Arrange through local tourist offices, the BTA offices or **The Farm Holiday Bureau**, National Agricultural Centre, Stoneleigh, Nr Kenilworth, Warwickshire CV8 2LZ; Tel. (0203) 696969.

Railway trips

Britain has several scheduled rail itineraries that offer outstanding scenery, even if the trains themselves no longer offer the kind of romantic wood-panelled, brass-fixtured luxury they once did. At least two companies try to recapture something of this past era with expensive pampered package tours. British Rail and its partners now offer some of these trips — less luxurious, but value-for-money one to three day packages. Also available are a number of steam-hauled excursions.

Recommended British Rail routes

The Cornish Riviera: London–Penzance
Take the sleeper at one minute to midnight. Arrive in the milder, palm-fringed Penzance. Return from Cornwall on a daytrain to see gorgeous seaside and hill scenery: St Michael's Mount, Victorian stations, the red cliffs at Dawlish and the Royal Albert Bridge.

Welsh Miniature Railways
Travel to Llandudno Junction, Wales, on a regular British Rail service, then enjoy the smaller-gauge interconnecting **Conwy Valley** and **Ffestiniog Line** services through the magnificent Welsh mountains and valleys to Cardigan Bay. Check with the British Rail Travel Centre at Euston Station to see if combined tickets are still available.

Trains to Scotland
You can travel up via an eastern route from King's Cross to Edinburgh, perhaps stopping at York and Durham. After the border at Berwick, the tracks parallel the sea for some distance. Or you can travel from Euston to Glasgow, skirting the Lake District and through the valleys of the rugged Scottish borders. From Edinburgh or Glasgow your goal should be Inverness. It's best to go up by one of the two eastern routes and back via the Kyle and West Highland lines. The most popular eastern route is through Perthshire and the Grampian mountain valleys. The other route goes past St Andrews and the seaside to Aberdeen, then through pleasant rolling farmland. The Kyle Line from Inverness to Kyle of Lochalsh is a spectacular trip through the Western Highlands to the sea. Be sure to visit the Isle of Skye. Then take the ferry to

Mallaig and ride the West Highland Line to Fort William. Along the way are tunnels, viaducts and hill-hugging stretches of track — a marvel of Victorian engineering. The trip from Fort William to Glasgow crosses lonely, unpopulated moors surrounded by spectacular mountains. The final part runs along the side of Loch Lomond.

Carlisle and Settle route

This 3-hour trip is England's most spectacular train trip, over the hills and moors of Yorkshire Dales National Park. The high cost of maintaining the numerous bridges, viaducts and tunnels means that the line is threatened with closure. The trip is not very accessible from London, but those with rail passes can arrange to make the journey as part of a London–Scotland route.

British Rail sponsored trips

In the past two years British Rail has begun to offer special Pullman day package tours with value prices to such destinations as the Lake District, Durham, Yorkshire, Hadrian's Wall, Stratford (steam-hauled) and the Carlisle and Settle Line. These are in addition to the long-established **Britainshrinker** day trips (01-379 0424).

British Rail Travel Centre, Euston Station, London NW1 2HF; Tel. 01-388 0510.

Intercity Land Cruises

This company works with British Rail to produce some very good-value two to four day rail trips inclusive of meals, accommodation and most side trips. The **West Highlander** leaves London on a Friday evening and takes in Edinburgh, the line to Oban, a trip to the Isle of Iona and the West Highland Line by steam, before returning to London for a Monday morning arrival. The **Highlander** has a longer, different itinerary that includes John O'Groats and the famous Kyle Line.

Intercity Land Cruises

104 Birmingham Road, Lichfield, Staffs WS14 9BW; Tel. (0543) 254076.

The Venice–Simplon Orient Express

Besides the famous London–Venice trip in the elegant wagon-lit carriages (£655 — high season single), the company runs numerous day trips to destinations like Bath, Bristol and Arundel Castle (£115–£125), and the Bournemouth Belle allows you to sample the luxury, including gourmet food, at lower prices (£125).

Orient Express

200 Hudsons Place, Victoria Station, London SW1; Tel. 01-928 6000.

or **One World Trade Center** Ste. 2565 New York NY 10048; Tel. (800) 524 2420.

The Royal Scotsman

This elegant luxury train has carriages, cuisine and service similar to the Orient Express (above) with routes around the Scottish Highlands similar to the two Pullman rail trips (above). Cost ranges from £960 per person for the three day trip to £2,610 for a six day trip.

Abercrombie and Kent

51 Sloane Square House, Holbein Place, London SW1; Tel. 01-235 9761. or 1420 Kensington Road, Oak Brook, Illinois 60521; Tel. (800) 323 7308.

Some surprising places

So you think you know Britain? Here are a few out-of-the-way or frequently-ignored places we've often successfully recommended to our readers.

Bradford

A very useful base for exploring Brontë country, the Dales and nearby historic towns, especially if you utilize a **Great English City Break** hotel discount (see *Minibreaks*). Leeds is only 20 minutes away. **Harry Ramsdens** — the World's Largest Fish and Chip Shop — is between the two cities. Within the city: interesting Gothic revival architecture, the fascinating do-it-yourself **National Museum of Film, Photography and Television**, the **Industrial Museum**, the restored Moorish Alhambra Theatre and a 'curry trail' around the city's outstanding Asian restaurants.

Burgh Island

Twice a day when the tide is out, Burgh Island is a ten-minute walk across the sands from the Devon mainland. Otherwise, it's only accessible by a quaint vehicle known as the 'sea tractor'. This tiny 28-acre island has only a few cottages, a medieval pub and a restored Art Deco hotel that once hosted Agatha Christie, King Faroukh, and Douglas Fairbanks. Cliffs, bird life, picturesque ruins and a palm tree.

Burgh Island Hotel

Bigbury on Sea, Devon; Tel. (0548) 810 514.

The Channel Islands

Airfare deregulation has brought some very cheap fares to these islands, more English than French, that lie only 18 miles off the French coast. Jersey, Guernsey, Alderney, Sark and Herm are the last remnants of medieval England's French empire. Today the islands are mini-states with all of the advantages and none of the disadvantages of belonging to Britain. They have separate control of domestic affairs, and their own Customs and taxation (a flat 20%). But you don't have to show your passport; the four TV channels are British ones (English is predominant), and the currency is pounds and pence.

All the islands have lovely beaches, seascapes and country lanes, and a slightly milder climate than the UK mainland. The food and the architecture are French-influenced. Some islanders still speak a patois as well as southern-accented English.

Jersey is the largest and most interesting; Guernsey is more rural; Alderney and Sark are delightful backwaters, whilst Herm is said to have the best beaches. The islands are connected to one another, Britain and France by plane and boat. Numerous packages are available from London. Check with the **British Travel Centre** or the **Jersey Tourist Office**, 35 Albemarle Street, London W1; Tel. 01-493 5278.

Glasgow and the Burrell Collection

Scotland's 'other major city' is rising fast in recognition and status. There is even some talk about it stealing the festival from Edinburgh. In 1988 Glasgow was the site of the National Garden Festival, and in 1990 it will be the 'European Culture Capital'. Though it is still true that parts of the city have very severe social problems, Glasgow has been enjoying something of a renaissance and recognition of its genuine attractions: Europe's largest intact Victorian city centre; highly-regarded art and historical museums, and an interesting heritage of designers like Charles Rennie Macintosh.

But above all else, Glasgow now has the **Burrell Collection**, which we would rate as one of Europe's best small art museums. It is also one of the best designed and located — in the middle of a park. Through the big glass windows you can watch deer graze and the seasons change. The windows also give the museum a light and airy feel. You seem to float between the thousands of objects on display: medieval furniture, Persian carpets, classical statuary, Egyptian and Babylonian tomb objects, jade, pottery, paintings — the list goes on and on — and all in the careful collection of the late William Burrell.

Hay-on-Wye
The 'second-hand book capital of the world'. There are 14 second-hand bookshops in this tiny town on the Welsh border, the biggest of which has some 350,000 volumes. The surrounding area has outstanding natural beauty and historic interest. Go by train to Hereford, then take a local bus.

Liverpool
Of course, the Beatles' city is full of shrines, and the views from the ferry 'cross the Mersey of the waterfront are stunning, but did you know that the revitalized **Albert Docks** has waterfront shops and restaurants in formerly derelict warehouses? A new branch of the **Tate** houses some of the London museum's modern collection. At the **Maritime Museum**, visitors can participate in a moving street theatre-type presentation that simulates something of the immigrant ship experience (Liverpool was a major port for European emigration to North America). Another tradition is tea at the once-elegant **Adelphi Hotel**. **Great English City Breaks** features this hotel, and more modern ones, at bargain rates (see *Minibreaks*).

Lundy
On a clear day you can see this high-cliffed island 24 miles out in the Bristol Channel. Take the boat from Bideford or Ilfracombe in Devon and spend the day. Or book the small hotel or one of the charming cottages and stay awhile. Otherwise, there's an old pub, a shop, some ruins and lots of wild ponies, fallow and sika deer, goats and nesting birds. Not much else to do but enjoy the beauty and splendid isolation. All accommodation is controlled by the Landmark Trust. The nearest railway station is at Barnstaple.

Portmeirion
This is a fantasy village built by a rich eccentric in a beautiful region of North Wales. It was also the place where the cult TV series *The Prisoner* was filmed. It is famous for the attractive and colourful pottery still made there, and can be enjoyed with the nearby miniatue railways.

Scilly Isles
(Pronounced 'Silly') Twenty-eight miles south-west of Cornwall's Land's End, in mid-Gulf Stream, lie 100 islands where spring flowers often bloom at Christmas time. Five of the islands are inhabited by people as well as palms and subtropical flowers. Many colourful legends spring from the shipwrecks that dot the aqua waters.
   St Mary's is the largest island, with the largest town, Hughtown, but we recommend the **Island Hotel** on Tresco (most rooms with private bath) to view the botanic gardens and enjoy the excellent beach-combing and shell collecting. Why not combine the Scilly Isles with a trip to Cornwall? Regular boat and helicopter services are available from Penzance. More information is available from BTA offices overseas.

Shetland
June is an excellent time to fly up to these northerly islands and experience the midnight sun. Shetland belonged to Norway until 1469, and many place-names, customs and festivals are derived from that time. There are few trees, but the hills, bays and headlands have a wild, desolate beauty. The famous ponies run free, and in the sea below killer whales and porpoises can often be spotted. Great fishing, bird-watching and walking. The famous Fair Isle and other Shetland sweaters can be bought for low prices. Getting there can be half the fun if you go on the excellent overnight ferry from Aberdeen. Alternatively, British Airways has flight/hotel packages from London.

Activities

'Murder' and other theme weekends

On a 'murder weekend' guests get a package including accommodation, meals and extras, usually at a seaside or country hotel. A 'murder' is staged, and guests are invited to guess 'whodunnit'. Who is telling the truth? An Agatha Christie-style denouement reveals all.

In the off season, hotels outside London stage a variety of themed weekends for interests ranging from chess to hot-air ballooning. We particularly recommend the 'murder' breaks staged by **Quality Hotels**, 72 King Street, Southport PR8 1LG; Tel. (051) 924 1125.

Canal cruising

You can rent narrowboats that sleep up to ten people and cruise Britain's vast network of inland canals, stopping at canalside pubs and enjoying the pleasant scenery. Book through **UK Waterways Holidays Ltd**, Welton, Hythe Daventry, North Hants NN11 5LG; Tel. (0327) 843773.

Walking holidays

Go with a group or independently with accommodation arranged in advance. Too many good companies and routes to list here, so enquire at BTA offices.

Tours

Special interest and theme tours are available to all parts of the country and about a wide variety of subjects (literary figures, magic, ghosts and wildlife to name a few). Because many of these tours are run by very small companies with limited budgets for publicity, it's a good idea to plan and book in advance. If you have a special interest, contact the offices of the BTA abroad or the British Travel Centre after you arrive in London. (Addresses are in the section 'Other Practical Matters'). Or, North Americans might want to write to *Wilson & Lake International*, 330 York Street, Ashland, Oregon 97520; Tel. (503) 488 3350. This travel agency publishes an annual directory of these tours: it also provides a one-stop agency that specializes in all aspects of British travel.

How to use London as a base for onward world travel

Few cities have as many air destinations, flight connections, cut-rate agencies and discount flights; London is the travel capital of the world. Those who plan to stay in London for a while should investigate the many bargains available.

Bucket shops

Travel sections of British newspapers and London give-away magazines contain plenty of ads for cheap air tickets to just about anywhere in the world. Most of these tickets are actually legitimate. In a process known as 'consolidation' in the United States, the airlines allocate a number of seats they either can't sell or think they won't sell to independent travel agents known as 'bucket shops'. They in turn sell to the general public at knock-down prices. Be careful. It's best to pick an agent who's an ABTA member, been in business for years and can answer the questions you should ask. These include: Are the tickets refundable? Is the agency bonded? Which airline is the likely carrier? Two reliable discount agents are **Trailfinders** (46 Earls Court Road W8; Tel. 01-938 3368) and **Reho Travel** (15 New Oxford Street WC1; Tel. 01-242 5555); and the **Air Travel Advisory Bureau** (Tel. 01-636 5000) gives free advice about which of its members are currently offering the best prices to a particular destination.

Regular Apex
If you plan to travel onwards from London and don't want or can't get a 'bucket ticket', many European and other airlines offer Apex (Advance Purchase) tickets to those who can buy a ticket a requisite number of days ahead. Even if you're flying within the United Kingdom, say to Edinburgh, flying Apex can make a substantial difference in price.

Package holidays
Several years ago, in the days of the high dollar, British-originating package holidays were a real bargain for American visitors. Now they are much less so, but continentals actually fly to Britain to take advantage of much cheaper British packages to the Mediterranean and beyond. British tour operators claim their average profit on each holiday is only £4! Nevertheless, many bargains are available to places — like Madeira and the Greek and Canary Islands — that are not on the way to anywhere and can be troublesome or expensive to reach travelling independently. Off-season holidays in Majorca, the Algarve, the Spanish Costas and other commonplace tourist centres can be dirt cheap, but remember — you get what you pay for. Check travel agents' windows for late bargains. In the summer, Gatwick airport sometimes has a late travel booth for on-the-spot bookings.

European rail travel
Those who want to travel onwards by train should contact the **European Travel Centre** at Victoria Station (Tel. 01-834 2345) and ask whether British Rail is currently offering any packages or bargains to your chosen destination. Under 26's should take advantage of the bargains offered by the nearby **Transalpino** agency (71 Buckingham Palace Road, London SW1; Tel. 01-834 6283).

Paris
Four years ago the big French company **Nouvelles Frontières** won an important court case which allowed them to sell cut-rate London–Paris fares. Their airfares are still some of the best. (1 Hanover Square; Tel. 01-629 7772). Check also the many cheap bus and rail deals offered by the bus, BR and the ferry companies. The **Travel Centre** (see above) and **Victoria Coach Station** are the places to ask.

Holiday homes
Many Britons own holiday homes in Spain, France, Italy, Greece and Portugal. Look at the ads in the papers or British travel agents' brochures to find out how to rent these homes at prices lower than those given by many overseas agents.

Camping tours
The days of the hippie trail to Australia via India are over, but several companies offer youth-oriented cheap camping trips to exotic places or nearby Europe. Try **Encounter Overland** (Tel. 01-370 6843) or **Dekkers** (Tel. 01-373 8345).

Travel information
London is a world centre par excellence. As such, it has vast numbers of embassies and government tourist bureaux. If you're like me, you'll probably agree that most government tourist offices are next to worthless; Third World governments have been known to exile political challengers or incompetent members of the head of state's family to them. But at the very least they should offer basic visa and travel information.
    You'll probably find that London's public libraries offer a good selection in the way of travel guides and information; after all, London writers practically invented travel writing. General bookstores, especially **Waterstones**, have big, comprehensive sections. A special gem is the **Travel Bookshop** (13 Blenheim Crescent W11; Tel. 01-

229 5260), just off Portobello Road, with sections on all parts of the world and interesting old Baedekers and antique travel books.

14 *A final word*

Thank you for buying our guidebook. We hope to make it an annual, and naturally we want to make it the best on offer. Perhaps some of you will want to become regular visitors to London and subscribers to our newsletter — at a special rate of US$39.95 per year (reg.$44.95), or (within UK) £22, for purchasers of this book (Visa, MC, Amex accepted for dollar orders only). Regardless, we'd like to hear from you with any constructive suggestions or recommendations.

UK: Siewert Publications Ltd, Box 662, London W10, United Kingdom.

USA: c/o US Agents Blackwood Business Services, Box 3884, Lubbock, Texas 79452, USA.

The author and contributors

Clark Siewert, the Texas-born editor and founder of *London Traveletter*, has been a keen traveller from an early age, but for the past five years he has happily made his home in the Notting Hill area of London with his Scottish wife, Lesley, and their son Keir. Although he keeps a foot firmly planted in the United States, his love of London, its history and culture, makes it his favourite city. Unless otherwise noted by the initials below, he wrote most of this book. 'The buck stops here.'

London Traveletter contributors with article material excerpted in this book:

Michael Apichella (M.A.) is an American writer who settled with his English wife in Oxford (England not Mississippi). *Daphne Ayles* (D.A.) is an editor of Methodist and Rechabite publications and thinks it wonderful that someone with her name is a life-long tee-totaller. *Alison Bremner* (A.B.) is a registered nurse, traveller and writer, born in England, but presently in Sydney, Australia. *Clive Brook* (C.B.) lives in Southampton and wrote a book about the sea soap 'Howard's Way'. *Morag Campbell* (M.C.) is a former editor of *Diner's Club Magazine* who has eaten her way through London — all in the line of duty, of course. *Joan Clayton* (J.C.) notes that despite her initials, she's a London journalist who has been happily finding new surprises for 30 years. *Andrew Crowe* (A.C.), author of *The Parks and Gardens of London*, was once a labourer in Battersea Park. *Jane Ehrlich* (J.E.) is an American freelance journalist in London well-known by her friends for her 'insatiable taste for anything elegant' but cursed by 'Steuben tastes and styrofoam budget'. *Audrey Groom* (A.G.) is a full-time writer as well as a full-time housewife, mother and granny. *Robert Hackler* (R.H.) is an anglophile from Indiana who frequently brings tour groups to Britain. *Elizabeth Kirby* (E.K.) lives in Stamford and writes about the area. *Arda Lacey* (A.L.) is a writer on art, antiques and collectables for many national newspapers. *Linda Keister* (L.K.) has covered London for many religious publications. *Genevieve Muinzer* (G.M.) lives in London and frequently writes about shopping, art, and expatriate matters. *Suzanne Myers* (S.M.) retired to writing after reading English at Sussex University. *Arthur Nicklin* (A.N.) is a contributor to many national publications and is currently writing a book on chastity belts. *Anthony Phillips* (A.P.) was born in Carshalton but now writes for many US and UK travel publications. *Brian Rourke* (B.R.) likes to write about haunted pubs. *Lesley Siewert* (L.S.) is a London social worker and theatre critic who is closely related to someone else involved with this book. *Cathy Smith* (C.R.S.) is a London travel writer who spent 20 years in Canada. *Gillian Thomas* (G.T.) has written frequent articles for *The Guardian* and other national newspapers. *Leslie Mandel-Viney* (L.V.) is a London American who specializes in travel, health and food (and writing about them). *John Wilcock* (J.W.), a nomadic columnist for 20 years, commutes between the past and future. *Martha Zenfell* (M.E.Z.) writes about London life for many US and UK publications, but even after 20 years, she still doesn't understand cricket. Thanks also to *Kathleen Fedouloff* for her word processing help.

We'd also like to thank these people who have contributed to our newsletter:

Harold Baldwin, Joan Brittaine, Jean Bellamy, April Carlucci, Edna Cass, E. Chroman, M. J. Crawford, Sarah Crowe, J. Emerson, Marjorie Goddard, Christine Green, Martin Green, Jean Harper, Jean Hawkes, Kathleen Herold, Herman Herst, Marion Hough, Pamela Howarth, Roger Jones, Jo Kerns, Peter Leather, Linda Moore, M. Muinzer, Graham Norton, Elaine O Gara, John Pattinson, Elizabeth Rae, Joanna Ralph, Sheila Ralph, Jenny Ridgwell, Hazel Speed, Judy Taylor, Nicholas Thornton, Ian Weightman, Rosemary Wells and Phyllis Zauner.

Our unique offer to purchasers: a free additional update before you leave home

Because all guidebooks have a press date, none can remain completely up-to-date. For this reason, **London Traveletter** is offering, *to purchasers of this guidebook only, a unique free opportunity to update the valuable information in this book* before you leave. Naturally, we can't check all prices and phone numbers, but we can let you know about the most exciting new London developments and recommendations.

Please detach this page and fill in the coupon below. Send it to us with a first class American or British letter stamp (or, if you live in neither place, sufficient international reply coupons). By return mail we'll send you a free update letter and some information about **London Traveletter**.

For obvious reasons, we cannot accept a photocopy of this page.

Name: ....

Address:..

....

....

Allow three weeks for delivery.
Send to Department 1–A;
UK and European readers:

   Siewert Publications Ltd, Box 662, London W10, United Kingdom.

US and other readers:

   Blackwood Business Services, US Agents for Siewert Publications Ltd, Box 3884, Lubbock, Texas 79452 USA.
Offer expires January 1, 1990.

Index